FOR DUMMIES™
COMPUTER BOOK SERIES FROM IDG

The Internet For Windows For Dummies Starter Kit

Cheat Sheet

Fill in your important information here

Hostname	The name of your PC, which is part of your PC's Internet address	
Username	Your username, which is the part of your e-mail address that comes before the @	
E-mail address	Your complete e-mail address	
Password	The password you have to enter to use your account (actually, Internet Chameleon always types it for you)	
Mail password	Separate password used to read the mail from your mailbox	
Support number	The (voice) phone number of your Internet provider, in case you run into trouble	
IP address	A four-part number that identifies your number on the Internet, something like 123.45.67.89	

Electronic mail addressing for different systems

To Send to	***With This Address***	***Use This Address***
AOL	Jen Smith	jensmith@aol.com
Delphi	jsmith	jsmith@delphi.com
Easylink	3141592	3141592@eln.attmail.com
GEnie	J.SMITH7	J.SMITH7@genie.geis.com
MCI Mail	555-2468	5552468@mcimail.com
	Jen Smith	jen_smith@mcimail.com
CompuServe	7123,4567	7123.4567@compuserve.com
BITNET	user@node	user@node.bitnet *or* user%node.bitnet@cunyvm.cuny.edu
Fido	Mary Smith 1:2/3.4	mary.smith@p4.f3.n2.z1.fidonet.org

. . . For Dummies: #1 Computer Book Series for Beginners

The Internet For Windows For Dummies Starter Kit

Cheat Sheet

COMPUTER BOOK SERIES FROM IDG

Quick start on installing the disks

1. Insert the Internet Chameleon Disk 1 in the disk drive.
2. In the Windows Program Manager, choose File⇨Run from the menu.
3. Type **a:\setup** in the Command Line box, and click OK. Chameleon asks where to install the software. Click Continue to accept its suggestion of C:\NETMANAG.
4. When you're asked for a disk, stick the disk it wants into the same disk drive you've been using and click Continue.
5. Click OK when the installation program says that it's done.
6. In the Program Manager, double-click the Internet Chameleon icon to see the Chameleon program group.
7. Double-click on Instant Internet to get signed up for an Internet account.

See Chapter 3 for more details on installation and signup.

E-mail address zones decoded

Zone	Type of site
com	Commercial
org	Noncommercial
net	Network
gov	Government
edu	Education
mil	Military
int	International organizations

Note: Two-letter zones are country codes such as *us* for the United States, *ca* for Canada, and *jp* for Japan.

How to read a URL

Type of Resource	Typical URL
WWW	http://dummies.com/starter.html
Gopher	gopher://dummies.com/
FTP	ftp://dummies.com/pub/file/
Local file	file://localhost/C:/NETMANAG/INTRO.HTM
News	news://rec.nude
Telnet	telnet://locis.loc.gov/

IDG BOOKS

Cheat Sheet $2.95 value. Item 237-6.

For more information about IDG Books, call 1-800-762-2974 or 415-312-0650.

. . . For Dummies: #1 Computer Book Series for Beginners

THE INTERNET FOR WINDOWS FOR DUMMIES™ STARTER KIT

THE INTERNET FOR WINDOWS FOR DUMMIES™ STARTER KIT

by Margaret Levine Young
and John R. Levine

Foreword by Ted Nelson

IDG BOOKS

IDG Books Worldwide, Inc.
An International Data Group Company

Foster City, CA ♦ Chicago, IL ♦ Indianapolis, IN ♦ Braintree, MA ♦ Dallas, TX

The Internet For Windows For Dummies Starter Kit

Published by
IDG Books Worldwide, Inc.
An International Data Group Company
919 East Hillsdale Blvd.,
Suite 400
Foster City, CA 94404

Library of Congress Catalog Card No.: 94-79313

ISBN: 1-56884-237-6

Printed in the United States of America

10 9 8 7 6 5 4 3 2 1

1D/SR/RS/ZU

Distributed in the United States by IDG Books Worldwide, Inc.

Distributed by Macmillan Canada for Canada; by Computer and Technical Books for the Caribbean Basin; by Contemporanea de Ediciones for Venezuela; by Distribuidora Cuspide for Argentina; by CITEC for Brazil; by Ediciones ZETA S.C.R. Ltda. for Peru; by Editorial Limusa SA for Mexico; by Transworld Publishers Limited in the United Kingdom and Europe; by Al-Maiman Publishers & Distributors for Saudi Arabia; by Simron Pty. Ltd. for South Africa; by IDG Communications (HK) Ltd. for Hong Kong; by Toppan Company Ltd. for Japan; by Addison Wesley Publishing Company for Korea; by Longman Singapore Publishers Ltd. for Singapore, Malaysia, Thailand and Indonesia; by Unalis Corporation for Taiwan; by WS Computer Publishing Company, Inc. for the Philippines; by WoodsLane Pty. Ltd. for Australia; by WoodsLane Enterprises Ltd. for New Zealand.

For general information on IDG Books in the U.S., including information on discounts and premiums, contact IDG Books at 800-434-3422 or 415-655-3000.

For information on where to purchase IDG Books outside the U.S., contact IDG Books International at 415-655-3021 or fax 415-655-3295.

For information on translations, contact Marc Jeffrey Mikulich, Director, Foreign & Subsidiary Rights, at IDG Books Worldwide, 415-655-3018 or fax 415-655-3295.

For sales inquiries and special prices for bulk quantities, write to the address above or call IDG Books Worldwide at 415-655-3000.

For information on using IDG Books in the classroom, or ordering examination copies, contact Jim Kelly at 800-434-2086.

About the Authors

Margaret Levine Young and **John R. Levine** were members of a computer club in high school — before high school students, or even high schools, *had* computers. They came in contact with Theodor H. Nelson, author of *Computer Lib* and inventor of hypertext, who fostered the idea that computers should not be taken seriously and that everyone can and should understand and use computers.

Margy has been using small computers since the 1970s. She graduated from UNIX on a PDP/11 to Apple DOS on an Apple][to MS-DOS and UNIX on a variety of machines. She has done all kinds of jobs that involve explaining to people that computers aren't as mysterious as they might think, including managing the use of PCs at Columbia Pictures, teaching scientists and engineers what computers are good for, and writing and cowriting computer manuals and books, including *Understanding Javelin PLUS, The Complete Guide to PC-File, UNIX For Dummies, MORE Internet For Dummies, WordPerfect For Windows For Dummies* (with David C. Kay), and *The Internet For Dummies Quick Reference.* She has a degree in Computer Science from Yale University.

John wrote his first program on an IBM 1130 (a computer roughly as powerful as your typical modern digital wristwatch, only harder to use) in 1967. His first exposure to UNIX was while hanging out with friends in Princeton in 1974. He became an official system administrator of a networked computer at Yale in 1975. He started working part-time for Interactive Systems, the first commercial UNIX company, in 1977 and has been in and out of the computer and network biz ever since. He got his company put on Usenet (see Chapter 11) early enough that it appears in a 1982 *Byte* magazine article, which included a map of Usenet sites. He used to spend most of his time writing software, but now he mostly writes and cowrites books (including *UNIX For Dummies, The Internet For Dummies* [with Carol Baroudi], *The Internet For Dummies Quick Reference,* and *MORE Internet for Dummies,* all published by IDG Books Worldwide) because it's more fun. He also teaches some computer courses, publishes and edits an incredibly technoid magazine called *The Journal of C Language Translation,* and moderates a Usenet newsgroup. He holds a B.A. and a Ph.D in Computer Science from Yale University, but please don't hold that against him.

ABOUT IDG BOOKS WORLDWIDE

Welcome to the world of IDG Books Worldwide.

IDG Books Worldwide, Inc. is a subsidiary of International Data Group, the world's largest publisher of computer-related information and the leading global provider of information services on information technology. IDG was founded more than 25 years ago and now employs more than 7,000 people worldwide. IDG publishes more than 220 computer publications in 65 countries (see listing below). More than fifty million people read one or more IDG publications each month.

Launched in 1990, IDG Books Worldwide is today the #1 publisher of best-selling computer books in the United States. We are proud to have received 3 awards from the Computer Press Association in recognition of editorial excellence, and our best-selling *...For Dummies*™ series has more than 12 million copies in print with translations in 25 languages. IDG Books, through a recent joint venture with IDG's Hi-Tech Beijing, became the first U.S. publisher to publish a computer book in the People's Republic of China. In record time, IDG Books has become the first choice for millions of readers around the world who want to learn how to better manage their businesses.

Our mission is simple: Every IDG book is designed to bring extra value and skill-building instructions to the reader. Our books are written by experts who understand and care about our readers. The knowledge base of our editorial staff comes from years of experience in publishing, education, and journalism — experience which we use to produce books for the '90s. In short, we care about books, so we attract the best people. We devote special attention to details such as audience, interior design, use of icons, and illustrations. And because we use an efficient process of authoring, editing, and desktop publishing our books electronically, we can spend more time ensuring superior content and spend less time on the technicalities of making books.

You can count on our commitment to deliver high-quality books at competitive prices on topics consumers want to read about. At IDG, we value quality, and we have been delivering quality for more than 25 years. You'll find no better book on a subject than an IDG book.

John Kilcullen
President and CEO
IDG Books Worldwide, Inc.

VIII
WINNER
Eighth Annual Computer Press Awards 1992

IX
WINNER
Ninth Annual Computer Press Awards 1993

IDG BOOKS

IDG Books Worldwide, Inc. is a subsidiary of International Data Group, the world's largest publisher of computer-related information and the leading global provider of information services on information technology. International Data Group publishes over 220 computer publications in 65 countries. More than fifty million people read one or more International Data Group publications each month. The officers are Patrick J. McGovern, Founder and Board Chairman; Kelly Conlin, President; Jim Casella, Chief Operating Officer. International Data Group's publications include: **ARGENTINA'S** Computerworld Argentina, Infoworld Argentina; **AUSTRALIA'S** Computerworld Australia, Computer Living, Australian PC World, Australian Macworld, Network World, Mobile Business Australia, Publish!, Reseller, IDG Sources; **AUSTRIA'S** Computerwelt Oesterreich, PC Test; **BELGIUM'S** Data News (CW); **BOLIVIA'S** Computerworld; **BRAZIL'S** Computerworld, Connections, Game Power, Mundo Unix, PC World, Publish, Super Game; **BULGARIA'S** Computerworld Bulgaria, PC & Mac World Bulgaria, Network World Bulgaria; **CANADA'S** CIO Canada, Computerworld Canada, InfoCanada, Network World Canada, Reseller; **CHILE'S** Computerworld Chile, Informatica; **COLOMBIA'S** Computerworld Colombia, PC World; **COSTA RICA'S** PC World; **CZECH REPUBLIC'S** Computerworld, Elektronika, PC World; **DENMARK'S** Communications World, Computerworld Danmark, Computerworld Focus, Macintosh Produktkatalog, Macworld Danmark, PC World Danmark, PC Produktguide, Tech World, Windows World; **ECUADOR'S** PC World Ecuador; **EGYPT'S** Computerworld (CW) Middle East, PC World Middle East; **FINLAND'S** MikroPC, Tietoviikko, Tietoverkko; **FRANCE'S** Distributique, GOLDEN MAC, InfoPC, Le Guide du Monde Informatique, Le Monde Informatique, Telecoms & Reseaux; **GERMANY'S** Computerwoche, Computerwoche Focus, Computerwoche Extra, Electronic Entertainment, Gamepro, Information Management, Macwelt, Netzwelt, PC Welt, Publish, Publish; **GREECE'S** Publish & Macworld; **HONG KONG'S** Computerworld Hong Kong, PC World Hong Kong; **HUNGARY'S** Computerworld SZT, PC World; **INDIA'S** Computers & Communications; **INDONESIA'S** Info Komputer; **IRELAND'S** ComputerScope; **ISRAEL'S** Beyond Windows, Computerworld Israel, Multimedia, PC World Israel; **ITALY'S** Computerworld Italia, Lotus Magazine, Macworld Italia, Networking Italia, PC Shopping Italy, PC World Italia; **JAPAN'S** Computerworld Today, Information Systems World, Macworld Japan, Nikkei Personal Computing, SunWorld Japan, Windows World; **KENYA'S** East African Computer News; **KOREA'S** Computerworld Korea, Macworld Korea, PC World Korea; **LATIN AMERICA'S** GamePro; **MALAYSIA'S** Computerworld Malaysia, PC World Malaysia; **MEXICO'S** Compu Edicion, Compu Manufactura, Computacion/Punto de Venta, Computerworld Mexico, MacWorld, Mundo Unix, PC World, Windows; **THE NETHERLANDS'** Computer! Totaal, Computable (CW), LAN Magazine, Lotus Magazine, MacWorld; **NEW ZEALAND'S** Computer Buyer, Computerworld New Zealand, Network World, New Zealand PC World; **NIGERIA'S** PC World Africa; **NORWAY'S** Computerworld Norge, Lotusworld Norge, Macworld Norge, Maxi Data, Networld, PC World Ekspress, PC World Nettverk, PC World Norge, PC World's Produktguide, Publish& Multimedia World, Student Data, Unix World, Windowsworld; **PAKISTAN'S** PC World Pakistan; **PANAMA'S** PC World Panama; **PERU'S** Computerworld Peru, PC World; **PEOPLE'S REPUBLIC OF CHINA'S** China Computerworld, China Infoworld, China PC Info Magazine, Computer Fan, PC World China, Electronics International, Electronics Today/Multimedia World, Electronic Product World, China Network World, Software World Magazine, Telecom Product World, **PHILIPPINES'** Computerworld Philippines, PC Digest (PCW); **POLAND'S** Computerworld Poland, Computerworld Special Report, Networld, PC World/Komputer, Sunworld; **PORTUGAL'S** Cerebro/PC World, Correio Informatico/Computerworld, MacIn; **ROMANIA'S** Computerworld, PC World, Telecom Romania; **RUSSIA'S** Computerworld-Moscow, Mir - PK (PCW), Sety (Networks); **SINGAPORE'S** Computerworld Southeast Asia, PC World Singapore; **SLOVENIA'S** Monitor Magazine; **SOUTH AFRICA'S** Computer Mail (CIO),Computing S.A.,Network World S.A., Software World; **SPAIN'S** Advanced Systems, Amiga World, Computerworld Espana, Communicaciones World, Macworld Espana, NeXTWORLD, Super Juegos Magazine (GamePro), PC World Espana, Publish; **SWEDEN'S** Attack, ComputerSweden, Corporate Computing, Macworld, Mikrodatorn, Natverk & Kommunikation, PC World, CAP & Design, Datalngenjoren, Maxi Data,Windows World; **SWITZERLAND'S** Computerworld Schweiz, Macworld Schweiz, PC Tip; **TAIWAN'S** Computerworld Taiwan, PC World Taiwan; **THAILAND'S** Thai Computerworld; **TURKEY'S** Computerworld Monitor, Macworld Turkiye, PC World Turkiye; **UKRAINE'S** Computerworld, Computers+Software Magazine; **UNITED KINGDOM'S** Computing / Computerworld, Connexion/Network World, Lotus Magazine, Macworld, Open Computing/Sunworld; **URAGUAY'S** PC World Uraguay; **UNITED STATES'** Advanced Systems, AmigaWorld, Cable in the Classroom, CD Review, CIO, Computerworld, Computerworld Client/Server Journal, Digital Video, DOS World, Electronic Entertainment Magazine (E2), Federal Computer Week, Game Hits, GamePro, IDG Books, Infoworld, Laser Event, Macworld, Maximize, Multimedia World, Network World, PC Letter, PC World, Publish, SWATPro, Video Event; **VENEZUELA'S** Computerworld Venezuela, PC World; **VIETNAM'S** PC World Vietnam.

11/16/94

Dedication

John would like to dedicate this book to Alison, Antonia, Margy, Jordan, Steve L, Dave, Steve D, Carol, Arnold, Barton, and Bob, without all of whom this book would never have been finished. Joshua Reinhold offered essential moral support.

Margy would like to dedicate this book to baby Zack, his big sister Meg, and Jordan, who never stops amazing me.

Credits

Executive Vice President, Strategic Product Planning and Research
David Solomon

Editorial Director
Diane Graves Steele

Acquisitions Editor
Megg Bonar

Brand Manager
Judith A. Taylor

Editorial Managers
Tracy L. Barr
Sandra Blackthorn

Editorial Assistants
Tamara S. Castleman
Stacey Holden Prince
Kevin Spencer

Acquisitions Assistant
Suki Gear

Production Director
Beth Jenkins

Project Coordinator
Cindy L. Phipps

Pre-Press Coordinator
Steve Peake

Project Editor
Corbin Collins

Editors
Rebecca Whitney
Kathy Simpson

Technical Reviewer
Samuel D. Faulkner

Production Staff
Paul Belcastro
J. Tyler Connor
Drew R. Moore
Carla Radzikinas
Dwight Ramsey
Patricia R. Reynolds
Gina Scott

Proofreader
Henry Lazarek

Indexer
Sherry Massey

Book Design
Kavish + Kavish

Acknowledgments

Margy would like to acknowledge the continuing interference of Christopher Isaac in utero, with thanks to him for holding off being born until we were almost entirely finished with the book.

Many of the tables in this book were adapted from material contributed gratis by people on the Internet itself. The list of newsgroups in Chapter 9 is condensed from the master lists maintained by David "Tale" Lawrence. The list of Whois servers in Chapter 5 was compiled by Matt Power at M.I.T.

The entire contents of this book was submitted by the authors to the publisher over the Internet. Edited chapters were returned for review the same way. We thank TIAC (Bedford, Massachusetts), CENTNet (Cambridge, Massachusetts) and IndyNet (Indianapolis, Indiana), our Internet providers.

(The Publisher would like to give special thanks to Patrick J. McGovern, without whom this book would not have been possible.)

Contents at a Glance

Foreword xxix

Introduction 1

Part I: Getting onto the Internet 7

Chapter 1: What Is the Internet? Why Use It? 9
Chapter 2: Ways to Get Connected 15
Chapter 3: SLIP-ing onto the Net with Chameleon 25

Part II: Mail and Gossip 43

Chapter 4: On-Line Gossip: Using Chameleon Mail 45
Chapter 5: Mail Tips 75
Chapter 6: Getting on Mailing Lists 97
Chapter 7: You Name It, They Talk About It:Usenet Newsgroups 113
Chapter 8: Using NEWTNews 123
Chapter 9: A Sampler of Nifty Newsgroups 141

Part III: Using Other Computers and Grabbing Files 157

Chapter 10: Using Far-Off Computers 159
Chapter 11: Some Interesting Computers to Log Into 171
Chapter 12: Elements of FTP-ing 183
Chapter 13: FTP's Greatest Hits 197

Part IV: Searching the Net 213

Chapter 14: Want a File? Ask Archie 215
Chapter 15: Gopher Baroque 231
Chapter 16: Swinging on the World Wide Web 253
Chapter 17: Using Chameleon WebSurfer 263

Part V: Neat Stuff from the Net 277

Chapter 18: Grabbing Software over the Net 279
Chapter 19: Other Cool Windows Internet Programs 295

Chapter 20: We Have WAIS of Finding Your Information 313
Chapter 21: Having a Problem? 327
Chapter 22: Ten Ways to Find Fun Things to Do 339
Appendix A: Listing of Software on the Starter Kit Disks 353
Appendix B: Manually Configuring Chameleon 357
Appendix C: International Internet Providers 377

Index 385

License Agreement and Installation Instructions 414

Reader Response Card .... Back of Book

Cartoons at a Glance

By Rich Tennant

page 74

"OH SURE! LEAVE IT TO THE FORESTRY SERVICE TO START TALKING DISTRIBUTED COMPUTING ENVIRONMENT JUST WHEN I GET THE MAINFRAME UP AND RUNNING."

page 182

"I JUST DON'T THINK THIS NEW SALES KID IS GONNA WORK OUT."

page 326

page 112

page 43

"RIGHT NOW I'M KEEPING A LOW PROFILE. LAST NIGHT I CRANKED IT ALL UP AND BLEW OUT THREE BLOCKS OF STREETLIGHTS."

page 213

"OH, SCARECROW – I DON'T THINK YOU'LL NEED YOUR LAPTOP IN THE EMERALD CITY ANYWAY."

page 157

"I'M ALWAYS AMAZED AT THE TECHNOLOGICAL ADVANCES MADE AT PR FIRMS."

page 277

"YOU MEAN TO TELL ME YOU KNEW THIS WAS SACRED INDIAN BURIAL GROUND AND YOU BUILT THE COMPUTER ROOM HERE ANYWAY?! YOU FOOL! YOU FOOL!"

page 252

"I THOUGHT HE WAS A VACUUM CLEANER SALESMAN. HE CAME IN, SPRINKLED DIRT ON THE CARPET, AND THEN TRIED TO SELL ME A SOFTWARE PROGRAM THAT WOULD SHOW ME HOW TO CLEAN IT UP."

page 7

Table of Contents

Foreword .... *xxix*

Introduction *1*

About This Book 1
About the Software in This Book 2
How to Use This Book 2
Who Are You? 3
How This Book Is Organized 3
Icons Used in This Book 4
What Now? 5
Feedback, Please 5

Part I: Getting onto the Internet *7*

Chapter 1: What Is the Internet? Why Use It? **9**

What Is the Internet? 9
What's So Cool About It? 10
- Just how big is it? 10
- Anybody can access it? 10
- Politically, socially, religiously correct 11

What's in It for Me? 11
- Electronic mail (e-mail) 12
- Bulletin boards (Usenet newsgroups) 12
- Information retrieval (FTP, Archie, and Gopher) 12
- Using other computers (Telnet) 13
- Hypertext and hypermedia (WebSurfer and the World Wide Web) 13
- On-line conversation (talk and IRC) 13

How Do I Begin? 14

Chapter 2: Ways to Get Connected **15**

You May Already Be Connected 15
Letting Your PC Talk on the Phone 16
Who Ya Gonna Call? 17
- Bulletin boards 17
- General on-line services 18
- Shell systems 18
- SLIP systems 19

Choosing an Internet Provider 22
Why SLIP Is Way Cool 23

Chapter 3: SLIP-ing onto the Net with Chameleon 25

The Master Plan 25
What You Need 26
Installing Internet Chameleon 27
Opening Your SLIP Account 29
  Instant Internet! 30
  What if it's not so instant? 34
Making a Connection 34
It Didn't Work! 36
Testing! Testing! 37
When You're Finished, Hang Up 38
Calling Again 39
Who Are You? 39
  Your PC's Internet address 40
  Your e-mail address 40
  Your password 41

Part II: Mail and Gossip 43

Chapter 4: On-Line Gossip: Using Chameleon Mail 45

Names and Numbers 46
  What's my address? 47
  Where's my mail? 47
Setting Up Chameleon Mail 48
Running Mail 49
  The Mail window 49
  Leaving Chameleon Mail 50
Sending Mail 51
  Making a signature for yourself 53
  When is your mail sent? 54
  Can we see that again? 54
  Send it now! 55
Receiving Mail 56
  Here's my answer 56
  Into the circular file 57
  Hot potato! Here's a message for you! 57
  Get it on paper 57
Saving Money 58
Your Little Black Book 59
  Making book 59
  Using your little black book 60
  Making your own mailing list 60

May We Have a Copy of That File? 61
Including text from a file 62
Attaching files 63
Receiving attached files 65
Including uuencoded stuff 65
Receiving uuencoded files 66
Hang Onto It 67
Using Folders 67
Make me a folder 68
What's in this folder? 68
File this message, please 69
I don't want this folder anymore 69
Taking out the trash 69
Your Automated Mail Sorter 70
Here's What I Prefer 71
Other E-Mail Programs 73

Chapter 5: Mail Tips 75

Where Is Everyone? 75
Whaddaya Mean, You Don't Know Your Own Address? 76
Giving Your Friends the Finger 76
Running Finger 76
The industrial-strength Finger 79
Whois Out There? 80
Running Whois 81
Know what? 85
Mailing to the Outside World 86
America Online (AOL) 86
Applelink 86
AT&T Mail 86
BITNET 87
BIX 87
CompuServe 87
Delphi 88
Easylink 88
FIDONET 88
GEnie 88
MCI Mail 89
Prodigy 89
Sprintmail (Telemail) 89
UUCP 89
X.400: We're from the government and we're here to help you 90

A Few Words from the Etiquette Ladies 92
E-mail always seems ruder than it's supposed to 93
Flame off! 93
How private is e-mail? 95

Chapter 6: Getting on Mailing Lists 97

Are You Sure This Isn't Junk Mail? 97
Getting on and off Mailing Lists 98
Manual lists: Say "Add me, please!" 98
Add me, LISTSERV! 99
Stupid LISTSERV tricks 101
Add me, Majordomo! 103
Stupid Majordomo tricks 104
Sending Messages to Mailing Lists 105
Replying to Mailing-List Messages 107
Mailing Lists versus Usenet News 108
Some Interesting Lists 108

Chapter 7: You Name It, They Talk About It: Usenet Newsgroups 113

All the News That Fits and Considerably More 113
Being a Newsgroupie 114
The newsgroup thicket 115
Regional groups 116
Honest, It's a Work of Art 118
Binary files 118
Groups of files 118
Anatomy of an Article 119
What's in a number? 119
Distributions are your friends 120
Serving You the News 122

Chapter 8: Using NEWTNews 123

Running NEWTNews for the First Time 123
NEWTNews Mission Control 126
Ta-Ta for Now 127
Running NEWTNews Later 127
Reading Articles 128
Let's see what it says 129
Saving and printing articles 130
When Is an Article Not Really an Article? 131
Whattizzit? 131
Reading uuencoded messages 132
Dealing with Articles That Demand a Response 133
Responding privately by e-mail 133
Possibly making a fool of yourself 136

Other Things You Can Do to a Newsgroup 137
Your News Options 137
These Newsgroups Are Boring! 138
Adding New Groups as They Appear 139
Other Newsreaders of Note 139

Chapter 9: A Sampler of Nifty Newsgroups 141

So What Is There to Read Already? 141
Not-to-Be-Missed Groups 141
Computers, on Computers, About Computers 142
Misc: None of the Above 146
Rec: Fun and Games 147
Sci: Ask Dr. Science 150
Soc: C'mon By and Stay a While 151
Talk: Blah, Blah, Blah 151
More Hierarchies 152

Part III: Using Other Computers and Grabbing Files 157

Chapter 10: Using Far-Off Computers 159

How Can You Be in Two Places at Once? 159
Emulation Madness 160
Any Port in a Storm 161
Tell It to the Net 162
Help! I've Telnetted and I Can't Get Out! 164
Other Stuff You Can Do 164
We've Got a Little List 165
 Creating an entry in your little list 165
 Fixing a mistake 167
Your Telnet Options 167
Other Telnet Programs 169

Chapter 11: Some Interesting Computers to Log Into 171

Come on by Any Time 171
Libraries 172
Other Libraries 174
Miscellaneous Databases 174
 Agriculture and nutrition databases 174
 Geography databases 175
 Ham-radio databases 175
 History databases 176
 Outer-space databases 176
 Aviation database 177
 Book databases 177

Gateway Systems 178
Commercial Services 178
Fun and Sheer Goofiness 180

Chapter 12: Elements of FTP-ing 183

You See It, You Can Almost Touch It, but Where Is It Anyway? 183
What's on File? 184
Get Copying 185
Put me through, FTP 185
The FTP window 188
Finding files on the remote computer 189
Choosing where to put the file on your computer 189
When is a file not a file? 190
Copying files from the FTP server to your computer 191
Copying files to the FTP server 192
Doing a little housekeeping 192
When you finish 193
Your Favorite FTP Servers 193
Telling FTP about a system that you like 194
Fixing a mistake 194
Enough with connection profiles 195
Using all this information 195
FTP Trouble? 195
Other FTP Programs 196

Chapter 13: FTP's Greatest Hits 197

How Many Kinds of Files Are There? 197
Text files 197
Executable files 198
Archives and compressed files 198
Data files 198
Dealing with Files 199
Just plain text 199
Any last requests before we execute you? 200
Packing it in 200
There's Gigabytes Out There 202
Ms. Manners says 202
Mirror, mirror, on the Net 203
A few words about navigation 203
The FTP Hit Parade 203
UUNET 204
WUARCHIVE 204
RTFM 204
InterNIC 205
NSFNET 205

Desperately seeking software 205
The list of lists 205
Of Academic Interest 206
Coombs Papers 206
Behavioral brain sciences 206
EJVC 206
Compilers 207
NIH 207
It's the Law 207
Supreme Court rulings 208
Congressional mail 209
Law libraries 209
Fun and Frolic 209
Hamming it up 209
Shop 'til you drop 209
For music lovers 210
Attention, sports fans 210
News 210
TV (and Movie) guide 210
Travel tips 211
Yummy finds 211

Part IV: Searching the Net 213

Chapter 14: Want a File? Ask Archie 215

I Know I Saw a Note About It Somewhere 215
Archie at Home 216
Troubleshooting 217
Types of searches: how much do you know about this file? 218
Another way to tell Archie what to look for 219
How long do you want to look? 220
Archie, get me that file 220
After you find it, what is it? 221
Which Server Should I Use? 221
Hello? Archie? 223
Tell Archie how to behave: the set and show commands 224
Searching is such sweet sorrow, or something 224
How many files would you like? 225
Find it! 225
What is it? 226
You can't get there from here 227
E-Mail Archie 227
Other Archie Programs 229

Chapter 15: Gopher Baroque 231

Welcome to Gopherspace 231
Running Chameleon Gopher 233
The Gopher Window 234
  Selecting something 235
  It didn't work! 236
  Closing a menu or menu item 237
  Getting rid of boring items 237
  Lost in Gopherspace 237
  Get me out of this Gopher burrow! 238
What Do You Do When You Find Something? 239
  Not another menu! 240
  This item does nothing 240
  Here's some text! 240
  It's a picture! 240
  It's a program! 241
  It's a sound! 241
  It's a World Wide Web page! 242
  Searching with Gopher 243
  Leaping tall systems in a single bound 244
  Other types of items 245
Searching Gopherspace 245
  Veronica, my darling 246
Rewriting the Map 248
  Making book 248
  Saving servers 249
Other Gopher Programs 251

Chapter 16: Swinging on the World Wide Web 253

What's the Big Deal? 254
What is WebSurfer? 256
A Sample Web Crawl 256
The Web Catches Gophers, Too 258
Fame and Fortune 259
The People's Hypermedia 260
Indexes Galore 261

Chapter 17: Using Chameleon WebSurfer 263

First, Get Some Viewers 264
Climbing onto the Web 264
  The WebSurfer window 264
  Stop the music! 266
  Some other pages 266
Tips for Browsing 267

Displaying Any Old WWW Page 268
Remembering Hot Places 269
Serious Searching 270
Files on the Web 271
Searching for Info 273
Changing the Fonts 274
Other Web Browsers 276

Part V: Neat Stuff from the Net 277

Chapter 18: Grabbing Software over the Net 279

Where to Put Things 279
Ready to Decompress: WinZip 280
Grabbing WinZip 281
Uncompressing WinZip 282
Setting it up 282
What's in that ZIP file? 285
Unzip it! 285
Zip it! 286
Making your own ZIP file 287
Zipped out? 287
Netting a Program 288
Getting hold of the program 288
Unzipping the program files 289
Installing the program 290
Configuring the program 291
Scanning for Viruses 291
If you use MS-DOS 6.2 (or later) 292
If you don't use MS-DOS 6.2 292
Doing Your Part 292
Free versus not-quite-free 293
Registering WinZip 293

Chapter 19: Other Cool Windows Internet Programs 295

Sock Me Some WinSock Programs 296
Mailers 296
Newsreaders 297
Telnet programs 298
FTP programs 299
Archie 299
Gopher 300
Web browsers 301
WAIS 302

IRC 303
MUD programs 303
Miscellaneous Internet stuff 304
Vying for Viewers 305
Seeing things 305
Hearing voices 306
Seeing ghosts 307
Miscellany 307
Uudecoders 307
UNIX uncompressors 308
Mac unstuffers 309
Win32S 309
Lost? Dumbfounded! 310
The Latest WinSock Programs 310
The Most Popular FTP Servers 311

Chapter 20: We Have WAIS of Finding Your Information 313

Where Does WAIS Come From? 314
The world's ugliest program 315
Gateways that usually aren't 315
WAIS, at last 316
Setting up WinWAIS 316
Hand-to-hand with WinWAIS 317
Let's go to the source 318
Are we ever going to do some real searching? 319
A four-star performance 320
On the button 321
That's irrelevant! 322
Back to the source 322
Adding sources by hand 323
Other WAIS Programs 325

Chapter 21: Having a Problem? 327

The Network's Dead, Jim! 327
Is your computer working? 328
Is your computer connected to your Internet provider? 328
Are you connected to your name server? 329
Is the other end OK? 329
What's in a Name? 331
When Networks Go Bad 331
"Connection refused" 331
"No route to host or Network unreachable" 332
. . . Utter silence 332
What's My Address? 333
Don't Be a Pig 334
A Not-So-CAPITAL Idea 334
How to Make Enemies by Way of E-Mail and News 335

Mailing List and Usenet News Etiquette 336
Why FTP Mangled Your Files 336
The FTP That Wouldn't 337
Dread Version Creep 337

Chapter 22: Ten Ways to Find Fun Things to Do 339

How to Get There 339
Travel 339
The Global Network Navigator 340
The Avid Explorer 340
U.S. State Department Travel Advisories 340
Countries around the World 341
Down Under 341
Europe 341
Toot, toot! 343
The Funnies 343
Dr. Fun 343
Dilbert and Doonesbury 344
Virtual Meetmarket 344
WWW Calc 344
The Metro Server 345
Making Gopher Harder to Use 346
And Now, Coming to a Network near You! 346
Femmes Femmes Femmes Je Vous Aime! 348
Horsing Around 348
Attention, Klutzes! 348
More Fun and Games 348
Food, Food, Wonderful Food 349
Where to Eat in the Hub of the Universe 349
On-line Coke Machines 349
The Trojan Room 350

Appendix A: Listing of Software on the Starter Kit Disks 353

Instant Internet 353
Chameleon Custom Program and NEWT 354
Chameleon Mail 354
Mail Utilities 354
NEWTNews 354
Chameleon Telnet 354
Chameleon FTP 355
FTP Server 355
Chameleon Archie 355
Chameleon Gopher 355
WebSurfer 355
Chameleon Ping 356
Finger 356
Whois 356

Appendix B: Manually Configuring Chameleon 357

Using a Non-Instant Internet Provider 357
The concept 357
Installing the software 358
Activating the software 358
Getting your own Internet account 360
Configuring Internet Chameleon for your account 363
If Internet Chameleon knows about your Internet provider 364
If Internet Chameleon has never heard of your Internet provider 364
Either way 365
Configuring Your Mail 369
Changing Your Software Configuration 372
If your Internet address and name change 372
If you change your modem 372
If you change the way you connect to your Internet provider 373
If your provider's network gateway or domain name server changes 374
If your mail server or mail gateway changes 374
If your news server changes 375
Other Things That May Go Wrong 375
How to change the password for your account 375
How to unlock your mailbox 375

Appendix C: International Internet Providers 377

Australia 377
Belgium 378
Canada 378
France 379
Germany 379
Italy 380
Japan 380
Mexico 380
Netherlands 380
Norway 382
South Africa 382
Spain 382
Switzerland 382
United Kingdom (U.K.) 383

Index 385

License Agreement and Instalation Instructions 414

Reader Response Card .... Back of Book

Foreword

Welcome to John and Margy's *The Internet For Windows For Dummies Starter Kit,* their fifth brother-and-sister book together. It is, of course, exactly the right thing to follow John and Margy's excellent *UNIX For Dummies* and John's phenomenally successful *The Internet For Dummies, 2nd Edition* (written with Carol Baroudi).

John is mischievous and clever and seems to know everything, Margy is clever and gentle and wise. Both are frighteningly competent.

I'm terribly pleased to have the opportunity to write a foreword for them, because we've been friends for a very long time. I first met John and Margy in 1970, when they were members of the famous R.E.S.I.S.T.O.R.S. computer club of Princeton, New Jersey (Radically Emphatic Students Interested in Science, Technology, and Other Research Studies). The group was playful, zany, and smart. They ranged in age from 12 to 16 but were doing professional-level work in computer languages and programming.

The Levine home in Princeton was one of the warmest homes I have ever seen. Bob and Ginny Levine, the kind, trusting, and astute parents of John and Margy, made it a kind of clubhouse where everyone was welcome.

For me the Levine household became a home away from home. My excuse for hanging out in Princeton was that I was learning so much from the kids, but in fact it was also a place where my work was appreciated, as it was not yet appreciated in the Official Computer World.

John was the know-it-all patrician of the club, Margy was warm and clever and eager. Both of them seemed to understand everything, but John managed to turn his insights into a constant stream of wisecracks.

With his glasses and curly hair, John bears a curious and unplanned resemblance to the academic-looking cartoon figure of the . . . *For Dummies* books, although the character preceded him in the series. (I had forgotten John has a Ph.D. till I looked over the previous volume — most Ph.D.-encumbered friends don't let you forget it.)

John is a Class A wag, but his one-liners generally take a moment to understand. His dry delivery enfolds a pithy wisecrack like a fortune cookie. You can't laugh quickly because you have to unpack it.

He was always like that. When he was 16, I was driving a car full of R.E.S.I.S.T.O.R.S. around Princeton. Boisterously they called out contradictory driving instructions. "I demand triple redundancy in the directions!" I barked. It was John who replied laconically, "Right up ahead you turn right right away."

The coolest subject of our day

Now the Internet is today's cool subject. Everybody wants in on the Internet because they hear it's important, but most people don't know what it is.

However, as you insiders already know from the first book, *The Internet For Dummies,* the Internet is just a bunch of computers talking to each other, kind of. The Internet is not a Thing any more than the highway system is a Thing. You connect to the highway system by building a stretch of road from your house to any other piece of road that's *already* connected to the highway system; that makes the "highway system" include your piece of road as well. The Internet is like that.

And like the highway, the Internet is there for the taking, awaiting your particular use (except that the asphalt is a data-sending procedure that makes sure the messages get back and forth).

The hottest topics

Not only is the Internet a cool place, but all the hot topics are piling into it, like overheated people into a midsummer swimming pool.

Everybody wants to get into interactive multimedia — ahem, the *correct* term is *hypermedia,* which I coined 30 years ago — and everybody wants to produce interactive texts, movies, whatever, for the TV screen or computer screen (which will no longer be distinct from one another). The computer world is getting to be just like Hollywood, where everybody says he's a producer. As a matter of fact, the computer world isn't getting to be just *like* Hollywood, it's turning *into* Hollywood, and vice versa — Hollywood itself is now treating hypermedia as the new frontier.

But the hypermedia are no longer just on disks that people buy. Till recently, many people have thought electronic media meant CD-ROM disks — but CD-ROM publishing isn't electronic publishing, it's *plastic* publishing. CD-ROM forces a pre-Columbian view of the world: When you get to the edge, you fall off. The limited size of the CD-ROM — 600 megabytes — means that much of the editorial effort is concerned with deciding what's in and what's out. And it's not connectable: Every CD-ROM is absolutely separate from every other CD-ROM.

Whereas with *true* electronic publishing — that is, publishing *electrons, over networks* — there are no boundaries, there is no limit on size, nothing has to be left out. The publisher can keep filling up more disks up to any size, all available on-line; and you the reader/viewer can keep sending for the stuff indefinitely.

And this has begun. Notably, World Wide Web, which you use through Chameleon WebSurfer (see Chapters 16 and 17), is already a wildly successful network hypermedia publishing system. We will see many more network hypermedia systems that will make available media of every kind, across the world, under many different schemes of copyright and royalty. (Each of us seems to think that he, she, or it has the answer to copyright. We shall see what works.)

Another key issue now raging on the Internet is freedom of privacy. The American government is giving an awfully good imitation of a police state, claiming that it has a God-given right to spy on all communications and demanding that something called the Clipper Chip be put in every electronic device so that users can *think* their communications are private — but the government can listen in at will. (Didn't a guy named Orwell talk about this quite a while ago?)

But the Clipper Chip is a fraud. First of all, no actual criminal will submit to it. Any high school kid can figure out a code that the government *can't* listen in on.

What, then, is the point of the Clipper Chip? What the advocates of the Clipper Chip *really* want is the laws that the chip was sneakily designed to impose on us — "enabling laws" that will make it illegal to aid and abet cryptography, enabling laws that will allow search and confiscation of computers, enabling laws that will allow search and confiscation of any private information and data by those suspected of actually trying to hide things in a way that the government cannot read. Welcome to the New Order.

But Americans are getting smart about such things. This book is intended to help make you smart.

Wasting time

People ask me: Do you surf the Internet?

Oh sure.

If your idea of fun is gossip columns, want ads, card catalogs, and graffiti, then the Internet is for you. A lot of Internet enthusiasts are people who apparently have nothing better to do than send and receive electronic chitchat and Hot News all day long.

But actually I'm talking sour grapes here. The problem really is that all that Internet stuff is *too* interesting. You can throw your every waking hour into it. Don't go near it unless you're good at Tearing Yourself Away.

So welcome back to the sequel

New kinds of moving data, winds of data, are sweeping across the world — eddies and gusts of data, hurricanes, cyclones of data.

Now, John and Margy guide you with their warmth and wit through this wild and windy world.

Ted Nelson
Sausalito, California

Ted Nelson is best known for coining the terms hypertext *and* hypermedia *and for designing a worldwide network publishing system with automatic royalty in 1960, now called* Xanadu *— soon, we hope, to become a reality. He is the author of many works.*

Introduction

Welcome to *The Internet For Windows For Dummies Starter Kit!* There are lots of books available about the Internet, but most of them assume that you have a degree in computer science, would love to learn every strange and useless wart of the Internet, and enjoy memorizing unpronounceable commands and options. We hope this book is different.

This book describes what you actually do to become an *Internaut* (someone who navigates the Internet with skill) — how to get started, what commands you actually need, and when to give up and go for help. And we describe it in plain old English.

About This Book

This book is designed to do two things: First, it gets your Windows PC onto the Net using the Internet Chameleon software contained on the disks in the back. Second, it's designed to be used when you can't figure out what to do next. We don't flatter ourselves that you are interested enough in the Internet to sit down and read the whole thing (though it should be a fine book for the bathroom). When you run into a problem using the Internet ("Hmm . . . I *thought* I ran a program that would log into another computer, but it didn't respond with any message . . ."), just dip into the book long enough to solve your problem.

Pertinent sections include:

- What the Internet is
- How to get connected to the Net
- Communicating with electronic mail
- Using other computers on the Net
- Moving files and other data around
- Ways to find useful stuff on the Internet
- Common mistakes and how to correct them
- Where to find services and software beyond what's in this book

About the Software in This Book

This book contains a special version of **Internet Chameleon** from NetManage, Inc. of Cupertino, California, a leading vendor of Internet software for the Microsoft Windows operating system. It includes all of the software you need to use the Internet, including the latest applications like Chameleon WebSurfer and Instant Internet. WebSurfer, sort of like a much faster version of Mosaic (the famous, free software product from NCSA), enables you to roam the reaches of the World Wide Web (see Chapters 16 and 17). Instant Internet automates the otherwise horribly tedious job of setting up your computer to work with the Net (see Chapter 3). In fact, *Starter Kit* is a misnomer — for most people, this book comes with all the software you need to effectively use the resources of the Internet like a pro. Most "starter kit" books come with the Chameleon *Sampler,* a bare bones shareware edition of an older version of Chameleon that leaves you needing to find and download lots more programs before you can really use the Net.

Note: The important difference between the software in this book and the Chameleon Sampler is that *this version requires activation.* That is, after you install this software, you must sign up with a cooperating Internet provider who will give you an activation key that turns on the software. Then, after the software is activated, you can continue using it with that provider or with any other Internet provider you want. If you want to use a provider other than the cooperating ones, however, you still need to get an activation key from NetManage or one of the other cooperating providers.

Most providers offer a 30-day free trial, during which they give you a temporary key that works for the duration of the trial. After the trial period is up, to continue using the software, you have to get a permanent key by signing up for a regular account with the provider.

How to Use This Book

First, use this book to get connected. Read Chapter 3 for how to install Internet Chameleon and get your own account. Then try the programs you are interested in, referring to the chapters that describe each one.

After that, use this book as a reference. Look up your topic or command in the Table of Contents or the Index, which refers you to the part of the book in which we describe what to do and perhaps define a few terms (if absolutely necessary).

When you have to type something, it appears in the book like this:

```
cryptic command to type
```

Type it in, just as it appears. Use the same capitalization we do — many systems care very deeply about CAPITAL and lowercase letters. Then press the Enter or Return key. The book tells you what should happen when you give each command and what your options are.

You'll find chapters that list error messages that you may run into as well as common user mistakes. You may want to peruse the latter topic (Chapter 21) in order to avoid these mistakes before they happen.

Who Are You?

In writing the book, we assumed that

- You have or would like to have access to the Internet.
- You want to get some work done (or have some fun) with it.
- You have a PC running the Windows operating system on which you want to run your Internet software.
- You are not interested in becoming the world's next great Internet expert.

How This Book Is Organized

This book has five parts. The parts stand on their own — you can start reading wherever you like, but you should at least skim Part I first to get acquainted with some unavoidable Internet jargon and learn how to get your computer on to the Net.

Here are the parts of the book and what they contain:

Part I: Getting onto the Internet

This part defines what the Internet is and why it's interesting (at least why we think it's interesting). Also, there's stuff on vital Internet terminology and concepts that will help you as you move through the later parts, and it walks you through the process of installing and configuring your Internet Chameleon software.

Part II: Mail and Gossip

In this part, you learn how to exchange electronic mail with people who may be down the hall or on other continents and how to use electronic mailing lists to keep in touch with people of like interests. You learn about using *Usenet news* to keep in touch even better, and there are even some suggestions for checking out the thousands of topics that Usenet addresses.

Part III: Using Other Computers and Grabbing Files

Here you learn how to log into other computers, how to retrieve useful files from computers around the world, and how to figure out what to do with the files once you've got them.

Part IV: Searching the Net

This part tells you about four extremely cool programs that help you find useful stuff among the millions (no kidding) of computers on the Net, mostly by clicking and pointing.

Part V: Neat Stuff from the Net

This part is a compendium of ready references and useful facts (which implies, we suppose, that the other chapters are full of useless facts, but we hope not). Part V includes how to find and install swell free and shareware Internet software from the Net itself, as well as a bunch of fun and useful places to start your network explorations. Plus three exciting Appendices.

Icons Used in This Book

This icon lets you know that some particularly nerdy, technoid information is coming up so that you can skip it if you want (on the other hand, you might want to read it).

This icon indicates that a nifty little shortcut or time-saver is explained.

Watch out! You're near a dangerous part of cyberspace.

This icon alerts you to particularly juicy information related to locating something or someone on the Net.

What Now?

That's all you need to know to get started. Whenever you hit a snag using the Internet, just look up the problem in the Table of Contents or Index of this book. You'll either have the problem solved in a flash or you'll know whether you need to find some expert help.

Because the Internet has been evolving for more than 20 years, largely under the influence of some extremely nerdy people, it was *not* designed to be particularly easy for normal people to use. So don't feel bad if you have to look up a number of topics before you feel comfortable using the Internet. After all, most computer users never have to face anything as complex as the Internet.

Feedback, Please

We love to hear from our readers. If you want to contact us, please feel free to do so in care of

IDG Books Worldwide
7260 Shadeland Station
Suite 100
Indianapolis, IN 46256

Or, better yet, send us Internet electronic mail at `starter@dummies.com`.

Part I

Getting onto the Internet

The 5th Wave **By Rich Tennant**

"I THOUGHT HE WAS A VACUUM CLEANER SALESMAN. HE CAME IN, SPRINKLED DIRT ON THE CARPET, AND THEN TRIED TO SELL ME A SOFTWARE PROGRAM THAT WOULD SHOW ME HOW TO CLEAN IT UP."

In this part . . .

The Internet is a big and happening place. But it's full of computers, so nothing there is quite as simple as it should be. First we take a look at what the Internet is and how it got that way. Then we get down to business figuring out how to get *your* computer onto the Net. If you are impatient to begin, skip straight to Chapter 3 to install your new Internet software and get your own account.

Chapter 1

What Is the Internet? Why Use It?

In This Chapter

- What is the Internet?
- What's so cool about it?
- What is it good for?

Before we launch right into getting your Windows computer connected to the Internet, let's review what this subject is all about and why you want to bother. If you already know what the Internet is, skip this chapter and jump right in with Chapter 2, "Ways to Get Connected."

What Is the Internet?

The *Internet* — also known as the *Net* — is the world's largest computer *network.* "And what is a network?" you might ask. Even if you already know, you might want to read the next couple of paragraphs to make sure we're speaking the same language.

A computer network is, basically, a bunch of computers hooked together somehow. (Here in computerland, we like these crisp, precise definitions.) In concept, it's sort of like a radio or TV network that connects a bunch of radio or TV stations together so that they can share the latest episode of "The Simpsons."

But don't take the analogy too far. TV networks send the same information to all the stations at the same time (in a process called *broadcast* networking, for obvious reasons); in computer networks, each particular message is usually routed to a particular computer. Unlike TV networks, computer networks are invariably two-way so that when computer A sends a message to computer B, B can send a reply back to A.

Some computer networks consist of a central computer and a bunch of remote stations that report to it (a central airline-reservation computer, for example, with thousands of terminals at airports and travel agencies). Others, including the Internet, are more egalitarian and permit any computer on the network to communicate with any other.

The Internet isn't really a network — it's a network of networks, all freely exchanging information. The networks range from the big and formal, such as the corporate networks at AT&T, Digital Equipment, and Hewlett-Packard, to the small and informal, like the one in the attic of one of the authors of this book (with a couple of old PCs bought through the "Want Advertiser") and everything in between. College and university networks have long been part of the Internet, and now high schools and elementary schools are joining up too.

What's So Cool About It?

So the Internet is a network, actually a network of networks, and it really is huge. Nobody knows exactly *how* big it is, in fact, because it is a collection of separately run smaller computer networks with no single place where all the connections are registered.

Just how big is it?

At least a million machines are connected to the Internet, and it has many millions of users on every continent (see the sidebar titled "Every continent?"). *That's* big. One thing we do know is that it's growing like crazy — as of August 1994, more than 46,000 networks were on the Internet, with 1,000 new networks per month being added. The Internet Society estimates (perhaps overenthusiastically) that more than *32 million people* use it.

Anybody can access it?

Another unusual thing about the Internet is that it's probably the most *open* network in the world. Thousands of computers provide facilities that are available to anyone who has Net access. This situation is unusual — most networks are very restrictive in what they allow users to do and require specific arrangements and passwords for each service. Although many pay services exist, the majority of Internet services are free for the taking. If you don't already have access to the Internet through your company, your school, or John's attic, you probably have to pay for access to the Internet by using one of the Internet access providers. We talk about providers in Chapter 2, "Ways to Get Connected."

Politically, socially, religiously correct

The final unusual thing about the Internet is that it is what one might call *socially unstratified*. That is, one computer is no better than any other, and no person is any better than any other. Who you are on the Internet depends solely on how you present yourself through your keyboard. If what you say makes you sound like an intelligent, interesting person, that's who you are. It doesn't matter how old you are or what you look like or whether you're a student, a business executive, or a construction worker. Physical disabilities don't matter — we correspond with several people who are blind or deaf. If they hadn't felt like telling us, we never would have known. Famous people are in the Net community, some favorably and some unfavorably, but they got that way through their own efforts.

What's in It for Me?

After you are connected to the Internet, you can use its various services. There are thousands of different services you can use, but this section describes only the major ones.

Every continent?

Some skeptical readers, after reading the claim that the Internet spans every continent, may point out that Antarctica is a continent, even though its population consists largely of penguins, who (as far as we know) are not interested in computer networks. Does the Internet go there? It does. A few machines at the Scott Base, on McMurdo Sound in Antarctica, are on the Net, connected by radio link to New Zealand. The base at the South Pole is supposed to have a link to the U.S., but it doesn't publish its electronic address.

At the time of this writing, the largest Internet-free land mass in the world seems to be Bali, or maybe Java. (Greenland got on the Internet in 1992.)

Electronic mail (e-mail)

Electronic mail is certainly the most widely used service — you can exchange e-mail with millions of people all over the world. And people use e-mail for anything they might use paper mail or the telephone for: gossip, recipes, rumors, love letters — you name it. (Some people even use it for stuff related to work.) The newer, fancier e-mail programs also let you attach files to your mail, so you can use e-mail to send word-processing documents, programs, or graphics files to your friends.

In addition to sending messages to friends and colleagues, you can join electronic *mailing lists,* which enable you to join in group discussions and meet people over the Net. *Mail servers* (programs that respond to e-mail messages) let you retrieve all sorts of information by way of e-mail.

This book comes with Chameleon Mail, a Windows-based mail-reading program that enables you to attach all types of files to your mail (see Chapter 4 for details).

Bulletin boards (Usenet newsgroups)

A system called *Usenet* is an enormous, distributed, on-line bulletin board with about 100 million characters of messages in more than 4,000 different topic groups flowing daily. Each topic is called a *newsgroup.* Topics range from nerdy computer stuff to hobbies such as cycling and knitting to endless political arguments to just plain silliness. The most widely read Usenet group features selected jokes, most of which *are* pretty funny.

You'll use NEWTNews (another inspiried program name) to choose which newsgroups to read, select which articles within each newsgroup that look interesting, read the articles, and respond to them, either by e-mail or by sending a follow-up article to the newsgroup (see Chapter 8 for details).

Information retrieval (FTP, Archie, and Gopher)

Many computers have files of information that are free for the taking. The files range from U.S. Supreme Court decisions and library card catalogs to digitized pictures (nearly all of them suitable for family audiences) and an enormous variety of software, from games to operating systems.

The trick, of course, is finding out what files are out there and what computer they are stored on. A program called *Archie* can help you search for files, assuming that you know the filename you are looking for. *Gopher* is a system of menus that can lead you to the information you want.

This book comes with Chameleon FTP, which lets you download files from public archives, Chameleon Archie, which lets you search for files, and Chameleon Gopher, which lets you browse all those menus in Gopherspace (see Chapters 12, 14, and 15 for details).

Using other computers (Telnet)

If you have permission to use another computer that is on the Internet, you can use Telnet to connect to it. Many college and university libraries, for example, allow anyone to Telnet to their card-catalog computers and search for books. You log on to the computer and use the commands that computer requires, just as though you were sitting at a terminal in the college library.

You'll use Chameleon Telnet, which comes with the disks in the back of this book (see Chapter 10 for details).

Hypertext and hypermedia (WebSurfer and the World Wide Web)

For the fanciest and zoomiest in on-line information, you can use the *World Wide Web* (WWW), a system of pages of information linked together like hypertext. When you see something interesting on one page in the WWW, you can usually click it to zoom to another, related page. Some pages also contain pictures, sound clips, and even video — take a look at Figure 1-1. To see WWW pages on your computer, you use a program called Chameleon WebSurfer (see Chapter 17 for details).

On-line conversation (talk and IRC)

You can "talk" in real time to other users anywhere on the Net. Although on-line conversation is pointless for someone down the hall, it's great for quick chats with people on other continents, particularly when one party or the other isn't a native English speaker (typing is easier and clearer than talking). *Internet Relay Chat* (IRC) is a party line over which you can have more or less interesting conversations with other users all over the place. IRC seems to be frequented primarily by bored college students, but you never know whom you'll encounter.

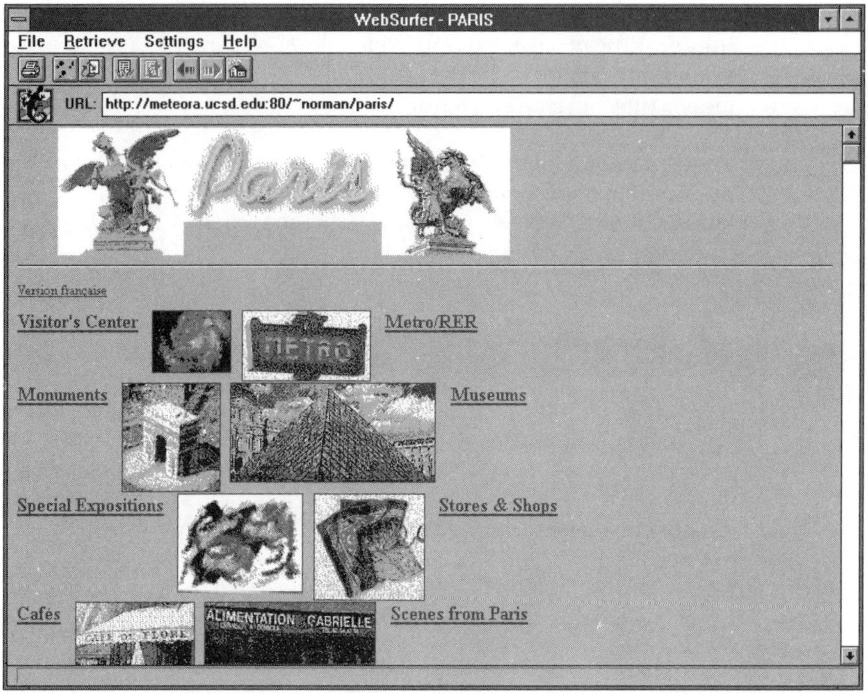

Figure 1-1: WebSurfer and the Web give you a hypertext window on the world.

If you are interested in using talk or IRC (that is, if you have loads of free time to kill), we tell you how to download easy-to-use talk and IRC programs right from the Net (see Chapters 18 and 19 for details).

How Do I Begin?

Your first step is to get your computer connected to the Internet. Then you can begin exploring all these fun Internet services. Chapter 2 describes the various ways you can connect to the Internet, and Chapter 3 contains step-by-step instructions for getting your own Internet account. Read on!

Chapter 2

Ways to Get Connected

In This Chapter

- Determining whether you are already connected to the Internet
- Connecting your computer to a phone line
- Who ya gonna call?
- Choosing an Internet provider
- Learning why SLIP is cool

A confusing thing about the Internet is that there are so many ways to be connected. In fact, you may already be connected without knowing it! This chapter describes the various ways that you, as the owner and operator of a computer that runs Windows, can get connected.

You May Already Be Connected

If you have access to a computer or a computer terminal, you may already be on the Internet. Here are some ways to check:

- If you have an account on an on-line service such as CompuServe, America Online, GEnie, or MCI Mail, you can use the service's electronic-mail system to exchange messages with anyone on the Internet. Some on-line services, notably Delphi, also provide other, more interactive Internet services.
- If you use a *bulletin board system* (BBS) that exchanges messages with other BBSs, again you can exchange e-mail with the Internet.
- If your company or school has an internal e-mail system, it may also be connected to the Internet. Ask a local mail expert.
- If your company or school has a local area network (LAN), it may be connected directly or indirectly to the Internet, either just for mail or for a wider variety of services. Ask your local network guru.

Letting Your PC Talk on the Phone

Okay, okay, you've checked around and your computer is *not* on the Internet. To rectify that situation, you have to give your computer a way to talk on the phone. Here's what you need:

- **A modem connected to your computer (or installed inside it):** A *modem* is a gizmo that lets your computer talk to other computers by using a telephone line. Get as fast a modem as you can afford. Most folks these days buy modems that communicate at 14,400 bps. You can get an internal modem that goes inside your PC (it installs in a slot) or an external one that sits next to your PC, connected to it by a cable to a serial port. We like external modems because they have neat lights that show whether you are on the phone and whether data is flowing. On the other hand, if you have a laptop PC (like John does) there's much to be said for the convenience of an internal modem.
- **A phone line:** You can use your regular phone line if you don't mind tying it up while you are using the Internet. (If you become a serious nethead, you probably will want a separate computer line, particularly if you live with someone who is not amused by the phone being busy for four hours at a time.) You need a phone wire from the modem to a phone jack too.
- **An account with an Internet provider:** Many commercial Internet providers have sprung up in the past few years. If you can get a free account with your company or school, so much the better. We talk about the types of Internet providers in the next section.
- **Communications software:** Your computer needs software to tell it to talk on the phone to your Internet provider. The type of Internet provider you use determines the kind of software you need. In the next section, we describe the software each type of Internet provider works with.

Here are some random tips you may find useful:

- If your phone line has a call-waiting feature, which beeps when another call comes in, it confuses your computer and your provider's system to no end. Therefore, you should turn off call-waiting. To turn off call-waiting for the duration of one outgoing call, dial *70 on your touchtone phone and wait for a confirming tone. To use this feature when you make calls from your computer, precede the phone number with *70, (include the comma too). This technique tells the modem to dial *70 and then wait a few seconds before dialing the number. (If you don't have a touchtone phone, dial 1170 instead.) In most places, *70 is automatically provided with call-waiting. In a few places, you have to call the phone company and ask for it, and in at least one (New Jersey is the only one we know of), it costs extra. (If *70 doesn't work to turn off call-waiting, try 70#, says one of our phone-geek editors.)

TIP

- When — notice we didn't say *if* — you get a separate line for your modem, be sure *not* to get call-waiting on that line.
- If you have to buy a modem, find the cheapest fax modem that runs at 14,400 bps (currently the fastest usable speed — you can pay more for things that go faster, but that speed isn't usually passed on to you by using your ordinary phone line just now). If it's an external modem, make sure that whoever's selling it to you gives you the correct cable for your computer. If it's an internal modem, make sure that it works with your computer and that you have a spare slot for it. If you want to find out more about modems, check out Tina Rathbone's *Modems For Dummies* (published by IDG Books Worldwide).

Who Ya Gonna Call?

Next, you need someone for your computer to call on the phone — your *Internet provider.* An Internet provider is a business that sells you access to its computers, which are on the Internet. There are lots of Internet services you can use, with more appearing every month.

Virtually all providers fall into four categories:

- Bulletin boards (BBSs)
- General on-line systems
- Shell systems
- SLIP systems

The first two don't really give you complete Internet access, but they can be interesting and fun, and they usually provide at least e-mail access to the rest of the Internet. The last two are the real McCoy, bringing the entire Internet world to your doorstep.

Bulletin boards

Electronic bulletin board systems (BBSs) provide on-line services generally on a small scale and many times with a particular focus. They are often local, usually very cheap, and sometimes even free to callers. They may provide an e-mail connection to the Internet, chatting (on-line conversations with other users), forums about special interests, games, ads, and lots, lots more. We've found bulletin board users to be very friendly and welcoming of newcomers. However, they *don't* give you real Internet access either — just e-mail.

General on-line services

On-line services are services provided to you by a computer or computers interactively. They include but are not limited to computerized banking, shopping, dating, entertainment, and study. *They may or may not have anything to do with the Internet.* For many years, such major on-line service providers as CompuServe existed independently of the Internet, enabling users to exchange electronic mail among other CompuServe users but failing to reach out to touch anyone else.

Almost all the popular on-line services are now adding Internet connectivity. America Online, CompuServe, and Prodigy — the most widely used on-line services — all let you at least send and receive mail from the Internet. At the time this book is being written, CompuServe and America Online give access to Usenet newsgroups, and America Online also provides access to Gopher and WAIS. However, *none of them provides true, complete Internet access.*

Some on-line services provide you with special software you use rather than a regular communications program. America Online works only with its own special software, which it gives you when you sign up — a nice, Windows-based program with friendly icons. CompuServe works with a normal terminal program, but it's much friendlier if you use WinCim or CSNav, two Windows-based programs.

Pipeline is another on-line service that comes with its own Windows software. Unlike CompuServe, America Online, and Prodigy, Pipeline *does* offer Internet services with few additional ones. Pipeline is in New York City, but several providers around the country use its software.

Shell systems

With a shell system, you use your PC as a terminal. Your PC isn't really "on the Internet" — instead, you use it to communicate with the provider's computer, which *is* on the Net. Delphi, NETCOM, and the World provide this type of access. The provider's system runs Internet applications such as Telnet and FTP. On your computer, you run a terminal emulator communications program such as Procomm, Crosstalk, or — everyone's third choice — Windows Terminal (its advantage is that it comes free with Windows). The shell provider tells you the phone number your modem should call, your ID, and your password. You use the communications program to make the call.

Some shell providers, such as the World and NETCOM, give you access to a machine running UNIX. It's up to you to learn the UNIX commands necessary to use the system. For details about the UNIX commands you need for UNIX shell providers, see *The Internet For Dummies,* 2nd Edition by John R. Levine and Carol Baroudi (1994, IDG Books Worldwide).

Other shell systems provide menus to make them easier to use. For example, Delphi displays an apparently endless succession of menus — they can get tedious after you are familiar with them, but they are great when you are getting started.

Shell systems usually give you full access to all Internet services, including e-mail, Usenet newsgroups, FTP file transfer, Telnet for logging in to other computers, and more. For details about using Internet shell providers, see *MORE Internet For Dummies,* by us same authors (1994, IDG Books Worldwide).

SLIP systems

With SLIP, your PC becomes part of the Internet. InterRamp, AlterNet, and many other providers can give you SLIP access. With SLIP, while you're dialed up to your provider, your computer *is* part of the Internet, with its own host name and everything. Network applications such as Telnet and FTP run on your own computer. Someone can FTP to *your computer,* in fact, if you allow it! Figure 2-1 shows the difference between a shell connection and a SLIP connection.

We think that SLIP access is the cat's pajamas, Internet-wise, and this book concentrates on how to use a SLIP account to get on the Net. Which Internet services you can use depends on which programs you have on your PC — to use FTP, you need an FTP program; to read newsgroups, you need a newsreader. Luckily, the disks in the back of this book provide almost all the software you need.

Other kinds of access, called CSLIP and PPP, do basically the same thing as SLIP, so to avoid saying "SLIP or CSLIP or PPP" a thousand times, we call them all "SLIP" here.

In case you were wondering, SLIP is the *Serial Line Internet Protocol* (a *serial line* is what network types call a phone-line-type hookup.) CSLIP is *Compressed* SLIP, which uses tricky techniques to send less data over the phone, thus improving performance. PPP is the *Point-to-Point Protocol,* a full-featured, all-singing, all-dancing successor to SLIP.

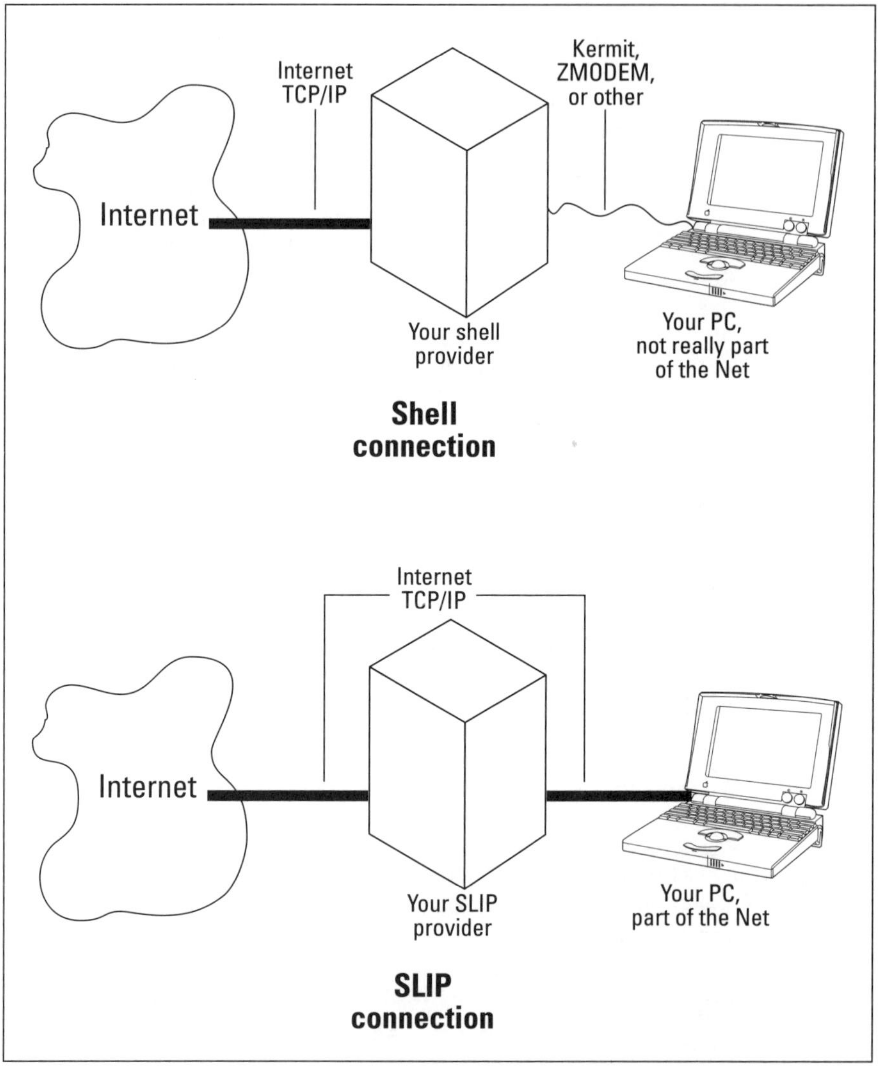

Figure 2-1: The difference between a shell and a SLIP connection.

TIP

For enhanced confusion, many providers provide both shell and SLIP accounts. Which gives you the best of both worlds: You can use one kind of access sometimes and the other kind at other times.

TIP

How the heck should I know whether I want shell or SLIP?

Here's some possibly helpful advice:

Advantages of shell systems

It's easier to get started because there's much less to set up on your system.

All the network applications are set up by the provider.

They usually cost slightly less per hour.

The provider's system is connected to the Net all the time, so you can arrange for files and documents to be available to the public.

Some shell systems provide lots of other services in addition to access to the Internet. Delphi provides lots of business and recreational information, for example, and the World provides a complete UNIX programming environment.

Disadvantages of shell systems

You can use only the applications your provider has set up.

Applications use plain old text — no fancy graphics.

File transfer is more complicated because you first have to transfer files to the provider's system and then to your own computer.

You can run only one application at a time.

You must stay on-line during all the time you are doing Internet-related work (it's not easy to set up your system so that you can read and compose your e-mail off-line, for example).

Advantages of SLIP systems

Applications can and usually do use graphics, mice, icons, and other groovy Windows stuff. Rather than use some yucky UNIX editor such as emacs or vi (*shiver*) to write e-mail messages, you can use a nice Windows-based editor or your own word processor. Check out the screen pictures throughout this book to see how nice these programs look.

You can run any network application you want, including cool, free ones you can get from the Net.

Multiple applications can run at the same time in different windows.

File transfer runs directly to and from the disk on your computer.

Disadvantages of SLIP systems

They can be more difficult to set up.

Because they're a part-time Internet connection, it is impractical to provide files and services to other people.

The Windows applications are not always as powerful as their UNIX equivalents are. The UNIX-based newsreading programs you use on a shell system, for example, are more powerful (though more difficult to figure out) than the Windows ones are, especially when it comes to skipping articles you don't want to read.

Here at Internet For Dummies Central, we have both kinds of systems, naturally. If we had to choose one or the other, we definitely would choose SLIP because the programs are so much more fun.

Choosing an Internet Provider

As you know, this book comes with the complete software necessary to connect your Windows computer to the Internet by using a SLIP connection. The software, called Chameleon, provides the connection itself in addition to programs that handle e-mail, Usenet newsgroups, FTP file transfer, Telnet (for logging on to other computers), web surfing (reading World Wide Web hypertext pages), and more.

The Chameleon software that comes with this book also includes the unique Instant Internet. This program lets you choose from a group of national Internet SLIP providers, calls up the one you choose, and automatically does the following:

- Sets up a new Internet SLIP account for you
- Downloads the information you need in order to configure your Chameleon programs, including your Internet address and the addresses of the computers that provide you with mail and newsgroup services
- Configures all the Chameleon programs with this information

So, assuming that you have your modem and phone line hooked up, you still have the disks that came with this book, and you're ready to make your SLIP connection with the Internet, you're ready for the next chapter.

Instant Internet works with *only* the Internet SLIP providers shown when you run the program. Only these providers have the software to do automatic configuration for you. If you want to use another provider, follow the instructions in Appendix B. If you are outside the U.S., Appendix C contains a partial listing of Internet providers in some other countries.

If your PC is on a local area network and you want to connect to the Internet through the LAN, you need the LAN version of Chameleon. The version that comes with this book is for PCs that connect to the Internet by directly dialing up using a modem inside the computer or attached to a serial port. The rest of the Chameleon programs that come with this book, such as Mail and Telnet and WebSurfer, are the same in the LAN version as in this version. If you're interested in the LAN version of Chameleon, contact NetManage for details on an upgrade offer.

Why SLIP Is Way Cool

There's another reason that SLIP connections are so cool — a standard has been developed for Windows programs that work with SLIP-type connections. The standard is called *WinSock* (which stands for *Win*dows *Sock*ets, if you can believe it). If you use a SLIP connection, you can install and use *any* WinSock-compatible program.

And lots of cool WinSock software is available, much of it free on the Internet. In addition to the programs that come with Chameleon, described in Parts II, III, and IV in this book, you can download and install any WinSock software that looks interesting — Part V, "Neat Stuff from the Net," tells you how.

Chapter 3

SLIP-ing onto the Net with Chameleon

In This Chapter

- Installing Internet Chameleon
- Using Instant Internet to activate your software and sign up for a SLIP or PPP account
- Calling your Internet provider for the first time
- Calling your Internet provider after that
- Hanging up on your Internet provider
- Who are you?

Okay, you've got your computer connected to a modem and phone line, you're clutching the disks from the back of this book, and you're ready to network. Here we go!

The Master Plan

Here's the general procedure for getting up and running with your SLIP account and Chameleon software:

1. **Install the Chameleon software from the disks.**
2. **Choose a provider from the ones available in Instant Internet.**
3. **Call your provider by using Instant Internet.**

   This step both activates your Chameleon software and sets up a SLIP, PPP, or ISDN account (which we'll henceforth refer to as a SLIP account, even though that's not strictly correct) with your provider. If you are not sure about this whole plan, most providers let you sign up for a free demo, which lasts from seven to 30 days, so that you can try out both the software and the provider's service before deciding.

4. **Make your very first SLIP connection to the Net, by using the Custom program.**
5. **Test your connection by using the Ping program.**

The rest of this chapter leads you through these steps. Don't worry — it's easy and fast!

If you already have an Internet provider, install the Internet Chameleon software by following the instructions in the section "Installing Internet Chameleon," later in this chapter. Then see Appendix B, "Manually Configuring Chameleon," to learn how to activate the software and set it up to work with your provider.

For readers outside the United States and Canada, some of the providers you see in the Instant Internet program may have international access numbers. If you want to use a provider from your own country rather than one of the U.S. providers in Instant Internet, see Appendix C, "International Internet Providers."

What You Need

Be sure that you have the following things handy:

- This book
- The disks that came with it
- A computer that runs Microsoft Windows 3.1; it must have a 386, 486, or Pentium chip (a 286 won't do — sorry.)
- A modem installed inside your computer or connected to it by using a serial cable — the modem should be capable of communicating at least as fast as 14.4K bps or else you will die of boredom waiting for information to appear on your screen
- At least 4MB of RAM in your computer
- At least 5MB of free space on your hard disk for the software
- A 3½-inch disk drive
- DOS 5.0 or newer and Windows 3.1 or 3.11, running in Enhanced mode (that's the usual mode, unless you have a very elderly computer with a 286, which won't work anyway)

Installing Internet Chameleon

The idea here is to install Internet Chameleon (the program that allows your computer to communicate with the Internet by using SLIP, PPP, or ISDN), Instant Internet (the program that signs you up with the Internet provider you choose), and a bunch of Chameleon WinSock Internet programs, including Mail, FTP, WebSurfer, and Telnet.

Grab the disks from the back of this book and follow these steps:

1. **Insert the Internet Chameleon Disk 1 in the disk drive.**
2. **In the Windows Program Manager, choose File⇨Run from the menu.**

   You see the Run dialog box.
3. **Type** `a:\setup` **in the Command Line box and click OK.**

   If the disk is in drive B:, type **b:\setup**. Either way, the Chameleon installation program runs, asks where you want to install the software, and displays the dialog box shown in Figure 3-1.

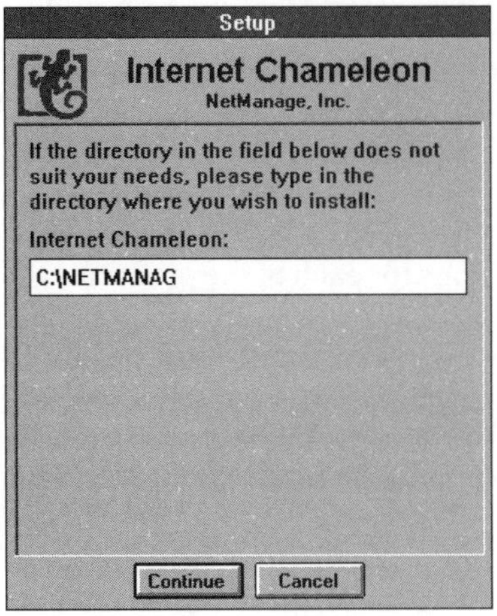

Figure 3-1: Where do you want your Chameleon software installed?

Chameleon suggests C:\NETMANAG as the directory in which it will install its software files. You can change this name if you would rather put the files somewhere else.

4. **Click Continue.**

   Chameleon creates the directory (if it doesn't already exist) and copies a bunch of files into it from the diskette. It also adds information to your AUTOEXEC.BAT and WIN.INI files.

   The setup program copies the program files and asks for each of the other disks.

5. **When you're asked for a disk, stick the disk it wants into the same disk drive you've been using and click Continue.**

   When it is finished, the setup program displays a message telling you that the installation is complete.

6. **Click OK to make the message disappear.**

   Sometimes, at this point your Program Manager window minimizes, so you may have to find the Program Manager icon near the bottom of your screen at this point.

7. **If your Program Manager window has disappeared, double-click the Program Manager icon at the bottom of the screen to bring it back to life.**

   In the Program Manager window, you see a new little program group icon named Internet Chameleon.

8. **In the Program Manager, double-click the Internet Chameleon icon to see the program group.**

   You can adjust the size, shape, and position of the program group by dragging its sides. The group should look something like Figure 3-2 — pretty empty. Don't worry — icons for each of the programs that come with Chameleon appear later, after you sign up for your Internet provider.

Figure 3-2: Your Chameleon program group.

So why is this SLIP program called Chameleon, anyway?

Chameleon is based on a program called NEWT, which stands for something like NetManage Enhanced Windows TCP/IP. You don't run NEWT directly, but all the other Internet programs use it to manage the connection to the Internet. When the folks at NetManage decided to write this nice Windows-based program that connects to NEWT, they chose the name Chameleon. (The next product will probably be called Gecko or Iguana.) You even see a cute little NEWT icon on your screen when NEWT is running.

Opening Your SLIP Account

The coolest thing about the software that comes with this book is the Instant Internet program. We have installed and configured SLIP software many times, and it has until now been a total and colossal bore, not to mention confusing. This program does the job for you in about five minutes by getting the various Internet parameters you need and plugging them in to the configuration parts of all the Chameleon programs. For example, when you're through, Chameleon Mail will know where to pick up your mail, and NEWTNews (the Chameleon newsreader) will know where to get your newsgroups.

TIP

Before you run Instant Internet, decide how to you want to pay for your SLIP account. Most Internet providers bill you every month. You have to choose a credit card on which to put the bill, and you have to type the card number and expiration date when you register your account. Even if you decide to start with a free demo version, you have to enter a credit-card number. Don't worry about security — Instant Internet uses a regular phone call, not an Internet connection, when it transmits your credit-card number to your provider.

In order to find out how much each provider charges, you have to connect to each provider and read its prices. Some offer free demos, and some charge extra to activate your software. Go ahead and choose Sign up and Send to call each provider — after you've read about its pricing, you can still cancel.

Instant Internet!

Actually, this process isn't totally instant because some Internet providers take a day or so to get your account set up. But at least *your* part is instant and doesn't involve any horrendous configuration process!

1. **Double-click the Instant Internet icon in the Internet Chameleon program group.**

   When you run Instant Internet, you see the Select Internet Provider window, shown in Figure 3-3. Across the top of the window are "tabs," one for each Internet provider that works with the Instant Internet program.

Figure 3-3: Which Internet provider have you decided to use?

2. **Browse through the Internet providers by clicking their tabs.**

   For more information about a provider, click the More Info button at the bottom of the window. Here's where you learn about their prices, terms, and conditions. When you've read the text, click the Cancel button to return to the Select Internet Provider window.

3. **When you've chosen a provider, click its tab and then click the Signup button.**

   You see the Instant Internet Account Sign-Up window, shown in Figure 3-4. There are two tabs at the top of the window, named "Please fill out this registration form" and "Fill out this also." These forms contain all the blanks you need to fill in to tell your new Internet provider all about yourself, where you live, and how you want to pay for your new Internet account. The forms vary from provider to provider — because different providers are interested in different information.

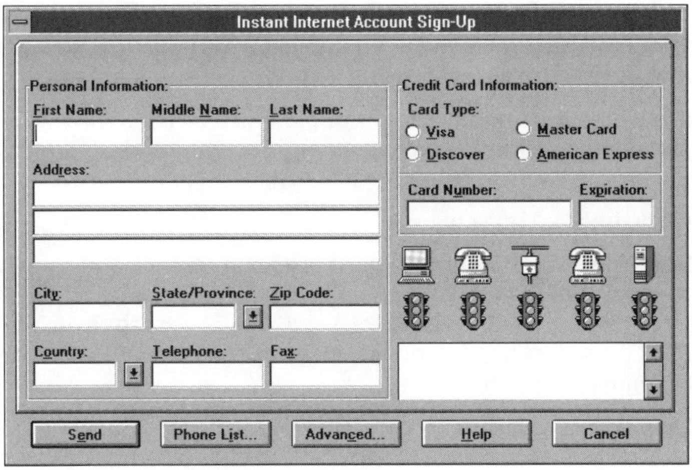

Figure 3-4: Time to tell your new Internet provider all about yourself.

4. **Fill in the blanks.**

   You can always click the Help button if you have questions. Don't worry about the little pictures of phones, cables, and traffic lights — the program uses those later to show you how it's doing while it communicates with your Internet provider.

5. **Click the Phone List button and choose the phone number that is closest to you.**

   That is, minimize your long-distance telephone charges by choosing a phone number that is a local call from where you are, or at least not too far away. Those of you in rural North Dakota may have to settle for a long-distance number.

   If you have to dial some extra digits to get an outside line, use the Phone List button to edit the phone numbers and add the extra digits to the beginning. For example, if your modem is connected through an office phone system that requires dialing 9 first for an outside call, you have to add a 9 and a comma (modem-ese for a short pause) in front of the phone number.

6. **If there is a "Fill out this additional form as well" tab in the upper corner of the window, click it.**

   You see another form, with more blanks. (Some providers may not use this form, if all their questions fit on the first form. In that case, the tab doesn't appear.)

7. **Fill in the blanks.**

8. **When you've answered all the questions on both forms, make sure that your modem is turned on (if it's an external modem). Also, make sure that no other program is using it and that it's plugged into a phone jack.**

   If you have a fax-modem, for example, close your fax software so that Instant Internet and your fax software don't argue about who's using the phone line. (It's a little like having teenagers in the house.)

9. **Click the Send button.**

   Instant Internet figures out which of your communication ports connects to your modem, calls your new Internet provider, and transmits the information you just typed. You see a "hello" message from your provider. Most providers let you choose between a real account and a demo account at this point.

   Depending on the Internet provider you chose, you may see various information messages. You may have to click OK to agree to the provider's sign-up agreement. And you may have to choose which type of account you want, if your provider offers different pricing packages. If your provider offers a free introductory account, this is the point where you can tell it that that's what you want.

   Then your provider gets approval for your new account and downloads your new Internet address and other configuration information. While it's at it, it configures all your Internet Chameleon software to work with this new Internet account.

   Your account may not appear immediately. Most providers require a few hours or a day to get everything set up, assign you an Internet address, and all that stuff.

   The last message from your provider contains some information about your new account — they are so well-organized that they can tell you the host name of your PC, your username, and your password right on the spot. Put this information in Table 3-1 (and into the Cheat Sheet in the front of the book) right now so that you can refer to it later.

   When Instant Internet is finished, it explodes into a bunch of fantastic icons in your Internet Chameleon program group. Your new, improved set of icons looks like Figure 3-5. Then you see a message that tells you that you've successfully registered for a new Internet account.

10. **Click OK to make the message go away.**

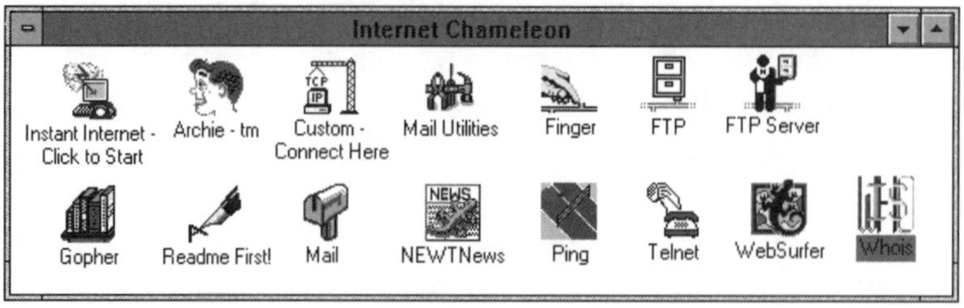

Figure 3-5: At last — your Chameleon programs appear!

11. **When you see the Account Registration Complete dialog box, read it and decide whether to restart your computer right away. Before you can use your new Internet applications, you need to reboot so the new configuration takes effect.**

    If you have an ISDN telephone connection, before you reboot, run the Custom application and select Setup⇨Hardware to set the type of ISDN card you have. Then exit from Custom, telling it to save the changes.

    If you are running other Windows programs and don't want to reboot your computer right now, click Restart Later, and remember to exit from Windows and reboot your PC before using Internet Chameleon. If you're raring to go, click Restart Now.

Table 3-1 (and the Cheat Sheet) provide convenient places for you to fill in information you will need to refer to in the future.

Table 3-1 Information About Your Account

Item	*Description*	*Your Account*
Host name	The name of your PC, which is part of your PC's Internet address	
Username	Your username, which is the part of your e-mail address that comes before the at-sign	
E-mail address	Your complete e-mail address	
Password	The password you have to enter to use your account (actually, Internet Chameleon always types it for you)	
Mail password	Separate password used to read the mail from your mailbox	
Support number	The (voice) phone number of your Internet provider, in case you run into trouble	
IP address	A four-part number that identifies your number on the Internet, something like 123.45.67.89	

If your provider doesn't display all the information listed in Table 3-1, you probably can figure it out. See the section "Who Are You?" at the end of this chapter.

What if it's not so instant?

If Instant Internet wasn't able to dial the phone, it might not have found your modem. After you click the Signup button for your provider, click the Advanced button. Set the Connector to the communications port to which your modem is attached and click OK. Then make sure your modem is turned on and connected to the phone line and try clicking Send again.

If you need to dial 9 or some other digit (or digits) to get an outside line, you must click the Phone List button. Then edit the Active Phone number, adding the digit (or digits) at the beginning.

If you have the call-interrupt feature on your phone line, the little beeps can really foul up computer conversations. Use the Phone List button to add *70 (or, in some areas, 70#) to the beginning of the phone number. This number tells your phone system to turn off the call-interrupt feature for the duration of this phone call.

Appendix B contains all the settings that Instant Internet sets — just in case you have to fool with them yourself. If your sign-up doesn't happen automagically, as it should, refer to Appendix B. In a pinch, call NetManage support (see Appendix A).

Some providers offer free trial periods. If you choose a free demo when you run Instant Internet, the provider gives you a demo serial number that lasts only for the duration of the free trial (7 days, or 30 days, or whatever). Once the time has expired on your demo account, you must run Instant Internet again to sign up for a permanent account. You can get one free demo for each credit card you use.

Making a Connection

You're on the Net! These steps show you how to make a connection, after your Internet provider has created your account, and after you've restarted your computer.

1. **Make sure that no other program is using your modem.**

   In particular, if you use fax software, exit from it.

2. **Double-click the Custom icon in the Internet Chameleon program group.**

   You see the Custom window, shown in Figure 3-6. Also, a little NEWT icon appears in the lower part of your screen, indicating that the communications-handling program that comes with Chameleon is loaded and working (good news).

3. **If the phone number doesn't look correct, choose Setup⇨Dial from the menu bar.**

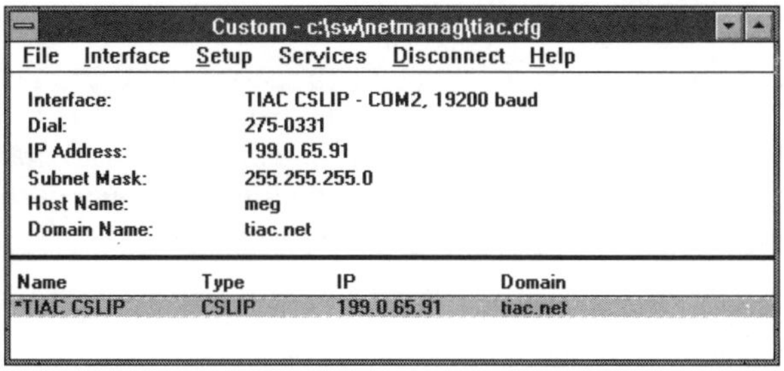

Figure 3-6: The Custom window, where you connect to and disconnect from the Internet.

   Look at the phone number for your Internet provider, which appears to the right of the Dial label in the Custom window. If it doesn't work as shown (for example, if it includes your own area code, or needs to start with a 1), fix it by choosing Setup⇨Dial from the menu bar, editing the phone number in the Dial box, and clicking OK.

   TIP: If the phone number is a long-distance call for you, you might want to call your Internet provider's support number to ask if they have added any more access numbers. Most providers are growing like Topsy, and a new number may be available closer to you.

4. **Choose Setup⇨Log from the menu bar.**

   This command opens a *Log window,* in which you can see what's going on between your computer and your Internet provider's. This step isn't absolutely necessary, but it's a good way to make sure that everything is working right.

5. **Move the Log window out of the way so that you can see the Custom window.**

   You can move the window by dragging its title bar with your mouse. You can also make the Log window larger if you want to see more of what's going on.

6. **In the Custom window, choose Connect.**

   You see a Connect box that tells you the phone number it is dialing. Then strange codes appear in the Log window as Chameleon dials the phone and makes the connection. You see your Internet provider's computer answer the phone, and Chameleon enters your username and password for you.

   After Chameleon enters your username and password, you should be connected. The Connect box disappears, and the Connect choice on the menu bar changes to Disconnect. That's about all the notification you get that your SLIP connection is now working.

Now you are ready to run programs that let you read your Internet mail, newsgroups, and so on. While you are connected to your Internet provider, you must leave the Custom program running. You can minimize it so that it shrinks to a little icon at the bottom of your screen by clicking the downward-pointing triangle in the upper right-hand corner of its window.

TIP

If you run into trouble and want to hang up the phone, choose Disconnect from the Custom window's menu bar.

It Didn't Work!

It would be lovely if everything worked right the first time, but that rarely happens. This section shows you some things to try.

If the Chameleon Custom program couldn't even dial the phone, try these suggestions:

- Make sure that you restarted your computer as Instant Internet suggested. If you didn't, exit from all Windows programs, exit from Windows, and then reboot your computer by pressing Ctrl+Alt+Del (that is, hold down the Ctrl and Alt keys while you press the Del key).
- Make sure that your modem is turned on (ignore this suggestion if your modem is inside your computer). Also make sure your modem is connected to a phone line.
- Make sure that you have set the right communications port for your modem. To test this port, use the Windows Terminal program to dial your own number. In Terminal, choose Settings⇨Phone Number to enter your number and then choose Phone⇨Dial to dial the number. If you have the right communications port, you should hear the phone dial and then a busy signal (because you are already using it!). Choose Phone⇨Hangup to hang up the phone.

If Chameleon dials the phone but doesn't connect to your Internet provider, try these suggestions:

- Make sure that you have the right phone number. Look at the entry in the Custom window labeled Dial. If it doesn't look right, you can run Instant Internet again to check the list of phone numbers (choose the provider, click Signup, click Phone List, look at the phone numbers, and choose Cancel a few times to stop yourself from signing up for *another* account.) If the phone number is wrong, choose Setup⇨Dial from the menu bar in the Custom program to change it.
- Make sure that your modem speed is one that your Internet provider supports. If your modem is talking at 28.8K bps and your Internet provider doesn't support that speed, for example, you see gobbledy-gook when they connect, or they may not connect after the provider's modem answers the phone. (Call your provider's support line for help with this.)

  To find out the support number of your Internet provider, run Instant Internet again, choose your provider, and click the More Info button. The phone number should be part of the information about the provider.

If Chameleon connects to your Internet provider and you see your username appear, communication is working fine as far as your port and modem are concerned. Try this technique: Make sure that Instant Internet entered the right username and password. One good way to check is to use the Windows Terminal program (or another communications program) to dial up your Internet provider and enter your username and password yourself. If everything is hunky-dory, you should see a message like `SLIP connection initiated` or some similar technobabble. (See the section "Who Are You?" at the end of this chapter to find out your username.)

After you make changes to your Chameleon Custom settings, be sure to choose File⇨Save from the menu, exit from the Custom program, and then restart it so that all the changes take effect.

Testing! Testing!

To see whether you are really communicating, you can use the Ping program, which sends a little message ("Ping!") to another computer on the Internet and waits for a response ("Pong!"). Make sure that you have connected to your Internet provider before trying this.

1. **Double-click the Ping icon in the Chameleon program group (it's the little Ping-Pong table icon).**

   You see the Ping window, shown in Figure 3-7.

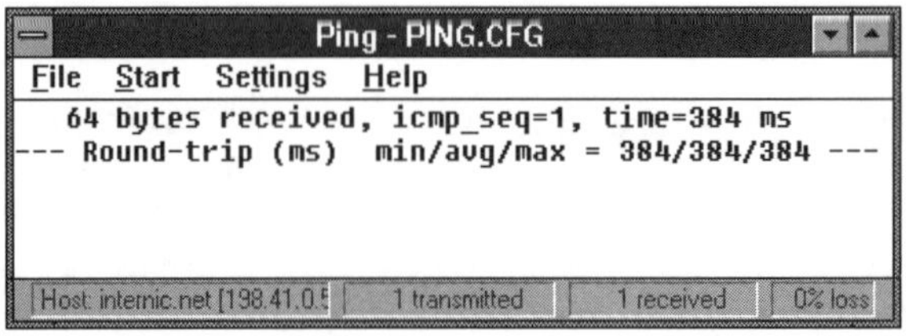

Figure 3-7: Ping has successfully exchanged a message with another computer.

2. **Choose Start.**

   Ping asks for the name of the host computer you want to ping. You can ping any computer you want.

3. **Enter the Internet address of a computer.**

   If you want to ping the Network Information Center for the U.S. part of the Internet (a good choice because it's a nice, big computer that is always up), enter **internic.net**.

4. **Click OK.**

   If the ping works, you see a message that some number of bytes of information (usually 64) were received — bingo! You've spoken to the outside world! Who cares what the computers said to each other?

   If the ping doesn't work, you see a message like `No message received`. Rats. It's probably time to talk to the technical-support people at your Internet provider.

5. **When you have had your fun pinging things, choose File⇨Exit from the menu bar. Then choose No so that you don't save the name of the computer you just pinged.**

   If you plan to ping that computer frequently, you can choose Yes to save it.

When You're Finished, Hang Up

When you are finished using your cool, new connection to the Internet, choose Disconnect from the Custom window's menu bar. Custom asks you to confirm that you want to disconnect — when you choose Yes, it hangs you up.

WARNING!

Remember to hang up, because many Internet providers charge you by the hour!

When you choose File⇨Exit to leave the Custom program, it may ask whether it should save any changes. Choose Yes.

You can leave the Custom program running if you plan to reconnect to the Net later. It doesn't cost anything except when you are actually connected. However, if you want to run another program that uses your modem (like a terminal program or fax software), you must exit from Custom first. Otherwise, the programs will argue like small children about who gets to use the phone, and neither will win.

Calling Again

The next time you call your Internet provider, you don't have to use the Log window to see the messages go by (unless you want to). The Log window is great for troubleshooting, but after everything works smoothly, you can skip it. Just run Custom and choose Connect from its menu bar. When the little Connect status box goes away, you're on.

If a Log window appears whenever you click Connect, and you don't want to see it, choose Setup⇨Dial and click the Open Log When Connecting box to remove the X from this box. Then click OK.

After you are connected, you can minimize the Custom window because nothing interesting happens there until you are ready to disconnect. As long as you are connected to the Internet, the Custom program must be running (it doesn't let you exit if you are still connected). So click the downward-pointing triangle in the window's upper right-hand corner to shrink it to an icon.

You're done! You're on the Net!

Who Are You?

You may be wondering what your e-mail address is. A good question! Here's how to figure out who exactly you and your computer are on the Internet.

Your PC's Internet address

In the Custom window, you see the *host name* and *domain name*. The host name is the name of your own little PC. The domain name is the name of your Internet provider's Internet domain. If you glue them together like this:

```
hostname.domainname
```

you get the Internet address of your own PC. For example, we have a PC with the host name `meg` and the domain name `tiac.net`. This PC's Internet address is therefore `meg.tiac.net`.

Your PC also has a numeric Internet address. It's listed right in the Custom window, as the IP Address. For example, your numeric Internet address might be 199.0.65.91. It always has four parts, separated by dots.

Some Internet providers don't fill in the Host Name and IP Address settings in the Custom window when you sign up — these providers use "dynamic addressing," which means that they assign you a name and number each time you connect. Don't worry — you don't need this information in ordinary usage. While connected, Custom shows the name and number you're using for your current connection.

Your e-mail address

But what about your e-mail address? Hmm . . . that's different from the Internet address of your PC and far more useful. To find out, run Chameleon Mail. (You don't have to be connected to the Internet to do this step.) It prompts you to log in with a username — click OK to accept its suggestion.

While you're in Chameleon Mail, choose Settings⇨Signature from the menu. You see the mail signature that Instant Internet created for you, including your real name and your e-mail address. For now, just make a note of what your e-mail address is. Then click OK and choose File⇨Exit to leave Chameleon Mail. (If you get a message that Mail is currently retrieving mail, choose Yes to abort.) For more information about Mail and how to change your signature, see Chapter 4.

TIP: Here's a way to confirm your e-mail address. Send a message to `starter@dummies.com`, telling us what you think of this book and the software that comes with it. Our friendly mail robot will send you back a message that tells you what your e-mail address is. (And we'll read your comments as well. Yes, really.)

Your password

With luck, your Internet provider told you your password in a message box when you ran Instant Internet to set up your account. And with more luck, you wrote it down. You can't find out your password by looking at the Custom program because it displays your password as a row of asterisks.

The only way to find out your password, or change it, is to contact your Internet provider and follow its instructions. Appendix B, "Manually Configuring Chameleon," contains the steps to follow to enter your new password into the Custom program.

If you want the full details of what you have just installed, double-click the Readme icon in the Chameleon program group. You see a full explanation in gruesome technical detail. When you're done, you might want to delete the icon— you can always read the file again by double-clicking the INETCHAM.WRI filename in File Manager.

Part II

Mail and Gossip

In this part . . .

Rumors, gossip, jokes, recipes, bad jokes, tourist travel tips, and really bad jokes (as if there weren't enough in here already): The Internet has them all, and you can read and write them using electronic mail and Usenet news. Read on to find out how.

Chapter 4

On-Line Gossip: Using Chameleon Mail

In This Chapter

- Names and numbers
- Setting up Chameleon Mail
- Leaving the program
- Sending mail
- Receiving mail
- Keeping an address book of e-mail addresses
- Attaching and detaching files
- Sorting your mail automagically
- Other e-mail programs

The most basic Internet service is e-mail (electronic mail). Not that you are particularly interested in mailing electrons to people, but if you get a bunch of electrons together, they can spell out a useful message.

You use Chameleon Mail to handle your e-mail. Before we tell you how to use it, let's spend a moment or two talking about e-mail addresses and the names and numbers the Internet uses to identify computers. You have to know the names of people and computers on the Net when you begin using Internet services.

Names and Numbers

If you've had anything to do with the Internet, you probably have seen Internet e-mail addresses, which look like this:

```
president@whitehouse.gov
```

An e-mail address has two parts: the part before the at-sign (@) and the part after it. The part before the at-sign is the *username,* or *mailbox name,* of the particular user on a computer, in this example, `president`. The part after the at-sign is the name of the computer that person uses (`whitehouse.gov`, for example). This `president@whitehouse.gov` address is real, by the way— write to it if you have any complaints or ideas!

Computers on the Internet are also called *hosts,* presumably because they graciously wine and dine you with gossip, files, hypermedia pages, and other Internet services. Hosts have names (such as `whitehouse.gov`) that consist of a bunch of words strung together with dots. The last word in the name tells you what kind of outfit owns the computer. You run into host names ending with `com` for companies, `edu` for educational institutions, `gov` for the government, `net` for networking organizations, `mil` for the military, and a few others. Some computers have names that end with country codes, such as `ca` for Canada, `uk` for the United Kingdom, `de` for Germany, and `us` for the United States.

Naturally, computers prefer to think of everything in terms of numbers, so all host computers have numeric addresses too, called *host numbers.* You almost never have to think about or use these numbers, but in case you run into one, they look like this:

```
140.186.81.3
```

(In fact, that's the host number of a computer at Internet for Dummies Central.) They always have four parts, separated by dots. Not every name translates directly to a numeric address, but that's a wart you don't have to worry about.

What's my address?

At the end of Chapter 3, we told you how to find out what your brand-new Internet address is. Your address depends on how your Internet provider assigns addresses. The last part of the address is certainly your provider's Internet address, but what comes before that varies.

Here's a way to find out your e-mail address: Start the Chameleon Mail program and choose Settings⇨Signature from the menu. Your computer's name and address are on a line like this: `E-mail: starter@dummies.com`. Then choose Cancel to leave your signature alone (we explain what a *signature* is in the section "Making a signature for yourself," later in this chapter).

If you ever have a question about what your e-mail address is, send a message to the address `starter@dummies.com`. A friendly robot sends you back a message that tells you your address. While you're at it, tell us whether you like this book, because we authors read the mail too.

Where's my mail?

Your Internet provider keeps a mailbox for you so that mail doesn't get lost when your PC isn't connected to the Internet. Your provider stores any incoming messages for you until you pick them up. To pick them up, you connect to the Internet (as described in Chapter 3) and tell Chameleon Mail to retrieve your messages. Mail downloads (copies) them to your PC and deletes them from your mailbox on your Internet provider's computer.

When you write e-mail messages, you use Chameleon Mail to compose them. Chameleon Mail (or just Mail, for short) stores them on your PC until they are uploaded to your Internet provider and sent out over the Net.

The computer at your Internet provider that accepts outgoing mail is called your *mail gateway*. The computer that holds your incoming mail for pickup is called your *mail server*. These devices are usually the same computer, although they can be two different computers. Don't worry — you don't have to know this stuff to use Chameleon Mail, because Instant Internet sets it all up for you.

POP goes the Internet provider!

Your Internet provider and Chameleon Mail use a system named POP3 for dowloading your mail. POP3 stands for Post Office Protocol, Version 3, and it lets Chameleon Mail ask your Internet provider for your messages, download your messages, and delete the messages in your mailbox on the Internet provider's computer (so that you don't retrieve them again the next time). POP3 is intended particularly for such programs as Chameleon Mail, which are connected to the Internet only while their human users are using them.

Chameleon Mail (and all other Internet mail programs) use a *different* system for sending mail from your PC to the Internet. It's called SMTP (the optimistically named Simple Mail Transfer Protocol), the standard way Internet systems send mail to each other. Chameleon Mail uses it to send your outgoing messages to your Internet provider, which in turn sends them along to their Internet destinations, again by using SMTP.

You might wonder why, if SMTP is the same way mail will be delivered anyway, why not send the mail directly to the recipient's computer. In fact, if Chameleon Mail doesn't have a mail gateway set up, that's what it does. But sometimes it can take two or three tries over a period of several hours to deliver a piece of mail if there is Internet congestion or a host is temporarily off the Net. When you use a mail gateway, the gateway automatically waits and retransmits the message. Without a gateway, Chameleon Mail will indeed retransmit after an hour or so, but you may not want to hang around and wait that long.

Setting Up Chameleon Mail

When you installed Internet Chameleon way back in Chapter 3, you also installed Chameleon Mail. And when Instant Internet signed you up with your Internet provider, it automatically configured Chameleon Mail to know your mail gateway and mail server. Part of what it did was to create a mailbox for you on your PC, that is, a directory on your PC in which to put your e-mail messages.

If you used Instant Internet to set up your account, your mailbox should be all set. If you didn't, see the section "Configuring Your Mail" in Appendix B for instructions on how to do this yourself.

Running Mail

These steps show you how to run Chameleon Mail — from here on out it's a piece of cake.

1. **Double-click the Mail icon in Program Manager.**

   You see the Mail Login window shown in Figure 4-1, but this time your name appears on the list of mailboxes. There should be only two mailboxes, yours and one for *Postmaster* (a nonexistent bureaucrat who is in charge of creating and managing mailboxes).

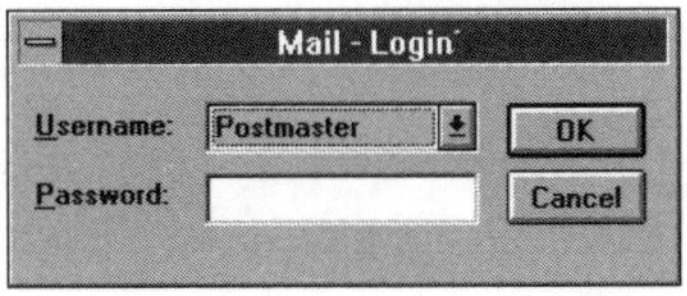

Figure 4-1: Chameleon Mail wants to know exactly who you are.

2. **Choose your username in the Username box.**

3. **Enter the password you entered when you created the mailbox.**

   If you didn't enter a password, or Instant Internet created this mailbox for you, leave it blank.

4. **Click OK.**

   You see the Chameleon Mail window. You're ready to retrieve some mail, read it, and send some of your own.

The Mail window

Figure 4-2 shows the Mail window with a bunch of messages listed. Usually the window shows a list of the messages in your inbox. You can create lots of different folders, however, to contain messages about different topics or from different people. The Folder box just below the menu bar lets you choose which folder to look at. (We talk about how to make folders and put messages in them in the section "Using Folders," later in this chapter.)

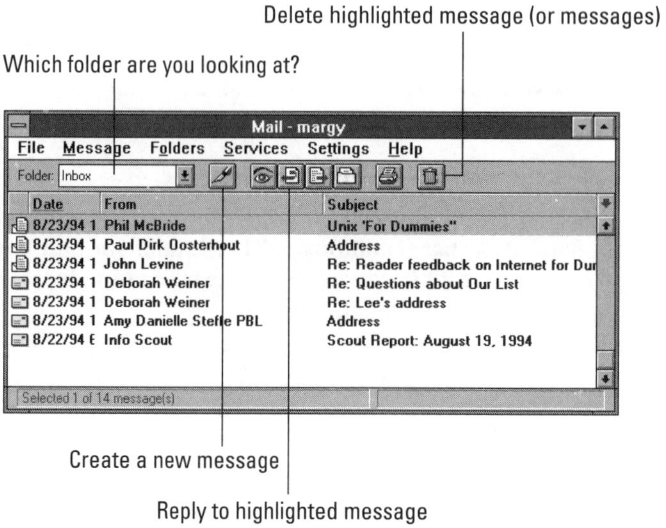

Figure 4-2: The Mail window lists messages in one folder, usually your inbox.

The list of messages includes four columns — one containing little icons that show whether the mail has been read, one with dates, one with the name or e-mail address of the person who sent the message, and one with the subject. You can make these columns wider or narrower by dragging the little vertical lines between the column heads to the left or right. You can even change the order of the columns by dragging the column heading to the left or right.

TIP: You can change the order of the messages in the list, which is usually in chronological order. To sort by the sender's name or subject, double-click the From or Subject heading. To reverse the order, double-click the blue arrow at the right end of the column heads.

Leaving Chameleon Mail

You can exit from the Chameleon Mail program by choosing File⇨Exit from the menu bar. If you have fooled with the settings, Mail asks whether you want to save your changes. Click Yes.

Sending Mail

To send a message:

1. **Choose Message⇨Create from the menu bar or press Ctrl+E.**

   Or click the fountain-pen icon on the toolbar (the leftmost one). You see the New Message window, shown in Figure 4-3. Your address already appears in the From box. (How nice!)

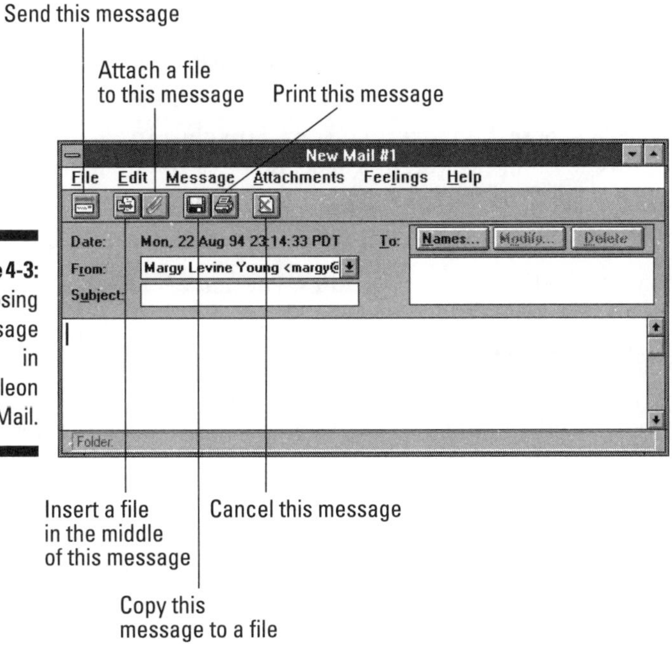

Figure 4-3: Composing a message in Chameleon Mail.

2. **To enter the address to which you want to send the message in the To box, click the Names button.**

   You see the Names dialog box, shown in Figure 4-4. Chameleon Mail lets you create an address book of Internet addresses you use (just choose Services⇨Address Book from the menu bar, as described in the section "Your Little Black Book," later in this chapter). This button displays the addresses in your address book, or you can type a new address.

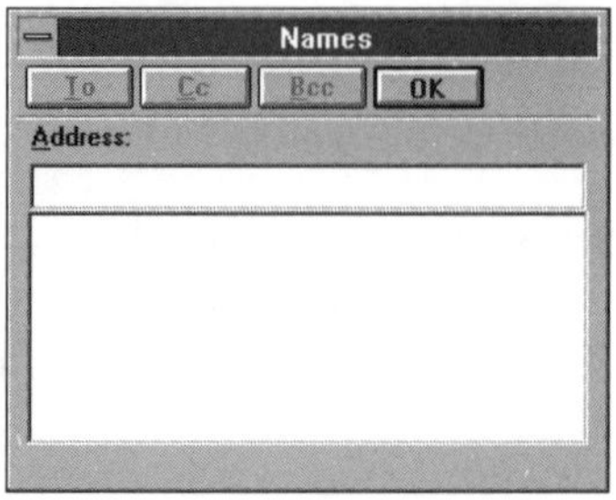

Figure 4-4: Chameleon Mail can show a list of names and addresses you usually write to.

3. **Type the address in the Address box or choose it from the list (if you have created an address book). Then click the To button.**

   Chameleon Mail puts the address you typed (or chose from the list) in the To box. You can repeat this step as many times as you want in order to send the message to a bunch of people.

4. **Click the OK button when you finish using the Names dialog box.**

   You're back in the New Message window. The name (or names) you entered appears in the To box.

5. **Enter a subject in the Subject box.**

   TIP

   Make it specific and informative, such as "What's with the new reporting procedure?" rather than general and vague, such as "Help!" or "message." Try never to use "Hi!" or "Help!" as subjects.

6. **In the big box at the bottom of the New Message window, enter the text of the message.**

   Don't press Enter at the end of each line — Chameleon Mail does word-wrapping for you.

   TIP

   Here's the cutest part about composing a message by using Chameleon Mail: If you want to include a *smiley* (a little face that indicates how you feel), just choose the Feelings command from the menu bar and then choose Happy, Sad, or Wink. Mail types the appropriate smiley. What service! (We guess the programmers must have been up really late the night before.)

7. **Click the Send button (the leftmost icon, with a picture of an envelope with a red arrow) when you are finished.**

   Alternatively, you can choose Message⇨Send from the menu bar. Chameleon Mail doesn't let you send a message until you've filled in all the boxes.

To print a message you have written, click the Print button (the fifth icon from the left, with a little picture of a printer) *before* you click the Send button.

If you decide not to send the message after all, click the Cancel button (the rightmost button, with the red X) *before* you click the Send button. If you've already clicked Send, read the section "Can we see that again?" later in this chapter to find out how to try to prevent the message from being sent.

Making a signature for yourself

Most people end their mail messages with a *signature,* a few lines of text that contain their name, their e-mail address, and perhaps a pithy saying. The following steps show how to make a signature for your mail:

1. **Choose Settings⇨Signature from the menu bar.**

   You see the Mail Signature window, shown in Figure 4-5.

2. **Type your signature in the Signature box.**

   It should contain your full name, e-mail address, and maybe some other information about you. ***Note:*** It shouldn't be more than three lines long or else folks will get tired of seeing it over and over! Some people have elaborate 20-line signatures, thinking that they look cool . . . but those people are mistaken.

3. **If you want the signature included at the end of each e-mail message you write, choose the Attach to Outgoing Mail box at the bottom of the window.**

   That is, click the box until it has an X in it.

4. **Click OK.**

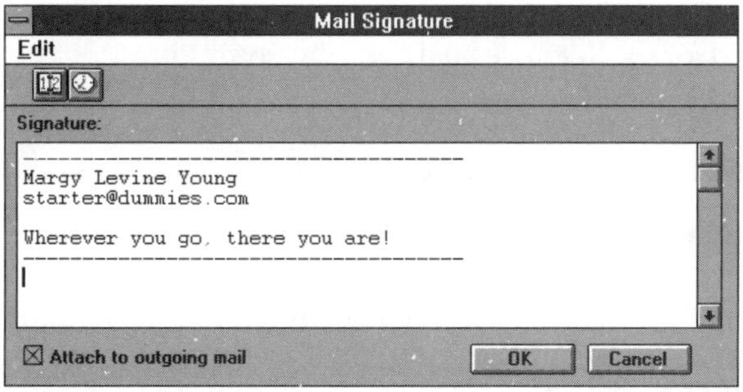

Figure 4-5: Your signature should identify you and be original, but keep it short!

Now whenever you compose a new message, your signature appears at the bottom. You can always delete it from messages that shouldn't include your standard signature. (Like, f'rinstance, messages to folks who wouldn't find your signature funny.)

When is your mail sent?

Having composed a message, you would think that it would be sent, outta here, history. But it ain't necessarily so. Chameleon Mail first puts your finished message in your outbox. Then it may send each message immediately or it may wait awhile, depending on what you tell it to do.

Chameleon Mail can send mail only when you are on-line with your Internet provider. (Chapter 3 tells you how to connect to your Internet provider). You can create or read messages at any time, but you have to be connected to the Internet to send the messages you've written and to receive new messages.

To tell Chameleon Mail how often to connect to your mail gateway (your Internet provider's computer that handles your outgoing mail), follow these steps:

1. **Choose Settings⇨Timers from the menu.**

   You see the Timers window, shown in Figure 4-6.

2. **In the Send box, in the "Retry every" boxes, enter how often you want to send messages you've composed by typing the frequency in days, hours, and minutes.**

   We usually set this option to send our mail every hour or so (at least, every hour during the time we are connected to the Internet).

3. **In the Retrieve box, enter how often you want Chameleon Mail to check for new mail.**

   We usually set this option to check our mailbox about every 15 minutes (at least, every 15 minutes while we are connected to the Internet). Leave the box checked for the Retrieve mail periodically option.

4. **Click OK.**

Can we see that again?

Until messages are sent, they are stored in your outbox. If you want to reread a message you just composed, you can look at it and, if you have second thoughts, delete it before it is sent.

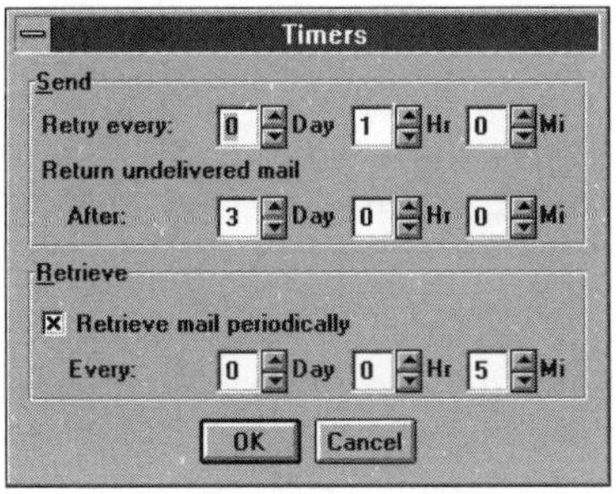

Figure 4-6: How often should Chameleon Mail connect to your mail server to send your mail?

To see a list of the messages in your outbox, choose Services⇨Outbox from the menu. You see the little Outbox window, shown in Figure 4-7.

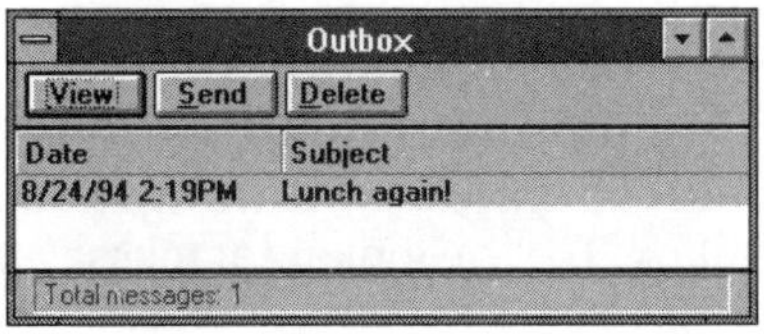

Figure 4-7: Messages that have not yet been sent to the Internet.

- To look at a message in your outbox, select the message (click on it) and click on the View button. Chameleon Mail displays the message, allowing you to look at it. You can't make any changes, however.
- To delete the message without sending it, select the message and click the Delete button. Mail asks whether you really want to delete it — click Yes.
- To print an outgoing message, select the message, click the View button, and click the Print button (the little picture of a printer). Then close the window displaying the message, by double-clicking the little white box in the upper left-hand corner of the window.

Send it now!

To send mail right now (assuming that you are connected to the Internet via the Custom program), view your outbox, select the message or messages, and click the Send button. Even if you don't do that, Mail sends all the outgoing messages automatically every hour, or whatever other time you've set in the Settings⇨Timers window.

Receiving Mail

Chameleon Mail checks your mail server for new messages when you run it and at regular intervals while it is running (see the section "When is your mail sent?" later in this chapter to set the frequency with which it checks). To get your incoming mail right now, just choose Message⇨Retrieve Mail from the menu bar or press Ctrl+T.

You can retrieve your mail only when you are connected to the Internet. Otherwise, you see the message `Failure to connect to POP server`. Don't worry — it just means that you have to use the Custom program to connect to your Internet provider before you can get your mail.

The Mail window usually shows a list of messages in your inbox. Messages you haven't read are preceded by a little, white folded-paper icon, and those you have read have a little, yellow envelope icon (refer to Figure 4-2).

To read a message, double-click it or select it and choose Message⇨View, or select it and press Ctrl+W, or select it and click the View button (the one with the eyeball in it). Jeez — they give you enough ways to do this!

To look at the next message, click the Next button (with the right-pointing red arrow) to see the next one in your inbox. To stop looking at messages, close the message window by choosing File⇨Exit from its menu bar or by double-clicking the box in the upper left-hand corner of the message window.

You can do a number of things with a message, including reply to it, forward it, throw it away, print it, and save it in a folder or a file. We talk about all these options in the following sections.

Here's my answer

It's easy to reply to a message, because you don't have to type in any dratted e-mail address. In the window that displays the message, click the Reply button (the one with a curved, blue arrow on it, the third button from the left). Mail displays a window in which you can compose your reply. It's already addressed to the person who sent you the message, and it has the same subject as the original message (with `Re:` tacked on the front). Compose your message and click the Send button to send it.

Rather than use the Reply button, you can also choose Message⇨Reply to. Mail gives you two choices: Choose Sender to reply to only the person who sent you the message, or choose All to send the reply to everyone who got copies of the message.

You can reply to a message without viewing it by selecting the message in the Mail window and clicking the Reply button (the one with a curved, blue arrow on it, to the right of the eyeball button). Don't you think, though, that you'd better read it first?

Into the circular file

You can delete a message by clicking the Delete button (the green trashcan) or by choosing Message⇨Delete or by pressing Ctrl+D.

If you are looking at the Mail window, you can delete a message by selecting it and using any of the same buttons or menu choices we just mentioned. You can select a bunch of messages, in fact (by clicking and dragging with the mouse), and delete them all at the same time.

Hot potato! Here's a message for you!

To forward a message to someone else, click the Forward button (the one with the white piece of paper and the right-pointing blue arrow), or choose Message⇨Forward, or press Ctrl+F. Chameleon Mail creates a new message that includes the text of the message you want to forward. Tell it whom to send the new message to, by using the Names button. You can add some introductory text at the beginning of the message, if you want ("Here's a message I just got from a bewildered client. Want to handle it?"). To send it off, click the Send button.

Get it on paper

To print a message, click the Print button (the little picture of a printer) or choose File⇨Print from the menu.

Saving Money

Aha! — a topic we knew you'd like. Because most Internet providers charge you by the hour (or minute) to be connected, it doesn't make sense to pay for Internet connect-charges while you read your mail. Instead, you can do the following:

1. **Run Chameleon Mail.**
2. **Write any messages you've been meaning to write. Leave Chameleon Mail running.**
3. **Connect to the Internet via the Custom program.**

   That is, run Custom and choose Connect.
4. **Switch back to Chameleon Mail, and send the messages in your outbox.**

   That is, view your outbox (by choosing Services➪Outbox from the menu), select all the messages, and click Send.
5. **Retrieve any new messages, by pressing Ctrl+T.**

   Or you can choose Message➪Retrieve Mail from the menu.
6. **Switch back to Custom and disconnect from the Internet by choosing Disconnect from the menu in the Custom window.**
7. **Back in Chameleon Mail, read your mail, write responses, forward messages, file messages, and so on.**

   There's no hurry — you aren't connected to your Internet provider, so you're not paying by the hour.
8. **Connect to the Internet again, by choosing Connect from the menu in the Custom window.**
9. **In Chameleon Mail, send all the messages in your outbox (see step 4).**
10. **While you're at it, check for incoming mail one last time by pressing Ctrl+T.**
11. **Disconnect from the Internet by choosing Disconnect from the menu in the Custom window.**

This method involves jumping back and forth between Custom and Chameleon Mail, but it saves on connect-time. It also lets you write much better mail, because it avoids the "gotta type fast, the meter's running" feeling that, we can tell you from experience, produces some spectacularly awful messages.

Your Little Black Book

Face it — typing e-mail addresses is annoying. Who can get all those little dots and @s straight? Far better to let Chameleon Mail keep track of the funky punctuation in e-mail addresses. That way, you can just choose the address you want from a list.

Making book

How? Create an address book of the e-mail addresses you use. To create one, choose Services⇨Address Book from the menu. You see the Address Book window, shown in Figure 4-8.

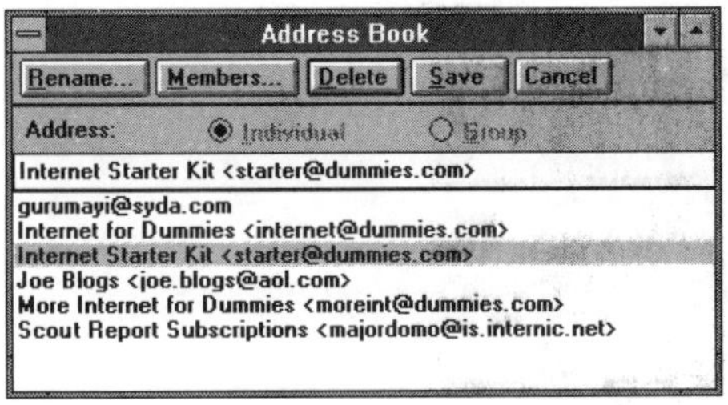

Figure 4-8: Your address book, an alphabetical list of your e-mail correspondents.

Here are some things you can do by using your address book:

- Add an address by typing it in the Address box and clicking the Add button. You can type either just the e-mail address or the person's name followed by the e-mail address enclosed in angle brackets. To add the address to use to write to Internet for Dummies Central about this book, for example, you type **Dummies Central <starter@dummies.com>**.
- Delete an address by selecting it and clicking the Delete button.
- Fix a fouled-up address by selecting it and clicking the Rename button.
- Minimize the address book so that you can look at it at any time by clicking the minimize button (the downward-pointing triangle in the upper right-hand corner of the window). The Address Book icon appears as a little yellow book.
- Close the Address Book window by double-clicking the box in the upper left-hand corner of the window. When Mail asks whether you want to save your changes to the address book, click Yes.

TIP

When you are viewing a message, you can easily add the sender's address to your address book. Choose Edit⇨Save 'From' Address from the menu. Nothing seems to happen, but if you look in your address book, the address appears there.

Using your little black book

After you've created an address book, you can use it whenever you create a message. When you compose a message and click the Names button, the Names window that appears contains all the addresses in your address book (shown in Figure 4-9).

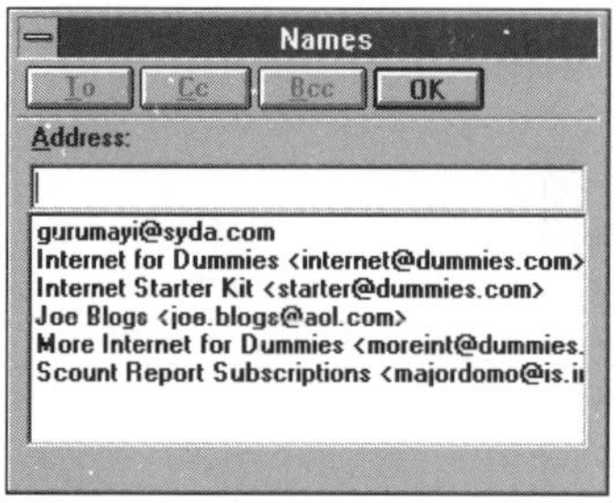

Figure 4-9: Using your address book to address a message.

To address a message to someone in your address book, choose the address and click the To button. If you want to send a copy of the message to someone, click the Cc or Bcc button. To close the Names window, double-click the box in the upper left-hand corner of the window.

Making your own mailing list

You can use the address book to create your own mailing list, to make it easier to send messages to a group of people. These steps show you how:

1. **Open your address book by choosing Services⇨Address Book from the menu.**

   You see the Address Book window, which was shown in Figure 4-8.

2. **Type the name of the mailing list in the Address box.**

   To make a mailing list of the folks with whom you play backgammon at lunch, for example, type **Backgammon**.

3. **Click the Group option and then click the Add button.**

   A window appears with the name you gave the group (see Figure 4-10).

4. **To add someone to the group, either choose the person's e-mail address from the list of addresses in your address book or, if the address isn't in your book yet, type it in the Address box. Then click Add.**

5. **When you've added all the people you want in the group, click OK.**

6. **You return to the Address Book window. The group appears on the list of addresses, at the end.**

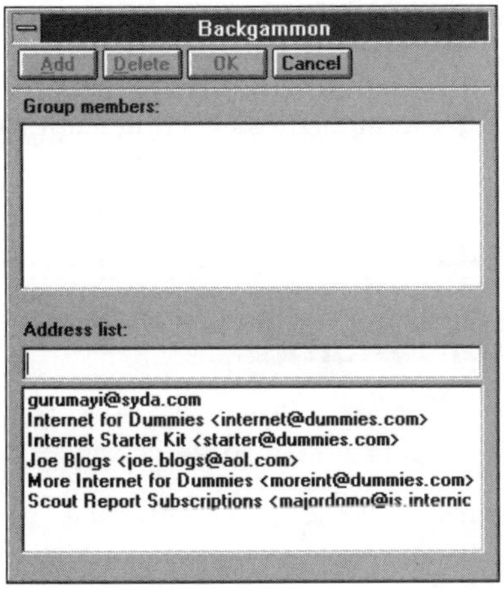

Figure 4-10: Creating a mailing list lets you send messages to lots of people at a time.

To address an e-mail message to a group, just choose the group name from the Names window when you are addressing the message. To see the list of the people in a group, open the Address Book, choose the group name, and click the Members button.

May We Have a Copy of That File?

E-mail messages usually consist of text, written by you in Chameleon Mail. You *can* attach other files to your mail messages, however. You may want to send a small spreadsheet file, for example, along with a message to your accountant. We submitted the chapters of this book to our publisher by attaching word-processing files to our messages and e-mailing them to Corbin, our long-suffering editor. (It's much faster and cheaper than overnight express.) Using attachments, you can e-mail any type of file, including *binary files* that contain nontext information.

Be sure to think about the person who will receive the file — what will he or she do with it? If you send a WordPerfect for Windows document, the person on the other end must have the same program or a program that can read that type of document. If you correspond with folks who use different types of computers, especially UNIX and mainframes, they may be out of luck. So find out beforehand which types of files your correspondent can deal with.

Including text from a file

If you want to include just the text from a text file in a message, you don't have to use attachments at all. Instead, put your cursor in the text of the message where you want the text to appear. Then choose File⇨Insert File (or press Ctrl+I). Mail asks for the directory and filename of the file to insert. Remember — it *has* to be a text file or you get an ugly-looking message that's not what you want.

Making attachments

Internet mail is set up to transmit only text files — that is, only files that use plain old text that can be stored as seven-bit ASCII character codes. So your mail program, and the mail program the recipient uses, have to cheat if you want to send anything other than plain text by e-mail. Luckily, there are several standard ways to cheat. The three most widely used are MIME, uuencoding, and BinHex.

MIME, which stands for Multi-purpose Internet Mail Extensions, enables you to attach any file to a mail message. MIME secretly encodes the file in ASCII characters (rather strange-looking ASCII characters, but computers don't care about that) so that the Internet mail system can handle it. At the other end, *if* the recipient's mail reader can also deal with MIME attachments, it turns the secretly encoded stuff back into the original file. If the recipient's mail program *cannot* handle MIME attachments, however, the person cannot read the attached file. Chameleon Mail handles MIME very well, as we describe in the section "Attaching files," later in this chapter.

In theory, uuencoding works the same way, although you use different commands in Chameleon Mail to make it happen. Because uuencoding is an older method, more mail readers know how to deal with uuencoded material. If you want to send stuff to someone whose mail reader cannot deal with MIME, try uuencoding. It's not as easy in Chameleon Mail, but it works (see the section "Including uuencoded stuff," a little later in this chapter).

The last way, BinHex, is not as widely used as either MIME or uuencoding, and Chameleon Mail cannot send or receive BinHex-encoded files. (BinHex is popular only among Macintosh users.) If you get one, send a message to the person who sent it, asking him or her to resend the file using MIME or uuencoding.

There is also an easy way to copy text stored in a word-processing document or in any other Windows program to an e-mail message that you are writing.

1. **View the document in your word processor or other Windows program.**
2. **Select the text and copy it to the Windows Clipboard.**

   In most programs, you select the text and then choose Edit⇨Copy from the menu or press Ctrl+C.
3. **Switch back to Chameleon Mail and put your cursor in the text of the message you are composing, where you want the copied text to appear.**
4. **Choose Edit⇨Paste from the menu or press Ctrl+V.**

   Poof! The text appears.

Attaching files

To attach a file to a message:

1. **Create the message.**

   Address it in the usual way (as described earlier in this chapter). Go ahead and type some text — be sure to mention that you are attaching a file, what it is called, what kind of file it is, and what it's for.
2. **Choose Attachments⇨New from the menu or press Ctrl+A.**

   You see the File to Attach dialog box, shown in Figure 4-11.

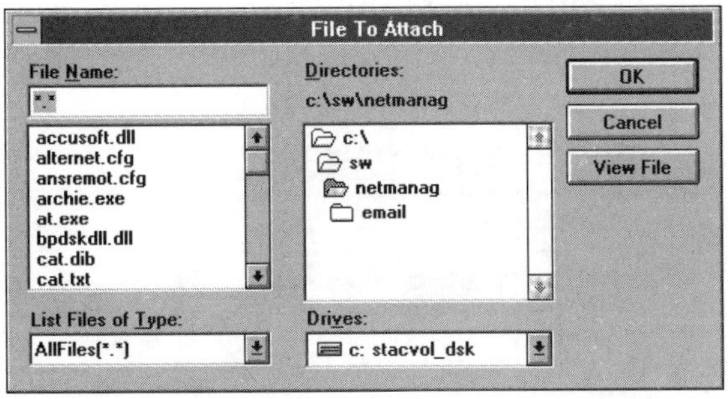

Figure 4-11: What file would you like to send along with your message?

3. **Choose a file to attach and click OK.**

   Next you see the Attachment Description dialog box, shown in Figure 4-12. To see the larger version of the dialog box, click the Advanced button.

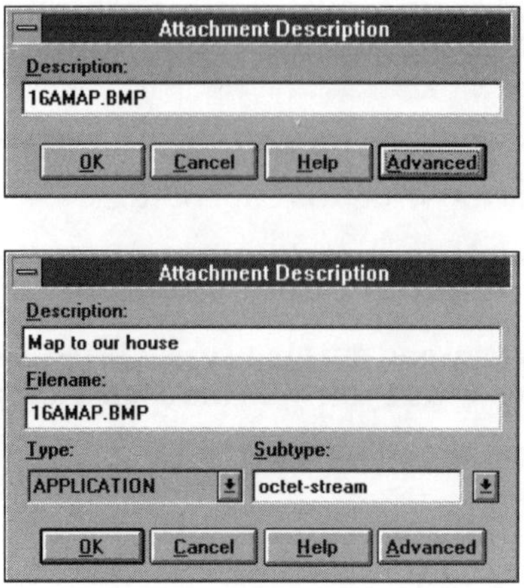

Figure 4-12: What the heck is in this attached file, anyway?

4. **In the Description box, type an explanation of what's in the file.**

   It's a good idea to mention what kind of file it is (DOC, TXT, BMP, whatever).

   For the Type and Subtype boxes, Chameleon Mail guesses what kind of file it is, based on the filename extension. You can choose a different type, if you want, although you usually don't. The choices of subtype depend on what type is selected. You usually want to leave these boxes alone.

5. **Click OK.**

   A line of information about the attached file appears at the bottom of the message, as shown in Figure 4-13. You can attach other files to the same message by repeating steps 2 through 5.

6. **Send the message as usual.**

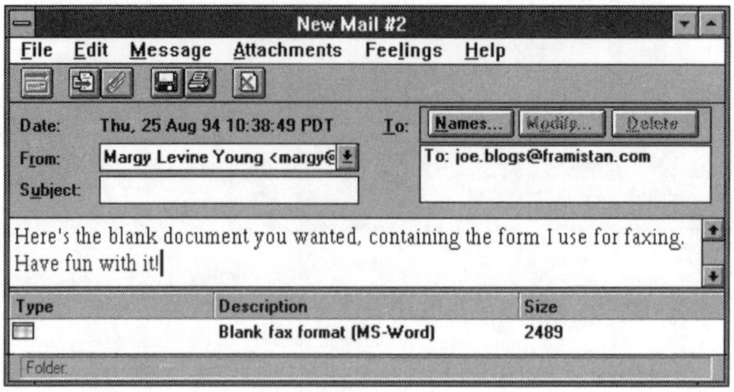

Figure 4-13: A file is attached to the bottom of this message.

If you change your mind about attaching a file, you can detach it. (Rip!) At the bottom of the message, highlight the attachment you want to deep six and choose Attachments⇨Delete. This command doesn't delete the file that contains the attachment; it just detaches it from the e-mail message.

You can also change the description of an attachment by selecting it and choosing Attachments⇨Modify. You see the Attachment Description dialog box again (refer to Figure 4-12).

Receiving attached files

When you receive an attached file, it appears with a little paper clip on its icon in the list of incoming messages. When you view it, the information about the attachments appears at the bottom of the message, just as it does when you send a message with attachments (refer to Figure 4-13).

To view the attached file, assuming that you have the right software to do so, double-click the information about the attachment (or select the attachment and choose Attachments⇨View from the menu). Chameleon Mail looks at the filename extension of the attached file and runs the appropriate program for viewing it. If the filename ends in DOC, for example, it runs Microsoft Word. If it ends in BMP, it runs Windows Paintbrush. And so on.

To save an attachment in its own file, select it and choose Attachments⇨Save from the menu. Chameleon Mail asks for the directory and filename to use in saving the attached file.

How does Chameleon Mail know which program to run to view an attachment? It uses the same information File Manager does: the so-called *associations* between filename extensions and programs. To tell File Manager (and also Chameleon Mail) which program to run for files with a particular extension, switch to File Manager and choose File⇨Associate from the File Manager menu. Refer to your Windows manual for more information or run out and get *Windows For Dummies* by Andy Rathbone (published by IDG Books Worldwide).

Including uuencoded stuff

If you want to send a file to someone whose mail reader cannot handle MIME attachments (pity the poor soul), you can try uuencoding. Many mail readers can handle uuencoding, and if they can't, you can get separate programs that can uudecode stuff. (An excellent shareware uuencoder-uudecoder is called WinCode, which is widely available on bulletin boards and FTP servers — see Chapter 18 for how to grab software from the Net and Chapter 19 for where to find WinCode.)

These steps show you how to include a uuencoded file in an e-mail message.

1. **Start a new message and address it as usual.**
2. **For the subject, type something like** `Uuencoded File`**: and the filename.**

   It's polite to give the recipient some inkling of what you are sending.
3. **Choose Message⇨uuencode from the menu.**

   Chameleon Mail asks for the directory and filename of the file to uuencode.
4. **Choose the directory and filename and click OK.**

   A bunch of total gobbledygook appears in the text of your message (as shown in Figure 4-14). Don't worry — it turns back into sensible information when it's uudecoded.
5. **Send the message as usual.**

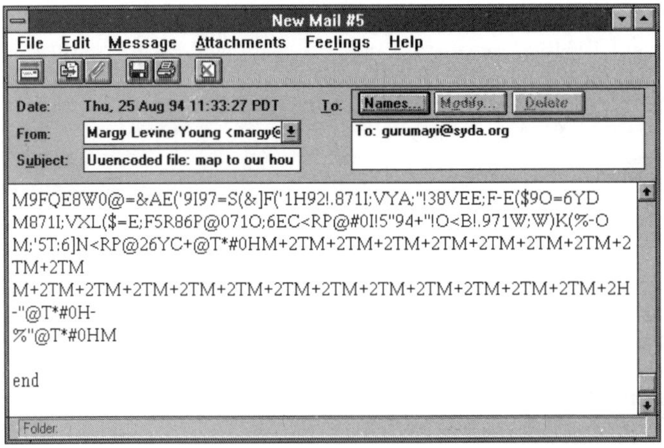

Figure 4-14: A uuencoded file — get out your secret decoder ring!

WARNING!

The size of a uuencoded file is limited to 50K — that is, Chameleon Mail encodes only the first 50K. If you want to send a larger file, you must use MIME (see the section "Attaching files," earlier in this chapter).

Receiving uuencoded files

When you get a uuencoded file, you see the same kind of meaningless garbage that was shown in Figure 4-14. The first line starts with the word *begin* (not shown) and ends with the name the file had when it was uuencoded. The last line contains the word *end.* In between: chaos.

To decode a uuencoded message, view it and choose Message⇨uudecode from the menu. Tell Mail the directory and filename in which to put the uudecoded file and click OK. Mail reconstructs the original file.

Hang Onto It

There are three different ways to save a message you want to hold on to:

- Just don't delete it. It hangs around in your inbox indefinitely. The problem with this method is that your inbox soon gets cluttered with messages you have already read.
- Save it in a folder within Chameleon Mail. This method is convenient if you want to read, forward, or reply to the message later. (We describe the process of creating and using folders in the next section.)
- Save it in a text file. This method is great if you want to use the text of the message in a word-processing document or other file.

If you want to save a message in a text file so that you can use it in a word-processing document or elsewhere, it's easy. Just select the message (or messages) from the list of messages in the Mail window and choose Message⇨Copy to File. Chameleon Mail asks for the directory and filename in which to put the mail message. If you selected more than one message, Mail asks you for a separate filename for each message.

You can save a bunch of messages in one file. You might want all messages in an ongoing discussion about travel plans, for example, to be saved in a file named TRAVEL.TXT. Save the first message by using the Message⇨Copy to File command. For all the rest of the messages, add them to the end of the same file by using the Message⇨Append to File command.

WARNING! You might think that you would use the File⇨Save command to save a message. *Don't do it!* That command saves your *mail configuration,* not the selected message. Your mail configuration is all the information about how to send and receive mail, and you don't usually have to worry about saving it.

Using Folders

So far you have been using one *folder* — your inbox. Chameleon Mail lets you create lots of folders so that you can sort your mail. We like to have folders for pending messages (messages we can't do anything about until someone else does something), folders for each book we are writing, a Personal folder, and folders about lots of other topics we exchange mail about.

After you have created some folders, you can move messages from one folder to another, look at all the messages in a folder, and even tell Mail to move incoming mail to a particular folder based on who it's from or what it's about (see the section "Your Automated Mail Sorter," later in this chapter).

Make me a folder

Poof — you're a folder. Sorry. Where were we?

1. **Choose Folders⇨Create from the menu.**

   Mail asks you for the folder name.

2. **Type the name of the new folder and click OK.**

   The folder name can have spaces, and you can use capital and small letters, so type something neatly.

   Mail makes you a folder. (Poof!)

TIP: To see a list of all your folders, with information about how many messages are in each one, choose Folders⇨Folder List from the menu (or press Ctrl+L). Figure 4-15 shows the Folder List window, which you can also use for opening, creating, and deleting folders.

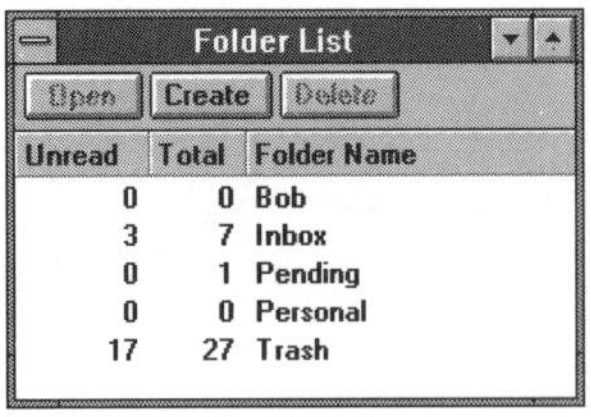

Figure 4-15: All your folders and how many messages are in each one.

What's in this folder?

To look at the messages in a folder, choose the folder name from the Folder box at the left end of the icon bar, right under the Message choice on the menu bar. (Alternatively, you can choose the Folders⇨Open command.) You see a list of the messages in your folder. They appear just as they do when they're listed in your inbox.

When you are looking at the messages in a folder, you can do most of the same things you did in your inbox — you can view messages, reply to them, forward them, print them, or throw them away.

File this message, please

When you are looking at a message, either in the Mail window or in a window that shows the text of the message, you can move the message to a different folder by choosing Message⇨Move to Folder (or pressing Ctrl+M). You see a little dialog box listing all your folders (as shown in Figure 4-16). Choose a folder and click OK. The message disappears from the folder it was in and appears in the new folder.

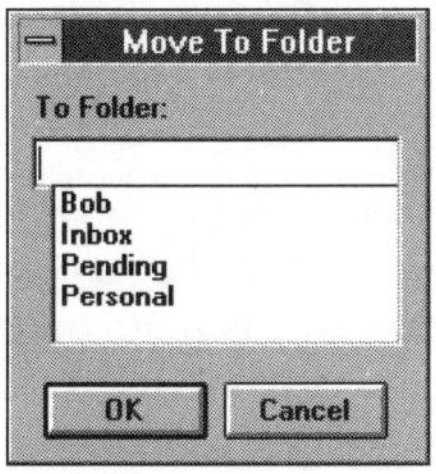

Figure 4-16: Where do you want to file this message?

I don't want this folder anymore

To delete a folder, choose Folders⇨Delete. Choose the name of the folder you never want to see again and click OK.

When you delete a folder, you also delete all the messages it contains. If you want to save the messages, you must first move them to another folder.

To rename a folder rather than delete it, choose the Folders⇨Rename command from the menu.

Taking out the trash

Yes, just as in real life, someone has to take out the garbage. Luckily, Chameleon Mail does it for you.

When you delete a message, Mail doesn't blow it away immediately. Instead, it moves it to a folder named Trash. Mail automatically empties the Trash folder when you exit from the program. To empty the Trash before then, choose Services⇨Empty Trash from the menu.

The point of a Trash folder is that if you delete a message by mistake, you can get it back at any time until you take out the trash. Just switch to Trash, find the message you want, and move it back to the folder where it belongs.

Your Automated Mail Sorter

Not many people have secretaries anymore. In the good old days, you could tell your secretary to throw away all mail from X or to put all mail from Y in a special pile or to give all mail from Z to someone else to deal with. It was a great time-saver.

In this modern age, software has to do that job. And what do you know: Chameleon Mail has a nifty mail-sorting feature that lets you throw away, forward, or move messages to a folder based on whom the message is from or what it's about. You define *rules* that tell the program what to do with incoming messages. Rules are particularly useful if you belong to any mailing lists — you can tell Mail to stick messages from the mailing list in a separate folder so that they are not mixed in with your personal messages.

These steps show you how to tell Chameleon Mail how to sort your mail. Now if we could just get it to make us coffee . . .

1. **Choose Services⇨Rules from the menu.**

   You see the Mail Rules dialog box, shown in Figure 4-17.

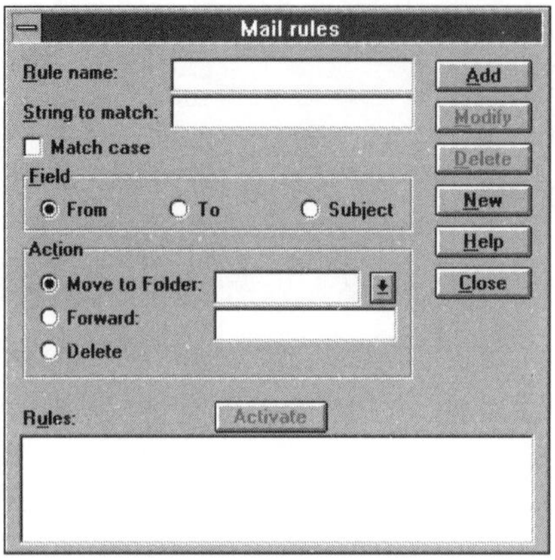

Figure 4-17: Defining rules that tell Mail how to sort your incoming messages.

2. **Type the name of the rule in the Rule name field.**

   You know that your spouse, for example, is interested in getting copies of all messages you receive from your mother. Name the rule something like **Forward to Jordan** (adjust the name of this rule as needed if you are not, in fact, married to Jordan).

3. **In the String to match box, type the name or word (or words) you want Mail to be on the lookout for.**

   Type your mom's e-mail address, for example.

4. **Choose From, To, or Subject for the field in which Mail should look for this name or word (or words).**

   Click the From option, for example.

5. **Tell Mail what to do with the messages it finds by choosing Move to Folder, Forward, or Delete.**

   If you choose Move to Folder, also choose the folder name to move the messages to. If you choose Forward, enter the e-mail address to forward the mail to (in our example, it'd be your spouse's address).

6. **Click Add to add the rule to Mail's list of rules.**

   The rule name appears in the Rules box at the bottom of the window.

7. **Enter additional rules, by repeating steps 2 through 6.**

8. **When you finish defining rules, click Close.**

TIP

If you tell Mail to file incoming messages in another folder automatically, you have to remember to read them in that folder!

Here's What I Prefer

You can tell Chameleon Mail how you want it to behave, by choosing Settings⇨Preferences from the menu. You see the Preferences dialog box, shown in Figure 4-18.

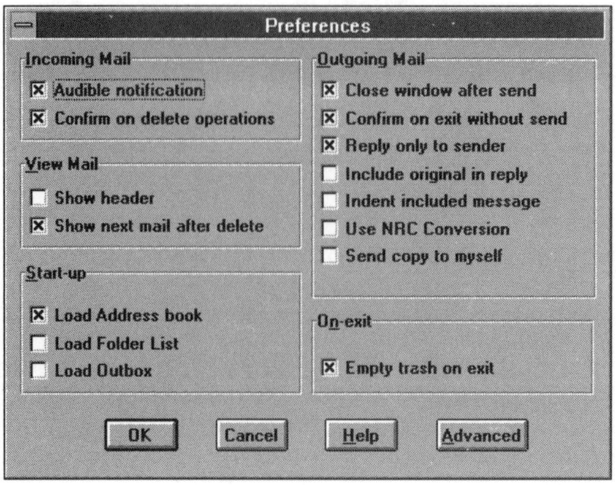

Figure 4-18: Telling Chameleon Mail how to behave.

We usually leave the settings alone, except for the following:

- If you use the list of folders often, choose the Load Folder List option.
- When you reply to messages, if you like to include parts of the original message in the reply, choose the Include original in reply option. To have Mail indent it, also choose the Indent included message option.
- If you like to keep copies of your messages, choose the Send copy to myself option. (It's a thoughtful way to help your future biographer.)

When you finish making changes, click OK. If you've made changes, the next time you exit from Chameleon Mail it asks whether you want to save your changes — click Yes.

TECHNICAL STUFF

Mail Utilities — forget 'em

In the Internet Chameleon program group in Windows Program Manager, you can find an icon that says Mail Utilities. Sounds interesting, but it turns out that we practically never use it.

If you need to combine the mailboxes for two people or if your mail files have gotten strangely large, try running the Mail Utilities. You must exit from Mail before you run it. It's also useful if your mailbox has gotten fouled up somehow — the Mail Utilities can look through your messages and reconstruct your mailbox.

Other E-Mail Programs

We like Chameleon Mail — it's easy to use and has lots of nice features, such as automated mail sorting and background mail sending and receiving. You do have some alternatives, however:

- Eudora, from Qualcomm, is a widely used mail reader. You can download a shareware version by FTP from `ftp.qualcomm.com`, in the directory `/quest/windows/eudora` or you can buy an inexpensive commercial version directly from Qualcomm.

- Trumpet, a widely used shareware newsreading program from Australia (see Chapter 7) is also an adequate mail program (and no, you don't have to turn your screen upside down to use it). It's on `ftp/utas.edu.au` in `/pc/trumpet/wintrump`.

See Chapter 18 if you want to find out how to download these programs from the Internet.

The 5th Wave
By Rich Tennant
The 500 channel multimedia future
©RICHTENNANT
The Dental Network is starting a 10-hour, 3-day, 16-part miniseries on gum disease. Wanna watch?

Chapter 5

Mail Tips

In This Chapter

- Finding people's e-mail addresses
- Using Chameleon Finger to find people's addresses
- Using Chameleon Whois for finding the addresses of people at big organizations
- E-mail addresses for folks who use on-line services
- Mail etiquette

Electronic mail is without a doubt the most widely used Internet service. Almost every system supports some sort of mail service, meaning that no matter what kind of computer you're using, if it's on the Internet, you can send and receive mail. Also, much morc than any other Internet service, e-mail is connected to many non-Internet systems, which means that you can exchange mail with a large number of people not on the Internet as well as with all the people who are on it.

If you want to send a message to the authors of this book, the address for Internet for Dummies Central is `starter@dummies.com`. You get a reply from a mail robot (also called a *mailbot*) and possibly from a real human being.

Where Is Everyone?

As you've probably figured out, one teensy detail is keeping you from sending e-mail to all your friends: You don't know their addresses. In this chapter, you learn lots of different ways to look for addresses. But we save you the trouble of reading the rest of the chapter by starting out with the easiest, most reliable way to find out people's e-mail addresses:

```
Call them on the phone and ask them.
```

Pretty low-tech, huh? For some reason, this seems to be the absolute last thing people want to do (see the sidebar titled "Top ten reasons not to call someone to get an e-mail address"). But try it first. If you know or can find out the phone number, it's much easier than any of the other methods.

Whaddaya Mean, You Don't Know Your Own Address?

It happens frequently — usually because a friend is using a proprietary e-mail system that has a gateway to the outside world that provides instructions for how to send messages to the outside but no hint for how outsiders send stuff in. Fortunately, the solution is usually easy: Tell your friend to send you a message. All messages have return addresses, and all but the absolute cruddiest of mail gateways put on a usable return address. Don't be surprised if the address has a great deal of strange punctuation. After a few gateways, you always seem to end up with things like this:

```
"blurch::John.C.Calhoun"%farp@slimemail.com
```

TIP

But usually if you type the strange address back in, it works, so don't worry about it. Better yet, use the Edit⇨Save 'From' Address command on the Chameleon Mail menu to copy the address directly into your address book.

Giving Your Friends the Finger

TIP

If you know the name of the computer your friend uses, you might be able to use the Chameleon Finger program to find her username. Then you can guess the address (it'll be *username@computername*).

Running Finger

Internet Chameleon comes with a Finger program. You can use it to find out information about a host computer or about an individual. These steps show you how to run it:

1. **Double-click the Finger icon in the Internet Chameleon program group in the Windows Program Manager.**

   You see a window like the one in Figure 5-1.

Top ten reasons not to call someone to get an e-mail address

10. Want to surprise long-lost friend.
9. Want to surprise long-lost *ex*-friend who owes you a large amount of money and thinks that he's given you the slip.
8. You or your friend don't speak English. (Really happens, because many Internauts are outside the U.S.)
7. You or your friend don't speak at all. (Really happens: Networks offer a uniquely friendly place for most people with handicaps because nobody knows or cares about the handicaps.)
6. It's 3 a.m. and you have to send a message right now or you'll never get to sleep.
5. You don't know the phone number and, because of an unfortunate childhood experience, you have a deathly fear of calling directory assistance.
4. Phone takes only quarters; nobody around can break your $100 bill.
3. Company installed a new phone system, nobody has figured out how to use it, and no matter what you dial you always end up with Dial-a-Prayer.
2. Inadvertently spilled entire can of soda into phone; can't wait for it to dry out to make the call.
1. You called yesterday, didn't write down the answer, and forgot it. Oops.

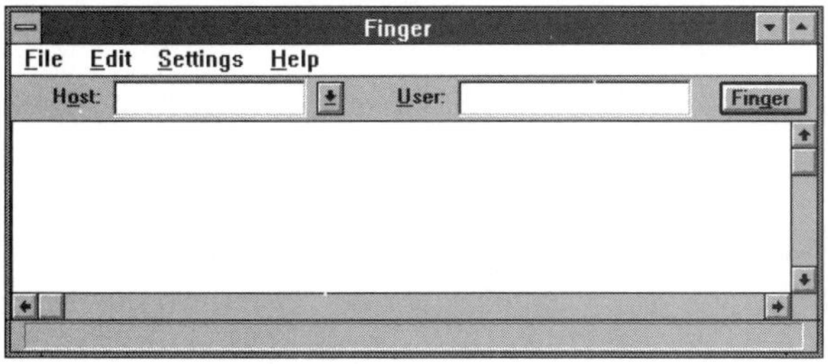

Figure 5-1: Chameleon Finger is ready to finger someone.

2. **To find out about a computer on the Internet, enter the computer's hostname in the Host box and click the Finger button.**

   To find out about the computer called `dummies.com`, for example, enter **dummies.com** in the Host box. When you run Finger without asking for any particular user, you get information about the computer itself, which frequently includes a list of who's logged in now, something like the following:

```
Login     Name                 TTY   Idle   When
johnl     John R. Levine       co    12:    Wed 16:04
margyl    Margy Levine Young   vt    1d     Wed  9:26
carol     Carol Baroudi        p0           Tue 17:31
davekay   David C. Kay         p2    1      Wed 12:34
alison    Alison Barrows       p3    8:04   Wed 10:25
```

With luck, you see a username that looks right for the person you are searching for. The information appears in the large box in the Finger window. If Finger can't get any information from the host computer, you see a message at the bottom of the Finger window, saying something like "Unable to resolve host" or "Unable to connect to host." Some host addresses, particularly those for large on-line services, are valid only for mail (called *mail exchange* or MX addresses), so you may have to find out the name of the user's computer before you can try Finger.

3. **To finger a particular person, enter his hostname in the Host box and his username in the User box. Then click the Finger button.**

   It's a good idea to finger the host computer first, to make sure that the host part of the person's address is right. Depending on the type of system the person uses, you see some information about him in the large box in the Finger window, like this:

```
— Host: dummies.com     User: margyl —

Login name: margyl      In real life: Margy Levine Young
On since Aug 26 15:08:26 on ttyp2   1day 21 hours Idle Time
Plan:
Write lots of best-selling books. Move to Brazil. Become
enlightened.
```

   If there is no such username on this computer, you don't see much information.

4. **To leave the Finger program, choose File⇨Exit from the menu.**

Here are some tips for using Finger:

- If you want to know more about the computer or person you are fingering, choose Settings⇨Verbose from the menu. In verbose mode, Finger displays all the information it gets about each user.
- You can print the contents of the Finger window by choosing File⇨Print from the menu.

- You can copy information from the Finger window to another Windows program. Select the information and choose Edit⇨Copy from the menu (or press Ctrl+C) — this command copies the selected text to the Windows Clipboard.
- If you can't get information about a host computer, try using the Ping program to communicate with it — if Ping can't talk to the host computer, probably the address is wrong or the computer is not working. See Chapter 3 to learn how to run Chameleon Ping.

The industrial-strength Finger

Some places, universities in particular, have attached their Finger programs to organizational directories. If you finger `bu.edu` (Boston University), for example, you get the following response:

```
[bu.edu]
Boston University Electronic Directory (finger access)
  This directory contains listings for Students, Faculty,
  Staff and University Departments. At present, most informa-
  tion about students is not accessible off-campus or via
  finger on bu.edu. The primary directory interface is ph; if
  this is not available, finger accepts <user>@bu.edu where
  <user> can be a login name or FirstName-LastName (note dash
  '-' not space). Also note that <user> can include standard
  UNIX shell patterns.  ...
```

So you can try fingering user `Jane-Smith` at host `bu.edu` to find the address. Other universities with similar directories include M.I.T. (see Figure 5-2) and Yale. It's worth a try — the worst that can happen is that it will say `not found`.

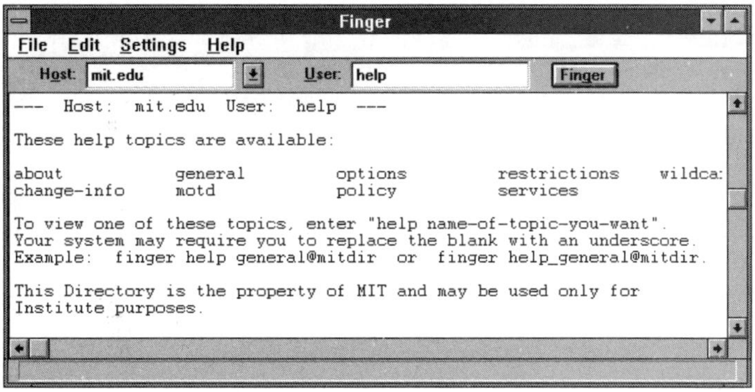

Figure 5-2: Some hosts have organizational directories built into Finger.

Hey, Mr. Postmaster

Sometimes you have a pretty good idea what machine someone uses, but you don't know the name. In that case, you can try writing to the *postmaster.* Every *domain* (the part of the address after the @) that can receive Internet mail has the e-mail address `postmaster`, which contacts someone responsible for that machine. So if you're pretty sure that your friend uses `moby.ntw.org`, you might try asking (politely, of course) `postmaster@moby.ntw.org` what the address is. (We assume that, for some reason, you can't just call your friend and ask what the e-mail address is.)

Most postmasters are overworked system administrators who don't mind an occasional polite question, but you shouldn't expect any big favors. Keep in mind that the larger the mail domain, the less likely it is that the postmaster knows all the users personally. Don't write to `postmaster@ibm.com` to try to find someone's e-mail address at IBM. (Fortunately, IBM has a Whois server — see the next section, "Whois Out There?")

Postmaster is also the appropriate place to write when you're having trouble with mail to or from a site. If your messages to someone are coming back with a cryptic error message which suggests that the mail system is fouled up or if you're receiving a flood of mechanically generated junk mail from a deranged automatic mail server (see Chapter 6), the postmaster at the relevant site is the one to write to.

Whois Out There?

Quite a long time ago (at least, a long time ago in *network* terms — 15 or 20 years ago), some network managers began keeping directories of network people. The system that lets you look up people in these directories is called *Whois.* And Internet Chameleon comes with a Whois program.

In practice, however, it isn't quite that simple. For one thing, around the end of 1992, the main system that keeps the Internet Whois database moved, and some Whois commands haven't been updated yet to reflect that move. The standard computer most Whois programs used to contact now holds only the names of people who work for the U.S. Department of Defense.

Fortunately, you can tell the Whois program to use a particular server — the civilian Internet service is now at `whois.internic.net`.

Running Whois

The following steps show you how to run Chameleon Whois:

1. **Double-click the Whois icon in the Internet Chameleon program group in the Windows Program Manager.**

   You see a window like the one in Figure 5-3.

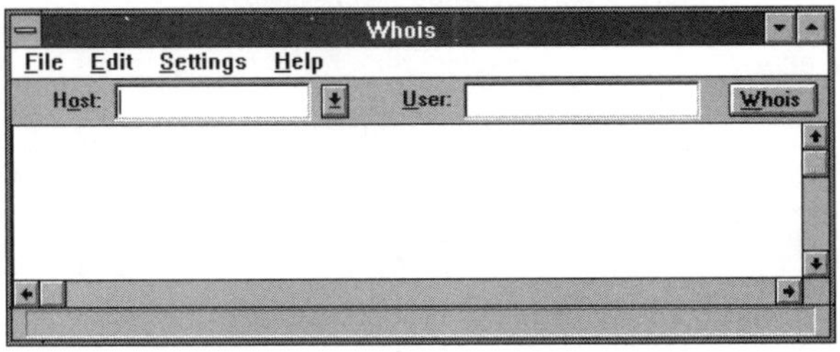

Figure 5-3: The Chameleon Whois program.

2. **Choose a Whois host from the list in Table 5-1 and type it in the Host box.**

   If you don't see an obvious choice, try `whois.internic.net` (Network Solutions, Inc., which helps run the Internet).

3. **Enter the person's last name in the User box.**
4. **Click the Whois button.**

   Your Whois program sends a query out the Whois server you chose. The answer appears in the large box in the Whois window.

5. **To leave Whois, choose File⇨Exit from the menu.**

But don't be surprised if you don't find the person you are looking for — only one of us world-famous authors here at Internet for Dummies Central (the one who runs the computers) is listed! You can also try entering just the person's first name or nickname.

Here are a couple of tips for using Whois:

- For the latest list of Whois servers, use FTP to get the file `whois-servers.list` from `sipb.mit.edu`, in the directory `/pub/whois`. (See Chapter 12 to learn how to get a file by using FTP). This list is maintained by Matt Power at M.I.T.
- If you get the message "Unable to resolve host," check the spelling of the Whois server in the Host box and try again.

To use the Whois program, you have to provide the name of the Whois server, that is, the host computer that stores the information about the organization your friend works for. Table 5-1 offers a partial list of Whois servers, taken from a complete list that was compiled by Matt Power of M.I.T. Questions, comments, and corrections about this list should be sent to the address `mhpower@mit.edu`.

Table 5-1 List of Internet Whois hosts

Server Name	*Associated Institution*
whois.bcm.tmc.edu	Baylor College of Medicine
caltech.edu	California Institute of Technology
csufres.csufresno.edu	California State University — Fresno
csuhayward.edu	California State University — Hayward
csus.edu	California State University — Sacramento
whois.cwru.edu	Case Western Reserve University
whois.doc.ca	Communications Canada (the Federal Department of Communications)
whois.dfci.harvard.edu	Dana-Farber Cancer Institute
cc.fsu.edu	Florida State University
gmu.edu	George Mason University
gettysburg.edu	Gettysburg College
gte.com	GTE Laboratories
hmc.edu	Harvey Mudd College
src.doc.ic.ac.uk	Imperial College (Great Britain)
indiana.edu	Indiana University
whois.lac.net	Latin America & Caribbean Whois Server
llnl.gov	Lawrence Livermore National Laboratory
mit.edu	Massachusetts Institute of Technology
vax2.winona.msus.edu	Minnesota State University — Winona
whois.msstate.edu	Mississippi State University
whois.monash.edu.au	Monash University (Australia)
x500.arc.nasa.gov	NASA Ames Research Center
x500.gsfc.nasa.gov	NASA Goddard Space Flight Center
larc.nasa.gov	NASA Langley Research Center

Server Name	*Associated Institution*
wp.nersc.gov	National Energy Research Supercomputer Center
whois.nrl.navy.mil	Naval Research Laboratory
earth.njit.edu	New Jersey Institute of Technology
pilot.njin.net	New Jersey Intercampus Network
acfcluster.nyu.edu	New York University, Courant Institute
whois.ncsu.edu	North Carolina State University
whois.oxy.edu	Occidental College
osu.edu	Ohio State University
ph.orst.edu	Oregon State University
whois.pacbell.com	Pacific Bell
info.psu.edu	Pennsylvania State University
whois.queensu.ca	Queen's University, Kingston, Canada
cs.rit.edu	Rochester Institute of Technology
whitepages.rutgers.edu	Rutgers University
whois.sdsu.edu	San Diego State University
seda.sandia.gov	Sandia National Laboratories
stjohns.edu	St. John's University
stanford.edu, camis.stanford.edu, hpp.stanford.edu	Stanford University
bingsuns.cc.binghamton.edu	State University of New York at Binghamton
sunysb.edu	State University of New York at Stony Brook
syr.edu	Syracuse University
wp.doe.gov	U.S. Department of Energy
whois.adelaide.edu.au	University of Adelaide (Australia)
zippy.telcom.arizona.edu	University of Arizona
whois.ubalt.edu	University of Baltimore
whois.berkeley.edu	University of California at Berkeley
directory.ucdavis.edu	University of California at Davis
oac.ucla.edu	University of California at Los Angeles
ucsd.edu	University of California at San Diego

(continued)

Table 5-1 *(continued)*

Server Name	***Associated Institution***
whois.ucsb.edu	University of California at Santa Barbara
uchicago.edu	University of Chicago
uc.edu	University of Cincinnati
whois.eng.ufl.edu	University of Florida
umd5.umd.edu	University of Maryland
whois.umass.edu	University of Massachusetts at Amherst
umn.edu	University of Minnesota
sun1.mcsr.olemiss.edu	University of Mississippi
whois.und.ac.za	University of Natal (Durban, South Africa)
ns.unl.edu	University of Nebraska at Lincoln
whois.unb.ca	University of New Brunswick (Canada)
nd.edu	University of Notre Dame
whois.uoregon.edu	University of Oregon
panda1.uottawa.ca	University of Ottawa (Canada)
whois.upenn.edu	University of Pennsylvania
whois.cc.rochester.edu	University of Rochester
whois.usask.ca	University of Saskatchewan (Canada)
jethro.ucc.su.oz.au	University of Sydney (Australia)
x500.utexas.edu	University of Texas at Austin
whois.virginia.edu	University of Virginia
whois.uwo.ca	University of Western Ontario (Canada)
wisc.edu	University of Wisconsin
whois.wfu.edu	Wake Forest University
ibc.wustl.edu	Washington University
wpi.wpi.edu	Worcester Polytechnic Institute
horton.yorku.ca	York University (Canada)

TIP

Okay, so how do I find people at IBM?

We thought you would never ask. IBM has a mail server that lets you look up people's names. Send to `nic@vnet.ibm.com` an e-mail message that contains a line like this:

```
whois Watson, T
```

It lists any users with e-mail addresses whose names match. Although nearly all IBM employees have internal e-mail addresses, only a fraction can receive mail from the outside, and you can see only those addresses. (Makes sense — no point in telling you about mail addresses you can't use.)

Many other companies have a straightforward addressing system that gives everyone at the company an alias such as *`Firstname.Lastname`*. This system works at AT&T, so mailing to this line:

```
Theodore.Vail@att.com
```

finds someone pretty reliably. This method also works at Sun Microsystems (`sun.com`). It's always worth a try because the worst that can happen is that you get your message back as undeliverable. If several people have the same name, you usually get a mechanical response telling you how to figure out which of them you want and what the correct address is.

Know what?

NAVIGATE

One more address-finding system worth trying is *Knowbot*. You telnet (see Chapter 10) to the following address:

```
nri.reston.va.us, port 185
```

(The port 185 means that you want to log in to the Knowbot server rather than to the usual login prompt.) It then displays a prompt. Just type the person's name and wait, sometimes for as long as several minutes, as it looks through a bunch of directories and tells you what it finds. Knowbot has access to some directories not otherwise easily accessible, including the one for MCI Mail, so it's worth checking. In our experience, though, it sometimes misses things — we have MCI Mail accounts, for example, but for some reason Knowbot can't find us there.

Mailing to the Outside World

One of the best things about Internet mail is that it is surprisingly well connected to all sorts of other mail systems and on-line services. In most cases, the connection is seamless enough that you send mail to off-Net users in exactly the same way as you send it to users directly on the Net. In other cases, you have to type the address by using strange punctuation (such as ! and * and %), but in every other way you send and receive mail the same as always.

Here is a short (well, *pretty* short) list of major mail and on-line systems connected to the Internet and a description of how to send mail to people on each system.

America Online (AOL)

An AOL user's username is usually her full name, up to ten letters long, or whatever cute derivative she chose. To send mail to a user named with the username `AaronBurr`, type this line:

```
aaronburr@aol.com
```

Note: Some AOL users have chosen mail names unrelated to their actual names — for them, you have to pick up the phone and call them.

Applelink

Applelink users typically use their last name as their usernames:

```
presley@applelink.apple.com
```

AT&T Mail

AT&T Mail users have arbitrary usernames. To send mail to a user whose username is `blivet`, type this line:

```
blivet@attmail.com
```

BITNET

BITNET is a network of mostly IBM mainframes. Each system name is eight characters long or fewer. System names often contain the letters *VM,* the name of the operating system used on most BITNET sites. Usernames are arbitrary, but they are usually also eight characters or fewer. Many BITNET sites also have Internet mail domain names, so you can send mail to them in the regular Internet way.

If your Internet provider's mail program is smart, it probably has a BITNET support setup to handle BITNET systems not directly on the Internet. So you can send mail to `JSMITH` at `XYZVM3`, for example, by typing this line:

```
jsmith@xyzvm3.bitnet
```

Failing that, you have to address mail directly to a BITNET gateway. Here are addresses using two gateways that tolerate outsiders' mail:

```
jsmith%xyzvm3.bitnet@mitvma.mit.edu
jsmith%xyzvm3.bitnet@cunyvm.cuny.edu
```

These two gateways are provided by M.I.T. and the City University of New York (CUNY), respectively, as a courtesy to the Net community.

BIX

BIX is a commercial system formerly run by *Byte* magazine and now run by Delphi Internet. Usernames are arbitrary short strings. To mail to user `NickDanger`, type this line:

```
NickDanger@bix.com
```

CompuServe

CompuServe is a large on-line service. For ancient, historical reasons, CompuServe usernames are pairs of *octal* (base eight) numbers, usually beginning with the digit 7. If a user's number is 712345,6701, the address is

```
712345.6701@compuserve.com
```

Note: The Internet form uses a *period,* not a *comma,* because Internet addresses can't contain commas.

Delphi

Delphi is an on-line service from Delphi Internet, the same people who run BIX, although the services are separate. (Delphi is now owned by Rupert Murdoch, the media baron.) Delphi usernames are arbitrary strings, most often the first initial and last name of the user. To send to user `joeblow`, type this line:

```
joeblow@delphi.com
```

Easylink

Easylink is a mostly mail service formerly run by Western Union and now run by AT&T. Users have seven-digit numbers beginning with 62. To mail to user `6231416`, type this line:

```
6231416@eln.attmail.com
```

FIDONET

FIDONET is a large, worldwide BBS network. On FIDONET, people are identified by their names, and each individual BBS (called a *node*) has a three- or four-part number in the form `1:2/3` or `1:2/3.4`. To send a message to Grover Cleveland at node `1:2/3.4`, type this line:

```
grover.cleveland@p4.f3.n2.z1.fidonet.org
```

If a node has a three-part name, such as `1:2/3`, type this line:

```
grover.cleveland@f3.n2.z1.fidonet.org
```

GEnie

GEnie is an on-line service run by General Electric. It's the consumer end of GE's commercial on-line service, which dates back into the 1960s. Each user has a username, which is an arbitrary and totally unmemorable string, and a mail name, which is usually related to the user's name. You have to know a user's mail name, something like `J.SMITH7`:

```
J.SMITH7@genie.geis.com
```

MCI Mail

MCI Mail is a large, commercial e-mail system. Each user has a seven-digit user number guaranteed to be unique and a username that may or may not be unique. You can send to the number, username, or the person's actual name, using underscores rather than spaces:

```
1234567@mcimail.com
jsmith@mcimail.com
john_smith@mcimail.com
```

If you send to a username or an actual name and the name turns out not to be unique, MCI Mail thoughtfully sends you a response listing the possible matches so that you can send your message again to the unique user number. MCI user numbers are sometimes written with a hyphen, like a phone number, but you don't have to type the hyphen in your address.

Prodigy

Prodigy is a large on-line system run by IBM and Sears. (We hear that it can have upward of 10,000 simultaneous users.) Users have arbitrary usernames like `KS8GN3`. Send mail to this address:

```
KS8GN3@prodigy.com
```

Sprintmail (Telemail)

Sprintmail is an e-mail system provided by Sprintnet. Sprintmail used to be called Telemail because Sprintnet used to be called Telenet. (It was a technological spin-off of the original ARPANET work that led to the Internet.) Sprintmail is the major X.400 mail system in the United States. See the section "X.400: We're from the government and we're here to help you," later in this chapter, to learn how to handle this type of address.

UUCP

UUCP is an old and cruddy mail system still used by many UNIX systems because (how did you guess?) it's free. UUCP addresses consist of a system name and a username, which are both short strings of characters.

The system here at Internet For Dummies Central, for example, has (for historical reasons) a UUCP address — `iecc` — in addition to its normal Internet address (`dummies.com`), so rather than mail us messages at `starter@dummies.com`, you can address mail to `iecc!starter`. (The !, pronounced "bang," is called a *bang path address.*)

Multihop UUCP addresses also exist: `world!iecc!starter` says to send the message first to the machine called `world`, which can send it to `iecc`, where the address is `starter`. (Think of it as e-mail's "whisper down the lane.") Most often, UUCP addresses are written relative to an Internet host that also talks UUCP, so you can address mail to

```
world!iecc!starter@uunet.uu.net
```

(although it gets here considerably faster and more reliably if you send it to `starter@dummies.com` because that avoids the UUCP nonsense). This address means to send the message to `uunet.uu.net` by using regular Internet mail, and then by UUCP to `world`, and then another UUCP hop to `iecc`, and from there to the mailbox called `starter`. If you think that this method is ugly and confusing, you're not alone.

UUNET Communications is a large, nonprofit outfit that, among other things, brings e-mail to the UUCP-speaking masses, so it's the Internet system most often seen with UUCP addresses. Most of UUNET's customers also have regular Internet addresses that internally are turned into the ugly UUCP addresses. If you know the Internet address rather than the UUCP address, use it.

X.400: We're from the government and we're here to help you

After the Internet had been around for several years and e-mail had been flowing for much longer than that, the international organization in charge of standards for telephones and stuff like that, known then as the *CCITT* (a French acronym for the International Telephone Committee), decided that it too was going to get into the e-mail business.

You might think that the obvious thing to do would be to adopt the existing standards because they had been shown to be reliable and robust. (Silly you — that just goes to show that *you'll* never get very far as an international telecommunications standards developer.) CCITT decided to come up with *X.400,* something all new, all singing, all dancing, and much, much more complex — as befits the grandeur of the international telecommunications establishment. In all fairness, X.400 does handle a few things that Internet mail (known as *RFC822,* after the document that describes it) doesn't, or at least didn't until recently. But X.400 is so complicated that it has taken nearly ten years from the publication of the first version for it to become at all common.

An X.400 address isn't just a name and a domain: It's a bunch of attributes. The official specification goes on for dozens, if not hundreds, of pages, but we spare you the detail (which would be fascinating if we had the space, you can be sure) and report on the bare minimum. The attributes that are usually of interest and the codes used to represent them are shown in this list:

- **Surname (S):** Recipient's last name
- **Given name (G):** Recipient's first name
- **Initials (I):** First or middle initial (or initials)
- **Generational qualifier (GQ or Q):** Jr., III, and so on (these folks think of everything)
- **Administration Domain Name (ADMD or A):** More or less the name of the mail system
- **Private Domain Name (PRMD or P):** More or less the name of a private system "gatewayed" into a public ADMD
- **Organization (O):** Organization with which the recipient is affiliated, which may or may not have anything to do with the ADMD or PRMD
- **Country (C):** Two-letter country code (see Appendix A)
- **Domain Defined Attribute (DD or DDA):** Any magic code that identifies the recipient, such as username or account number

You encode these attributes in an address, by using / (a slash) to separate them and writing each attribute as the code, an equal sign, and the value. Is that clear? No? (Can't imagine why.)

Here's a concrete example: Suppose that your friend uses Sprint's Sprintmail service (formerly known as Telemail, the ADMD), which has an X.400 connection to the Internet. Your friend's name is Samuel Tilden, he's in the United States, and he's with Tammany Hall. His attributes are

- **G:** Samuel
- **S:** Tilden
- **O:** TammanyHall
- **C:** US

so his address is

```
/G=Samuel/S=Tilden/O=TammanyHall/C=US/ADMD=TELEMAIL/
          @sprint.com
```

because the Internet domain for the gateway is `sprint.com`. Notice that a slash appears at the beginning of the address and just before the @. The order of the slash-separated chunks doesn't matter.

Exactly which attributes you need for a particular address varies all over the place. Some domains connect to only a single country and ADMD, so you don't use those attributes with those domains. Others (such as Sprintmail) connect to many, so you need both. It's a mess. You have to find out for each X.400 system which attributes it needs. In theory, redundant attributes shouldn't hurt, but in practice, who knows?

One minor simplification applies to the hopefully common case in which the only attribute necessary is the recipient's actual name. If the user's name is Rutherford B. Hayes, the full attribute form is

```
/G=Rutherford/I=B/S=Hayes/
```

But instead you can write

```
Rutherford.B.Hayes
```

Pretty advanced, eh? You can leave out the given name or the initial if you want. You can hope that most X.400 addresses can be written this way, but you are probably doomed to disappointment.

TIP

In most cases, the easiest way to figure out someone's X.400 address is to have your recipient send you a message and see what the "From:" line says. Failing that, you have to experiment.

A Few Words from the Etiquette Ladies

Sadly, the great Etiquette Ladies such as Emily Post and Amy Vanderbilt died before the invention of e-mail. But here is what they might have suggested about what to say and, more important, what *not* to say in electronic mail.

E-mail is a funny hybrid, something between a phone call (or voice mail) and a letter. On the one hand, it's quick and usually informal; on the other hand, it's written rather than spoken, so you don't see any facial expressions or hear tones of voice.

E-mail always seems ruder than it's supposed to

This means:

- When you send a message, watch your tone of voice.
- Feel free to stick in little "smiley" faces to show when you are joking, like this: :-) or this: ;-) or this: :-D or this: >8^).
- If someone sends you an incredibly obnoxious and offensive message, as likely as not, it is a mistake or a joke gone awry. In particular, be on the lookout for failed sarcasm.

Flame off!

Pointless and excessive outrage in electronic mail is so common that it has a name of its own: *flaming.* Don't flame. It makes you look like a jerk.

When you get a message so offensive that you just *have* to reply, stick it back in your electronic in-box for a while and wait until after lunch. Then, don't flame back. The sender probably didn't realize how the message would look. In about 20 years of using electronic mail, we can testify that we've never, ever regretted *not* sending an angry message. (But we *have* regretted sending a few. Ouch.)

When you're sending mail, keep in mind that someone reading it will have no idea of what you *intended* to say — just what you *did* say. Subtle sarcasm and irony are almost impossible to use in e-mail and usually come across as annoying or dumb instead. (If you are a truly superb writer, you can disregard this advice, but don't say that you weren't warned.)

Sometimes it helps to put in a :-), or *smiley,* which means "This is a joke." (Try leaning way over to the left, if you don't see why it's a smile.) In some communities, notably CompuServe, <g> or <grin> serves the same purpose. Here's a typical example:

```
People who don't believe that we are all part of a warm,
caring community who love and support each other are no
better than rabid dogs and should be hunted down and shot. :-)
```

Smileys sometimes help, but if a joke needs a smiley, maybe it wasn't worth making. It may sound like all your e-mail is supposed to be totally humorless. It's not that bad, but until you have the hang of it, limit the humor. You'll be glad that you did.

TIP

Chain letters: Arrrrrggghhh!

One of the most obnoxious things you can do with e-mail is to pass around chain letters. Because all mail programs have forwarding commands, with only a few keystrokes you can take a chain letter and send it along to hundreds of other people. Don't do it. Chain letters are cute for about two seconds, and then they're just annoying.

A few chain letters just keep coming around and around, despite our best efforts to stamp them out. Learn to recognize them now and avoid embarrassment later. Here are some of the hangers-on:

Dying boy wants greeting cards: (Sometimes it's business cards.) Not anymore, he doesn't. Several years ago, an English boy named Craig Shergold was hospitalized with what was thought to be an inoperable brain tumor. Craig wanted to set the world record for most greeting cards. Word got out, and Craig received millions and millions of cards and eventually got into the *Guinness Book of World Records.* When it turned out that maybe the tumor *wasn't* inoperable, U.S. TV billionaire John Kluge paid for Craig to fly to the United States for an operation, which was successful. So Craig is OK now and definitely doesn't want any more cards. (You can read all about this story on page 24 of the July 29, 1990, edition of the *New York Times.*) Guinness is so sick and tired of the whole business that it closed the category — no more records for the most cards are accepted. If you want to help dying children, give the two dollars that a card and stamp would have cost to a children's welfare organization, such as UNICEF.

The modem tax rumor: In 1987, the Federal Communications Commission (FCC) briefly floated a proposal for a technical change to the rules governing the way on-line services, such as CompuServe and GEnie, are billed for their phone connections. Implementing the proposal would have had the effect of raising the prices these services charge. Customers of on-line services made their opposition clear immediately and loudly, members of Congress made concerned inquiries, and the proposal was dropped — permanently. Unfortunately, undated alarmist notices about the proposal have circulated around bulletin boards ever since. If you see yet another modem tax scare, demand the FCC's current docket number because the FCC — as a government bureaucracy — can't blow its nose without making announcements, accepting comments, and so on. So no docket means no action, which means that it's the same old rumor you should ignore.

Make big bucks with a chain letter: Usually these letters, signed by "Dave Rhodes," contain lots of testimonials from people who are now rolling in dough and tell you to send $5 or so to the name at the top of the list, put your name at the bottom, and send the message to a zillion other suckers. Some even say "This isn't a chain letter" (you're supposedly helping to compile a mailing list or something, which is your 100 percent guaranteed tip-off that it *is* a chain letter). Don't even think about it. These chain letters are extremely illegal, and besides, they don't even work. (Why send any money? Why not just add your name and send it on?) Think of them as highly contagious gullibility viruses. Just ignore them or perhaps send a polite note to the sender's postmaster to encourage her to tell users not to send any more chain letters.

The "two-fifty" cookie recipe: According to this one, someone was eating chocolate chip cookies somewhere (Mrs. Fields and Neiman-Marcus are frequently cited) and asked whether she (it was always a she) could have the recipe. "Sure," came the answer, "that'll be two-fifty, charged to your credit card." "OK." When the credit card statement came, it turned out to be two hundred and fifty *dollars,* not two dollars and fifty cents. So in retribution, the message concludes with the putative Mrs. Fields or Neiman-Marcus recipe, sent to you for free. The story is pure hooey: Mrs. Fields doesn't give out her recipes, for money or otherwise; Neiman's has never even served chocolate chip cookies. The recipe, which varies somewhat from one version to the next, makes perfectly OK cookies, but we don't think that it's any better than the one on the back of the bag of chips. This same story, by the way, circulated hand-to-hand in the 1940s and 1950s, except that the recipe was for a red-velvet cake served at the restaurant in one of the big New York department stores. It wasn't true then either.

How private is e-mail?

Relatively, but not totally. Any recipient of your mail might forward it to other people. Some mail addresses are really mailing lists that redistribute messages to many other people. In one famous case, a mistaken mail address sent a message to tens of thousands of readers. It started out, "Darling, at last we have a way to send messages that is completely private."

TIP

The usual rule of thumb is to not send anything you wouldn't want to see posted next to the water cooler or perhaps scribbled next to a pay phone. The latest e-mail systems are starting to include encryption features that make the privacy situation somewhat better so that anyone who doesn't know the keyword used to scramble a message can't decode it. There's no standard for encrypted mail yet, so you have to ask the folks with whom you exchange sensitive mail whether they use any e-mail encryption.

Another possibility to keep in the back of your mind is that it is technically not difficult to forge e-mail return addresses, so if you get a totally off-the-wall message from someone that seems out of character for that person, somebody else may have forged it as a prank.

BTW, what does IMHO mean? RTFM!

E-mail users are often lazy typists, and many abbreviations are common. Here are some of the most widely used abbreviations:

Abbreviation	*What It Means*
BTW	By the way
IMHO	In my humble opinion
PMJI	Pardon my jumping in
ROFL	Rolling on floor laughing
RTFM	Read the funny manual — you could have and should have looked it up yourself
TIA	Thanks in advance
TLA	Three-letter acronym

Chapter 6

Getting on Mailing Lists

In This Chapter

- How mailing lists work
- LISTSERV, Majordomo, and regular old lists
- Do's and don'ts
- Some interesting mailing lists

Now that you know all about how to send and receive mail, only one thing stands between you and a rich, fulfilling, mail-blessed life: You don't know many people with whom you can exchange mail. Fortunately, you can get yourself on lots of mailing lists, which ensures that you arrive every morning to a mailbox with 400 new messages. (Maybe you should start out with one or two lists.)

Are You Sure This Isn't Junk Mail?

The point of a mailing list is simple. The list itself has a mail address, and anything (more or less) someone sends to that address is sent to all the people on the list, who often respond to the messages. The result is a running conversation. Different lists have different styles. Some are relatively formal, hewing closely to the official topic of the list. Others tend to fly off into outer space, topic-wise. You have to read them for a while to be able to tell which list works which way.

TIP: Usenet news is another way to have running e-mail-like conversations, and the distinction between the two is blurry. (Some topics are available both as mailing lists and on Usenet, so both people with and without access to news can participate.) Chapters 7 through 9 discuss Usenet.

Getting on and off Mailing Lists

The way you get on or off a mailing list is simple: You send a mail message. Two general schools of mailing-list management exist: *manual* and *automatic.* Manual management is the more traditional way: Your message is read by a human being who updates the files to put people on or take them off the list. The advantage of manual management is that you get personal service; the disadvantage is that the list *maintainer* may not get around to servicing you for quite a while if more pressing business (such as her real job) intervenes.

These days it's more common to have lists maintained automatically, which saves human attention for times when things are fouled up. The most widely used automatic mailing managers are programs known as *LISTSERV* and *Majordomo.*

Manual lists: Say "Add me, please!"

For manual lists, there is a widely observed convention regarding list and manager addresses. Suppose that you want to join a list for fans of James Buchanan, the 15th President of the United States (the only one who never married, in case you slept through that part of history class), and the list's mailing address is `buchanan-lovers@blivet.com`. The manager's address is almost certainly `buchanan-lovers-request@blivet.com`. In other words, just add `-request` to the list's address to get the list manager's address. (Add it *before* the at-sign.)

Send all messages about getting on or off the list, or problems with getting messages from the list, to the list manager. Because the list is maintained by hand, your request to be added or dropped doesn't have to take any particular form, as long as it's polite. "Please add me to the buchanan-lovers list" does quite well. When you decide that you've had all the Buchanan you can stand, another message saying "Please remove me from the buchanan-lovers list" does equally well.

Messages to `-request` addresses are read and handled by human beings who sometimes eat, sleep, and work regular jobs as well as maintain mailing lists. This means that they don't necessarily read your request the moment it arrives. It can take a day or so to be added to or removed from a list, and after you ask to be removed, you usually get a few more messages before they remove you. If it takes longer than you want, be patient. And *don't* send cranky follow-ups — they just cheese off the list maintainer.

TIP

How to avoid looking like an idiot

Here's a handy tip: After you subscribe to a list, don't send anything to it until you've been reading it for a week. Trust us, it has been getting along without your insights since it began, and it can get along without them for one more week.

This gives you a chance to learn the sorts of topics people really discuss, the tone of the list, and so on. It also gives you a fair idea about which topics people are tired of. The classic newcomer gaffe is to subscribe to a list and immediately send a message asking a dumb question that isn't really germane to the topic and that was beaten to death three days earlier. Bide your time and don't let this happen to you.

The number-two newcomer gaffe is to send a message directly to the list asking to subscribe or unsubscribe. Such a message should go to a `-request`, LISTSERV, or Majordomo address, where the list manager (human or robotic) can handle it, and *not* to the list itself, where all the other subscribers can see that you screwed up.

Add me, LISTSERV!

Maintaining a mailing list can be a great deal of work, so some folks at BITNET came up with a program called LISTSERV, which runs on great, big IBM mainframe computers. (The IBM mainframe types have an inordinate fondness for eight-letter uppercase names EVEN THOUGH TO MOST OF US IT SEEMS LIKE SHOUTING.) Originally, only users on machines that were directly connected to BITNET could use LISTSERV, but current versions have been improved so that anyone with an Internet address can use them. Indeed, LISTSERV has grown to the point that it is an all-singing, all-dancing mailing-list program with about 15 zillion features and options, almost none of which you care about.

LISTSERV is a little klunky to use, but it has the great advantage of being able to handle with ease enormous mailing lists containing thousands of members, something that makes regular Internet mail programs choke. (LISTSERV can send mail to 1,000 addresses in about five minutes, for example, whereas that would take the regular Internet `sendmail` program more than an hour.)

You put yourself on and off a LISTSERV mailing list by sending mail to `LISTSERV@`*`some.machine.or.other`*, where *`some.machine.or.other`* is the name of the particular machine where the mailing list lives. Because they're computer programs, LISTSERV list managers are pretty simpleminded, so you have to speak to them clearly and distinctly.

Suppose that you want to join a list called AARDVARK-L (the names of LISTSERV mailing lists usually end with *-L*), which lives at ntw.org. To join, send a message to LISTSERV@ntw.org that contains this line:

```
SUBSCRIBE AARDVARK-L Roger Sherman
```

(This line assumes that your name is Roger Sherman.) You don't have to add a subject line or anything else to this message. You can type just **SUB** rather than **SUBSCRIBE** — LISTSERV knows what you mean. After that, you type the name of the list you want to subscribe to (*AARDVARK-L,* in this example). Anything after that is supposed to be your real name. (You can put whatever you want there, but keep in mind that it shows up in the return address of anything you send to the list.) Shortly afterward, you should get two messages back:

- A chatty, machine-generated welcoming message, telling you that you've joined the list, along with a description of some commands you can use to fiddle with your mailing-list membership.
- An incredibly boring message telling you that the IBM mainframe ran a program to handle your request and reporting the exact number of milliseconds of computer time and number of disk operations the request took. *Whoopee.* (It is sobering to think that somewhere people find these messages interesting.)

TIP

To get off a list, you again write to LISTSERV@*some.machine.or.other* and replace *some.machine.or.other* with the computer the mailing list lives on (for example, ntw.org), this time sending this line:

```
SIGNOFF AARDVARK-L
```

or whatever the list's name is. You don't have to give your name again because, after you're off the list, LISTSERV has no additional interest in you and completely forgets that you ever existed.

Some lists are more difficult to get on and off than others. Usually, you ask to get on a list and you're on the list. In some cases the list isn't open to all comers, however, and the human list owner screens requests to join the list. In other cases, after you ask to subscribe, LISTSERV sends you a message to make sure that it got your address right, and you have to respond with "OK" or something. (These messages tend to say pretty clearly what you're expected to do.)

TIP

To contact the actual human being who runs a particular list, the mail address is *OWNER-* followed by the list name (OWNER-AARDVARK-L@ntw.org, for example). The owner can do all sorts of things to lists that mere mortals can't do. In particular, the owner can fix screwed-up names on the list or add a name that for some reason the automatic method doesn't handle.

Don't put your LISTSERV command (such as `subscribe` or `signoff`) in the subject line of the e-mail message. Put the command in the text of the message. LISTSERV ignores subject lines.

Stupid LISTSERV tricks

The people who maintain the LISTSERV program have added so many bells and whistles to it that it would take an entire book to describe them all, and, frankly, they're not that interesting. But here are some stupid LISTSERV tricks. For each of them, you send a message to `LISTSERV@`*`some.machine.or.other`* to talk to the LISTSERV program itself (substitute for *`some.machine.or.other`* the name of the machine on which the mailing list lives). You can send several commands in the same message, one command on each line, if you want to do two or three tricks at one time.

Hey, it bounced

LISTSERV mailing lists usually live on computers that are on BITNET, a network of mostly IBM mainframes. BITNET is a separate network from the Internet, although there are gateways that connect BITNET to Internet.

If you try to subscribe to a LISTSERV mailing list and the message bounces back to you marked "undeliverable," you probably used a BITNET address rather than an Internet address. Many lists of mailing lists include only BITNET addresses, not the Internet addresses.

BITNET sites have names with up to eight characters, frequently including the letters *VM*. For example, the BITNET address of a LISTSERV site might be `LISTSERV@xyzvm3`.

The first thing to try when sending a message to a BITNET address is adding `.bitnet` to the end of it, like this: `LISTSERV@xyzvm3.bitnet`. If a message to this address bounces, address it using a BITNET gateway. Here are three BITNET gateways to try:

`LISTSERV%xyzvm3.bitnet@mitvma.mit.edu`

`LISTSERV%xyzvm3.bitnet@cunyvm.cuny.edu`

`LISTSERV%xyzvm3.bitnet@uga.cc.uga.edu`

Replace the `xyzvm3` with the name of the BITNET site where the mailing list lives.

BITNET, which was originally entirely separate from the Internet, has been slowly merging into it, which means that most BITNET machines have both a BITNET name and an Internet name. (You might hope there'd be a systematic way to convert one kind of name to another, but unfortunately there isn't.) This means, for example, that the BITNET machine known as AUVM is now also the Internet host `american.edu`, and you can use the Internet name directly. Eventually all BITNET machines will have Internet names and we will finally be able to forget about the funky names and address punctuation.

- **Temporarily stop mail:** Sometimes you're going to be away for a week or two and you don't want to get a bunch of mailing-list mail in the meantime. But because you're planning to come back, you don't want to take yourself off the list either. To temporarily stop mail from the AARDVARK-L mailing list, send this line:

  ```
  SET AARDVARK-L NOMAIL
  ```

  It stops sending you messages. To turn the mail back on, send this line:

  ```
  SET AARDVARK-L MAIL
  ```

- **Get messages as a digest:** If you're getting a large number of messages from a list every day and would rather get them all at the same time as a daily digest, send this line:

  ```
  SET AARDVARK-L DIGEST
  ```

  Remember that not all lists can be digested (think of burritos), and the indigestible ones let you know.

- **Find out who's on a list:** To find out who subscribes to a list, send this line:

  ```
  REVIEW AARDVARK-L
  ```

  Some lists can be reviewed only by people on the list, and others not at all. Some lists are enormous, so be prepared to get back an enormous message listing thousands of subscribers.

- **Get or don't get your own mail:** When you send mail to a LISTSERV list of which you're a member, it usually sends you a copy of your own message to confirm that it got there OK. Some people find this copy needlessly redundant. ("Your message has been sent. You'll be receiving it shortly." Huh?) To avoid getting copies of your own messages, send this line:

  ```
  SET AARDVARK-L NOACK
  ```

  To resume getting copies of your own messages, send this line:

  ```
  SET AARDVARK-L ACK
  ```

- **Find out which lists are available:** To find out which LISTSERV mailing lists are available on a particular host, send this line:

  ```
  LIST
  ```

  Note: Keep in mind that just because a list exists doesn't necessarily mean that you can subscribe to it. But it doesn't hurt to try.

- **Get LISTSERV to do other things:** Lots of other commands lurk in LISTSERV, most of which apply only to people on IBM mainframes. If you are this type of person, or if you're just nosy, send a message containing this line:

  ```
  HELP
  ```

  and you'll receive a helpful response listing other commands.

Add me, Majordomo!

Majordomo is a program, written by a guy named Brent Chapman, that works much like LISTSERV does. To subscribe to a list maintained by Majordomo, you send a message to `majordomo@`*`some.computer`*. Replace *`some.computer`* with the name of the computer on which the mailing list lives.

To get yourself on a mailing list, send a message like this:

```
subscribe listname
```

Replace *`listname`* with the name of the list you want to be on. (Suppose that you want to subscribe to a list called `net-happenings`, which lives on the computer `acpub.duke.edu`. You send the message `subscribe net-happenings` to `majordomo@acpub.duke.edu`.) You receive from Majordomo a friendly message confirming that you are on the mailing list, giving you instructions about how to get off, and usually describing the list itself. If for some reason you want it to send the messages to an address different from the one from which you're sending the request, put that address after the listname. (Note to the mischievous: The origin of the request is easily traced, in case the person whose address got added didn't want to be on the list.)

To get off a list, send this message:

```
unsubscribe net-happenings
```

If the address you want it to remove isn't the one from which you're sending the request (if your system manager has changed your address, for example), put the address you want to remove after the listname.

Don't put your Majordomo command (such as `subscribe` or `signoff`) in the subject line of the e-mail message. Put it in the text of the message. Majordomo ignores subject lines.

Stupid Majordomo tricks

Here are some other things Majordomo can do:

- **Find out which files are in the archive for a mailing list:** Some mailing lists maintain archives. To get a list of the files in the archive for a mailing list, send the following command to the Majordomo where the mailing list lives:

  ```
  index listname
  ```

  Replace *listname* with the name of the mailing list.

- **Get a file:** For mailing lists that maintain archives, you can retrieve copies of the files by e-mail. You have to know the name of the file you want. Send this command:

  ```
  get listname filename
  ```

  Replace *listname* with the name of the mailing list, and replace *filename* with the name of the file you want.

- **Find out which list (or lists) you are on:** Send this message to the Majordomo:

  ```
  which
  ```

- **Find out who is on a mailing list:** To get a list of all the e-mail addresses of the folks on a mailing list, send this command:

  ```
  who listname
  ```

- **Get introductory information about a mailing list:** To get the introductory message for a mailing list, send this command:

  ```
    info listname
  ```

- **Find out which mailing lists live at this Majordomo site:** To see a list, send this message:

  ```
  lists
  ```

- **Get a list of the commands this Majordomo understands:** Send this message:

  ```
  help
  ```

- If you have to contact the human manager of a Majordomo system because you can't get off a list you want to leave or if you otherwise have an insoluble problem, send a polite message to `owner-majordomo@`*`some.computer`*. Remember that humans eat, sleep, and have real jobs, so it may take a day or two to get an answer.

WARNING!

LISTSERV and Majordomo: They could have made it the same, but n-o-o-o-o

Because LISTSERV and Majordomo work in sort of the same way, even experienced mailing-list mavens get their commands confused. Here are the important differences:

- The address for LISTSERV is `LISTSERV@`*`hostname`*, and the address for Majordomo is `majordomo@`*`hostname`*.
- To subscribe to a LISTSERV list, send `subscribe` followed by the list name followed by your real name. To subscribe to a Majordomo list, just send `subscribe` and the list name.

TIP

Urrp! Computer's Digest messages

Some mailing lists are *digested.* No, they're not dripping with digital gastric juices — they're digested more in the sense of *Reader's Digest.* All the messages during a particular period of time (usually a day or two) are gathered into one big message with a table of contents added at the front. Many people find this method more convenient than getting messages separately, because you can easily look at all the messages on the topic at one time.

Some mail and newsreading programs give you the option of dividing digests back into the individual messages so that you can see them one at a time yet still grouped together. This option is sometimes known as *undigestification* or *exploding* a digest. (First it's digested and then it explodes — sort of like a burrito.) Ask a nearby guru whether and how you can turn on digest exploding in your local mail program.

Sending Messages to Mailing Lists

Okay, you're signed up on a mailing list. Now what? First wait a week or so and see what sort of messages arrive from the list — that way, you can get an idea of what you should or should not send to it. When you think that you've seen enough to avoid embarrassing yourself, try sending something to the list for all its readers to see (assuming that you have something to say).

That's easy — you mail a message to the mailing list's address: `buchanan-lovers@blivet.com` or `AARDVARK-L@ntw.org` or whatever. Keep in mind that hundreds or thousands of people will read your pearls of wisdom, so try at least to spell things correctly.(You may have thought that this was obvious, but you would be sadly mistaken.) On popular lists, you may begin to get responses within a few minutes of sending a message.

Be sure to provide a descriptive `Subject:` for the multitudes who will benefit from your pearls of wisdom. Within a matter of minutes, people all over the world will read your message.

Some lists encourage new subscribers to send in a message introducing themselves and saying briefly what their interests are. Others don't. So don't send anything until you have something to say.

After you watch the flow of messages on a list for a while, all this stuff becomes obvious.

Be sure to use your Chameleon Mail address book to keep track of mailing list addresses. Add both addresses for each mailing list you belong to — the address to use for administrivia (the `-request` address) and the one to use when you're writing to all readers of the list.

Some mailing lists have funny rules about who is allowed to send messages, meaning that just because you're on the list doesn't automatically mean that any messages you send will appear on the list. Some lists are *moderated,* meaning that any message you send in gets sent to a human *moderator,* who decides what goes to the list and what doesn't. This method may sound sort of fascist, but in practice the arrangement makes a list about 50 times more interesting than it would be otherwise, because a good moderator can filter out the boring and irrelevant messages and keep the list on track. Indeed, the people who complain the loudest about moderator censorship are usually the ones whose messages most deserve to be censored.

Another rule that sometimes causes trouble is that many lists for some reason allow messages to be sent only from people whose addresses appear on the list. This rule becomes a pain if your mailing address changes. Suppose that your e-mail address changes from `jj@shamu.pol.ntw.org` to `John.Jay@ntw.org`, although your old address still works. You may find that some lists begin *bouncing* your messages (sending them back to you rather than to the list) because they don't understand that `John.Jay@ntw.org`, the name under which you now send messages, is the same as `jj@shamu.pol.ntw.org`, the name under which you originally subscribed to the list. What's worse is that, for the same reason, LISTSERV doesn't let you take yourself off the list. To resolve this mess, you have to write to the human owners of any lists in which this problem arises and ask them to fix the problem by hand.

TIP

Boing!

Computer accounts are created and deleted often enough and mail addresses change often enough that a large list always contains, at any given moment, some addresses that are no longer valid. So if you send a message to the list, your message is forwarded to these invalid addresses, and a return message reporting the bad addresses is generated for each of them. Normally, mailing-list managers (both human and computer) try to deflect the error messages so that they go to the list manager, who can do something about them, rather than go to you. But as often as not, a persistently dumb mail system sends one of these failure messages directly to you. Just ignore it because there isn't anything you can do about it.

Replying to Mailing-List Messages

Lots of times you receive an interesting message from a list and want to respond to it. But when you send your answer, does it go *just* to the person who sent the original message or does it go to the *entire list?* It depends, mostly on how the list manager set up the software that handles the list. About half the list managers set it up so that replies automatically go to just the person who sent the original message, on the theory that your response is likely to be of interest only to the original author. The other half set it up so that replies go to the entire list, on the theory that the list is like a running public discussion. In messages coming from the list, the mailing-list software automatically sets the `Reply-To:` header to the address where replies should be sent.

Fortunately, you're in charge. When you start to create a reply, Chameleon Mail shows you the address it's replying to. If you don't like the address it's using, change it.

While you're fixing the recipient's address, you may also want to fix the "Subject:" line. After a few rounds of replies to replies to replies, the topic of discussion often wanders away from the original topic, and it is nice to change the subject to better describe what is really under discussion.

Mailing Lists versus Usenet News

Many mailing lists are *gatewayed* to Usenet newsgroups (see Chapter 8), which means that all the messages you would receive if you subscribed to the mailing list appear as items in the newsgroup and vice versa. Most gateways are two-way, meaning that anything you mail to the list also shows up in the newsgroup and that anything you post as a news item also goes to the list. A few are one-way, usually because of sloppy gateway code, and many of them are moderated — which means that you have to mail any items to the moderator, who filters out inappropriate messages.

Whether you get a particular list as mail or as Usenet newsgroups is largely a matter of personal taste. The advantages of receiving lists as mail are that mail items tend to arrive faster than newsgroup items do (usually by only a few hours) and that mail items stick around until you explicitly delete them (whereas newsgroup articles are deleted automatically, usually after a few days). The advantages of Usenet newsgroups are that items are collected in a newsgroup rather than mixed in with your mail; items are automatically deleted unless you save them; and NEWTNews does a better job than Chameleon Mail does of collecting threads of related messages so that you can read them in order.

If you don't care which way you get your stuff, get it as news because the load on both your provider's computer and the network in general is considerably lower that way.

Some Interesting Lists

A great many mailing lists reside on the Internet — so many, in fact, that entire *books* have been written that just enumerate all the lists. So to get you started, here are a bunch of lists we find interesting, along with short descriptions of what they are. Each is accompanied by at least one of the following codes, describing what kind of list it is:

- **Internet:** Internet-type list, maintained by a regular human being. To get on or off or to contact the human who maintains the list, write to `listname-request@sitename`.
- **Majordomo:** Majordomo-type list. To get on or off, send a `subscribe` or `signoff` message to `majordomo@sitename`.
- **LISTSERV:** LISTSERV-type list. To get on or off, send a `subscribe` or `signoff` message to `LISTSERV@sitename`. To contact the relevant human, send mail to `owner-whatever@sitename`.

- **Moderated:** Moderated list. Messages are filtered by the human list owner (moderator).
- **News:** List is also available as Usenet News, which is usually the best way to receive it (see previous section "Mailing Lists versus Usenet News"). Nearly all LISTSERV lists are also available as a special kind of newsgroup, so this marks only lists available as regular newsgroups. (See Chapter 7 to learn how to read newsgroups.)
- **Digest:** Messages normally arrive as a digest rather than one at a time.

For a huge list of mailing lists (all those maintained by LISTSERV), mail a message containing the line `list global` to `LISTSERV@VM1.NODAK.EDU`. The list is so long that it arrives as nine (or more) separate mail messages. Note that it lists BITNET addresses, not Internet addresses (see the sidebar "Hey, it bounced"). Alternatively, read the Usenet newsgroup entitled `news.lists` (see Chapter 7 to learn how).

Frequent Flyers (Internet)

Manager address: `frequent-flyer-request@ames.arc.nasa.gov`

List address: `frequent-flyer@ames.arc.nasa.gov`

`Frequent-flyer` is for and about frequent air travelers. It has lots of tips and war stories. Neophytes are welcome to join and listen in, but this isn't the right place to ask "How do I buy a plane ticket from New York to Chicago?"

Internet Use (LISTSERV)

Manager address: `LISTSERV@emuvm1.bitnet`

List address: `INETUSE@emuvm1.bitnet`

Discusses the use of the Internet.

Net-happenings (Majordomo, moderated)

Manager address: `majordomo@acpub.duke.edu`

List address: `net-happenings@acpub.duke.edu`

Announcements of upcoming Internet-related events. It's a service of InterNIC Information Services and the list moderator, Gleason Sackman (of North Dakota's SENDIT Network), for K-12 educators.

Net-stuff (Majordomo, Moderated)

Manager address: `majordomo@acpub.duke.edu`

List address: `net-stuff@acpub.duke.edu`

Announcements about Internet-related items for sale on a not-for-profit basis. Items have included T-shirts that make fun of various netiquette outlaws.

Risks Digest (Internet, Moderated, News, Digest)

Manager address: `risks-request@csl.sri.com`

List address: `risks@csl.sri.com`

Forum on risks to the public in computers and related systems. Discusses the risks of modern technology, particularly of computer technology. Lots of great war stories.

Roots (LISTSERV, Digest)

Manager address: `LISTSERV@ndsuvm1.bitnet`

List address: `ROOTS-L@ndsuvm1.bitnet`

Genealogy discussion, with questions and answers about on-line genealogy databases. Also lots of folks asking about their distant ancestors.

Scout Report (Majordomo, Moderated)

Manager address: `majordomo@is.internic.net`

List address: `scout-report@is.internic.net`

A weekly newsletter listing new Internet resources, including Gopher sites, World Wide Web pages, FTP servers, and more. It's put out by InterNIC Information Services.

Sorehand (LISTSERV)

Manager address: `LISTSERV@ucsfvm.bitnet`

List address: `SOREHAND@ucsfvm.bitnet`

Discussion of carpal tunnel syndrome, tendonitis, and so on, for all you folks who spend a little too much time pounding away at the keyboard. You receive a detailed FAQ (list of frequently asked questions and their answers) when you join.

NAVIGATE

Telecom Digest (Internet, Moderated, News, Digest)

Manager address: `telecom-request@eecs.nwu.edu`

List address: `telecom@eecs.nwu.edu`

Discussions of telephones ranging from the technical to the totally silly, such as what the official telephone song should be. This high-volume list is heavily moderated, with the only full-time moderator on the Net.

NAVIGATE

Tourism Discussion (LISTSERV)

Manager address: `LISTSERV@trearn.bitnet`

List address: `TRAVEL-L@trearn.bitnet`

Travel and tourism, airlines, guidebooks, places to stay — you name it. Participants come from all over the world (the system host is in France), so you get lots of tips you would never get locally.

NAVIGATE

Weather Talk (LISTSERV)

Manager address: `LISTSERV@vmd.cso.uiuc.edu`

List address: `WX-TALK@vmd.cso.uiuc.edu`

Relatively technical weather discussions. You may want to join `WX-NATNL`, which gets you the National Weather Service's nationwide forecasts twice daily, which may be more weather than you want in your mailbox. You can also send the command `INDEX WX-TALK` to the manager address to get a listing of the archives for this mailing list.

NAVIGATE

White House Press Releases (Moderated)

Manager address: `clinton-info@campaign92.org` (send the message `help`)

Press releases and transcripts of press conferences direct from the White House. (Much goes on in press conferences that never gets reported.) When you send the message `help` to the manager address, you get back a subscription form to fill out and send back. This service was set up during the 1992 presidential campaign, hence the address, but it proved so popular that it has continued.

The 5th Wave
By Rich Tennant
©RICH TENNANT
MEN
PRINTER PAPER

Chapter 7

You Name It, They Talk About It: Usenet Newsgroups

In This Chapter

- What is Usenet?
- Subscribing and unsubscribing to newsgroups
- Files that may be included in articles
- Where are articles distributed?

All the News That Fits and Considerably More

Mailing lists are an okay way to send messages to a small number of people, but they're a lousy way to send messages to a large number of people. For one thing, just maintaining a big list with thousands of people is a great deal of work for a list manager, even if you automate most of it with something like LISTSERV, which was discussed in Chapter 6. (On a large list, every day a few of the addresses go bad as people move around and system managers reconfigure addresses.) For another thing, just shipping the contents of messages to thousands and thousands of addresses puts a huge load on the system that sends them out.

Usenet (also referred to by the name of the system that manages and transports its messages, *Net news*) solves that problem and creates a whole host of others. Usenet is a large, distributed *BBS (bulletin board system).* The principle is simple: Every Usenet site ships a copy of all *articles* (news-speak for messages) it has received to all its neighbors several times a day. (To avoid wasted effort, each article contains a list of sites it has already been sent to.) It's sort of a global game of "whisper down the lane," although computers don't scramble the messages at each stage, as people do. Different host-to-host connections run at different speeds, but for the most part, news articles slosh around to nearly every directly connected Usenet site within a day or two of being sent. If your machine is directly on the Internet rather than connected over the phone, most news arrives within a few hours.

You have to learn three Important News Skills:

- How to read the news that interests you
- How not to read the news that doesn't interest you, because far more news is sent every day than any single human could ever read
- How to post articles of your own (definitely optional)

This chapter talks about the principles of Usenet newsgroups, and the next chapter guides you through NEWTNews, the newsreader that comes with Internet Chameleon. Chapter 9 lists some interesting newsgroups you might want to read.

Being a Newsgroupie

Every day more than 50,000 articles appear at a typical, well-connected news machine, such as your Internet provider's. To make it possible to sort through this mass of stuff, all items are assigned to *newsgroups,* which are topic headings. In all, several thousand newsgroups exist, ranging from the staid and technical (computer data communications, for example) to the totally goofy (such as urban legends, like the one about the poodle in the microwave). Most people pick a small number of groups to read and ignore the rest (a good plan, unless you have enough time to read 50,000 articles a day).

You can easily *subscribe* and *unsubscribe* to any group received by your Internet provider — unlike getting on and off mailing lists, newsgroups just require an update to a file on your own or your provider's computer. Many people subscribe to a group, look at a few articles, and then unsubscribe if it looks boring. Depending on how much time you plan to spend reading news, you may add a number of groups when you're less busy and then drop all but the ones directly related to work when the crunch hits. (We suppose that, theoretically, you *could* stop reading news altogether, just like you *could* stop drinking coffee altogether — but that's way too painful to contemplate.)

TIP

Where did Usenet come from?

North Carolina, originally. In 1980 two students came up with the first version to run on a couple of UNIX machines. Their original version, now known as *A* news, seemed pretty cool because it could transfer as many as a dozen articles a day from one machine to another by using a networking scheme called UUCP (UNIX-to-UNIX Copy), which is a clunky but reliable dial-up communications program that comes with all UNIX systems. Within a few years, Usenet had spread to several other universities and several software companies in a completely rewritten version called *B* news, then transferring as many as a thousand messages a day. Usenet was established enough to be featured in an article in the October 1983 issue of *Byte* magazine, which boasted that more than 500 news sites were in existence. (John can't resist pointing out that his site was called `ima` — you can find it near the upper right-hand corner of the network map on page 224 of the issue.)

Throughout the ensuing decade, Usenet has spread like a disease. Now more than 30,000 sites send out news, and probably at least that many more sites just read it. Most of the original dial-up links have been replaced by permanently connected Internet network links using a communication scheme called *NNTP*, for *Net News Transfer Protocol*. (And you thought that all acronyms were obscure.) A great deal of news is still sent over the telephone by way of UUCP, but an increasing amount of it is sent by way of exotic means, including satellite using a spare channel that belongs to a national beeper company; CD-ROM; and even magnetic tapes (the tapes are sent to such countries as Malaysia, where long modem phone calls are impractical, and also to such places as the FBI, where internal computer users are prohibited from connecting to outside networks).

The volume of news has increased from a few hundred articles per day in 1983 to upward of 70,000 articles (more than 100 MB of text) per day now. And Usenet is still growing.

Many sites still use B news, even though its own authors officially pronounced it dead more than five years ago. Current news systems include *C news*, which is a faster, more maintainable, complete rewrite of B news, and *INN*, a new version designed to work well in Internet networked environments. Fortunately they all function in pretty much the same way, so you don't have to worry about which version you're using.

The newsgroup thicket

TIP

If you're eager to begin reading newsgroups, you can skip this section and come back to it later when you want to refine your newsreading skills. Go directly to Chapter 8 so you can start using NEWTNews.

Newsgroups have multipart names separated by dots, as in `comp.dcom.fax` (a group devoted to fax machines and fax modems). The plan is that newsgroups are arranged in *hierarchies*. The first part of the name describes the general kind of newsgroup. When a bunch of newsgroups are related, their names are related too. So, for example, all the newsgroups having to do with data communication are filed as `comp.dcom.`*`something`*. Here are the top-level names (that is, the first part of the names) of the *official* Usenet hierarchies distributed to nearly every news site:

- **comp:** Topics having something to do with computers (lots of fairly meaty discussions)
- **sci:** Topics having something to do with one of the sciences (also fairly meaty)
- **rec:** Recreational newsgroups (sports, hobbies, the arts, and other fun endeavors)
- **soc:** Social newsgroups (both social interests and plain socializing)
- **news:** Topics having to do with Usenet itself (a few groups with introductory material and the occasional important announcement should be read by everyone — otherwise, not very interesting unless you're a news *weenie*)
- **misc:** Miscellaneous topics that don't fit anywhere else (the ultimate miscellaneous newsgroup is called `misc.misc`)
- **talk:** Long arguments, frequently political (widely considered to be totally uninteresting except to the participants)

Note: Lots of less widely distributed, or less widely sanctioned, sets of newsgroups are mentioned in Chapter 9.

Regional groups

All the mainstream groups are of interest, in theory at least, to people regardless of where they live. But many topics are quite specific to a particular place. Suppose that you live near Boston and you want recommendations for restaurants where you can take small children and not be snarled at (this topic came up recently). Although some newsgroups in the `rec` hierarchy discuss food, because most readers are likely to be nowhere near Boston, you're likely to get more snappy comments than useful restaurant tips (someone in Texas may note, for example, that if you don't mind driving to Dallas for dinner, you can find one there).

Fortunately, local and regional groups exist for local and regional discussions. An `ne` hierarchy for topics of interest to New England includes such groups as `ne.food`, which is just the place to ask about kiddie restaurants in Boston. (The answers, by the way, turned out to be practically any ethnic restaurant and one yuppie place in the suburbs that makes a big deal about having an annex featuring hot dogs and babysitters so that Mom and Dad can eat their fancy meal in elegant silence.) State and regional hierarchies exist for most places that have enough Usenet sites to make it worthwhile: `ny` for New York, `ba` for the San Francisco Bay Area, and so on.

Universities and other organizations big enough to have many Usenet users often have hierarchies of their own, such as `mit` for MIT. Many companies have their own local sets of newsgroups for announcements and discussions about company matters. At a software company where one of us used to work, for example, every time someone logged in a change to one of our programs, the description of the change was sent out as a local news item so that everyone else could keep up with what was changing. Naturally, local company groups are sent around only within the company. Some Internet providers have their own groups too. When you run NEWTNews (described in the next chapter), you can see a list of all the newsgroups your Internet provider carries. If it doesn't carry a newsgroup you are interested in, complain to your Internet provider, because it decides which groups to carry.

TIP

Arrgh! It's a kill file

In most newsgroups, a bunch of running discussions go on, and some of those discussions are much more interesting than others are. You can arrange to permanently ignore the uninteresting ones by using a *kill file.* After you add a topic or author to your kill file, whenever you enter that newsgroup, your newsreading program checks for any new articles with titles in the kill file and automatically kills them so that you never see any of them. Using kill files can save a great deal of time and lets you concentrate on discussions that are actually interesting.

Unfortunately, NEWTNews doesn't handle kill files. We hope that a future version will, because they are great time-savers.

Honest, It's a Work of Art

Usenet allows exactly one kind of article: plain old text. (A few versions of newsreaders handle MIME messages, which we mentioned in Chapter 4; and there are versions for Japanese and Russian characters, but this chapter is confusing enough without worrying about them.) A few widely used conventions exist, though, for sneaking through other kinds of files.

Binary files

Some newsgroups consist partly or entirely of encoded binary files, most often executable programs for IBM PCs, Macs, or other personal computers, or GIF or JPEG bitmap files (see Chapters 18 and 19 for how to get programs to read graphics files in these formats) of, um, artistic images. (If you must know, the newsgroup with the largest amount of traffic, measured in megabytes per day, is called `alt.binaries.pictures.erotica`, and it contains exactly what it sounds like. An equal-opportunity group, it has about the same number of pictures of unclad men as of unclad women.)

The usual way to pass around binary files of whatever type is called *uuencoding*. You can recognize uuencoded articles because they start with a `begin` line followed by lines of what looks like garbage, as in the following:

```
begin plugh.gif 644
M390GNM4L-REP3PT45G00I-05[I5-6M30ME,MRMK760PI5LPTMETLMKPY
ME0T39I4905B05Y0PV30IXKRTL5KWLJR0JT0U,
6P5;3;MRU050I4J50I4
```

You unscramble this with a program called `uudecode`. One way to uudecode articles is to mail them to yourself and then use the uudecode feature built into Chameleon mail. (We come back to this subject in Chapter 8.)

Groups of files

Sometimes an article contains a group of files. These are packed up as *shell archive* or *shar* files, which are UNIX shell (command language) scripts that, when executed, re-create the files you want. Shar files usually begin with something like this:

```
—cut here—
# This is a shar file created on 4 Jul 1826 ...
```

If you don't have access to a UNIX system, you can't do much with a shar file other than load it in a text editor and pick out the files by hand. Bummer. The good news is that the growing numbers of Windows- and Mac-based folks out there won't be making and sending shar files, only UNIX users.

Don't say we didn't warn you

You may occasionally find an article that is just plain gibberish, neither uuencoded nor a shar file (see the section, "Honest, It's a Work of Art," earlier in this chapter). Such articles use the infamous *rot13 cipher.* Rot13 is a simple-minded scheme that replaces each letter of the alphabet with the letter that is 13 places ahead of or behind it. For example, A turns into N and vice versa, B turns into O, and so on. This isn't a very secure code (we believe that it was cracked about 2,000 years ago by the Carthaginians), but it's not supposed to be.

The point of rot13 is to warn you that an article contains rude words or something else gross and offensive, so you shouldn't read it if you think that you may be offended. If you want to read it anyway, you have to save it to a file and use an external program to read it. It's rarely worth the effort, and NEWTNews doesn't help you with rot13 decoding.

Don't expect much sympathy if you complain about an offensive rot13 article. After all, you didn't have to read it.

Anatomy of an Article

Each Usenet article consists of a *header* and some text. The header contains a bunch of lines that say who sent the article, where replies should be directed, the subject of the article, the date it was written, when your Internet provider got it, its message number, and a bunch of other boring information.

What's in a number?

Every Usenet article has a *message ID,* which is supposed to be different from the message ID of any other article ever, from the beginning to the end of time. (These people thought big.) A typical message ID looks like this:

```
<1994Jul9.055259.15278@chico.iecc.com>
```

The part after the @ is the name of the site where the article originated, and the part before the @ is some garbage made up to be unique and usually includes the date, time, phase of the moon, and so on.

Articles also have numbers, which are assigned in order at each newsgroup as articles arrive. So the first article in `comp.fooble` is number 1, the second is number 2, and so on.

Note: An important difference distinguishes message IDs and the numbers: The IDs are the same everywhere, but the numbers apply to only *your local system.* So don't refer to articles' message numbers when you write a response because people at other sites can't tell which articles you mean.

If you use NEWTNews to write a follow-up article, it automatically sticks in a line that begins with `References:`, which has the message ID of the original article, along with any articles it in turn referenced. Some news programs use the references to gather articles into related groups, called *threads*.

Distributions are your friends

Note: NEWTNews does not yet handle distributions, but a future version probably will. In the meantime, this section describes what distributions are.

Even though Usenet is a worldwide network, you may want to post an article that doesn't really need to go to the entire world. If you're posting something to `misc.forsale.computers`, for example, to advertise an old disk drive you want to sell and you're in the United States, there's no point in sending the article outside the country because it's not worth the shipping and customs hassles to sell it overseas. Usenet *distributions* enable you to limit where an article is sent. A line like the following in your article header limits its distribution to the United States:

```
Distribution: usa
```

If you're sending a follow-up, the news system guesses that you want to use the same distribution the original article did. You can edit the `Distribution:` line in the article yourself as necessary.

A long list of possible distributions exists. Some commonly used distributions are shown in this list:

- **world:** Everywhere (default)
- **na:** North America

- **usa:** United States
- **can:** Canada
- **uk:** United Kingdom
- **ne:** New England
- **ba**: Bay Area (California)

All the regional hierarchy names, such as `ne`, `ny`, `uk`, `ba`, and so on, are also used as distributions. (People occasionally use worldwide hierarchy names such as `comp` and `rec` as distributions by mistake — that doesn't do anything useful.)

TIP

Unless you're sure that people on the other side of the world will be as fascinated by what you say as people next door will be, you should use the smallest appropriate distribution for any articles you post, both originals and follow-ups.

In practice, distributions are pretty leaky, and articles often get sent to places the distribution says that they shouldn't go because of peculiarities in the way news is passed from one system to the next. But it's a courtesy to faraway readers to at least *try* to avoid sending articles to places where the articles are not interesting. Keep in mind that international phone links are expensive, so if you avoid sending an article to countries where people aren't interested, you can save people some money.

TIP

Dying boy makes mailing list about modem tax

Back in Chapter 5, a sidebar lists well-known topics about which you should never, *ever* write to any mailing list. The same warning applies to Usenet news. For review, the top four topics not to write about are shown in this list:

- Dying boy wants cards to set Guinness world record
- FCC will pass modem tax and impoverish us all
- Make big bucks with a chain letter
- Friend got ripped off for cookie recipe

See Chapter 5 for details about why nobody wants to hear about any of these things.

Serving You the News

For your NEWTNews program to show you news articles, you must have access to a *news server,* that is, an Internet host computer from which NEWTNews can get the text of the articles. Luckily all Internet SLIP providers include this service as part of your SLIP account (at least, all the ones avaialble through Instant Internet do).

When you used Instant Internet (back in Chapter 3) to sign up with your Internet provider, the program automatically configured your copy of NEWTNews to know the address of your news server. So you should be all set to waste time and read newsgroups!

Chapter 8

Using NEWTNews

In This Chapter

- Running NEWTNews for the first time and selecting some newsgroups to read
- Leaving NEWTNews
- Reading the articles in a newsgroup
- Replying to an article by using e-mail or by posting a follow-up article
- Subscribing to other newsgroups later
- Selecting NEWTNews options
- Using other newsreaders

Are you ready to read some newsgroups for yourself? Be sure that you've got a half-hour or more to spare, because you (like most new newsgroupies) will probably find lots of interesting things to browse through.

Running NEWTNews for the First Time

The first time you run it, you've got to tell NEWTNews which newsgroups you are interested in. (Don't worry — you can always add or remove groups later.) Follow these steps:

1. **Run Custom and connect to your Internet provider.**

   This procedure is described in Chapter 3.

2. **Double-click the NEWTNews icon in the Internet Chameleon program group in Program Manager.**

   NEWTNews runs and asks you for your name and password.

3. **Enter the same name and password that you used for your mailbox in the Mail program, and then click OK.**

   When you ran Instant Internet (back in Chapter 3), it created a mailbox with your username and no password. Most people leave their password blank. This is the same mailbox you used in Chapter 4, in the section "Running Mail."

   The first time you run it, NEWTNews asks you to subscribe to some newsgroups (see Figure 8-1). It warns you that the process could take a while, because it must download the list of available newsgroups, of which there are about 6,000, from your Internet provider. If you don't have time right now, click the No button, and then choose File➪Exit.

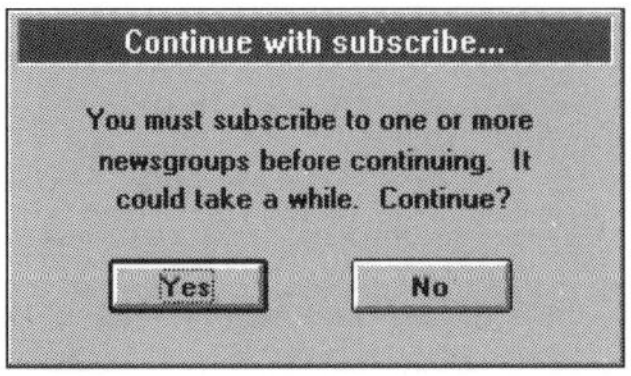

Figure 8-1: Before you can enter NEWTNews, you've got to subscribe to some newsgroups.

4. **Click the Yes button.**

   NEWTNews asks your Internet provider which newsgroups are available — providers don't always carry every single newsgroup. For example, many providers skip `alt.barney.dinosaur.die.die.die` and `alt.nosebeeping`. You can peruse the list and choose the groups that look interesting, or you can look for specific groups. Later, as new groups form (which happens almost every day), you can decide which new ones to subscribe to.

   You see the message `Fetching list of newsgroups`, and newsgroup names flicker by. If you use a 14,400-baud modem, the list could take a minute or two to download to your PC; if your modem is slower, it'll take even longer. This would be a good time to refill your coffee cup or attend to personal hygiene. When the download is done, you see the Subscribe - All Groups window, as shown in Figure 8-2.

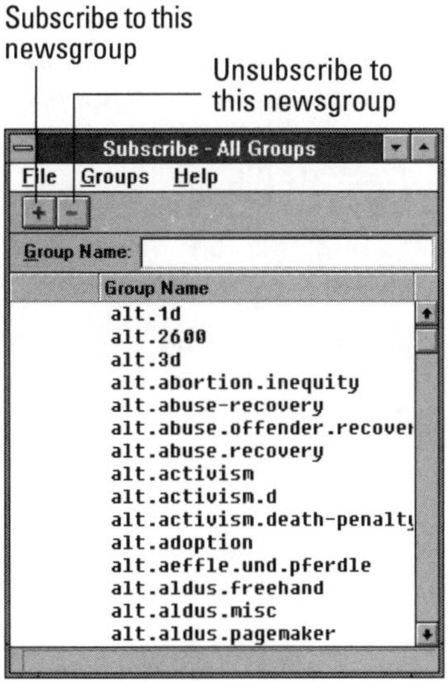

Figure 8-2: The beginning of a long, long list of Usenet newsgroups.

5. **Scroll down the list. When you see a group that looks interesting, click the Subscribe button (the one with the plus sign) to subscribe to it.**

   Another way to subscribe to a group is to double-click its name on the list. You can tell which groups you have already subscribed to, because an *S* appears to the left of the group name.

   You don't have to scroll down the entire list right now; it probably has more than 5,000 entries. Just choose a few groups to get started with. You can always look at the list again later and choose some more.

6. **To move directly to a group, click in the Group Name box and start typing the group's name.**

   NEWTNews skips down to find the group in the list, if it is there.

   TIP: You can select several groups at the same time and click the Subscribe button.

7. **To unsubscribe to a group to which you are subscribed (an *S* appears to the left of the group name), double-click it.**

   Alternatively, select the group and then click the Unsubscribe button (the one with the minus sign).

8. **When you are done perusing the list, choose File⇨Exit in the Subscribe - All Groups window.**

Alternatively, you can double-click the little button in the upper-left corner of the window. NEWTNews closes the window and displays a series of messages about how it is updating the information on the newsgroups you subscribed to (see Figure 8-3). This can take a while — say, 10 or 15 minutes — especially if you have selected a bunch of groups that have a lot of messages, because NEWTNews has to check the status of every message in every subscribed newsgroup. (Maybe you can make a new pot of coffee while you wait.) Finally, you see the main NEWTNews window, described in the following section.

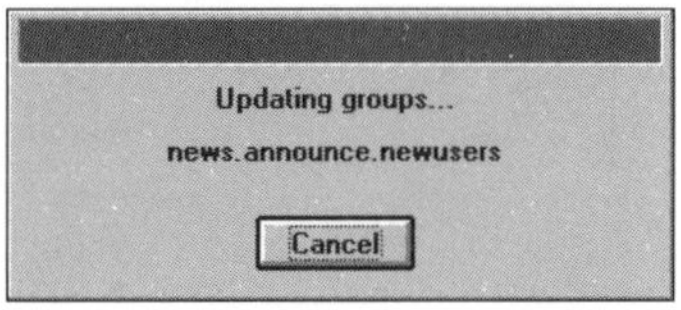

Figure 8-3: NEWTNews takes a moment to download info about a group you subscribed to.

TIP: We recommend that you subscribe to `news.announce.newusers` and read the articles in it. These articles are an excellent introduction to Usenet and to the rules that Usenetters should follow. Chapter 9 contains information about other interesting newsgroups.

NEWTNews Mission Control

When you have selected some newsgroups, you see the NEWTNews window, as shown in Figure 8-4.

Right now, for each newsgroup to which you subscribe, you see the number of messages in the group and the number of messages that you haven't read yet. Later, this window will show lists of articles in individual newsgroups.

TIP: You can switch the order of the columns of information about your newsgroups just by dragging the column headers to the left or right. You can also sort the list of subscribed newsgroups by any column; just double-click the header of the column you want to sort by.

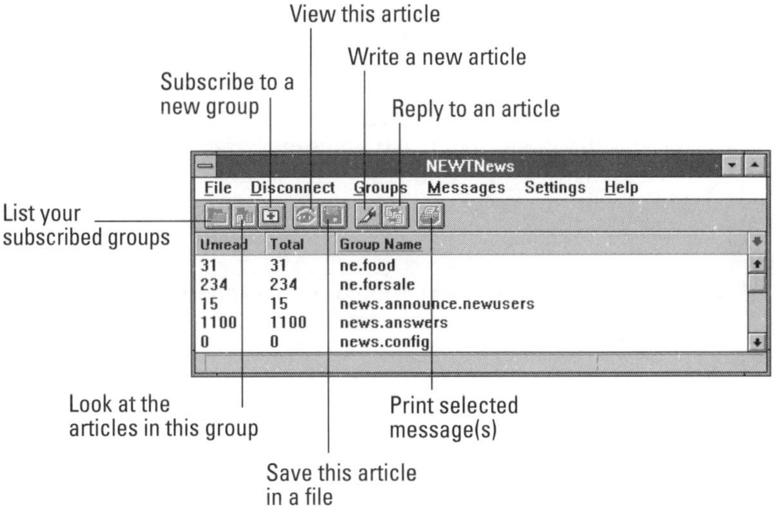

Figure 8-4: The NEWTNews window with the list of newsgroups that you selected.

Ta-Ta for Now

When you are done running NEWTNews, choose File⇨Exit. NEWTNews asks whether you want to save your configuration changes. Always click the Yes button so that information about subscribed groups is saved.

Running NEWTNews Later

After the first time you run NEWTNews, you don't have to tell it again which groups you want to read; NEWTNews remembers which groups you have subscribed to. Here's how to run NEWTNews once you have subscribed to some newsgroups.

1. **Run Custom and connect to your Internet provider.**

   This procedure is described in Chapter 3.

2. **Double-click the NEWTNews icon in the Internet Chameleon program group in Program Manager.**

   NEWTNews runs, and asks you for your name and password.

3. **Enter the same name and password that you used the first time you ran NEWTNews and then click OK.**

   NEWTNews checks for new articles in each of the newsgroups you are subscribed to. If you subscribe to many newsgroups, this search can take several minutes. (Hmmm — you've probably had too much coffee by now. Perhaps a brisk jog around the office would be in order.) When NEWTNews is ready and raring to go, you see the NEWTNews window, shown back in Figure 8-4.

If you don't want NEWTNews to check for new newsgroups, you can tell it not to. For information, see "Your News Options," later in this chapter.

Reading Articles

After you select some newsgroups, you are ready to read the articles in a group. You can read articles in at least three ways:

- Double-click the name of the newsgroup.
- Click the name of the newsgroup, and then click the Articles button (the second one from the left in the toolbar).
- Click the name of the newsgroup, and then choose Groups⇨Articles (or press Ctrl+A).

You see the list of articles in the NEWTNews window, as shown in Figure 8-5. For each article, NEWTNews shows the name of the sender, the subject, and a column for *flags* (indicators that show what you've done with the article).

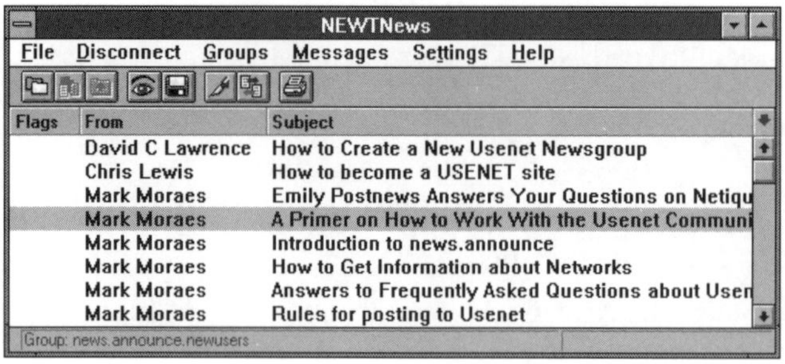

Figure 8-5: Articles in a newsgroup.

TIP

The list doesn't include articles that you've already read unless you tell NEWTNews to display them. For information, see "Your News Options," later in this chapter.

Let's see what it says

NEWTNews gives you a few different ways to read an article:

- Double-click it.
- Click it and then click the View icon on the toolbar (the fourth from the left — yes, the one with the eyeball).
- Click it and then choose Messages⇨View (or press Ctrl+W).

Whichever way you choose, the article appears in its own window, as shown in Figure 8-6.

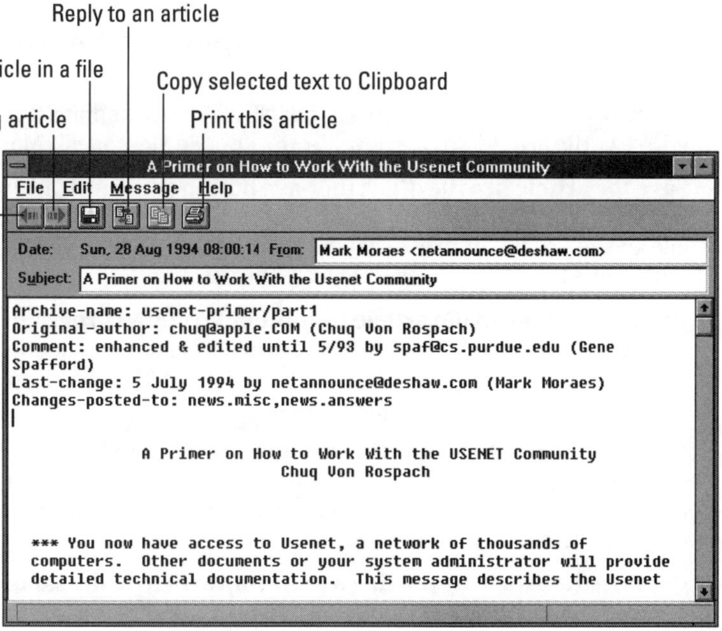

Figure 8-6: A Usenet article.

Saving and printing articles

After you read an article, you can do a number of things with it:

- **Move along to the next message.** Click the Next article button (the next-to-leftmost one in the toolbar, with the right-pointing red arrow).
- **Close its window and return to the list of articles.** Choose File⇨Exit in the article's window.
- **Print the article.** Click the Print button (the rightmost one in the toolbar, with the little picture of a printer). NEWTNews displays a Print dialog box that allows you to select the pages to print and the number of copies. Click OK to start printing. Alternatively, you can choose File⇨Print.
- **Mark this article with a flag.** A what? *Flag* is NEWTNewsese for marking an article that you want to hang on to. Usually, NEWTNews doesn't display articles that you've already read. To mark an article so that it will stick around in the newsgroup, choose Messages⇨Set Flag (or press Ctrl+F). If you change your mind later, you can choose Messages⇨Clear Flag (or press Ctrl+Shift+F). Notice that newsgroup articles don't stick around forever; your news server deletes them after a while. To really save an article, see the following bullet item.

  To mark the article as unread, so that NEWTNews displays it the next time you read the articles in this newsgroup, choose Messages⇨Mark Unread.
- **Save the article in a file.** Click the Save button (the third one from the left in the toolbar, with the floppy disk). Alternatively, you can choose File⇨Save To File (or press Ctrl+S). NEWTNews asks for the directory and path name to which you want to save the text file.
- **Copy some or all of the article to another Windows program.** You can copy text from an article to the Windows Clipboard by selecting the text and pressing Ctrl+C. After text is in the Windows Clipboard, you can paste it into most other Windows programs.
- **Reply to the article by sending e-mail to the person who wrote it.** This is the thing to do if you have comments that are of interest mainly to the person who wrote the article. For information, see "Responding privately by e-mail," later in this chapter.
- **Reply to the article by posting a follow-up article in the same newsgroup.** Do this only if your response to the article is so fascinating that everyone in the entire newsgroup will want to read it. For information, see "Possibly making a fool of yourself," later in this chapter.

TIP

Rot how many?

Usenet has a system that protects you from gross, disgusting, obscene, or otherwise offensive articles. Offensive articles can be posted with a simple code called *Rot13*. If you try to read an article and it appears as gibberish, it's probably encoded using Rot13. Unfortunately, NEWTNews doesn't have a built-in Rot13 decoder for those of you whose sensibilities aren't easily offended, so for the time being, you'll have to do without it.

When Is an Article Not Really an Article?

Sometimes, an article contains not plain text but a coded version of a binary file or a group of files. For example, an article may contain an executable program or a graphics file. There are two common ways to sneak files into articles:

- Uuencoding
- Shar files

Whattizzit?

In a *uuencoded* message, a single binary file is turned into a lot of ugly-looking text, like the following example:

```
begin 664 sample
M5V]W(2!)9B!Y;W4@86-T=6%L;'D@='EP960@:6X@=&AI<R!W:&]L92!F:6QE
M(&%N9"!U=61E8V]D960@:70@<W5C8V5S<V9U;&QY+'IY;W4G<F4@82!R96%L
M;'D@9&5D:6-A=&5D(')E861E<BX@($1R;W`@=7,@82!N;W1E(&%T(&UI9'5M
K;6EE<T!I96-C+F-O;2!A;F0*;65N=&EO;B!S96-R970@8V]D92!8,3(N"G5M
'
end
```

Usually, uuencoded files are a lot longer than this, but they're all equally ugly. Really long ones are often split across several news messages to keep each article a reasonable size. Uuencoded files are most often found in groups such as `comp.binaries.ms-windows`, in which case they're runnable programs, or in groups such as `alt.binaries.pictures.erotica`, in which case they're digitized pictures of . . . er, various stuff.

A *shar* file (short for *shell archive*) contains a group of files. Most often, shar files contain program source code, but they can contain any text files. You can run shar files only on UNIX machines, so they don't do DOS and Windows folks (or Mac users) much good. Luckily, you are unlikely to run into them except in UNIX-related newsgroups.

Shar files usually begin with a line like this:

```
#!/bin/sh
```

Uuencoded files of pictures are unlikely to cause any trouble, other than the hair you may get on your palms from looking at some of them. But program files do present a potential security hole through which a virus could crawl into your system. Instead of displaying a picture, for example, a file could turn into a program that, when run, installs a virus on your computer and *then* displays a picture. Uuencoded files from moderated groups (groups in which all messages are examined and approved by a third party before being sent out) are generally okay, but files from other groups are only as reliable as the people sending them. It's always appropriate to use a virus checker to scan any program that arrives from the Net.

Reading uuencoded messages

NEWTNews doesn't have a built-in uudecoder. Instead, you can e-mail the article to yourself and then use Chameleon Mail's uudecoding feature to convert it. Follow the instructions in "Responding privately by e-mail," later in this chapter, and address the e-mail to your own e-mail address. Be sure to include the entire original message except for the headers and to delete the > characters at the beginning of each line.

When you receive the article in Chameleon Mail, view the message and then choose Message⇨Uudecode (as described in Chapter 4). This command decodes the article and stores it in a file.

If a uuencoded file arrives divided into several articles because it is too long for one article, this method of uudecoding it won't work. Luckily, files this large are usually available some other way. If you want the file, ask on the newsgroup whether the file is available for FTP, and see Chapter 12. Better yet, grab the excellent WinCode program to uudecode it (see Chapter 19).

Dealing with Articles That Demand a Response

If you read an article that demands a response, you have two options: You can respond privately by sending e-mail to the person who wrote it, or you can post a follow-up article to the newsgroup. Here's how to decide which way to go:

- If your response will be of interest only to the person who wrote the article, send e-mail.
- If you are really mad, take a walk before doing anything. If you're still mad and you just *have* to reply, send e-mail.
- If the original article contains errors that everyone reading it should know about, post a follow-up article — but only after checking to make sure that 12 other people haven't already done the same thing.
- If you have further information on the subject that will be of universal interest to those reading the original article, post a follow-up article.

Responding privately by e-mail

When you are looking at an article that you want to respond to privately, here's what to do:

1. **Choose Messages⇨Followup/E-Mail (or press Ctrl+R), or click the Reply button on the toolbar (the fourth from the left, with the blue and red arrows).**

   NEWTNews displays a window in which you can compose your message (shown in Figure 8-7). The title of the window is the subject of the article to which you are responding. NEWTNews includes the text of the article, with each line preceded by a > character. This is the standard way to "quote" text from another article.

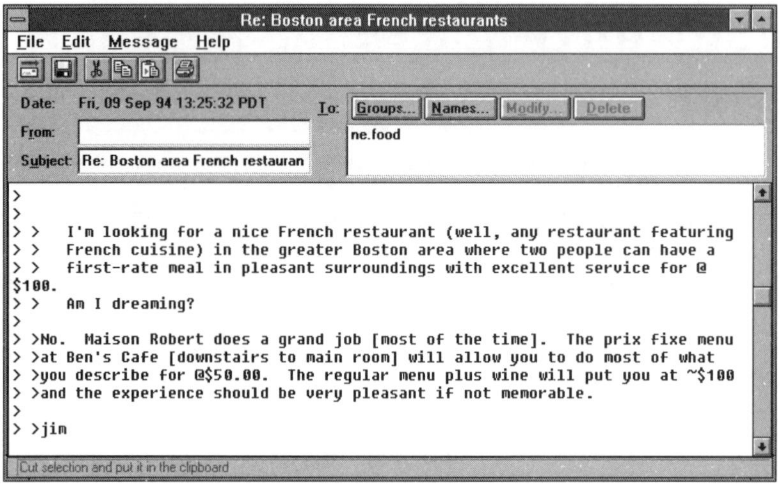

Figure 8-7: Respond to articles either by posting follow-ups or sending private e-mail.

2. **In the From box, type your own e-mail address (if it's not already there).**

   The Subject box contains a subject line based on the subject of the article to which you are replying. You can edit it, if you like.

3. **Select the name of the current newsgroup in the To box, and then click the Delete button.**

   This action deletes the newsgroup name from the To box, which contains all the newsgroups to which you want to post this article and all the e-mail addresses to which you want to mail it. To avoid posting this response (you want to e-mail it, right?), delete the newsgroup name.

4. **In the text of the article to which you are responding, select the e-mail address of the person who wrote it. Then press Ctrl+C to copy it to the Windows Clipboard.**

   You're going to need this address in a minute, to address this reply.

5. **Click the Names button to see a list of e-mail addresses in your address book.**

   You see the Names window — the same address book that you created and used in Chameleon Mail (see Chapter 4). In all probability, the person to whom you are replying isn't in your address book, but this is the only way to type an e-mail address (sigh).

6. **Press Ctrl+V so that the writer's e-mail address appears in the Address box of the Names window.**

7. **Click the To button so that this address appears in the To box of the message window.**

   While you are at it, you can type another address in the Address box and then click the To button if you want to send this message to anyone else.

8. **Click the OK button to close the Names window.**

   You are looking at the message window again.

9. **Delete all the quoted header lines in the text window, along with the boring parts of the quoted article.**

   That is, delete all but the interesting parts of the article; keep only the parts that you want to talk about.

10. **Write your response, typing the text above the quoted article. Be clear, polite, and reasonable.**

11. **When the message is ready to send, choose Message➪Send (or press Ctrl+D), or click the Post button (the leftmost one on the toolbar, with the envelope and the blue arrow).**

    NEWTNews mails the message to the address(es) you entered.

If you decide not to send a reply after all, you can choose File➪Exit to cancel your reply — but you've got to do it before choosing the Message➪Send command.

Actually, you can use the Messages➪Followup/E-Mail command to send an e-mail message to anyone, not just to the person who wrote the article you just read. If you suddenly get the urge to write a note to your mom, choose Messages➪Followup/E-Mail, delete the newsgroup name from the To box (so that you don't post the letter to your mom to the newsgroup), enter your mom's e-mail address, change the contents of the Subject box to any subject, delete the quotes article, and type your message! More to the point, it's also the easiest way to forward a Usenet message via e-mail to someone who won't have seen it as news.

Possibly making a fool of yourself

Okay, you've decided to take the plunge. You have something so interesting to say in response to an article that you want to post it publicly, where it can be read, appreciated, savored, misconstrued, or laughed at. The procedure is almost the same as replying by e-mail. Follow these steps:

1. **Choose Messages⇨Followup/E-Mail (or press Ctrl+R), or click the Reply button (the fourth from the left on the toolbar, with the blue and red arrows).**
2. **In the From box, type your own e-mail address (if it's not already there).**

   The Subject box contains a subject line based on the subject of the article to which you are replying. You can edit it, if you like.
3. **Delete all the quoted header lines in the text window, along with the boring parts of the quoted article.**

   That is, delete all but the interesting parts of the article; keep only the parts that you want to talk about.
4. **Write your response, typing the text above the quoted article. Be clear, polite, and reasonable.**
5. **Consider carefully whether all the folks who read this newsgroup really need your opinion on this matter or the new information that you are providing. If not, choose File⇨Exit to cancel your reply.**

   Remember, thousands of people will be reading your article!
6. **When the message is ready to send, choose Message⇨Send (or press Ctrl+D), or click the Post button (the leftmost one, with the envelope and the blue arrow).**

   NEWTNews posts the reply to the same newsgroup that the original article was in. A little message tells you that your post succeeded — that is, your article was successfully transmitted to your news server. Who knows what will happen to it after that.
7. **Click OK to make the message go away.**

TIP

You can also post the article to other groups or e-mail it to people. To post it to other newsgroups, click the Groups button. NEWTNews displays a list of the newsgroups to which you have subscribed. Choose a newsgroup and then click OK; the newsgroup name appears in the To box. See the preceding section for directions on entering e-mail addresses in the To box.

WARNING!

This world already has enough newsgroup messages to read, so don't post an article to more than one newsgroup unless absolutely necessary.

Other Things You Can Do to a Newsgroup

When you return to the list of articles in the newsgroup, the articles that you have read appear with an *R* in the Flags column. You can do the following things when you are looking at the article list:

- **Skip the unread articles.** If you decide that you have read all the articles of interest and that you want to skip the rest of them, you can tell NEWTNews to pretend that you have read all the articles — that is, mark them all as having been read. Just choose Groups➪Catch Up (or press Ctrl+U). NEWTNews marks all the articles as read and returns you to the list of newsgroups. You may notice that the number of unread articles in the newsgroup you were reading is now zero.
- **Leave for now.** When you finish looking at the articles in a newsgroup, you can return to the list of newsgroups by clicking the List Groups button (the leftmost button on the toolbar, with two yellow folders) in the NEWTNews window.
- **Leave forever.** If you decide that the newsgroup is so boring that you never want to read it again, consider unsubscribing. Click the List Groups button (the leftmost one, with the two yellow folders) to see the list of your newsgroups. Select the newsgroup that you were just reading. Then choose Groups➪Unsubscribe. The group disappears from your list of subscribed groups, never to bother you again.

Your News Options

Like most programs, NEWTNews has a bunch of options that you can set. Some of those options are actually useful. To see and change your news-reading options, choose Settings➪Preferences. You see the Preferences dialog box, shown in Figure 8-8.

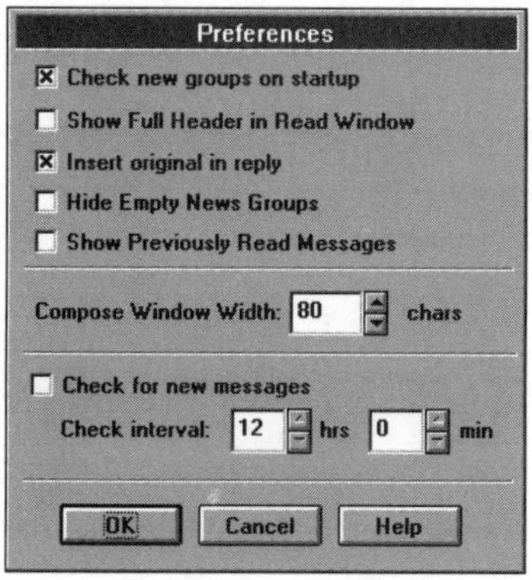

Figure 8-8: The settings that NEWTNews uses, unless you change them.

Consider these questions as you decide which settings to use.

- **Do you want to check for new newsgroups each time you run NEWTNews?** It's not a bad idea — sometimes, good new groups come along. Make sure that the Check new groups on startup option is selected.
- **When you reply to an article, do you want NEWTNews to include the text of the article that you are replying to?** It's a good idea to do this. The text of the original article is included in your reply, with each line preceded by the > character (the standard Usenet way to quote material from another article). Be sure to delete the quoted headers and any parts of the article that you don't plan to talk about. To tell NEWTNews to include article text, make sure that the Include original in reply option is selected.
- **Do you want to see articles that you've already read?** Probably not. But if you do want to see them, make sure that the Show Previously Read Messages option is selected.
- **Do you want NEWTNews to check for new messages every few hours or minutes?** If you stay connected to your Internet provider for hours at a time, you can tell NEWTNews to check for new articles periodically. Select the Check for new messages option, and enter the number of hours and minutes that NEWTNews should wait between checks.

When you finish looking at or changing your settings, click the OK button.

These Newsgroups Are Boring!

Stay calm — you can subscribe and unsubscribe to newsgroups any time you want to.

To see the entire list of newsgroups again, choose Groups⇨List All, or click the Subscribe button (third button from the left; a little folder with a plus sign). You see the Subscribe - All Groups window again. Follow steps 5 through 8 in the section "Running NEWTNews for the First Time" to subscribe and unsubscribe to groups.

Adding New Groups as They Appear

New newsgroups appear every day. It's easy to see a list of the groups that have appeared since the last time you checked; simply choose Groups⇨Check New Groups. NEWTNews downloads an updated list of groups and displays the Subscribe - All Groups window again. Alternatively, you can tell NEWTNews to check for new newsgroups each time you run it (as described in the preceding section, "Your News Options").

If you tell NEWTNews to check for new newsgroups each time you run it, you see the Subscribe - New Groups window, shown in Figure 8-9. If you want to subscribe to a newsgroup, double-click it. When you finish, double-click the box in the upper left-hand corner of the Subscribe - New Groups window to close it.

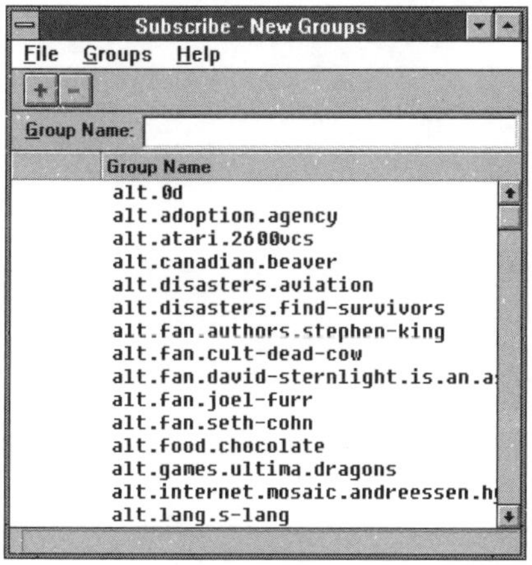

Figure 8-9: New groups created since the last time you ran NEWTNews.

Other Newsreaders of Note

We like the NEWTNews newsreader, but others are available, including the following:

- **Trumpet:** A news-reading program written by Peter R. Tattam of the University of Tasmania (yes, that Tasmania — just south of Australia) and distributed as shareware. Trumpet can also send and receive your e-mail.

- **WinVN:** Doesn't have all the fancy features of Trumpet and NEWTNews, but it does do *threading*, which means that it organizes the articles in each newsgroup by topic. If you find yourself reading a lot of news, it's worth trying WinVN to see whether it speeds your news reading.
- **WinQVT/Net:** A program that has a built-in newsreader, along with about 150 other features.

See Chapter 18 for directions on downloading and installing software from the Internet, and Chapter 19 for the FTP sites that have these programs.

Chapter 9

A Sampler of Nifty Newsgroups

In This Chapter

- Favorite groups
- Standard and not-so-standard hierarchies
- Lots of newsgroups

Now that you learned all about how to read and write Usenet news in Chapter 8, the only little detail remaining is to figure out what there is to read.

So What Is There to Read Already?

This chapter lists some of the more interesting groups that exist as of late 1994. Remember that new groups appear practically every day, old groups occasionally go away, and your Internet provider can reject any groups it wants to for lack of interest or other reasons. First we present some popular groups to get you acquainted with the mainstream hierarchies. Then you learn about hierarchies that are a tad more obscure. And finally, Tables 9-1 through 9-6 list numerous groups in the various hierarchies you may want to explore.

Not-to-Be-Missed Groups

This section presents a few groups you may want to start with:

news.announce.newusers

Every new user should at least skim this group, which contains introductory material for new news users. One of the messages is pretty funny, but you have to read them to find out which one.

news.answers

This group contains all the periodic (weekly and monthly, mostly) postings to all the groups on the Net. Many of these have evolved into pithy and well-written introductions to their subjects. When you want to learn something fast about something that might have been discussed on the Net, start here.

rec.humor.funny

This highly competitive, moderated group contains jokes, most of which are pretty funny. Compare to `rec.humor`, which contains articles that the authors think are funny but that usually aren't.

comp.compilers

This one has discussions of systems to translate one computer language into another. John thinks that it's interesting, but then he's the moderator.

alt.sex

Everybody reads it, but nobody admits to doing so. We certainly don't.

Computers, on Computers, About Computers

Traditionally, the largest set of newsgroups have been the computer-related ones under the hierarchy `comp` (many of which are listed in Table 9-1). It's not surprising: If you listen in on ham-radio conversations, you realize that they're mostly about ham radio. So you may expect that when people used computers to create Usenet, they mostly talked about computers.

The `comp` groups can tend toward the esoteric and the technoid, but they're also a treasure trove when your computer acts up and you need advice from people who have seen it all before.

Many groups offer usable computer programs. The ones under `comp.binaries` are the places to look for free programs for PCs, Macs, and other personal systems.

TIP

For newsgroups about Microsoft Windows, look at groups whose names begin with `comp.os.ms-windows`.

Table 9-1 Groups in the Comp Hierarchy

Name	*Discussion*
comp.ai	Artificial intelligence
comp.ai.nat-lang	Natural language processing by computers
comp.ai.neural-nets	All aspects of neural networks
comp.ai.philosophy	Philosophical aspects of artificial intelligence
comp.ai.shells	Artificial intelligence applied to shells
comp.answers	Repository for periodic Usenet articles (moderated)
comp.apps.spreadsheets	Spreadsheets on various platforms
comp.arch	Computer architecture
comp.arch.storage	Storage-system issues, both hardware and software
comp.archives	Descriptions of public-access archives (moderated)
comp.archives.admin	Issues relating to computer archive administration
comp.bbs.misc	All aspects of computer bulletin board systems
comp.bbs.waffle	The Waffle BBS and Usenet system on all platforms
comp.benchmarks	Benchmarking techniques and results
comp.binaries.apple2	Binary-only postings for the Apple II computer
comp.binaries.atari.st	Binary-only postings for the Atari ST (moderated)
comp.binaries.ibm.pc	Binary-only postings for IBM PC and MS-DOS (moderated)
comp.binaries.ibm.pc.d	IBM PC binary postings
comp.binaries.ibm.pc.wanted	Requests for IBM PC and compatible programs
comp.binaries.mac	Encoded Macintosh programs in binary (moderated)
comp.binaries.ms-windows	Binary programs for Microsoft Windows (moderated)

(continued)

Table 9-1 *(continued)*

Name	*Discussion*
comp.binaries.os2	Binaries for use under the OS/2 ABI (moderated)
comp.cog-eng	Cognitive engineering
comp.compilers	Compiler construction, theory, and so on (moderated)
comp.compression	Data-compression algorithms and theory
comp.databases	Database- and data-management issues and theory
comp.dcom.fax	Fax hardware, software, and protocols
comp.dcom.lans.ethernet	Ethernet/IEEE 802.3 protocols
comp.dcom.modems	Data communications hardware and software
comp.dcom.servers	Choosing and operating data communications servers
comp.dcom.telecom	Telecommunications digest (moderated)
comp.doc	Archived public-domain documentation (moderated)
comp.doc.techreports	Lists of technical reports (moderated)
comp.dsp	Digital-signal processing using computers
comp.edu	Computer-science education
comp.emacs	EMACS editors of different flavors
comp.fonts	Type fonts — design, conversion, use, and so on
comp.graphics	Computer graphics, art, animation, image processing
comp.human-factors	Issues related to human-computer interaction (HCI)
comp.infosystems	Any discussion about information systems
comp.infosystems.gis	All aspects of geographic information systems
comp.infosystems.gopher	The Gopher information service
comp.infosystems.wais	The Z39.50-based WAIS full-text search system

Name	*Discussion*
comp.infosystems.www	The World Wide Web information system
comp.internet.library	Electronic libraries (moderated)
comp.lang.c	C
comp.lang.c++	The object-oriented C++ language
comp.lang.fortran	FORTRAN
comp.lang.lisp	LISP
comp.misc	General topics about computers not covered elsewhere
comp.multimedia	Interactive multimedia technologies of all kinds
comp.newprod	Announcements of new products of interest (moderated)
comp.object	Object-oriented programming and languages
comp.os.ms-windows.advocacy	Speculation and debate about Microsoft Windows
comp.os.ms-windows.announce	Announcements relating to Windows (moderated)
comp.os.ms-windows.apps	Applications in the Windows environment
comp.os.ms-windows.misc	Windows issues
comp.os.ms-windows.programmer.misc	Programming Microsoft Windows
comp.os.ms-windows.programmer.tools	Development tools in Windows
comp.os.ms-windows.setup	Installing and configuring Microsoft Windows
comp.os.msdos.apps	Applications that run under MS-DOS
comp.parallel	Massively parallel hardware and software (moderated)
comp.patents	Patents of computer technology (moderated)
comp.periphs	Peripheral devices
comp.programming	Programming issues that transcend languages and OSs
comp.risks	Risks to the public from computers and users (moderated)

(continued)

Table 9-1 *(continued)*

Name	***Discussion***
comp.robotics	All aspects of robots and their applications
comp.security.misc	Security issues of computers and networks
comp.simulation	Simulation methods, problems, uses (moderated)
comp.society	The impact of technology on society (moderated)
comp.society.cu-digest	The Computer Underground Digest (moderated)
comp.society.development	Computer technology in developing countries
comp.society.folklore	Computer folklore and culture, past and present (moderated)
comp.society.futures	Events in technology affecting future computing
comp.society.privacy	Effects of technology on privacy (moderated)
comp.sources.misc	Posting of software (moderated)
comp.speech	Research and applications in speech science and technology
comp.text	Text-processing issues and methods
comp.unix.questions	UNIX neophytes group
comp.unix.shell	Using and programming the UNIX shell
comp.unix.wizards	Questions for only true UNIX wizards
comp.virus	Computer viruses and security (moderated)

Misc: None of the Above

Despite all the careful (well, sort of careful) arrangement of Usenet into meaningful hierarchies, some topics just didn't fit anywhere else; these topics ended up in `misc`, the miscellaneous hierarchy (see Table 9-2). Topics range from the totally staid to the hopelessly argumentative. The ultimate miscellaneous group is `misc.misc`, for discussions that don't fit *anywhere*.

Table 9-2 Groups in the Misc Hierarchy

Name	*Discussion*
misc.answers	Repository for periodic Usenet articles (moderated)
misc.books.technical	Books about technical topics
misc.consumers	Consumer interests, product reviews, and so on
misc.consumers.house	Owning and maintaining a house
misc.education	The educational system
misc.entrepreneurs	Operating a business
misc.fitness	Physical fitness, exercise, and so on
misc.forsale	Short, tasteful postings about items for sale
misc.int-property	Intellectual property rights
misc.invest	Investments and the handling of money
misc.jobs.contract	Contract employment
misc.jobs.misc	Employment, workplaces, careers
misc.jobs.offered	Announcements of positions available
misc.jobs.offered.entry	Job listings only for entry-level positions
misc.jobs.resumes	Postings of résumés and *situation wanted* articles
misc.kids	Children and their behavior and activities
misc.kids.computer	The use of computers by children
misc.kids.health	Children's health
misc.kids.pregnancy	Pregnancy (not kids getting pregnant, but having kids via pregnancy)
misc.legal	Legalities and the ethics of law
misc.legal.computing	The legal climate of the computing world
misc.misc	Various discussions that don't fit in any other group

Rec: Fun and Games

Even computer weenies like to have fun. (Stop laughing. It's true.) Usenet has lots of recreational groups (in the `rec` hierarchy; see Table 9-3) for hobbies ranging from the strenuous, such as watching fish in an aquarium, to the totally relaxing — mountain climbing, for example. There are certainly a few here that you'll like.

Table 9-3	Groups in the Rec Hierarchy
Name	***Discussion***
rec.answers	Repository for periodic Usenet articles (moderated)
rec.antiques	Antiques and vintage items
rec.aquaria	Keeping fish and aquaria as a hobby
rec.arts.books	Books of all genres and the publishing industry
rec.arts.movies	Movies and movie making
rec.arts.movies.reviews	Reviews of movies (moderated)
rec.arts.poems	For the posting of poems
rec.arts.prose	Short works of prose fiction and follow-up discussion
rec.arts.sf.announce	Major announcements of the SF world (moderated)
rec.arts.startrek.current	New "Star Trek" shows, movies, and books
rec.arts.startrek.info	Information about the universe of "Star Trek" (moderated)
rec.arts.startrek.misc	General discussions of "Star Trek"
rec.arts.startrek.reviews	Reviews of "Star Trek" books, episodes, films, and so on (moderated)
rec.arts.theatre	All aspects of stage work and theatre
rec.arts.tv	The boob tube, its history, and past and current shows
rec.audio	High-fidelity audio
rec.audio.car	Automobile audio systems
rec.autos	Automobiles, automotive products, and laws
rec.autos.antique	All aspects of automobiles more than 25 years old
rec.autos.driving	Driving automobiles
rec.autos.tech	Technical aspects of automobiles
rec.backcountry	Activities in the great outdoors
rec.birds	Bird-watching
rec.boats	Boating
rec.climbing	Climbing techniques, competition announcements, and so on
rec.crafts.brewing	The art of making beers and meads
rec.crafts.metalworking	All aspects of working with metal

Name	*Discussion*
rec.crafts.misc	Handiwork arts not covered elsewhere
rec.crafts.textiles	Sewing, weaving, knitting, and other fiber arts
rec.equestrian	Things equestrian
rec.food.cooking	Food, cooking, cookbooks, and recipes
rec.food.preservation	Drying, canning, and freezing food
rec.food.recipes	Recipes for interesting food and drink (moderated)
rec.food.restaurants	Dining out
rec.games.chess	Chess and computer chess
rec.games.corewar	The Core War computer challenge
rec.games.design	Game design and related issues
rec.gardens	Gardening methods and results
rec.humor	Jokes and the like — may be somewhat offensive
rec.humor.d	The content of rec.humor articles
rec.humor.funny	Jokes that are funny (in the moderator's opinion)
rec.nude	Naturist and nudist activities
rec.railroad	For fans of real trains
rec.roller-coaster	Roller coasters and other amusement park rides
rec.running	Running for enjoyment, sport, exercise, and so on
rec.scouting	Scouting youth organizations worldwide
rec.scuba	Scuba diving
rec.skate	Ice skating and roller skating
rec.skiing	Snow skiing
rec.sport.football.college	U.S.-style college football
rec.sport.football.misc	American-style football
rec.sport.football.pro	U.S.-style professional football
rec.travel	Traveling all over the world
rec.travel.air	Airline travel around the world

Sci: Ask Dr. Science

Many Usenetters are in university or industrial research labs, so you encounter a number of scientists in the `sci` hierarchy (both professional and amateur). You also find many computer-science types, although (despite its name) this area isn't really a science.

In this hierarchy, you find pretty much any kind of pure or applied science you can think of, from archaeology to zoology and everything in between. Table 9-4 shows you a choice few.

Table 9-4 Groups in the Sci Hierarchy

Name	*Discussion*
sci.aeronautics	The science of aeronautics and related technology (moderated)
sci.aeronautics.airliners	Airliner technology (moderated)
sci.answers	Repository for periodic Usenet articles (moderated)
sci.archaeology	The study of antiquities of the world
sci.astro	Astronomy discussions and information
sci.classics	The study of classical history, languages, art, and more
sci.crypt	Different methods of data encryption and decryption
sci.math	Mathematics and its pursuits
sci.med	Medicine and its related products and regulations
sci.military	Science and the military (moderated)
sci.misc	Short-lived discussions on subjects in the sciences
sci.skeptic	Skeptics discuss pseudoscience
sci.space	Space, space programs, space-related research, and so on

Soc: C'mon By and Stay a While

Usenet is a sociable place, so naturally a great deal of socializing goes on in the `soc` hierarchy. About half the `soc` groups are in `soc.culture`, where they discuss particular countries or ethnicities; and the other half are devoted to other sociable topics (see Table 9-5). This is also where you find religious groups, ranging all the way from fundamentalist Christianity to paganism to Buddhism.

Table 9-5 Groups in the Soc Hierarchy

Name	*Discussion*
soc.answers	Repository for periodic Usenet articles (moderated)
soc.college	College, college activities, campus life, and so on
soc.couples	For couples (compare with soc.singles)
soc.culture.british	Issues about Britain and those of British descent
soc.culture.canada	Canada and its people
soc.culture.tamil	Tamil language, history, and culture
soc.history	Things historical
soc.men	Issues related to men and their problems and relationships
soc.misc	Socially-oriented topics not in other groups
soc.religion.unitarian-univ	A hangout for Unitarians, Universalists, and their noncreedal friends
soc.singles	For single people, their activities, and so on
soc.women	Issues related to women and their problems and relationships

Talk: Blah, Blah, Blah

A few topics provoke running arguments that never, *never* get resolved. Usenet puts these in the `talk` hierarchy, mostly to warn you to stay away (see Table 9-6). Most find these groups to be argumentative and repetitious and populated mostly by students. *You* may not mind this, however, or you may feel differently — so take a look at any that seem interesting to you.

Table 9-6	Groups in the Talk Hierarchy
Name	***Discussion***
talk.abortion	All sorts of discussions and arguments about abortion
talk.answers	Repository for periodic Usenet articles (moderated)
talk.bizarre	The unusual, bizarre, curious, and often stupid
talk.religion.newage	Esoteric and minority religions and philosophies
talk.rumors	For the posting of rumors

More Hierarchies

Along with the standard hierarchies are a bunch of less widely distributed ones.

alt

This name designates so-called *alternative* groups. Setting up a group in a regular hierarchy is relatively difficult, requiring a formal charter and an on-line vote by its prospective readers and nonreaders. On the other hand, any fool can (and often does) set up an `alt` group. During the O.J. Simpson pretrial media extravaganza, for example, one or two Simpson-related groups appeared per day. Often, after an `alt` has been around awhile, its proponents go through the procedure to create a corresponding mainstream group, and the `alt` group goes away.

bionet

This bunch of groups is of interest to *biologists,* with the latest news about fruit flies and the like. If you're not a biologist, don't bother.

bit

These BITNET mailing lists (see Chapter 6) are passed around as Usenet news.

biz

Designates *business* groups that are more commercial than the generally noncommercial traffic in the mainstream groups.

clari

This one refers to ClariNet (see the sidebar "Listen to the ClariNet," later in this chapter).

gnu

The *GNU project* develops freely available software, including, eventually, a complete reimplementation of the UNIX system. (GNU, by the way, stands for *Gnu's Not UNIX.*)

hepnet

This is HEPnet (High Energy Physics). Like bionet, you know whether you're interested.

IEEE

This is IEEE, the professional organization for electrical and electronics engineers.

k12

The K-12 newsgroups are for elementary and high-school students and teachers. Students and teachers are welcome on all the other groups, of course, but these groups contain topics of particular interest.

relcom

These are Russian-language groups. They are unintelligible unless you have a newsreading program that handles Cyrillic characters. You have to be able to read Russian too.

vmsnet

Groups discuss the VMS system that runs on some Digital (DEC) computers. Primarily, they are for VMS fans.

Of all these hierarchies, only `alt` has many groups that are of general interest. A few of them can be found in Table 9-7. The character of `alt` groups varies wildly. Some, like `alt.dcom.telecom`, are just as staid as any `comp` group. Others, like `alt.buddha.short.fat.guy`, verge on the indescribable.

Table 9-7 Groups in the Alt Hierarchy

Name	*Discussion*
alt.activism	Activities for activists
alt.angst	Anxiety in the modern world
alt.answers	As though anyone on alt has the answers (moderated)
alt.appalachian	Appalachian-region awareness, events, and culture
alt.backrubs	Lower, to the right — aaaah!
alt.bbs	Computer BBS systems and software
alt.binaries.pictures.erotica	Gigabytes of erotic copyright violations
alt.binaries.pictures.erotica.d	Erotic copyright violations
alt.binaries.pictures.fine-art.d	The fine-art binaries (moderated)
alt.binaries.pictures.utilities	Posting of pictures-related utilities
alt.books.isaac-asimov	For fans of the late sci-fi/science author Isaac Asimov
alt.buddha.short.fat.guy	Religion and not religion, both, neither
alt.cobol	Relationship between programming and stone axes
alt.dcom.telecom	Telecommunications technology
alt.dreams	What do they mean?
alt.drugs	Recreational pharmaceuticals and related flames
alt.evil	Tales from the dark side
alt.flame	Alternative, literate, pithy, succinct screaming
alt.folklore.college	Collegiate humor
alt.folklore.computers	Stories and anecdotes about computers (some true!)
alt.folklore.urban	Urban legends, à la Jan Harold Brunvand
alt.hackers	Descriptions of projects under development (self-moderated)
alt.manga	Non-Western comics
alt.online-service	Large, commercial on-line services and the Internet

Name	*Discussion*
alt.paranormal	Phenomena that are not scientifically explicable
alt.parents-teens	Parent-teenager relationships
alt.party	Parties, celebration, and general debauchery
alt.rhode_island	The great little state
alt.save.the.earth	Environmentalist causes
alt.sex	Postings of a prurient nature
alt.sources	Alternative source code, unmoderated — caveat emptor
alt.sources.d	Posted sources
alt.sources.index	Pointers to source code in alt.sources (moderated)
alt.supermodels	Famous and beautiful models
alt.surfing	Riding the ocean waves
alt.tv.mash	Nothing like a good comedy about war and dying
alt.tv.mst3k	Hey, you robots! Down in front!
alt.tv.muppets	Miss Piggy on the tube
alt.tv.prisoner	"The Prisoner" television series from years ago

TIP

Listen to the ClariNet

It had to happen someday — Usenet meets real life. A guy named Brad (same guy who created rec.humor.funny, Usenet's most widely read group) had a simple goal for his computer: He wanted to get his weekly Dave Barry column in his electronic mail. How hard could that be, considering that newspaper features are all distributed by satellite, anyway? Pretty hard, it turned out, mostly because of the legal issues of who owns what on the satellite.

Brad kept at it, though, and ended up with the right to distribute by network not just Dave Barry but also the entire UPI newswire and many other features too. That was *far* too much data to send out as e-mail, so Brad did the obvious thing and decided to use Usenet software instead. The result is a group of about 250 newsgroups known as ClariNet. Each group contains a particular category of news (actual newspaper-type news, not just Net news), such as clari.news.economy for stories about the economy.

If your Internet provider subscribes to it, you can get ClariNet news about as fast as the news comes off the ticker. It costs your provider money, of course, but for a site with dozens or hundreds of users, the price per user is low. Most commercial providers include ClariNet as part of their basic price.

If your provider doesn't get ClariNet, for information, send e-mail to info@clarinet.com. Remember — you can't subscribe to it by yourself (except for a few columns available by e-mail). Your Internet provider has to agree to do it.

Brad also did get his Dave Barry e-mail, for about two years until the syndicate that distributed him decided that there was more copyright piracy of Dave's articles than it cared for. You can still get other syndicated columns, including Mike Royko, Miss Manners, and Joe Bob Briggs, for less than $10 per year (less than the cost of a Sunday paper each week). If your system gets ClariNet news, they may already be filed under clari.feature.*. If not, send e-mail to info@clarinet.com to get subscription details.

Part III
Using Other Computers and Grabbing Files

The 5th Wave **By Rich Tennant**

"OH, SCARECROW – I DON'T THINK YOU'LL NEED YOUR LAPTOP IN THE EMERALD CITY ANYWAY."

In this part . . .

So far we've been looking at staid, stately, slow-moving ways to communicate with other people and other computers. Let's face it: Even though e-mail is a lot faster than regular mail, it's *still* mail. In this part, we go for instant gratification, connecting directly to far-off computers around the world, using them directly from your PC, and downloading files that look interesting.

Chapter 10

Using Far-Off Computers

In This Chapter

- What is telnet, anyway?
- Why your smart computer has to pretend to be a stupid terminal
- What's a port, and why you don't care?
- Using Chameleon Telnet
- A few words from IBM

In this chapter, you'll use Chameleon Telnet — the program that comes with this book — to use other computers on the Internet.

How Can You Be in Two Places at Once?

After e-mail and Usenet newsgroups, the most widely used interactive Internet service is *telnet* (and some related commands that are available only on UNIX systems). What telnet does is simple: You log in to a remote *host* (telnetese for a computer) as though your *terminal* (PC) were attached directly to that host. Because all hosts on the Internet are officially equal, you can log in to a host on the other side of the world as easily as you can log in to one down the hall, with the only difference being that the connection to the distant host may be a little slower.

Telnet is in principle simplicity itself, but because computers are involved, simplicity isn't what it used to be.

TIP

To use telnet, you must know the Internet address of the computer that you want to use. (Check Chapter 1 for a description of what Internet addresses look like.) Chapter 11 lists some interesting computers to log in to.

Some computers — indeed, most computers — don't allow strangers to use them. These computers require that you have an account on them; otherwise, they refuse to let you use telnet to access them. After all, there's no law that says that every computer on the Internet has to let you use it for free! It's actually remarkable how many computers *do* allow strangers free access.

Emulation Madness

If you plan to use a full-screen program — such as the UNIX text editors `emacs` and `vi` or the mail programs `elm` and `pine` — on the remote host computer, you have to tell Chameleon Telnet to *emulate* (pretend to be) the right kind of terminal, and you have to tell the remote computer what kind of terminal Telnet is pretending to be. This problem shouldn't exist in the first place, because all the 400 possible terminals that Telnet can emulate do the same thing except for some tiny details, but you have to deal with it.

The problem is that about a dozen different commands exist for screen controls such as *clear screen, move to position (x,y),* and so on. The program that you're using on the remote host has to use the same commands that Chameleon Telnet does.

If the commands are not the same, you get *garbage* (funky-looking characters) on the screen when you try to use a full-screen program. In most cases, the remote system asks you what terminal type to use. The trick is knowing the right answer:

TIP

- If you are telnetting to a computer that expects to talk to PCs, the best answer usually is ANSI, because most PC terminal programs use ANSI terminal conventions. (*ANSI* stands for the *American National Standards Institute.* One of its several thousand standards defines a set of terminal-control conventions that are invariably used by MS-DOS PCs — which otherwise wouldn't know an ANSI standard if they tripped over one.)
- If you're telnetting to a UNIX system or an X Windows-based system, such as Motif or Open Look, the answer is more likely to be VT-100, a popular terminal from the 1970s that became a de facto standard.
- If you are telnetting to an IBM mainframe, you may need your PC to pretend to be an IBM 3270 terminal, which is a completely different breed from most other terminals. Chameleon Telnet, however, can't emulate a 3270; see Chapter 18 for how to get a telnet program that can.

The ANSI and VT-100 conventions are not much different from each other, so if you use one, and your screen is only somewhat screwed up, try the other.

More than you want to know about terminal types

Back in the good old days (oh, say, about 1968), only one kind of terminal was used: a genuine Teletype-brand teletype. Teletype machines — direct descendants of the news teletypes that are familiar from old movie footage of newspaper production — were simple beasts. That is, they were simple conceptually; physically, they had an incredible number of moving parts. The only things that these machines did other than type text was return the carriage and ring the bell.

Then people realized that you could combine a keyboard with a slightly modified television screen and build a video terminal. Dozens of manufacturers appeared (most of them long forgotten now), and they all noticed that you could do a great deal more with a screen than you could with an old teletype. You could clear the screen, draw text in specific places, shift text up and down — all sorts of handy stuff. So each manufacturer assigned otherwise-unused character codes as control characters to handle these special functions. Naturally, no two terminals used the same assignment.

Meanwhile, on a small planet far, far away ... oops, sorry; wrong book. Meanwhile, in the late 1970s in Berkeley, California, what is now known as Berkeley UNIX was taking shape. People at Berkeley had amassed large and completely miscellaneous collections of incompatible terminals. Which terminals would Berkeley UNIX support? Here's a hint: Terminals, which cost real money, had to be bought from outside, whereas software was written by students and was free. Naturally, Berkeley UNIX supported every single terminal type on the campus, using a database of hundreds of terminal types with the particular control sequences needed for each terminal.

By the early 1980s, it was apparent that the dominant terminal in the non-IBM market was the DEC VT-100. Many clone terminals began to appear that understood exactly the same control sequences as VT-100s, so they would work in all the places that VT-100s did. ANSI, the organization in charge of technical standards in the United States, adopted as an official standard control sequences almost identical to the VT-100 sequences.

So now you can assume that every terminal is a VT-100, right? Well, no. For one thing, many of those old terminals refuse to die. For another thing, terminal manufacturers progressed far beyond the VT-100, adding features (such as color and graphics) that the VT-100 didn't have. Most terminals made today are more or less ANSI-compatible, but with their own warts. The world is stuck with multiple terminal types for the foreseeable future. But at this point, if you don't know what kind of terminal you have, either VT-100 or ANSI is your best guess.

Any Port in a Storm

When you telnet into a remote host, you have to select not just the host but also a port on the host. The *port* is a small number that identifies what service you want. The usual port for telnet is (for obscure historical reasons) 23, which is taken to mean that you want to log in to the host.

Port 13, for example, is the *daytime* port; it tells you that host's idea of the time of day and then disconnects. This exercise is not terribly useful, although occasionally you may need to see what time zone another host is in. Other ports are used for mail transfers, news transfers, on-line chatting, and other Internet services.

Tell It to the Net

To use the Chameleon Telnet program (which you installed in Chapter 3), follow these steps:

1. **Connect to your Internet provider, using the Custom program.**

   This procedure is described in Chapter 3, too.

2. **Double-click the Telnet icon (the little picture of a telephone) in the Internet Chameleon program group.**

   You see the Telnet window, which is completely blank and so boring that we're not going to show you a picture of it yet.

3. **Choose Connect.**

   You see the Connect To dialog box, shown in Figure 10-1. You use this dialog box to tell Chameleon Telnet what computer you want to log in to.

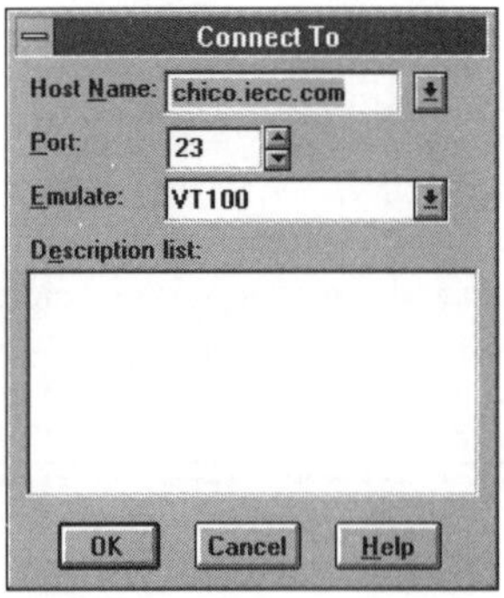

Figure 10-1: Which computer do you want to connect to?

4. **In the Host Name box, type the Internet address of the computer that you want to use.**

5. **In the Port box, type the port number — usually, 23.**

Unless someone tells you to use a different port number to connect to a particular computer, use port 23, which is the standard telnet port. Other port numbers are used for other types of Internet services, such as mail transmission.

6. **In the Emulate box, choose the type of terminal that you want Chameleon Telnet to pretend to be.**

   Remember, your PC is pretending to be a terminal connected to the host computer. Different terminals use different codes to move the cursor on-screen, display different colors, and do other stuff. We recommend choosing VT-100 or ANSI.

7. **Click the OK button.**

   If everything goes well, you are then connected to the host computer, and you see whatever login screen the computer wants to show you (see Figure 10-2).

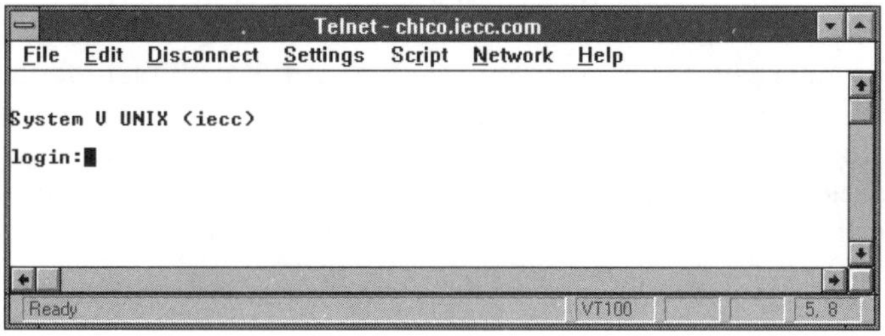

Figure 10-2: You are ready to log in to a computer over the Internet.

8. **If the remote host requires you to log in, type your user name and password.**

   If you don't have a user name and password for this computer, it probably won't let you log in.

If you frequently telnet to the same computer, you can store its address and other information. See "We've Got a Little List," later in this chapter.

After you're logged in, you can work pretty much as though you were directly logged in to the remote host. The main difference is that characters take a little longer to appear on-screen — a full second or more. In most cases, you can keep typing even when what you typed hasn't yet appeared; the host eventually catches up.

If you can't get through to the remote host computer, use the Ping program (described in "Testing! Testing!" in Chapter 3) to determine whether that computer is on-line. Within Telnet, Help⇨Diagnose Connection starts Ping for you.

Help! I've Telnetted and I Can't Get Out!

The normal way to leave telnet is to log out of the remote host computer by typing whatever command that computer uses. Try **logout, exit, off**, and **bye**, along with pressing Ctrl+D. When you log out, the remote host computer closes its end of the telnet connection, which tells the Chameleon Telnet program that it's finished. Easy enough — normally. Sometimes, though, the other end gets stuck and pays no attention to what you type. At other times, the host doesn't get permanently stuck, but it responds so slowly that you have no interest in waiting for it anymore. (This sometimes happens when network congestion occurs.)

If you have trouble logging off, just choose Disconnect from the Telnet menu. Then choose either Disconnect or Disconnect and Exit. Telnet severs the connection, and the other computer eventually gets the idea that you've lost interest.

If the other end gets really, really stuck, you can get into a situation where Telnet goes catatonic and doesn't respond to anything you type. In this situation, as an emergency exit, you can press Ctrl+Alt+Del, the same combination that normally restarts your computer. In this case, though, Windows should display a screen of text that says that your program TELNET.EXE has stopped responding, press Enter to kill it. Press Enter and Telnet goes away, letting you do something else. If Windows shows any other screen, though, press Esc to get back to where you were, and wait for Telnet to wake up.

Other Stuff You Can Do

While you are using Chameleon Telnet to talk to the remote host computer, you may want to do some of the following things:

- **Save incoming text in a file.** If it looks as though interesting information is about to start appearing on-screen, you can tell Telnet to begin saving all the incoming text in a text file. Choose File⇨Capture to file. Telnet asks for the directory and name of the file (it suggests the filename `telnet.cap`). From here on, all the text that Telnet receives from the remote host computer is saved to this file as it appears on your screen (a message to this effect appears at the bottom of the Telnet window). To stop saving text to the file, choose File⇨Capture to file again.
- **Print what's in the Telnet window.** Choose File⇨Print. Alternatively, you can choose File⇨Printer Auto Mode to send all incoming text to the printer, starting now. To stop, choose the same command again.

Watch out — you can waste a lot of paper this way! The printer doesn't start spewing out paper until after you issue the command to stop. It may be more prudent to save all the incoming text in a file and print the interesting parts later, after some editing.

- **Copy information from the Telnet window to another Windows program.** You can copy information from the Telnet window to the Windows Clipboard; just highlight it with the mouse and choose Edit⇨Copy. (Ctrl+C doesn't copy text to the Clipboard; instead, Ctrl+C is sent to the remote host computer, which reacts to it.) Then paste the contents of the Clipboard into the other Windows program (usually by using the Edit⇨Paste command).
- **Copy information from another Windows program to the Telnet window.** You can paste information from the Windows Clipboard into the Telnet window. Telnet sends the text (it had better be text!) to the remote host computer. Don't paste too much text; limit yourself to a screenful of text at a time, because your telnet connection can be slow at times and characters can be lost.

We've Got a Little List

If you regularly telnet to one or more host computers, why type the same boring information over and over? You can create a *connection profile* in Chameleon Telnet, so that the program already knows all that yucky port and emulation stuff. You can even tell Telnet to log you in automatically.

Creating an entry in your little list

To create a connection profile, follow these steps:

1. **Choose Settings⇨Connection Profile.**

   You see the Connection Profile dialog box, shown in Figure 10-3. (For information on SpaceLink, the host shown in this figure, see Chapter 11.)

2. **In the Description box, type a description of the system.**

   This description is the name that you'll choose later when you want to connect to this remote host.

3. **In the Host box, type the Internet address (or IP number) of the remote host computer.**

4. **Leave the Port set to 23, unless you've been specifically told to use a different port with this remote host.**

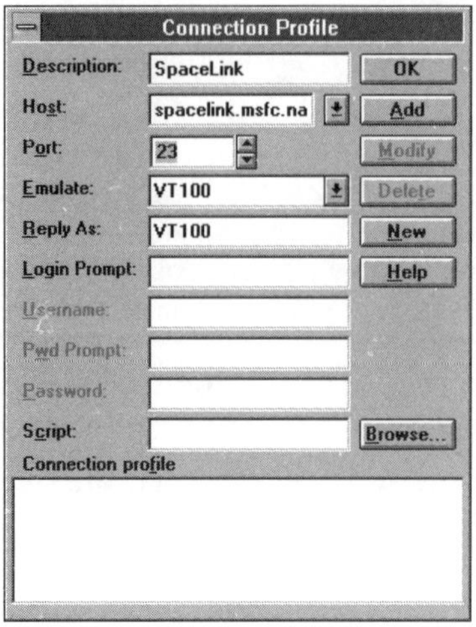

Figure 10-3: Creating a connection profile for computers that you use via Telnet.

5. **For the Emulate setting, choose a terminal for Telnet to pretend to be.**

   Refer to "Emulation Madness" earlier in this chapter for details. The correct choice is usually ANSI or VT-100.

6. **In the Reply As box, type whatever you have to type when the remote host computer asks what kind of terminal you are using.**

   Most remote host computers ask you what kind of terminal you are using, usually right after you enter your user name and password. If you enter the correct response in this box, Telnet types it for you each time you connect to the remote host. (We've found, however, that this doesn't work with all remote systems; it probably depends on how the remote system asks for your terminal type.)

7. **In the Login Prompt box, type the text that you see on-screen when the remote system prompts you to log in.**

   For most computers, this text is **login:**. If you don't want Telnet to log you in automatically, skip this step and go directly to step 11.

8. **In the Username box, type your user name on the remote host.**

   If you don't have your own account on the remote host computer, type whatever you usually type when logging in. This may be something like **guest** or **visitor**.

9. **In the Pwd Prompt box, type the text that you see on-screen when the remote system asks for your password.**

   This is usually something like **password:**.

10. **In the Password box, enter your password.**

    The password appears on-screen as asterisks (so that no one can read it over your shoulder), so type it carefully.

11. **Click the Add button to create this connection profile.**
12. **Click OK to leave the dialog box.**
13. **To try out your new connection profile, disconnect from the remote host, if you are currently using one.**
14. **Choose Connect.**

    You see the name of the connection profile that you just created in the Description list box.

15. **On the Connect To dialog box, in the Description list, double-click the connection you want to use.**

    Telnet connects to the host computer and, if you entered the right information, logs you in.

Fixing a mistake

To change the information in a connection profile, follow these steps:

1. **Choose Settings⇨Connection Profile.**
2. **Double-click the description of the system in the Description List.**

   The information about it appears in all the rest of the boxes.

3. **Make your changes.**
4. **Click the Modify button.**

   This step saves the changes you entered.

5. **Click OK to leave the dialog box.**

Your Telnet Options

You can change lots of tiny details about the way that Chameleon Telnet works. Choose Settings⇨Preferences to see the Terminal Preferences dialog box, shown in Figure 10-4.

You may need to change the following settings:

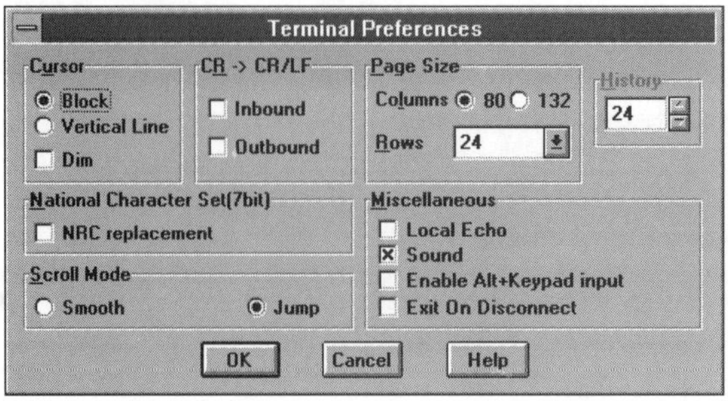

Figure 10-4: The standard Chameleon Telnet settings.

- **Cursor.** If you have trouble seeing the cursor, select Block rather than Vertical Line.
- **CR->CR/LF.** Say what? This setting tells Telnet to convert carriage returns to carriage returns followed by line feeds. If the text in your Telnet window doesn't advance to the next line properly, try choosing Inbound. Unless you telnet to some pretty strange systems, however, you won' t need to use this option.
- **Page Size.** If the remote host computer thinks that you have a terminal that can display 132 characters on each line (instead of the usual 80), choose 132 as the Columns setting.
- **History.** You can tell Telnet to store text temporarily after it scrolls off the top of the Telnet window. In the History box, enter the number of lines you want it to store. When you are using Telnet to connect to a computer, you'll be able to scroll the window upward to see information that has disappeared off the top. ***Note:*** You can't change this setting when you are connected. Disconnect first and then set it.
- **Local Echo.** If you can't see the characters that you type, select Local Echo.
- **Exit on Disconnect.** If you want Telnet to exit automatically when you disconnect from the remote host computer, select Exit on Disconnect.

When you are done fooling around with your settings, choose OK.

To change the way your Telnet window looks, you can choose Settings⇨Fonts to choose a different font for the text in the window. We find the default font to be a little pale, so we usually change our font to Terminal. You can change the colors of your Telnet window, too, by choosing Settings⇨Colors. In the Colors dialog box, you can choose the foreground color (the color of the text; usually black) and the background color (usually white). If you end up with a totally unreadable combination, click the Default button to set the colors back to normal.

If you have trouble using the remote host computer because key combinations that you type on your keyboard don't get through to the remote computer, you can actually change the meanings of the keys on your keyboard. We recommend staying away from this unless you have a specific problem, though. Choose Settings⇨Keyboard to see the keyboard-setup window.

Later, when you exit Telnet, be sure to choose Yes when it asks whether you want to save changes to your configuration.

Other Telnet Programs

Lots of other Telnet programs are available on the Net, but we've never found one that we like as well as the one that comes with Chameleon. The best of the rest is the Telnet part of a Swiss-Army-knife-type program called Win QVT/NET. If you need a telnet program that can emulate an IBM 3270 terminal, try QWS3270. See Chapter 19 if you want to check these two out.

Chapter 11

Some Interesting Computers to Log Into

In This Chapter

- Telnetting around the world
- More useful information than any sane person would want

Come on by Any Time

The Internet is a remarkably friendly place. Many systems let you telnet in with little or no prearrangement. Most systems let you telnet in without restriction. Other systems require that you register the first time you log in but still don't ask you to pay anything; they just want to have some idea who their users are.

This list doesn't include any of the many places you can telnet to Gopher, Archie, WAIS, or WWW servers; those servers are covered in Chapters 14 through 17 and Chapter 20.

TIP

In the list of services in this chapter, the access codes have the following meanings:

Table 11-1 Your Secret Decoder Ring

Codes	*Meaning*
Telnet	Connect by way of regular Chameleon Telnet or other telnet program.
Port 111	Specify a port number other than 23. (See Chapter 10 for information on where to enter the port number.)
TN3270	You should use a version of telnet that emulates an IBM 3270 terminal. (See Chapter 19 for information on how to get QWS3270.)
Register	Registration required. The first time you log in, you have to say who you are to get an account. No money is required, though.
Account	Account required. You have to sign up and arrange to pay money. (Not many of these services are listed in this chapter.)

Libraries

Nearly every large library in the country (indeed, in the developed world) now has a computerized catalog, and most of those catalogs are on the Internet. Most of the on-line catalogs also have other research info that is more interesting than the catalogs themselves. This section lists some of the most prominent library systems and explains how to access them.

Library: Library of Congress
Address: `locis.loc.gov`
Access code: Telnet or TN3270

The Library of Congress is the largest library in the world, and it certainly has the biggest catalog system, called LOCIS. (It's your tax dollars at work — or maybe at play.) In addition to the regular card catalog, in which you can look up almost any book ever published in the United States, the Library of Congress has an extensive and useful congressional legislation system that you can use to look up the bills that are in Congress. You can find out what bills have been introduced, what has happened to them (getting a bill through Congress is somewhat more complicated than getting someone canonized as a saint), who sponsored them, and what they say (in summary).

Figure 11-1 shows the menu that you see if you decide to search for a particular House of Representatives or Senate bill. You also can check for a bill by the name of its sponsor, if you're wondering what your representative or senator has been up to.

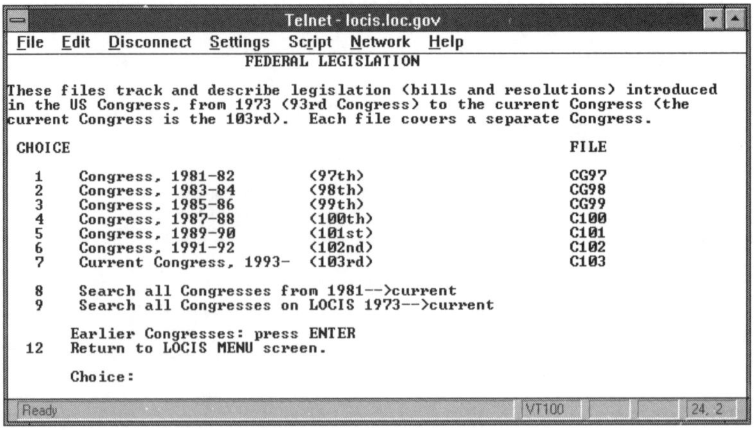

Figure 11-1: LOCIS showing how to search for a bill in the U.S. Congress.

Note: LOCIS is normally available only during the hours when the library is open — generally 9 a.m. to 9 p.m. weekdays (Eastern Standard Time), with shorter hours on weekends. At other times, LOCIS disconnects immediately.

Library: Dartmouth College Library
Address: `library.dartmouth.edu`
Access code: Telnet

In addition to the card catalog, this service includes the full text of William Shakespeare's plays and sonnets, along with the works of other great authors. To search the plays, type **select file s plays**; for sonnets, type **select file s sonnets**.

Figure 11-2 shows a search string found in *Hamlet,* which was written by our literary colleague Bill Shakespeare.

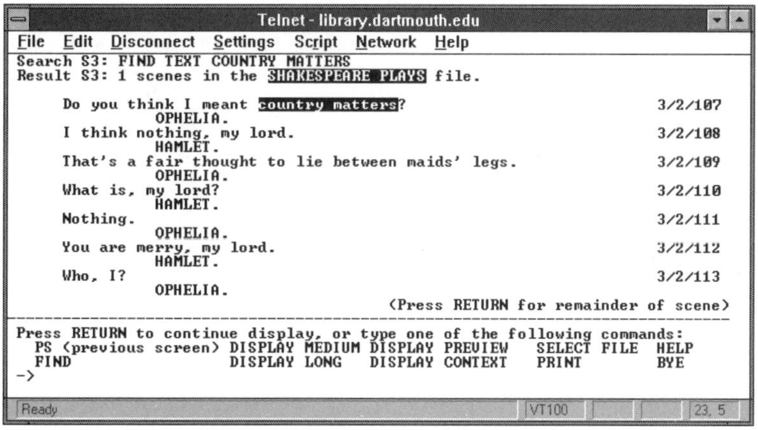

Figure 11-2: A memorable scene in *Hamlet.*

Library: Harvard Library
Address: `hollis.harvard.edu`
Access code: Telnet or TN3270

Harvard has another huge library, and the service also provides campus info.

Library: Yale Library
Address: `orbis.yale.edu`
Access code: TN3270

This is yet another large library (and the only one, by the way, in which you can find a copy of John's thesis, *A Data Base System for Small Interactive Computers*, which may not matter to you, but he thinks it's interesting).

Library: Victoria University of Wellington
Address: `library.vuw.ac.nz`
Access code: Telnet

This library catalog is in New Zealand, if you're planning to head down that way. After you connect, press Enter a few times until the service asks you to log in, and then type **OPAC**.

Other Libraries

A service called *hytelnet* is a database of, and gateway to, many other libraries. If you log in to any hytelnet service, it will help you find catalog information for hundreds of libraries. Current hytelnet servers include the following:

- `access.usask.ca` (login: **hytelnet**)
- `info.ccit.arizona.edu` (login: **hytelnet**)
- `laguna.epcc.edu` (login: **library**); located in Australia
- `info.anu.edu.au` (login: **library**)
- `nctuccca.edu.tw` (login: **hytelnet**); located in Taiwan

Large lists of on-line libraries also are available by FTP (see Chapter 13 for more information). For most purposes, we find that the Library of Congress is the most useful for finding the names of books, unless you're planning to physically visit one of the other libraries.

Miscellaneous Databases

On-line information on an astounding range of topics is only a few keystrokes away, as you see in the following sections.

Agriculture and nutrition databases

Database: PENpages
Address: `psupen.psu.edu`
Access code: Telnet

Log in with your two-letter state abbreviation. This database provides a wide range of agricultural info. It's handy if you are (or like to think of yourself as) a farmer.

Database: Clemson Forestry and Agriculture Network
Address: `eureka.clemson.edu`
Access code: Telnet, Register

Log in as **PUBLIC**. This database offers plenty of forestry facts.

Geography databases

Database: Geographic Server
Address: `martini.eecs.umich.edu`
Access code: Telnet, Port 3000

This database has the name, location, and other facts about every place in the United States. If you've ever wondered where Surf City, U.S.A. really is, this database is for you. (It's in New Jersey, by the way — eat your heart out, California.) The database doesn't tell you not to miss the world-famous Surf City Fire Breakfast, held on the fourth Sunday in August from 8 to 12 a.m., but we just did.

Database: Earthquake info
Address: `geophys.washington.edu`
Access code: Telnet

Log in as **quake**, and use the password **quake**. Did you know that the United States has earthquakes almost every day? And you thought you were paranoid!

Database: GLIS
Address: `glis.cr.usgs.gov`
Access code: Telnet, Register

This database is the government's Global Land Use Info System (GLIS). An enormous amount of map data is available in computer form, and GLIS enables you to locate and order it. Impress your friends by whipping out a computerized map of your town, state, or planet.

Ham-radio databases

Ham-radio call signs are available on-line, indexed by call, by name, and by address. If you're a ham or want to find hams in your area, you'll be interested in this one.

Database: Ham call signs
Address: `ns.risc.net`
Access code: Telnet

Log in as **hamradio**.

Database: Ham call signs
Address: `callsign.cs.buffalo.edu`
Access code: Telnet, Port 2000

Database: Ham call signs
Address: `pc.usl.edu`
Access code: Telnet, Port 2000

NAVIGATE

History databases

History buffs can find lots of good stuff in a variety of history databases around the Net.

Database: University of Kansas
Address: `ukanaix.cc.ukans.edu`
Access code: Telnet

Log in as **history** for databases on history or as **ex-ussr** for databases on Russia and its neighbors. These databases list documents, bibliographies, and other info that's of interest to historians.

Other history resources are available through Gopher (see Chapter 15) and FTP (see Chapters 12 and 13.) Also see the Usenet group `soc.history` for announcements about any newly available resources.

NAVIGATE

Outer-space databases

Care to roam the far reaches of the universe (or talk to people who do)? Then the outer-space databases are for you.

Database: NASA
Address: `nssdc.gsfc.nasa.gov`
Access code: Telnet, Register

Log in as **nodis**. This database is NASA's National Space Science Data Center, which contains many facts for the outer-space crowd.

Database: Spacelink
Address: `spacelink.msfc.nasa.gov`
Access code: Telnet, Register

This database contains NASA news, including the shuttle launch schedule.

Database: European Space Agency
Address: `esrin.esa.it`

Access code: Telnet

This database tells you what's new in the European part of outer space.

Database: FIFE
Address: `pldsg3.gsfc.nasa.gov`
Access: Telnet

Log in as **FIFEUSER**. This database has lots of satellite science data available for perusal and downloading.

Aviation database

Interested in the wild blue yonder? Here's a place you can roam.

Database: DUATS
Address: `duats.gtefsd.com`
Access code: Telnet, Register

This database provides pilot info, briefings, and flight plans. Use your last name as the login name. (If you're a real certified pilot, log in to `duat.gtefsd.com` instead.)

Book databases

Looking for books, tapes, and CDs? Here are a few starting points.

Database: CARL
Address: `pac.carl.org`
Access code: Telnet, Account

This database of book reviews, magazines, and articles includes fax article delivery. For many of the services, you need a library card (or at least the number of a library card) from a participating library in Colorado or Wyoming, such as the Denver Public Library.

Database: Consumer Access Services
Address: `columbia.ilc.com`
Access code: Telnet, Register

Books, CDs, and videotapes are listed in this database. If you register, you can order these goodies by using a credit card. Log in as **CAS**.

Database: Wordsworth Books
Address: `wordsworth.com`
Access code: Telnet

Wordsworth is a large, general-interest, discount bookstore in Cambridge, Massachusetts. Among other things, the store has an excellent selection of *Dummies* books. (One of your authors happens to live within walking distance of Wordsworth and drops by to autograph copies of his books from time to time.) Log in as **wordsworth** to search the catalog or as **order** to order or ask a question.

Gateway Systems

The following systems act as gateways to other systems, as hytelnet does for libraries.

Gateway: World Window Gateway at Washington University
Address: `library.wustl.edu`
Access code: Telnet

This gateway to hundreds of other services around the Net is the best place to begin browsing. When you find an interesting service, make a note of its name (and port and login, if necessary) so that you can telnet in directly next time.

Gateway: MERIT Network
Address: `hermes.merit.edu`
Access code: Telnet, Account

MERIT is the regional network that serves Michigan; it also runs some national network facilities. MERIT offers access to some commercial services at a modest hourly rate. The publicly available service is a gateway to Sprintnet, a commercial packet network from which you can reach many commercial services that are not otherwise connected to the Internet. You can sign up for a paid (but inexpensive) service that allows you to dial out to local Detroit numbers, which for some services ends up being several dollars per hour less expensive than Sprintnet.

Commercial Services

Several commercial on-line services are available, too. The services listed in this section all have local dial-in numbers as well as telnet access, but if you already have an Internet connection through school or work, telnet can be easier, faster, and cheaper than dialing in.

Service: DELPHI Internet
Address: `delphi.com`
Access code: Telnet, Account

Log in as **joindelphi** and use the password **info** to find out about Delphi's terms and services, or use the password **dummies** to sign up for an account. You get five free hours; thereafter, Delphi charges you.

Service: The World
Address: `world.std.com`
Access code: Telnet, Account

The World is a large on-line provider in suburban Boston, offering a complete suite of Internet services. Log in as **new** to get information and to sign up.

Service: NETCOM
Address: `netcom.com`
Access code: Telnet, Account

NETCOM is one of the largest national Internet providers. To look around, log in as **guest**.

Service: CR Labs
Address: `crl.com`
Access code: Telnet, Account

CR Labs is another large national Internet provider. To look around, log in as **guest**.

Service: CompuServe
Address: `compuserve.com`
Access code: Telnet, Account

If you don't already know what CompuServe is, we don't have room to explain it. Type **CIS** or **CISAGREE** when you're asked for the host name. Be sure you know your CompuServe account number and password.

Service: PC Travel
Address: `pctravel.com`
Access code: Telnet, Register

PC Travel allows you to look at airline schedules on-line, make reservations, and order tickets. It is (as far as we know) the only no-charge on-line reservation system.

Service: QUOTE.COM
Address: `quote.com`
Access code: Telnet, Register

This service offers daily on-line stock quotes and other stock-market information delivered by e-mail or other means. Some services are free; others cost money. You have to register, and the service sends occasional e-mail to remind you of its services.

Fun and Sheer Goofiness

Following are a few services you can access if you're in a frolicsome mood — or if you're just plain bored.

Service: Thought for the Day
Address: `astro.temple.edu`
Access code: Telnet, Port: 12345

Every time you telnet to this service, you get a pithy saying like this one:

```
Nihilism should commence with oneself.
```

When you use Chameleon Telnet to connect to this system, the saying flashes by pretty fast. You may want to tell Telnet to capture the text in a file (by choosing File⇨Capture to file) before making the connection.

Service: Internet Relay Chat
Address: various
Access code: Telnet

You can telnet to various systems to join the running on-line IRC (Internet Relay Chat) discussion. In each case, log in as **irc**. Following are a few servers that currently work, but be warned: They come and go frequently. To limit network load, try to use one on your continent.

- `sci.dixie.edu` (Port 6677)
- `exuokmax.ecn.uoknor.edu` (Port 6677)
- `caen.fr.eu.undernet.org` (Port 6677); located in France
- `obelix.wu-wien.ac.at` (Port 6996); located in Austria
- `irc.tuzvo.sk` (Port 6668); located in Slovakia
- `irc.nsysu.edu.tw` (login: **irc**); located in Taiwan

TIP

IRC servers tend to come and go with disconcerting rapidity. Consult the Usenet group `alt.irc` for the most recent information.

Service: Scrabble
Address: `next7.cas.muohio.edu`
Access code: Telnet, Port: 8888

or

Address `seabass.st.usm.edu`
Access code: Telnet, Port 7777

Play the game Scrabble against the computer or other people.

Service: Network Go
Address: `hellspark.wharton.upenn.edu`
Access code: Telnet, Register, Port 6969

Play the Oriental strategy game Go against other people.

Service: Sports info
Address: `culine.colorado.edu`
Access code: Telnet, Port (see below)

You should telnet to port 859 for NBA schedules, 860 for the NHL, 862 for major league baseball, or 862 for the NFL.

Service: Chess server
Address: `rafael.metiu.ucsb.edu` ***or*** `telnet ics.uoknor.edu`
Access code: Telnet, Register, Port 5000

Chess lovers can telnet to either of these two systems to find fellow chess lovers for a game, gossip, or advice. The server takes care of the mechanics of tracking moves in a game, matching players of similar ratings, and handling other chessabilia.

Service: The Tübingen Game Server
Address: `herx1.tat.physik.uni-tuebingen.de`
Access code: Telnet

Game lovers can come here to find everything from Tetris to multiuser Colossal Cave. Log in as **games**.

"OH SURE! LEAVE IT TO THE FORESTRY SERVICE TO START TALKING DISTRIBUTED COMPUTING ENVIRONMENT JUST WHEN I GET THE MAINFRAME UP AND RUNNING."

Chapter 12

Elements of FTP-ing

In This Chapter

- Getting files from all over the Net
- Stashing files all over the Net
- Saving information about your favorite FTP servers
- Troubleshooting
- Setting up your own FTP server
- Other FTP programs

You See It, You Can Almost Touch It, but Where Is It Anyway?

Being on the Internet feels, at times, like being in a hall of mirrors. It's easy to lose track of where you are and how you got there, especially if you're using Gopher or the World Wide Web. Often, it doesn't really matter where you are, as long as you're having a good time and finding what you're looking for. When it's time to go home, however, and you want to take some souvenirs with you — such as some of those nifty games to play on your own computer — it begins to matter where you are. You have to know where stuff is if you want to make a copy of it; it's that simple.

Luckily, because you use a modern, up-to-date, with-it SLIP or PPP connection (thanks to the Chameleon software that comes with this book), copying files to your PC is a one-step process, using Chameleon FTP. Folks who use shell connections or on-line services usually first have to copy files to their Internet provider's computer and then to their own computers. Time for you to feel smug!

Where do files live? Hundreds of computers out there on the Internet act as *FTP servers* — that is, they allow folks like you to download files from them. Chapter 13 lists some useful FTP servers that you may want to check out.

If you're truly ambitious, you can use the Chameleon FTP Server so that other people can log on to *your* computer to upload and download files. Who'd have thought that your lowly PC could be an FTP archive? Read on!

What's on File?

File transfer means copying files from one system to another. You can copy files from other systems to your system and from your system to others.

The Internet features two different and (how did you know that we were going to say this?) incompatible file-copying programs: FTP and RCP. This chapter discusses FTP because it's more widely available and because you've already got the software to do it — Chameleon FTP.

Before you can start copying files around the Internet, you have to know the host name of the computer that has the files, the directory in which the files are stored, and the filenames. You also have to know whether the files are available by *anonymous FTP* (that is, anyone can have them) or whether you need a login and password on that host computer. (Chapter 13 has a list of host computers that have interesting files to FTP. Or you can use Archie, described in Chapter 14, to find the files you want.)

Basically, copying a file from one place to another is pretty simple (but don't forget — computers are involved). Here's how it works: Connect to the other computer for FTP, tell the computer what you want to copy and where you want it copied to, copy the file(s), and disconnect. You'll use the Chameleon FTP program to make the connection and do the copying.

TIP

Why is it called FTP?

We could say that FTP is short for *file-transfer program*, and you probably would believe us, but that would be wrong. FTP really stands for *file-transfer protocol*. Way back in 1971, the Internet Powers That Be decided on a *protocol*: a set of conventions for copying files from one place to another on the Net. Then many people wrote programs that implemented the protocol, and all these programs were called FTP. Is this clear? Never mind.

TIP

Anonymous what?

Many files are available over the Internet by *anonymous FTP*. In case you're wondering what that is, anonymous FTP means that a host computer on the Internet will allow you to copy the file if you log in with the user name **anonymous**. When you're asked for your password, always enter your e-mail address.

It's darned nice of all those FTP hosts out there to let us copy files from them! It's kind of amazing that so much terrific software, text, and graphics are available for free just for the FTP-ing.

Get Copying

To use Chameleon FTP to copy a file from an FTP server on the Internet to your PC, you first make the connection, then copy the files, and finally disconnect.

Put me through, FTP

To connect to an FTP server, you run the Chameleon FTP program. Follow these steps:

1. **Connect to your Internet provider, using the Custom program.**

   Chapter 3 describes how to do this.

2. **Minimize the Custom window, if you want to get it out of the way.**

3. **Double-click the FTP icon (the little picture of a filing cabinet) in the Internet Chameleon program group.**

   This step runs the FTP program, which looks like Figure 12-1. After you get connected to a computer that has some interesting files, we'll show you how to use all these confusing lists and buttons.

4. **To connect to the computer from which you want to FTP a file, choose Connect.**

   You see the Connect dialog box, shown in Figure 12-2.

Figure 12-1: Using Chameleon FTP to grab files.

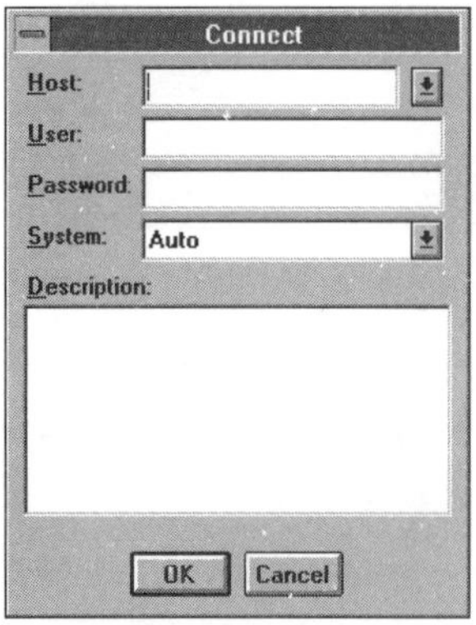

Figure 12-2: Who ya gonna call?

5. **In the Host box, enter the host name of the computer that has the files you want.**

For example, all the FAQs (lists of frequently asked questions and their answers) from USENET newsgroups are available by anonymous FTP from `rtfm.mit.edu`. (RTFM usually stands for "read the fine manual," so this may be a subtle nudge to read the relevant FTPs before posting dumb questions to newsgroups.)

6. **In the User box, type the user name that you want to use when you log in.**

For anonymous FTP, enter — you guessed it — **anonymous**.

7. **For the password, enter the password required for that user name.**

For anonymous FTP, enter your own e-mail address.

What you type appears as asterisks for security purposes (you never know who may be looking over your shoulder).

8. **If you know the type of operating system that the host computer runs, choose it from the System list.**

   Because hardly anyone ever knows this, leave System set to Auto so that the FTP program can figure it out by itself.

9. **Click OK to make the connection.**

   The Connect window closes, and you see a message at the bottom of the FTP window, telling you that Chameleon FTP is connecting. Then a message appears at the top of the FTP window, telling you that the FTP server is ready. (Yay!)

   If FTP cannot connect to the other computer, you see a message to that effect. Click OK to dismiss the message. Then see "FTP Trouble?," later in this chapter, for ideas on how to fix the problem.

Now you are connected to an FTP server. You are ready to move some files!

Chameleon FTP works beautifully 99 percent of the time, displaying the files and directories on the remote system in nifty lists in a dialog box. It does this by issuing commands that the other system can understand to ask for the file and directory information, which it then displays in the windows on your screen. Every once in a while, however, you may try to connect to an FTP server that sends back a filename and directory format in a strange way, and you are completely out of luck. Chameleon FTP and the FTP server can't figure out which files are where, and everything gets totally confused. When this happens, you have to find some other program to FTP with. We recommend a program called WS_FTP, which is described in Chapter 19.

TIP

A few anonymous FTP tips

Some hosts limit the number of anonymous users or the times of day that anonymous FTP is allowed. Please respect these limits, because no law says that the owner of the system can't turn off anonymous access.

Don't store files on the other computer unless the owner invites you to do so. Usually, a directory called INCOMING (or something similar) is available for you to put stuff.

Some hosts allow anonymous FTP only from hosts that have names. That is, if you try to FTP anonymously from a host that has a number but no name, those hosts don't let you in. This most often is a problem with PCs (like yours) that use SLIP or PPP connections. (Remember what a SLIP connection is, as opposed to a shell connection? We described it back in Chapter 2.) Depending on your Internet provider, your computer may or may not have its own Internet host name.

The FTP window

The FTP window has a large area labeled Local on the left side and another large area labeled Remote on the right. The local computer is your own computer. The remote computer is the one you connect to by using the FTP program. As soon as you connect to the remote computer (the FTP server), directory and file information appears in the Remote area, showing you where you are on the remote computer and what files are available. Figure 12-3 shows the FTP window after you connect to the FTP server at `rtfm.mit.edu`.

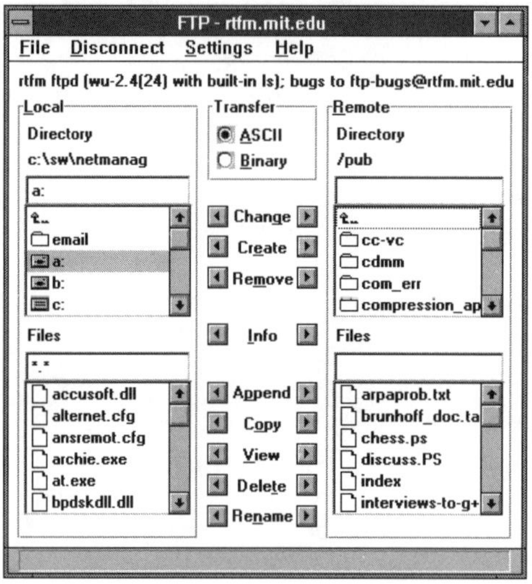

Figure 12-3: The Remote area shows directories and files on the other computer.

At the top of each of these areas is the name of the current directory (in the figure, it's `c:\sw\netmanag` for the local computer). Below that is the list of the current directory's subdirectories, if any. Then comes information about the files in that directory; the box that contains `*.*` tells you which files you have chosen to include in the list, and below that is the list of files.

This display of files and directories is pretty neat, and far nicer than using the FTP programs that are available by using shell Internet providers — you can easily see which files are where.

Finding files on the remote computer

Before you can transfer files from the other computer, you have to find them. To change directories on the remote computer, use either of these techniques:

- Double-click the directory name in the list of directories in the Remote part of the window.
- Click the directory name, and then click the arrow button to the right of the label Change.

There is a delay while the FTP program asks the remote computer to change directories; then you see the new list of subdirectories and files.

To move the parent directory of the current directory (that is, to move up one level), double-click the double-dot entry (..) in the directory list.

After you find the directory that you are looking for, look at the list of files that it contains for the one (or ones) you want.

TIP: Although the FTP window contains buttons labeled Create and Remove, you usually cannot create directories on remote FTP servers; neither can you remove directories. What a mess folks would make if anyone could make these kinds of changes! If you try to click the buttons to the right of Create or Remove, you get an error message from the remote computer.

Because the Files list isn't very wide, long filenames may be truncated, making it hard for you to choose among files.

TIP: To see the complete information about a file, click the arrow button to the right of the word `Info`. A little window appears, displaying full information about the file (at least, whatever information the FTP server provides). When you've read the information (scroll it sideways if the information goes off the side of the window), click the Close button.

Choosing where to put the file on your computer

Before starting to transfer the file, you should tell the FTP program where you want to put the file on your computer. Change to the directory in which you want to put the files by doing either of the following things:

- Double-click the directory name in the list of directories in the Local part of the window.
- Click the directory name and then click the arrow button to the left of the label Change.

TIP

To change to the parent directory of the current directory, double-click the double-dot entry. To change to a different disk drive, click `[-a-]` for drive A, `[-b-]` for drive B, and so on.

As you change directories on your local computer, the list of files in the Local part of the FTP window shows the files that are in that directory.

When is a file not a file?

When it's a text file. The FTP definition specifies six types of files, of which only two types are useful: ASCII and binary. An *ASCII file* is a text file; a *binary file* is anything else. FTP has two modes — ASCII and binary (also called *image* mode) — to transfer the two kinds of files. When you transfer an ASCII file between different kinds of computers that store files differently, ASCII mode automatically adjusts the file during the transfer so that the file is a valid text file when it is stored on the receiving end. A binary file is left alone and transferred verbatim.

WARNING!

The most common error made by inexperienced Internet users (and by experienced users, for that matter) is transferring a file in the wrong mode. If you transfer a text file in binary mode from a UNIX system to an MS-DOS or Macintosh system, the file looks something like this (on a DOS machine):

```
This file
     should have been
              copied in
                  ASCII mode.
```

If, on the other hand, you copy something that isn't a text file in ASCII mode, it gets scrambled. Compressed files don't decompress; executable files don't execute (or they crash or hang the machine); images look unimaginably bad. When a file is corrupted, the first thing you should suspect is the wrong mode in FTP.

Copying files from the FTP server to your computer

Well, it's about time! You have found the file you want, and you have decided where to put it on your computer. To grab the file, follow these steps:

1. **Choose the file from the list of files in the Remote part of the FTP window.**

   If you want to grab several files, click the first one and then Ctrl+click the other ones. To grab a bunch of files that are listed together, click the top one and then Shift+click the bottom one.

2. **Choose the type of transfer: ASCII or Binary.**

   Choose ASCII for files that are entirely text; choose Binary for any other kind of file. (You can use Binary for all files, but text files may arrive with extra or missing carriage returns or with line feeds at the ends of the lines, which makes the files look strange in the Windows Notepad. Windows Write can usually handle them, no matter what.)

3. **To copy the file to your computer, click the button to the left of the word Copy.**

   The FTP program displays the dialog box shown in Figure 12-4.

   When the transfer is finished, the little dialog box disappears, and the file appears in the list of files in the current directory of your local computer.

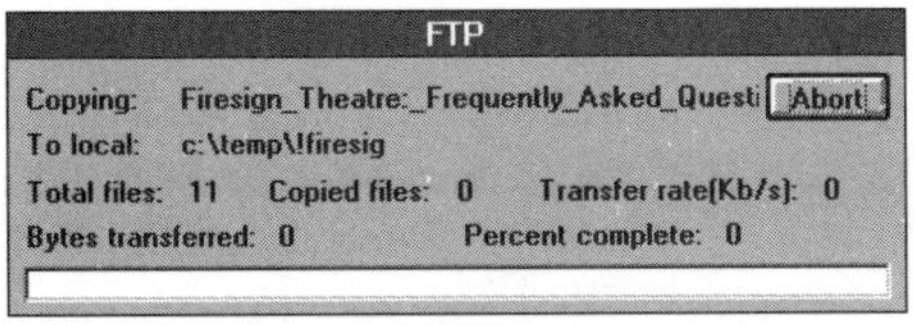

Figure 12-4: The FTP program tells you how it's doing while it transfers files.

Frequently, the filename on the remote computer would be illegal on your own computer, especially when you are copying from UNIX machines. If you want to copy the file `INDEX.readme`, for example, you cannot use that filename on a PC running MS-DOS. Don't worry — when the FTP program copies the file, it renames it to make it legal (in this case, the new filename is `!index.rea`). If you don't like the strange names that Chameleon invents, just type the name that you want it to use in the Files box in the Local section of the FTP window.

Patience is a virtue

The Internet is pretty fast, but not infinitely so. When you are copying stuff between two computers on the same local network, information can move at about 200,000 characters per second. When the two machines are separated by a great deal of intervening Internet, the speed drops — often to 1,000 characters per second or less. So if you're copying a file that's 500,000 characters long (the size of your typical inspirational graphics file), the transfer takes only a few seconds over a local network, but it can take several minutes over a long-haul connection.

Copying files to the FTP server

Occasionally, you may have to transfer a file *to* an FTP server. Not every FTP server accepts uploads (that is, files transferred to it), but you can try. Generally, don't try uploading files unless the system displays a message saying that you can. Also, make sure that the files you want to upload are appropriate for the FTP server; most servers concentrate on certain types of information.

If you are sure that you want to transfer a file *to* the FTP server, follow these steps:

1. **In the Local part of the FTP window, select the directory that contains the file, and then select the filename (or filenames) to be transferred.**
2. **In the Remote part of the window, select the directory in which you have been invited to upload the file (or files).**

   If you want to use a different name on the remote computer, enter that name in the Remote Files window.
3. **Choose the type of transfer to use: ASCII or Binary.**
4. **Click the button to the right of the Copy label.**

   The transfer begins!

Doing a little housekeeping

A useful feature of Chameleon's FTP program is that you can rename and delete files on your own computer without having to switch to the Windows File Manager. If you decide that you don't want the file that you transferred to your computer, select the file in the FTP window, and then click the button to the left of the Delete label. If you don't like the name that a transferred file ended up with, you can rename it; select it, and then click the button to the left of the Rename label.

Most (if not all) FTP servers prevent you from deleting or renaming their files, so you can try clicking the button to the right of the Delete or Rename label, but it probably won't work. (And it *shouldn't* work — it's impolite to delete files on someone else's system!) One place in which deleting or renaming files is useful is when you have both a shell account and a SLIP account. When you're running SLIP, you can use FTP to log in to your own shell account and then copy files back and forth. In this case, you're allowed to delete and rename files on the remote system, because they're your files in your own shell account.

When you finish

When you finish transferring files, choose Disconnect in the FTP window. A little dialog box pops up. Click Disconnect again to hang up but remain in the FTP program, or click Exit to hang up and close the program. The FTP program logs you off and closes the connection.

After you are disconnected, you can choose File⇨Exit to leave the FTP program.

Your Favorite FTP Servers

If you plan to connect to the same FTP server regularly, you can store the information about it (address, login, and password) so that you don't have to type it all again. The Chameleon FTP program calls this information a *connection profile*, which sounds like a reasonable name to us.

To create a connection profile or change an existing one, choose Settings⇨Connection Profile. You see the window shown in Figure 12-5.

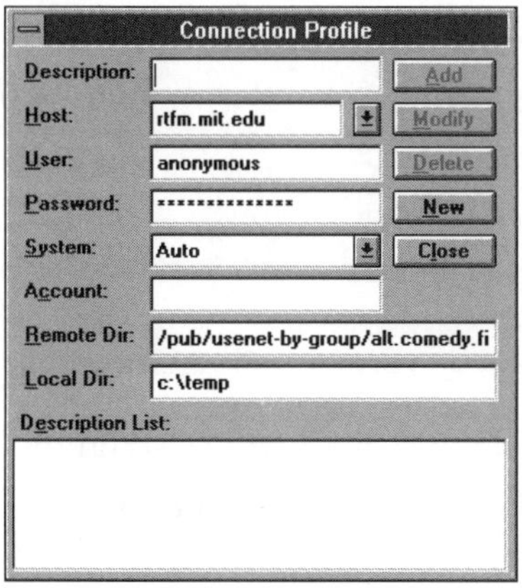

Figure 12-5: Creating a list of your favorite FTP spots.

Telling FTP about a system that you like

To create a new connection profile, follow these steps:

1. **Enter a description in the Description box of the Connection Profile dialog box.**
2. **Enter the Internet address of the system (such as** `spies.wiretap.com`**) in the Host box.**
3. **Enter the user name that you log in with (usually,** anonymous**) in the User box.**

   If you have an account on the system, enter your user name.
4. **In the Password box, enter the password that you use when you log in.**

   For anonymous FTP-ing, enter your e-mail address. If you have an account, enter your password. The password shows up as asterisks.
5. **In the System box, enter the type of operating system that the computer uses.**

   Choose Auto if you don't know.
6. **We don't know what the Account box is for, so skip it.**

   Well, actually, we *do* know, but it's not worth explaining — which amounts to the same thing.
7. **If you usually move files to or from the same remote directory, enter it in the Remote Dir box.**

   If you enter a directory in this box, Chameleon FTP moves right to it when it makes the connection.
8. **If you usually transfer files to or from the directory on your hard disk, enter it in the Local Dir box.**
9. **When everything looks right, click the Add button.**

   The description appears in the Description List at the bottom of the window.

Fixing a mistake

To change the information in a connection profile, follow these steps:

1. **Double-click the description of the system in the Description List.**

   The information about it appears in all the rest of the boxes.
2. **Make your changes.**

3. **Click the Modify button.**

   This step saves the changes that you entered.

Enough with connection profiles

When you finish entering or updating connection profiles, click the Close button. When you leave FTP, it asks whether it should save your changes. Be sure to click Yes.

Using all this information

TIP

What good does this information do you? Well, the next time you want to FTP files from a system for which you have created a connection profile, it's a snap. When you choose the Connect command from the menu bar to make an FTP connection, the Description box lists the descriptions that you entered in your connection profiles. Choose a description, and its information appears in the rest of the boxes automatically. Then just click OK.

FTP Trouble?

If Chameleon FTP can't connect to the computer that has the files you want, first make sure that the computer is up, running, and available. Use Ping to verify that the computer is alive. (You don't have to exit FTP to run Ping; see Chapter 3 for instructions on how to run it.)

TIP

If you can Ping the system and you get a response, the system lives and breathes (so to speak). If you still can't connect by using FTP, look at the user name and password that you entered in the Connect dialog box; maybe one is wrong. Also, if you chose a setting for System other than Auto, try changing the setting to Auto and connecting again.

If you can connect by using FTP but the files that you get look bogus, make sure that you choose the right transfer type (ASCII or Binary). If you cannot get the files to transfer, make sure that you have permission to make the transfer. To check any problems, choose Settings⇨Log to see the Log window that shows all the commands and responses sent to and received from the FTP server.

If you cannot upload a file to the FTP server, it may not want you to. Most FTP servers allow you to copy files *from* them but not *to* them. This policy prevents the servers from filling up with extraneous unsolicited material.

If you have a file that you think an FTP server can use, send e-mail to the manager (use the address `postmaster@server`, where *server* is the name of the FTP host) and offer the file. If the manager wants it, he or she will tell you where to copy it.

If FTP is acting odd — for example, it can connect, but it can't tell you which files are out there — you may have some bogus Internet connections (sockets, in SLIP parlance) lying around. It may help to disconnect from the Internet, exit all your programs, and restart Windows.

Other FTP Programs

Although we like Chameleon FTP, we've also had good luck with WS_FTP, a freeware program written by John A. Junod at the United States Military Academy. See Chapter 19 for how to get it.

Sharing your files with the world

What if you have some files that you want to make available for FTP? What if you have written a charming alphabet game for four-year-olds, for example, and you want to offer it as shareware? No problem — you can make your computer an FTP server, too!

Your computer is only an FTP server, of course, when it is connected to the Net, so unless you want to pay lots of connect-time charges to your Internet provider, this situation can get a little expensive. You can let folks on the Net know, however, that your files will be available only during certain hours of the day.

Create a directory with a name such as `\pub` (for *pub*lic) for your public files. If you have a bunch of files to share, you also can create subdirectories for this directory. All the rest of the directories on your hard disk will be off-limits.

To set up your system as an FTP server, you use the FTP Server program (it's in your Internet Chameleon program group — we love the little icon of a waiter). Choose the Users command to tell FTP the names of people who can log in and what directory they can access. Click Add to create a new user. If you want, you can make separate entries for your friends and colleagues, giving them separate directories to access. Enter the user names and passwords that people must use to connect to your FTP server. If you want to allow anonymous FTP-ing, enter **anonymous** as the user name, leave the password blank, and specify the `\pub` directory as the directory to which these folks have access.

Now your FTP server is up and running. You can turn it on and off at any time by running or exiting the FTP Server program. To find out whether anyone is using your server, look in the Active Connections section of the FTP Server window to see who is connected.

Chapter 13

FTP's Greatest Hits

In This Chapter

- A phantasmagoria of phile types
- Ways to squash a file and how to undo it
- The world's greatest FTP sites and what they contain

Now that you know how to use Chameleon FTP, you probably have already retrieved zillions of files (well, maybe three or four). But when you look at them with your text editor, you may notice that they appear to contain garbage. In this chapter, we consider the various kinds of files on the Net, how to tell what they are, and what to do with them. Then we tell you about some FTP servers that contains files you may want to grab.

TIP

You may also want to take a look at Chapter 18, which talks more about grabbing Windows software from the Internet and installing it on your PC.

How Many Kinds of Files Are There?

Hundreds, at least. Fortunately, they fall into some general categories.

Text files

Text files contain readable text (what did you expect?). Sometimes the text is human-readable text (such as the manuscript for this book, which we typed into text files the first time we wrote it). Sometimes the text is source code to computer programs in languages such as *C* or *Pascal*. And occasionally the text is data for programs. PostScript printer data is a particular kind of text file, discussed later in this chapter.

Executable files

Executable files are programs you can run on a computer. Executable programs are particularly common in archives of stuff for PCs and Macs. Some executable programs are also available on the Net for other kinds of computers, such as various workstations. Any single executable file runs on only a particular kind of computer: A Mac executable is useless on a Windows machine and vice versa.

Archives and compressed files

Often a particular package requires a bunch of related files. To make it easier to send the package around, the files can be glommed together into a single file known as an *archive.* (Yes, the term *archive* also refers to a host from which you can FTP stuff. Sorry. So sue us. In this chapter, at least, archive means a *multifile file.*) After you retrieve an archive, you use an *unarchiving program* to extract the original files.

Some files are also *compressed,* which means that they're encoded in a special way that takes up less space but that can be decoded only by the corresponding uncompressor. Most files you retrieve by anonymous FTP are compressed because compressed files use less disk space and take less time to transfer over the Net. In the PC world, archiving and compression usually happen together by using utilities such as PKZIP or WinZip.

Data files

Some files are not text, executable, archived, or compressed. We refer to these files, for lack of a better term, as *data files.* Programs often arrive with some data files for use by the program. Microsoft Windows programs usually come with a data file that contains the help text.

The most common kinds of data files you find on the Net are pictures, most often digitized photographs in *GIF* or *JPEG* format. An increasing number of digitized movies are also being made available in *GL* and *MPEG* formats.

You also occasionally find formatted word-processor files to be used with such programs as WordPerfect and Microsoft Word. If you encounter one of these files and don't have access to the matching word-processor program, you can usually load them into a text editor, where you see the text in the file intermingled with nonprinting junk representing formatting information. In a pinch, you can edit out the junk to recover the text.

Before you resort to that, however, try loading them with whatever word processor you have. Many word-processing programs can recognize a competitor's format and make a valiant effort to convert it to something usable by you so that you aren't tempted to buy the other product.

The most commonly used text-processing programs on the Internet remain the elderly but serviceable TeX and troff, which run primarily on UNIX. Both of them take as their inputs plain text files with formatting commands in text form, something like this:

```
\begin{quote}
Your mother wears army boots.
\end{quote}
```

If you want to know more about TeX, see the Usenet newsgroup `comp.text.tex`. Free versions of TeX are available for most computers, described in a monthly posting on the newsgroup.

Troff is commonly distributed with UNIX systems; see the `comp.text.troff` newsgroup. Most ordinary human beings find troff something worth avoiding. For one thing, it's not *wysiwyg,* common desktop publishing jargon for *what you see is what you get.* This means that it's really difficult to figure out what something will look like after it has gone through the program that interprets all the little codes you stick in. Some people, however (we won't mention any names, but his initials are JRL), get a strange satisfaction from using it, and much of the material in this book was written using troff, which JRL then filtered into something more usable by our regarded publisher. What can you say?

Dealing with Files

This section tells you what to do with each of these types of files.

Just plain text

There isn't much to say about text files — you know them when you see them. As mentioned in Chapter 12, the way text is stored varies from one system to another, so you should FTP text files in ASCII mode to convert them automatically to your local format.

If you encounter a text file that starts out something like the following, you have a PostScript document:

```
%!PS-Adobe-2.0
%%Title: Some Random Document
%%CreationDate: Thu Jul 5 1990
/pl transform 0.1 sub round 0.1 add exch
 0.1 sub round 0.1 add exch itransform bind def
```

A PostScript document is a program in the PostScript computer language that describes a document. Unless you are a world-class PostScript weenie, the only sensible thing to do with this type of document is to run the program and see the document. And the normal way to do that is to send it to a PostScript printer. PostScript interpreter programs, such as Ghostscript and Ghostview, are also available that can turn PostScript into other screen and printer formats for users without PostScript printers.

A few text documents are really archives or nontext files in drag. See the discussions of shar and uuencoded files later in this chapter.

Any last requests before we execute you?

Executable programs for DOS and Windows have filenames like `FOOG.EXE`, `FOOG.COM`, or (sometimes for Windows) `FOOG.DLL`. You run them in the same way as you run any other DOS or Windows program. See Chapter 18 for details about installing programs from the Net and running them under Windows.

Some chance always exists that any new PC or Mac program may be infected with a computer virus. (Because of the different ways in which the systems work, it's much less likely for workstation executables to carry viruses.) Stuff from such well-run repositories as SIMTEL-20 and wuarchive (look later in this chapter for details) are unlikely to be infected; but if you run a random program from a random place, you deserve whatever you get. We don't belabor the issue of safe software practices here — for more details, see *DOS For Dummies* by Dan Gookin (IDG Books Worldwide).

Packing it in

If you retrieve many files from the Net, you have to learn how to uncompress stuff. The four main compression schemes are shown in this list:

- compress
- gzip
- ZIP
- Stuffit

Compression classic

Back in 1975, a guy named Terry Welch published a paper on a swell, new compression scheme he had just invented. A couple of UNIX programmers implemented it as the program compress, and it quickly became the standard compression program. Better compressors are available now, but compress is still the standard.

You can easily recognize a compressed program because its name ends with `.Z`. A DOS version of compress called COMP430D (short for compress version 4.3, apparently) is available in the SIMTEL repository to decompress them (see Chapter 19 for where to find them).

It's patently obvious

Something that the people who wrote compress didn't realize is that Welch not only published the scheme that compress uses but also patented it. (Two guys at IBM named Miller and Wegman independently invented the same scheme at the same time and also got a patent on it — something that's not supposed to happen, because only the first person to invent something is allowed to patent it. But the patents are definitely there.) UNISYS, which employs Welch, has said from time to time that it may someday begin to collect royalties on compress, although to date it has never done so.

So the Free Software Foundation, which runs the GNU free software project, wrote gzip, which uses 100 percent nonpatented algorithms. Files that are gzipped end with `gz`.

A DOS version of gzip is in the SIMTEL repository — see Chapter 19 for details.

ZIPping it up

The most widely used compression and archiving program for DOS and Windows is the shareware program PKZIP. All zipped files end with .ZIP and can be uncompressed and unarchived with PKUNZIP, available at SIMTEL as well as at virtually every BBS in the world. Windows users generally prefer WinZip (also shareware), which handles the same files but is much easier to use from Windows.

We talk more about WinZip in Chapter 18.

Just StuffIt!

The favorite Macintosh compression and archiving program is a shareware program, known as StuffIt, by Raymond Lau. StuffIt comes in many flavors, including a commercially available version called StuffIt Deluxe. StuffIt files of all varieties generally end in .SIT.

Chapter 19 lists programs that can unstuff SIT files.

Other archivers

Dozens of other compressing archivers are out there with names like LHARC, ZOO, and ARC. You can find unarchivers for all of them in the SIMTEL repository — see Chapter 19.

There's Gigabytes Out There

Hundreds of gigabytes of stuff are available for FTP, if you know where to find them. (Remember that FTP stands for *file transfer protocol*. It's the way you can get files from one place to another on the Net, as discussed in Chapter 12). Before we suggest some places to look, a few words about strategy.

Ms. Manners says . . .

Please recall that all *anonymous FTP* servers (hosts that allow you to log in for FTP without having to have an account there) exist purely because someone feels generous. Any or all can go away if the provider feels taken advantage of. So remember these rules:

- **Pay attention to restrictions on access times noted in the welcome message.** Remember that servers are in time zones all over the world. So if the server says to use it only between 6 p.m. and 8 a.m., but it's in Germany and you're in Seattle, you can use it between 9 a.m. and 11 p.m. your time.
- **Do not upload material unless you're invited to.** (And don't upload material inappropriate to a particular archive — we would hope that this advice would be obvious, but experience suggests otherwise.)

Mirror, mirror, on the Net

Many archives are *mirrored,* which means that the contents of an archive are mechanically copied from the home server to other servers. Usually the mirroring systems are larger and faster than the home server is, so it's easier to get material from the mirror than from the home system. Mirrors are usually updated daily, so everything on the home system is also at the mirrors.

When you have a choice of mirrors, use the one closest to you. You want the one that's closest in terms of the number of network links between you and it. But because the number of hops is practically impossible to figure out, use the mirror that's physically closest. In particular, use one in your own country if at all possible because international network links are relatively slow and congested.

A few words about navigation

All the FTP servers discussed in this chapter require you to log in by using the username `anonymous`. For the password, use your e-mail address. When we say "log in," remember that we're talking about using the Chameleon FTP program that requires you to log in when it reaches the machine you have specified. Chameleon FTP gets you to the remote site through a specific entrance. Many FTP servers (machines that support FTP) don't allow you to log in through telnet, for example, or with any method other than anonymous FTP.

Many servers have a small file called README that you should retrieve the first time you use the server. That file usually contains a description of the material available and the rules for using the server.

If you log in to an FTP server and don't see any interesting files, look for a directory called `pub` (for *public*). For reasons lost in the mists of history, it's a tradition on UNIX systems to put all the good stuff there.

The FTP Hit Parade

The rest of this chapter lists some available FTP systems. Each section includes the following information:

- Name and location of the system
- Particular rules for use
- Mail or other non-FTP access, if any
- What's there

For more information about grabbing and installing programs from FTP servers, see Chapter 18.

UUNET

UUNET Communications, Virginia
Accepts FTP only from hosts with registered names.

UUNET is probably the largest archive available on the Net. It has masses of software (mostly for UNIX in source form), archives of material posted on Usenet, files and documents from many publishers and vendors, and mirrors of many other archives around the Net.

WUARCHIVE

wuarchive.wustl.edu
Washington University, Missouri

This large program and file archive includes mirrors of many other programming archives, with megabytes of stuff for DOS, Windows, Macintosh, and other popular computer systems. WUARCHIVE also contains the largest collection of GIF and JPEG pictures (all suitable for family viewing, by the way) on the Net.

RTFM

rtfm.mit.edu
Massachusetts Institute of Technology, Massachusetts
Mail server: mail-server@rtfm.mit.edu

RTFM is the definitive archive of all the *FAQs (frequently asked questions)* messages on Usenet. RTFM is therefore a treasure trove of information for everything from the state-of-the-art in data compression to how to apply for a mortgage to sources of patterns for Civil War uniforms. Look in the directories `pub/usenet-by-group` and `pub/usenet-by-hierarchy`.

RTFM also has an experimental Usenet address database, containing the e-mail address of every person who has posted a message to Usenet in the past several years. That database is in `pub/usenet-addresses`.

RTFM is one of the most popular FTP sites on the Net, but it lets only 50 outside users on at a time. (It also lets in 50 people from within M.I.T., where it's located, but that's not helpful unless you live in certain parts of Cambridge, Massachusetts.) As a result, it can be difficult to connect to RTFM, particularly at popular times. So try it during off hours, such as really early in the morning, or use the mail server.

InterNIC

ftp.internic.net
Internet Network Information Center, California

This central repository for information about the Internet itself includes copies of all the standards and RFC documents that define the network. Also, InterNIC has information about many other FTP archives available on the Net.

NSFNET

nis.nsf.net
National Science Foundation c/o MERIT, Michigan

The NSFNET is (or at least used to be) the largest backbone network in the Internet. It has a great deal of boring administrative stuff and some interesting statistics on how big the Net is and how fast it's growing. Look in `statistics/nsfnet`. The NSFNET Traffic Distribution Highlights for July 1994, for example, indicate a total of 74,941,251,400 packets or 15,947,658,867,700 bytes, of which 33.798 percent was FTP data.

Desperately seeking software

archive.umich.edu or sumex-aim.stanford.edu
The software archives at the University of Michigan and Stanford University

If you're looking to expand your computer's skills, check out the software for the PC, Macintosh, Amiga, Apple][, Apollo — you name it.

oak.oakland.edu
The Oak Software Repository, Oakland University, Rochester, Michigan

Here's software for your UNIX machine and more for your PC. It includes a mirror of the enormous SIMTEL archive of PC software.

The list of lists

sri.com
SRI International, California
Mail server: mail-server@sri.com

Look in the directory `netinfo` for the file `interest-groups`, or the compressed version, `interest-groups.Z`. This is a relatively complete list of public mailing lists on various topics. From 1992 to 1994 it languished unchanged, but as of mid-1994, it appears as though it's being updated again.

The contents of this list are published in book form and sold for about $25, but you can get it by FTP or e-mail for free!

Of Academic Interest

Many sites are full of information that is fascinating to sections of the academic community.

Coombs Papers

Coombs.anu.edu.au
Australian National University

This data bank of social-science papers, offprints, bibliographies, directories, abstracts of theses, and other materials is in Australia, so the slant is different from what you get in the United States.

Behavioral brain sciences

princeton.edu in directory pub/harnad/BBS
Behavioral Brain Sciences Archive
Princeton University, New Jersey

This site is the main meeting point for brain and cognitive scientists. It's also tied in to a conventional print journal for those seeking publications necessary for tenure.

EJVC

byrd.mu.wvnet.edu in directory /pub/ejvc
Arachnet Electronic Journal of Virtual Culture, West Virginia

We wouldn't dream of telling you what *virtual culture* is. You have to look for yourself. For more information about this journal, e-mail a polite note asking for info to `m034050@marshall.wvnet`.

For an historical database — no, wait, make that a history database — check out `/pub/history`.

Also at the same site is an archive on fractals, chaos, and more of that kind of stuff, in `/pub/estepp/fracha`.

Compilers

iecc.com
I.E.C.C., Massachusetts
Mail server: compilers-server@iecc.com

Complete archives of the `comp.compilers` Usenet group, in addition to various documents, bibliographies, and programs of interest to compiler writers, are available from this service. It also contains documents for the *Journal of C Language Translation.*

Incidentally, unlike most archives sponsored by large organizations, this one is maintained and funded by a single individual who thinks that having an Internet node in his house is fun.

NIH

ftp.cu.nih.gov
National Institutes of Health, Maryland

This system contains many NIH documents, including sometimes interesting reports from the General Accounting Office in the directory GAO-REPORTS, such as this one:

```
Although GAO notes much good news in the enforcement of federal
milk bid-rigging laws, more work needs to be done. On the plus
side, the Justice Department continues to aggressively
investigate milk bid-rigging cases and has taken legal action
against a number of violators. . . .
```

The messages from the NIH's FTP system look pretty strange, but it really does work like any other.

It's the Law

Finally you can take the law into your own hands. Well, at least to your computer. Don't rely on bigoted media reports. Check out the unedited goings-on on-line.

Supreme Court rulings

ftp.cwru.edu

This archive is maintained by Case Western Reserve University. For text files containing the Supreme Court rulings, look in `/hermes`.

Decisions are available in plain ASCII (in the `ascii` subdirectory), Atex800 format (in the `atex` subdirectory), WordPerfect (in the `word-perfect` subdirectory), and XYWrite (in the `xywrite` subdirectory). The filenames are based on the docket number, so you have to do some guessing to find what you want. The extensions are .O for the opinion, .S for the syllabus, .C for concurring opinions, and .D for dissenting opinions. Be sure to read the various README files before downloading anything so that you know what type of compression (if any) has been used.

Note: Some of the directories are enormous, so getting the list of files can take a couple of minutes.

Here's a typical shorter decision:

WEDNESDAY, MAY 11, 1994
CERTIORARI DENIED

93-9087 WHITMORE, JONAS H. V. GAINES, MIKE, ET AL, (A-937)

The application for stay of execution of
sentence of death presented to Justice Blackmun
and by him referred to the Court is denied.
The petition for a writ of certiorari is denied.
Justice Blackmun dissenting:
Adhering to my view that the death penalty
cannot be imposed fairly within the constraints of
our Constitution, see my dissent in *Callins v.*
Collins, 510 U.S. _, _ (1994), I would grant
the application for stay of execution and the
petition for a writ of certiorari and would remand
with instructions to enjoin petitioner's execution.

Congressional mail

ftp.senate.gov
Mail server: congress@hr.house.gov
The United States Senate

Provided by the Office of the U.S. Senate Sergeant at Arms and the Senate Committee on Rules and Administration, this server contains general information files about the Senate in addition to files posted by each state's senatorial office.

Law libraries

sulaw.law.su.oz.au
The Sydney University Law School, Sydney, Australia

From Florida to Ghana, if you need to know the law, look in Australia, of course. If you're into doing your own legal research, log in as `lawlib` and look into `/pub/law`.

Fun and Frolic

There's plenty of fun as well as work on the Net. Here are some of our favorite fun spots.

Hamming it up

oak.oakland.edu
The Oak Software Repository, Oakland University, Rochester, Michigan
Mail server info@arrl.org

Amateur radio talk on the Internet might seem redundant to most people, but if it's your thing, check out `pub/hamradio`.

Shop 'til you drop

ftp.netcom.com
Netcom On-line Communications Services

When the malls close everywhere else, you can still drop by the Internet Mall. You may find the selection better than the store next door. Look at `/pub/Guides`.

For music lovers

ftp.uwp.edu
The University of Wisconsin at Kenosha, Wisconsin

You can find lyrics, chords and tablature, and even music pictures in `/pub/music`.

Attention, sports fans

etext.archive.umich.edu
A volunteer-staffed archive at the University of Michigan

Check out the baseball archives in `pub/Sports/Baseball`.

News

ftp.voa.gov
The Voice of America

"Every week tens of millions of listeners around the world tune their radios to the Voice of America. They know that they can rely on VOA. . . ." It also has CNN Headlines and European news and weather. You can find overview information, schedules, and programs. If your computer has a sound card and a fast network connection (or you have a great deal of patience), you can download copies of their audio programs too. Note that by law VOA materials are not intended for domestic U.S. listeners but that anyone can retrieve material from the server.

TV (and Movie) guide

quartz.rutgers.edu
Rutgers University

When you're ready to trade your computer screen for a TV screen or the Big Screen, look at `/pub/tv+movies`.

Travel tips

ftp.cc.umanitoba.ca
The University of Manitoba, Winnipeg, Canada

Draw from a world of experience and check out travelogues, guides, and answers to frequently asked questions, gleaned from the Usenet group `rec.travel`. They're in the directory `rec-travel`.

Yummy finds

You'll never want for a new dish if you look for recipes on the Net!

FTP To	*And See*
`gatekeeper.dec.com`	pub/recipes
`mthvax.cs.miami.edu`	pub/recipes
`ftp.neosoft.com`	pub/rec.food/recipes
`cs.ubc.ca`	pub/local/RECIPES

One of the authors points with pride to his key-lime pie recipe at `gatekeeper`, but he wants you to know that contrary to what the recipe says, you *can* in fact now get bottled key-lime juice.

NAVIGATE

Go ask Archie

This chapter gives you only a handful of the FTP sites available on the Net. *Far* too many exist to list them all here, and new sites appear daily.

Fortunately, you have an ally to help you find the FTP material you need: Archie. See Chapter 14 to learn all about Archie, the on-line FTP locator.

Part IV

Searching the Net

The 5th Wave By Rich Tennant

"RIGHT NOW I'M KEEPING A LOW PROFILE. LAST NIGHT I CRANKED IT ALL UP AND BLEW OUT THREE BLOCKS OF STREETLIGHTS."

In this part . . .

The Internet is really, *really* big. (Did we already say that 40 times? Oh, right. Sorry.) It's *so* big that finding stuff on it has become a bigger challenge than using the stuff you find. The Net is sort of like a giant library with no card catalog, where each room is arranged at the whim of the person who runs it. Fortunately, swell new programs including Archie, Gopher, and particularly WebSurfer are your digital machetes to hack through the on-line jungle.

Chapter 14

Want a File? Ask Archie

In This Chapter

- How do you find a file you want?
- Using Chameleon Archie to search for files
- Telnetting to Archie
- Requesting an Archie search by e-mail
- Other WinSock Archie programs

Somewhere on the Internet probably is everything that you really want — and a great deal more that you might want if you knew it existed. "But how do I *find* it?" you ask. Good question.

I Know I Saw a Note About It Somewhere

If it's software you're looking for, ask Archie.

If you know the name of what you're looking for — or know the name enough to come up with a reasonable guess — Archie goes running around the world, checking FTP server after FTP server, looking for files that match your description.

You can access Archie servers in several ways:

- **You can run Chameleon Archie right from your PC.** See "Archie at Home," later in this chapter.
- **You can telnet to an Archie server.** See "Hello? Archie?" later in this chapter.
- **You can e-mail your request to an Archie server.** See "E-Mail Archie," later in this chapter. This is a good way to cut down on your connect time, because Archie searches can take hours.

Archie at Home

The easiest way to use Archie is to run your own Chameleon Archie program. Here's how:

1. **Connect to the Internet by using the Custom program.**

   This procedure is described in Chapter 3.

2. **Double-click the Archie icon in your Internet Chameleon program group.**

   You see the Archie window, shown in Figure 14-1. Below the menu bar and the row of little icons are two white boxes. The left box tells you what type of search Archie plans to do (see "Types of searches: how much do you know about this file?" later in this chapter). The right box is blank; this is where you can enter the name of the file you are looking for.

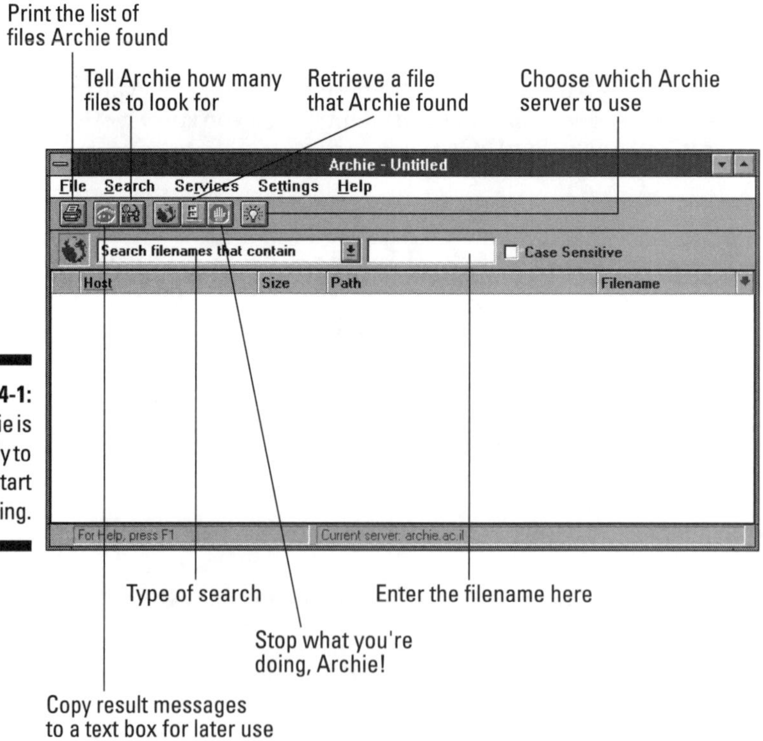

Figure 14-1: Archie is ready to start searching.

3. **Choose a server, if this is the first time you've used Archie.**

   Unless you tell it otherwise, Archie sends its request to a server in Israel (it's first in alphabetical order on Chameleon Archie's internal list of servers). You should use a server in your own country. Click the little light bulb to display a window in which you can select an Archie server. Click the arrow to the right of the server name to see a list of servers, and choose one that's relatively nearby. Likely candidates in the United States include `archie.ans.net`, `archie.internic.net`, `archie.sura.net`, `archie.rutgers.edu`, and `archie.unl.edu`. In other countries, look for a server whose name ends with a code for your country, such as `ca` for Canada, `uk` for Great Britain, or `au` for Australia.

4. **In the right box, type the name of the file you are looking for, and press Enter.**

   Archie begins searching. Actually, it uses the Chameleon Telnet program to connect to an Archie server, poses your question, and waits for the response.

One of the nicest things about running Archie under Windows is that you can start your query, shrink Archie to an icon, and go do something else until the answer comes back.

When Chameleon Archie gets the result of the search, you see a list of hosts and files that matched your request.

Troubleshooting

To see what Archie is up to, choose Settings⇨Log. A window entitled Log - Archie appears (see Figure 14-2), showing the messages that Chameleon Archie sends and receives from the Archie server.

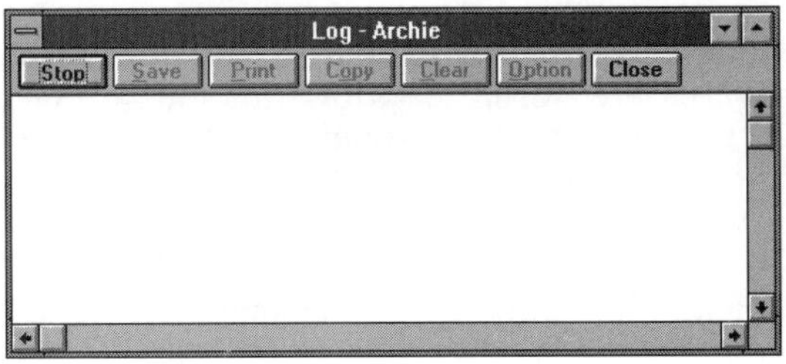

Figure 14-2: A conversation between Chameleon Archie and the Archie server.

If the Archie server refuses to talk to Chameleon Archie, try another server (see "Which Server Should I Use?" later in this chapter). If the other server tells you when it will be available, make a note of the time and try again later. (Remember that the Archie server may be in a different time zone than you are.)

Types of searches: how much do you know about this file?

Normally, Archie searches for a name that contains the string you type, disregarding uppercase and lowercase. So if you search for *pine,* it matches *PINE, Pineapple,* and *spineless,* among other things. If you use Archie much, you'll find that you want more control of the searching process, so you probably want to use one of the other search methods for matching what you type. How much you know about the name of the file that you're looking for should determine the search method that you use.

To set the search method, click the down-arrow button to the right of the box that says `Search filenames that contain`. You see five choices:

- **Search filenames that contain:** Look for filenames that contain the set of characters that you entered. The letters can appear anywhere in the file name, not just at the beginning. This search is case-insensitive, meaning that case doesn't matter. If you have an idea of a character string that's likely to be contained in the filename, choose this method.
- **Search filenames that match exactly:** Look for files with the exact filename that you entered. This search method is the fastest, and you should use it if you know exactly what file you're looking for.
- **Search filenames that start with:** Look for filenames that start with the characters that you entered.
- **Search filenames that end with:** Look for filenames that end with the characters that you entered.
- **Regular expression:** Look for filenames that match the UNIX-style *regular expression* that you entered. UNIX geeks love this stuff — you can use it to indicate that you want files that have a number as the second character in the filename and that end with *tex* or *troff.* See the sidebar "Regular what?," if you care. The rest of you can just skip this method.

After you choose the type of search, enter the filename (or part thereof), and press Enter. Archie starts to search.

Regular what?

Here's a quick introduction to UNIX regular expressions.

- If you know that the string begins the filename, start your string with the ^ character (caret) to tie the string to the first position of the filename.
- If you know that the file ends with a particular string, end your string with the $ character (dollar sign) to tie the string to the end of the filename.
- The . character (period) is used to specify any single character.
- The * character (asterisk) means zero or more occurrences of the preceding regular expression.
- Use [and] (brackets) to list a set of characters or a range of characters to match. Combined with ^ (caret) in the first position, square brackets list a set of characters to exclude or a range not to include.
- You can specify more than one range in the same search. If you need to use a special character as part of your string, place a \ (backslash) in front of it.

To find any files that contain the string *birdie* and end with *txt,* type

prog ^birdie.*txt$

To find filenames that contain numeric digits, type

prog [0-9]

To exclude filenames that contain lowercase letters, type

prog [^a-z]

Another way to tell Archie what to look for

If you want to get really specific, choose Search from the menu. You see the Search dialog box, shown in Figure 14-3.

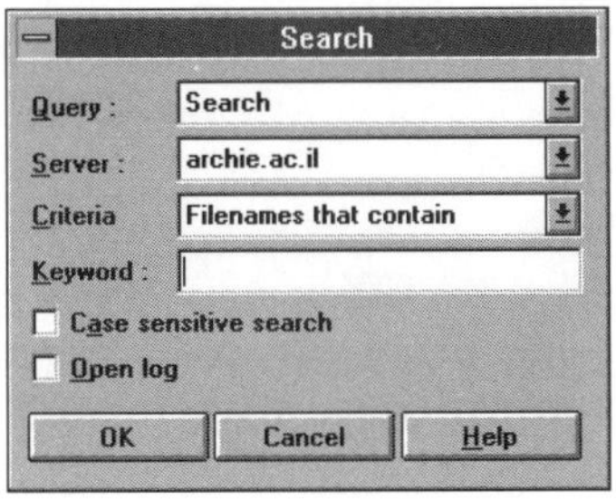

Figure 14-3: The Search dialog box lets you tell Archie more about how to search.

The Criteria box gives you the same five ways to search. The Keyword box is where you enter the filename (or part thereof) to search for. If you know exactly how the filename is capitalized, you can select the Case sensitive search box.

Selecting the Open log box is a great idea. That option tells Archie to open a log window when it starts the search so that you can see the progress of the search. You may see a lot of funny lines with slashes, dashes, and Os — that's normal. In a telnet window, those funny lines would look like a spinning cursor, but in a log window, they just look strange.

How long do you want to look?

You can tell Archie the maximum number of files that you want to know about. For example, Archie may find 1,500 files that contain the letters *win* (actually, there are more than that). On many Archie servers, the default setting for the maximum number of files is 1,000 — but for most searches, that setting is ridiculous. If you know the name of the file you want, how many copies do you want to choose among? Ten or 20 should give you sufficient choice.

Remember, too, that Archie's output is going to your screen and maybe to your log file, so think about how much data you can handle.

To tell Archie how many files to find, choose Settings⇨Preferences. You see the Archie Preferences dialog box, shown in Figure 14-4.

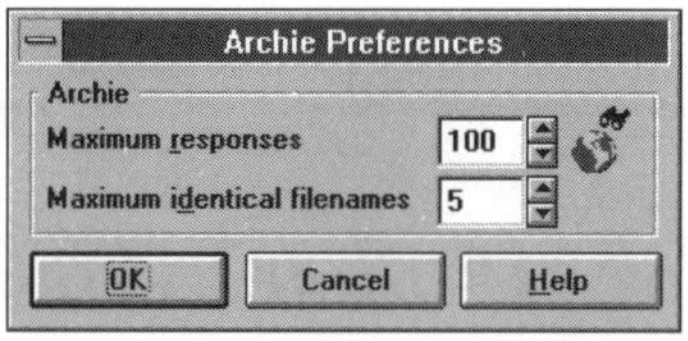

Figure 14-4: How many files do you want Archie to tell you about?

You can set the maximum number of responses and the maximum number of different locations that Archie reports for each filename. Click OK when you finish making changes.

Archie, get me that file

After you get a list of files, Archie can automatically retrieve any file in the list by using FTP. Here's how to retrieve a file that Archie found.

1. **In the list of files, click the one you want.**

   The file is highlighted.

2. **Click the file-cabinet icon in the toolbar.**

3. **In the window that appears, make sure that the FTP parameters are correct.**

   The user name should be `anonymous`, and the password should be your e-mail address. (If you're wondering why, see Chapter 12.) Choose ASCII if the file contains plain text; otherwise, choose Binary. The box at the bottom of the window contains the name under which the retrieved file will be stored on your machine. By default, Chameleon FTP retrieves files into Chameleon's own directory — not a great choice. Click the folder icon to the right of the filename and select an appropriate directory — usually, a scratch directory with a name like `\TEMP`.

4. **Click OK to retrieve the file.**

Retrieving a large file can take a while. On a fast SLIP or PPP link, file retrieval takes about a minute for each 50K of file retrieved.

After you find it, what is it?

There sure is a lot of *stuff* out there. But what the heck is it? Sometimes, Archie can help you figure that out. We say *sometimes* because Archie's information is only as good as that provided by the folks who hung the stuff out there in the first place. But for packages that have been supplied with a description, a service called *whatis* may give you useful information. This service is actually another kind of search; it searches a database of software descriptions provided by the individual FTP server managers, looking for the string that you specify instead of searching directories for filenames. If you're looking for software of a specific nature, regardless of its name, you can use the whatis service to augment your search.

To use whatis, choose Search from the menu; you see the Search dialog box. Click the down-arrow button to the right of the Query box, and choose What is. You set the term to search for and the search type the same way you do when you are searching for files.

Instead of giving you a list of filenames, Archie provides a list of whatis lines, some of which will (with luck) define the term. Choose File⇨Close to close the window in which whatis terms are displayed.

Which Server Should I Use?

Archie servers exist all over the world, but you should pick one close to home to help minimize traffic on the Net. Different Archie servers get different amounts of use, so you may have to try a few before you find one with a reasonable response time. Some servers are available only at night (that is,

8 p.m. to 8 a.m., local time). If everything that you try seems to be painfully slow, try early in the morning or late at night, or try sending your Archie request by e-mail (see "E-Mail Archie" at the end of this chapter).

In Chameleon Archie, the Search dialog box (refer to Figure 14-3) allows you to choose which Archie server to use. Just click the down-arrow button to the right of the Server box.

Table 14-1 lists several Archie servers that you can try. If you try one of these servers and it doesn't let you on because it's too full, chances are that it provides a list of other Archie servers that you can try. (Look in your log to see the list.) Eventually, you'll get on.

Table 14-1 Archie Servers

Server Name	*Location*
`archie.ad.jp`	Japan
`archie.ans.net`	New York
`archie.au`	Australia
`archie.cs.huji.ac.il`	Israel
`archie.doc.ic.ac.uk`	United Kingdom
`archie.funet.fi`	Finland
`archie.internic.net`	U.S.
`archie.kuis.kyoto-u.ac.jp`	Japan
`archie.luth.se`	Sweden
`archie.mcgill.ca`	Canada
`archie.ncu.edu.tw`	Taiwan
`archie.nz`	New Zealand
`archie.rutgers.edu`	New Jersey
`archie.sogang.ac.kr`	Korea
`archie.sura.net`	Maryland
`archie.th-darmstadt.de`	Germany
`archie.univie.ac.at`	Austria
`archie.unl.edu`	Nebraska
`ds.internic.net`	United States (run by AT&T)

If you find out about an Archie server that Chameleon Archie doesn't list, you can tell Chameleon Archie about it. Choose Services⇨Server, type the address of the Archie server, and click the Add button.

Hello? Archie?

Another way to use Archie is to telnet to an Archie server. Follow these steps:

1. **Choose an Archie server from the list in Table 14-1.**

   Try to choose the closest one to you.

2. **Run Chameleon Telnet.**

   Refer to Chapter 10 if you don't know how.

3. **Choose Settings⇨Log, select the Log to disk setting, and click OK.**

   This setting tells Chameleon Telnet to store a transcript of your conversation with Archie. It is frequently handy to keep a log of Archie sessions, since filenames and FTP servers go flying off the top of your screen.

4. **Choose the filename and directory for the log file, and then click OK.**

   Telnet suggests that the file be named `telnet.log` and be stored in your NetManage program directory.

5. **Choose Connect.**

   You see the Connect To dialog box.

6. **In the Host Name box, enter the address of the Archie server; then click OK.**

   Leave Port set to 23 and Emulate set to VT-100. Telnet connects to the other computer, which should ask you to log on.

7. **Type** archie **as your login, and press Enter.**

   You see some welcoming information and the `archie>` prompt.

8. **Type Archie commands to tell Archie what to search for, as described in the next few sections.**

   Be sure to press Enter after each command and to wait for the response. Some Archie servers can be very slow, especially in the middle of the day.

9. **When you finish, type** exit, quit, **or** bye **to tell Archie that you are leaving, and then press Enter.**

10. **Choose File⇨Exit.**

TIP

To see your Telnet log file, use the Windows Notepad program or your word processor to edit the file. Unless you choose otherwise, the file is called `telnet.log`, and it's in your C:\NETMANAG program directory.

Chameleon Archie works by running a telnet session on your behalf, typing just what you would, so there's usually no advantage to telnetting yourself. You can, however, use a few extra commands if you do your own telnet. To find out what these commands are, type the command **help** when you are connected to Archie.

Tell Archie how to behave: the set and show commands

Every Archie server is set up with features that you can fine-tune to suit your needs. When you telnet to Archie, you may have to change certain features to make Archie do what you want. Not all Archie servers are alike, and you have to pay attention to how things are set up on the server that you land on.

To see how the server that you're on is set up, type **show** and press Enter. You see a list of settings and their current values, like this:

```
# 'autologout' (type numeric) has the value '15'.
# 'mailto (type string) is not set.
# 'maxhits' (type numeric) has the value '100'.
# 'pager' (type boolean) is not set.
# 'search' (type string) has the value 'sub'.
# 'sortby' (type string) has the value 'none'.
# 'status' (type boolean) is set.
# 'term' (type string) has the value 'dumb 24 80'.
```

You can also use the show command to see specific values one at a time (try typing **show term**, **show search**, and so on). These values are explained in the following sections of this chapter. The variables to which you need to pay careful attention are *search* and *maxhits*. We also suggest setting the *pager,* which tells Archie to stop after every screen of text and wait for you to press the spacebar, to avert the extremely irritating situation in which you wait 15 minutes for an Archie search and then the output flies off the screen before you can read it.

Searching is such sweet sorrow, or something

As we mentioned earlier in this chapter, Archie usually searches for a name that contains the string you type, disregarding uppercase and lowercase. As with Chameleon Archie, you can set the search method depending on how much of the filename you know.

To set the search method, type **set search** followed by the search method — *sub, subcase, exact,* or *regex*. Here's how each method works:

- **sub:** Look for filenames that contain the set of characters that you entered, regardless of capitalization.
- **subcase:** Look for filenames that contain the set of characters that you entered, with the same capitalization.
- **exact:** Look for files with the exact filename that you entered. This search method is the fastest.
- **regex:** Look for filenames that match the UNIX-style *regular expression* that you entered. (See the sidebar "Regular what?," earlier in this chapter, if you care.)

How many files would you like?

Remember, too, that Archie's output is going to your screen and maybe to your log file — so think about how many files you want to hear about. After you decide just how much you want to know, set `maxhits` equal to that number (suppose that it's 100).

Type **set maxhits** followed by the maximum number of files you want to know about, for example:

```
archie> set maxhits 100
```

Table 14-2 lists more settings.

Find it!

Archie's basic command is the prog command, and it takes this form:

```
prog searchstring
```

To look for files that contain the characters *font*, for example, set the search type to *sub* and enter this command:

```
prog font
```

That's it — that command launches the whole search. The nature and scope of the search are determined by the variables that you set or didn't set.

Table 14-2 Other Nifty Features to Set

Variable	*What It Does*
autologout	Sets how long Archie waits for you to do something before automatically logging you out.
pager	Stops after each screen of output and waits for you to press the spacebar. The command **set pager** switches this setting from off to on or from on to off, so use the command **show pager** before you change the pager setting so that you don't do the opposite of what you intend.
sortby	Sorts Archie's output in one of the following orders: by *hostname* in alphabetical order or reversed (*rhostname*); by most recently modified (*time*) or oldest (*rtime*); by *size,* largest first, or by smallest first (*rsize*); by *filename* in lexical order, or reverse (*rfilename*); *unsorted* (usually the default). You type something like **set sortby time.**
status	Makes Archie shows the progress of the search (reassuring when Archie is very slow).
term	Sets the type of terminal that you're using, so that Archie can tailor your output (try VT-100 if you're not sure).

TIP

Many Archie servers tell you how long you are going to have to wait, in minutes and seconds. Also, many Archie servers accept the command find instead of the more forgettable prog.

What is it?

For those files that have been supplied with a description, the whatis command may provide useful information about what is in them. The whatis command searches a database of software descriptions provided by the individual FTP archive managers, looking for the text that you provide rather than searching directories for filenames.

For example, to find out what files contain the text *font* in their descriptions, type **whatis font.** You see something like this:

```
archie> whatis font
afm2tfm    Translate from Adobe to TeX
fage support)
gftodvi     Converts from metafont to DVI format
gftopk     Converts from metafont to PK format
gftopxl     Converts from metafont to PXL format
```

```
her2vfont  Hershey fonts to 'vfont' rasterizer
hershey    Hershey Fonts
hershey.f77Hershey Fonts in Fortran 77
hershtools  Hershey font manipulation tools and data
hp2pk      HP font conversion tool
jetroff/bfont       Jetroff Basic Fonts
jis.pk      The JTeX .300pk fonts (Japanese language support)
k2ps       Print text files with Kanji (uses JTeX fonts)
             (Japanese language support)
mkfont      Convert ASCII font descriptions <-> device-inde-
             pendent troff (ditroff) format
ocra-metafont       METAFONT sources for the OCR-A
"Alphanumeric Character Sets for
Optical Recognition"
```

Note: The string *font* appears in some of these filenames but only in the description of others.

You can't get there from here

Telnetting to Archie is great for finding stuff but no help at all for actually retrieving stuff. To actually get stuff off the Net, you have to use Chameleon FTP to copy it from the archive where it lives back to your computer. On the other hand, if you use the Archie program, it will perform the FTP for you.

TIP

If you're on a quest for related software, after you FTP to a host that has relevant stuff, you may want to look around in the directory that contains the file you know about and in any subdirectories near it.

E-Mail Archie

If you're having trouble logging in to an Archie server, or if you don't feel like paying the connect charges while Archie does its thing, you can send your request to Archie by using e-mail. If you're planning to launch a major search and don't want to wait for the response, using Archie from e-mail is a good way to go.

TIP

Archie has become extremely popular — so popular that it's common for each server to handle several dozen requests at a time, all the time, all day. That means that Archie — either Chameleon Archie or telnetting to Archie — can be *s-l-o-o-o-w-w,* taking 10 or 15 minutes to do a search. If it's going to be *that* slow, you may as well send in your request by e-mail and go do something else. As soon as Archie finishes your request, it drops its answer in your mailbox, where you can peruse it at your leisure. This method also can save you connect charges to your Internet provider.

Not all of Archie's capabilities are available through e-mail, but you can still carry out a substantial search. To send a request to Archie, send mail to `archie@`*`servername`*, where *servername* is any of the Archie servers mentioned in Table 14-1 earlier in this chapter.

The body of the e-mail message that you send contains the commands you want to issue to Archie. Enter as many commands as you like, each beginning in the first column of a line. These commands are pretty much the same ones you use when you telnet to Archie (see all the sections from "Hello? Archie?" up to this section for details). Choose among the commands listed in Table 14-3.

Table 14-3 E-Mail Archie Commands

Command	*What It Does*
set	Sets how Archie searches, the maximum number of files to find, and so on
prog	Searches for matching names (be sure to set the search type first)
whatis	Supplies the keyword for the software description database search
servers	Returns a list of Archie servers
path	Gives the e-mail address you want Archie to use to respond to your mail request, if the automatically generated return address on your e-mail isn't correct
help	Returns the help text for e-mail Archie
quit	Ends the request to Archie

The most common commands are prog and whatis. For example, the following commands search for files that contain *font* in their name or description:

```
prog font.*txt
whatis font
```

To set the search method, use the set command, as follows:

```
set search sub
```

For details on setting the search method, refer to "Searching is such sweet sorrow, or something," earlier in this chapter.

Other Archie Programs

At least one WinSock Archie client program is available as freeware or shareware. We recommend that you look at David Woakes's Wsarchie, which uses a different network communication technique than does Chameleon Archie — and which can be considerably faster than Chameleon Archie. See Chapter 18 for information on using FTP to download and install programs from the Internet, and see Chapter 19 for details on Wsarchie.

Chapter 15

Gopher Baroque

In This Chapter

- What is Gopher?
- Running Chameleon Gopher
- Searching with Gopher
- What to do with interesting files you find, such as pictures, sound, and hypertext
- Using Gopher to download files (including software)
- Using Gopher to telnet to other systems
- Using Veronica to wade through the swamp of Gopher menus
- Remembering interesting Gopher menus
- Other Gopher programs

As the Internet has grown, users have run into two related problems. One problem is that so much information is available, nobody can find it all. (Archie addresses the same problem.) The other problem is that umpteen different ways exist to get to different resources (telnet, FTP, finger, Archie, and so on), and it's getting hard to remember what you say to which program to make it do its tricks.

Welcome to Gopherspace

Gopher solves the aforementioned problem quite well by reducing nearly everything to menus. You start Gopher; it shows you a menu. You pick an item; Gopher shows you another menu. After a certain amount of wandering from menu to menu, you get to menus that contain actual useful stuff. Some of the menu items are files that Gopher can display, mail to you, or (usually) copy to your computer. Some items are *telnet* items that start a telnet session to a host that provides a particular kind of service. And some items are search items that ask you to enter a *search string* — the name (or partial name) of what you're looking for — and then use the search string to decide what to get next (more menus, files, or whatever).

Another way to look at Gopher is to think of it as being directories on your disk, in which some of the entries are files of various sorts and other entries are other directories. Whether you think of it as menus or directories, Gopher gets much of its power from the fact that any item in any menu can reside on any host in Gopherspace. It's quite common to have a menu in which every item refers to a different host. Gopher automatically takes care of finding whatever data you want, no matter where that data is. You may use a dozen or more Gopher servers in a single session, but you hardly know it.

This extremely simple model turns out to be very powerful. Gopher is usually the fastest, easiest, and most fun way to wander around the Net looking for — and frequently finding — the information you need.

TIP

The World Wide Web is another solution to the same problem. Like Gopher, the WWW allows you to peruse many types of information (including Gopher information) from different sources without having to use different programs. Whereas Gopher uses menus, the World Wide Web uses hypertext. For more information on the WWW, see Chapters 16 and 17.

You can use Gopher in several ways, but we recommend that you try running your own Chameleon Gopher program, which you have already installed (return to Chapter 3 if you haven't). Chameleon Gopher is a big step up from the UNIX text-based Gopher programs that don't use the mouse and can't display pictures.

TIP

Why did they name it Gopher?

They named it Gopher for two reasons. One reason is that the gopher is an industrious little animal, always busy, scurrying about on behalf of its family. The other reason is an obvious pun: Gopher *goes fer* your files.

The fact that the mascot of the University of Minnesota — where Gopher was written — is a gopher is, of course, completely irrelevant.

Gopher has been so successful that an improved version, called Gopher+, has appeared. Fortunately, the main difference between the two versions is that Gopher+ can handle more and different kinds of information than plain Gopher can. Other than that, the Gopher versions are so similar that you can think of them as being interchangeable. Plain Gopher and Gopher+ items can intermix in the same menu.

Running Chameleon Gopher

Enough of this Theory of Pure Gopherology — let's take Gopher for a test drive. To run the program, follow these steps:

1. **Connect to your Internet provider, using the Custom program.**

   Refer to Chapter 3 for directions on how to do this.

2. **Double-click the Chameleon Gopher icon in your Internet Chameleon program group.**

   You see the Gopher window, shown in Figure 15-1.

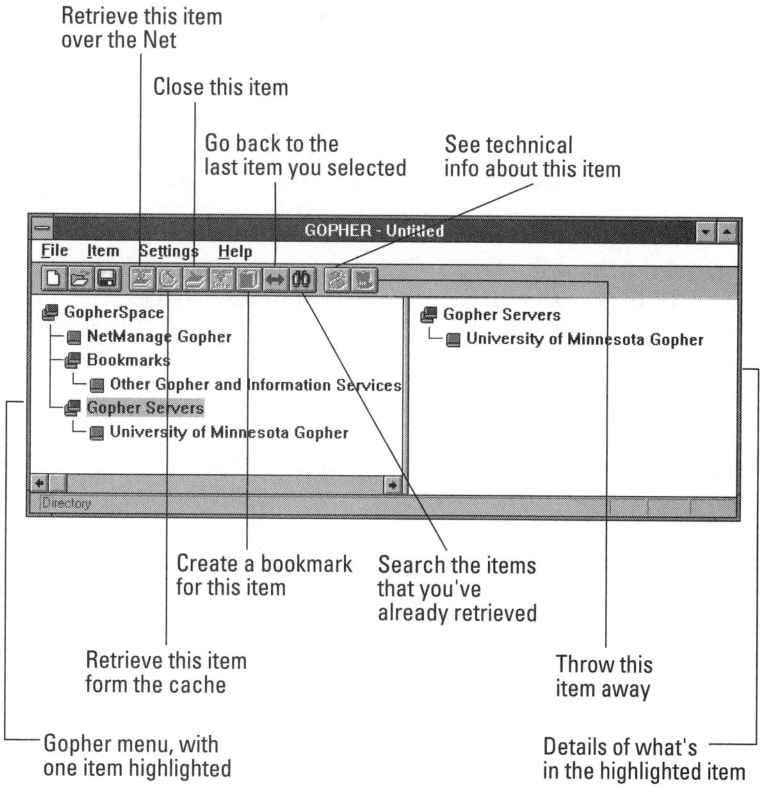

Figure 15-1: You're ready to travel through Gopherspace!

The Gopher Window

The Gopher window (refer to Figure 15-1) is divided into two sides. The left side shows a directory-style map of Gopherspace, with one item highlighted. The right side shows the detail of the highlighted item from the left side. The sides of the window look almost the same — pretty confusing.

According to the map on the left side of the window, Gopherspace has three general areas:

- **NetManage Gopher.** NetManage is the company that wrote Internet Chameleon. It decided to give a prominent position to its own Gopher — and why not?
- **Bookmarks.** These are interesting Gopher menus that you might want to return to later. You can add your own items to this part of Gopherspace (see "Making book," later in this chapter).
- **Gopher Servers.** These are host computers that provide Gopher services. To begin with, only one is listed: the home of all Gophers, at the University of Minnesota, where Gopher was invented. You can, however, add other servers (see "Saving servers," later in this chapter).

What about those little red and blue boxes to the left of the items in this map? Actually, they're supposed to look like little closed books. These icons tell you what kind of item this is. Figure 15-2 shows a list of icons that you may see and explains what they mean. (You can see this list at any time by choosing Help⇨Symbol Legend.)

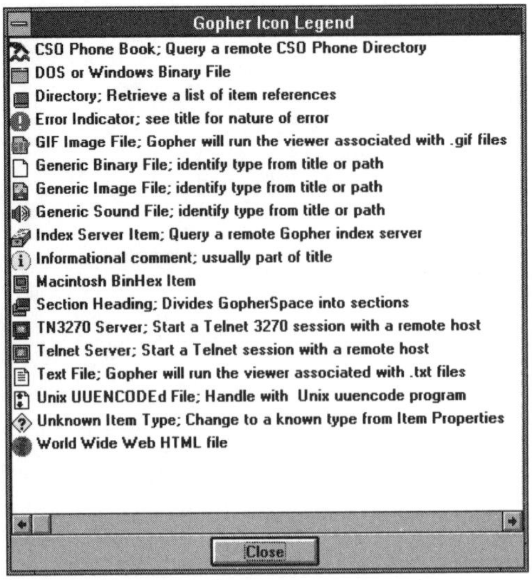

Figure 15-2: List of little icons that appear at the left of menu items.

You can move the dividing line between the left and right halves of the window. Just drag the vertical dividing line to the left or the right.

We personally find the right side of the Gopher window to be useless, so we always move the dividing line way over the right-hand edge of the window, to make the left side large and the right side nonexistent. To each his or her own!

Try thinking of this map of Gopherspace as being a menu. You can select any item in the menu, and Gopher will get more information about that item.

Selecting something

If you see something interesting in a menu, you can tell Chameleon Gopher to get more information about it. You can use any of the following methods:

- Double-click the item.
- Select the item and then press Enter or the down-arrow key.
- Select the item and then click the Retrieve icon (the fourth from the left on the toolbar).
- Select the item and then choose Item⇨Retrieve.

Gopher contacts the Gopher server that contains the information you want. The cool thing is that you don't have to worry about where in the world this Gopher server is — Minnesota, California, or Australia. Gopher knows where to find each menu item that you see.

While Gopher is getting information from a Gopher server, you see a Gopher Network Connection box like the one shown in Figure 15-3.

Figure 15-3: Gopher is going fer some information.

When Gopher finds the information that you want, the message box disappears, and the information appears in the Gopher window. If you double-clicked the NetManage Gopher item, for example, the Gopher window looks like Figure 15-4. Sharp-eyed readers will notice that the little book to the left of the NetManage Gopher item is now a little picture of an *open* book, showing that we opened this item. (Aren't all these little icons adorable?)

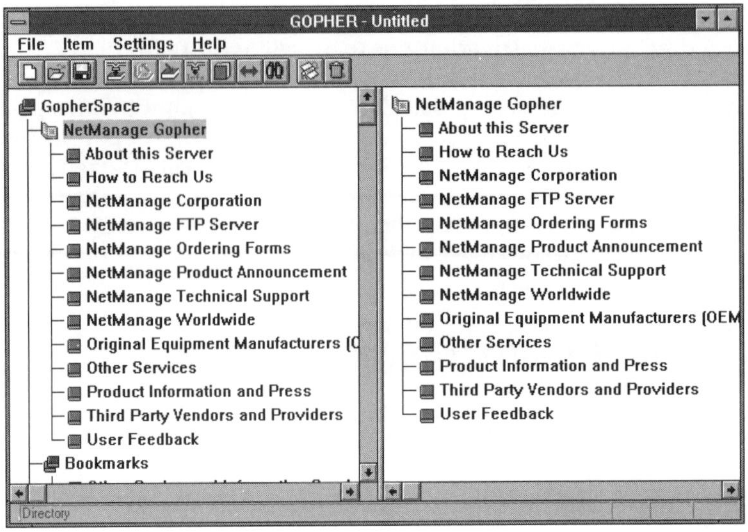

Figure 15-4: The Gopher from the folks who wrote Internet Chameleon.

Now you have lots of new items to choose among. If any of these items looks interesting, double-click it.

If you want to know the straight dope about a menu item — such as what Gopher server it lives on and what its name is — you can select it and then choose Item➪Item Properties (or press Ctrl+Y), or you can click the second-to-last icon (the little yellow card file). You see the Gopher Item Properties window, displaying lots of techie stuff.

It didn't work!

Gopher servers can be busy, and sometimes it takes a while for the information to arrive. Your Gopher may get a tiny bit of information (maybe 5MB) and then nothing for a while. But hang in there. After a minute or two, the information will probably start to flow. If it doesn't, click the Cancel button and try again later.

You may get a message such as `Server connection timed out` or `Gopher server returned no information`. This type of message means that your Chameleon Gopher had trouble contacting the Gopher server or that the Gopher server was too busy to respond. As often as not, if you try the request again, it'll work.

You can also find out whether the Gopher server is out there by choosing Help➪Diagnose Connection. This command runs the Chameleon Ping program, which sends a message to the Gopher server. If the server responds, it's out there, but it's just too busy; if it doesn't respond, it's broken in some way. Either way, try again later.

Closing a menu or menu item

If nothing in a menu looks interesting, you can double-click the title of the menu to close it. If you don't want any information on NetManage services right now, for example, double-click the NetManager Gopher item. The items that you just retrieved disappear.

When you close a menu, Chameleon Gopher is too clever and cagey to throw away all the information on that menu. Instead, Gopher stores the information for a while in a special place called a *cache*. Actually, the cache is in one or more files stored in your NetManage program directory. If you want to change where Chameleon Gopher stores menu information, choose Settings⇨Preferences, and then change the Gopher Cache File setting.

If you think that the information in a menu may have changed since Gopher transferred it and stored it in your cache, you can select the item and then choose Item⇨Retrieve Item (or press Ctrl+R). Gopher contacts the Gopher server where the item lives and downloads the item again.

Getting rid of boring items

You can get rid of items that you know you'll never want to use — that is, you can delete them from the information that you have retrieved. You can't delete items from the actual Gopher servers, however — someone else may be interested in them.

To delete an item from your Gopher menus, select the item and then choose Item⇨Remove Item or click the trash-can icon (the rightmost one).

Lost in Gopherspace

There are two good ways to get started wandering around Gopherspace:

- **Double-click the Other Gopher and Information Services item indented below the Bookmarks item.** Because there are too many Gophers to include in one list (hundreds, if not thousands), you see a list of areas of the world, plus items such as International Organizations. You can click the area that you are interested in, homing in on what you want.
- **Double-click the University of Minnesota Gopher item indented below the Gopher Servers item — the mother of all Gophers.** You get the list shown in Figure 15-5, displaying the types of information that are available. Choose what looks interesting, and browse the menus until you find what you want.

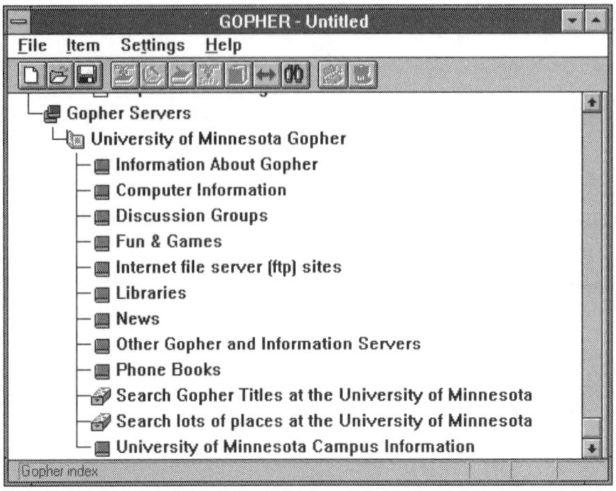

Figure 15-5: The mother of all Gophers shows a list of interesting things in Gopherspace.

TIP

These menus are a mess

If you use Gopher much, you quickly notice that there isn't a great deal of consistency from one menu to another. That's because Gopher is a totally decentralized system — that is, anyone who wants to can create a Gopher server. Creating a Gopher server is pretty easy, requiring only that the system manager install a few programs and create some index files containing the text of the menus. If one site wants to include in its Gopher menu a link to an item or a menu somewhere else, it can do so without any cooperation from the manager of the linked item or menu.

The *good* news is that thousands of Gopher servers are on the Net, created by volunteers who want to make the process of getting to their data easier. The *bad* news is that almost none of these people has any experience in indexing and information retrieval (for that, you need a degree in library science). The same item may appear in five menus under five names, and no two Gopher menus are quite the same.

Figuring out where people have hidden stuff, therefore, takes some experimenting and poking around, but it's usually worth the effort.

Get me out of this Gopher burrow!

To leave Chameleon Gopher, choose File⇨Exit. Before you leave, though, Gopher wants to save your configuration information in a configuration file, so it asks something like `Save changes to Untitled`? This peculiar question means that Gopher wants to know whether you want to save any configuration changes that you've made, if you haven't saved this stuff before. Don't worry about exactly what information Gopher is talking about — you want to save it.

Choose Yes so that your changes are saved. You see a File Save As window, suggesting that the configuration information be saved in a file named `untitled.cfg` in your NetManage program directory. (We usually change the filename to `gopher.cfg`, just for the heck of it.) Then click OK. Gopher saves whatever this terribly valuable information is and allows you to exit.

In the future, Gopher remembers where you saved this information. When you exit, Gopher usually asks you whether to save the information again, but it doesn't ask about a filename.

What Do You Do When You Find Something?

These menus are all very nice, but what about some actual information? We thought you'd never ask.

Eventually, you'll see a menu item with something other than a little red book icon to its left. Another icon indicates that this item is *not* just going to show you another menu. What happens when you click the item depends on what little icon appears to its left. The menu item can be a text file, a picture, a video clip (rare, at this point), a connection to an FTP server, or even a way to search a database.

TECHNICAL STUFF

With whom do you associate?

How does Chameleon Gopher know what to do with each kind of menu item? In a few cases, it has its own ideas, but it generally asks Windows File Manager for help. In File Manager, you can set up *associations* between types of files (as determined by their file extensions) and the programs that can handle them.

File Manager knows that if you want to deal with a text file (a file with the extension TXT), for example, you can use the Windows Notepad program. If you want to see a bitmap graphics file (with the extension BMP), you can use Windows Paintbrush.

You can set up other associations between file types and programs. If you use WinZip to handle your ZIP files (as described in Chapter 18), you can create an association between the program and the file type by choosing File⇨Associate in the File Manager, typing a file extension, pressing Tab, and typing the full path name of the program that handles files of that type.

For more information about *viewers* — programs that allow you to look at files of various types — see Chapter 18.

Not another menu!

When you see this little red book icon, the item is just another menu. Double-click it to see what's in the menu.

This item does nothing

When you see the little blue and red books, the corresponding items are not really Gopher menu items. These items are Chameleon Gopher's headings for all of Gopherspace, for your menu of bookmarks, and for your menu of Gopher servers. Nothing happens when you click these items.

Here's some text!

When you see this little picture of a dog-eared piece of paper, the item is a text file. When you double-click the item, Chameleon Gopher gets the text file, runs Windows Notepad, and uses Notepad to display the text.

After you read the text, you can save it by choosing the File⇨Save As command in Notepad. You can print the text by choosing File⇨Print. When you finish, choose File⇨Exit to leave the Notepad program.

It's a picture!

When you see this little icon, the item is a GIF file, which is a type of picture. To see the file, you need a program that can display GIF files — a program called a *GIF viewer.*

When you double-click a GIF item, Gopher tries to run your GIF viewer program. If you don't have one, Gopher complains, displaying the message `Unable to start viewer for xxx.GIF. Check file associations.` If this happens, see Chapter 18 for information on how to download and install a GIF viewer.

If you have a properly installed GIF viewer, when you double-click a GIF item, Gopher downloads the item, runs the GIF viewer, and displays the picture.

If you see this little icon (is it a sailboat? hard to say), the item is some kind of picture. The item could be a GIF file, a BMP file (a Windows bitmap, which you can view by using Windows Paintbrush), a PCX file (another standard type of image file that Windows Paintbrush can display), a PostScript file, or some other kind of picture. With luck, the item's title tells you what kind of image it is.

To confirm the type of image that you are dealing with, select the item and then press Ctrl+Y to see the gory technical details about it. Click the Selector/Path box, and scroll to the end of the list to see the name of the file that contains the image. Look at the file extension to see whether it is GIF, BMP, PCX, or something else. Then click OK to close the window filled with gory technical details.

When you double-click one of these items, Gopher asks for a filename. Use a file, name with the correct extension — that is, use the same extension that you saw in the Selector/Path box. When you click OK, Gopher retrieves the image. If you have a viewer for that type of image file, Gopher runs the viewer and loads the picture into it. If you don't have a viewer, see Chapter 18 for information on finding, downloading, and installing viewers.

If you are dying to see some pictures, you can use Veronica to find GIFs or other images in Gopher. For information, see the sidebar "Veronica tips," at the end of this chapter.

It's a program!

When you see this picture (a gray box with a blue–green top border), you're looking at a PC program. When you double-click the picture, Gopher asks you for the directory and filename to put the program in, and then downloads it, just like that. How could there be an easier way to download software to your PC?

Frequently, in addition to the program itself, you see an HLP file (a Windows Help file), an INI file (a Windows configuration file), and a file named something like README.TXT. It's a good idea to double-click the README file first, to make sure that you know what you are getting. Then download the program itself, along with its HLP and INI files. The README file should tell you what to do with all these files. (See Chapter 18 for more information on downloading and installing Windows programs from the Internet.)

It's a sound!

When you see the little icon of a speaker, you're looking at a sound file. You can play the file if your PC has a soundboard and speakers, and if you have a sound viewer program — that is, a program that can interpret and play the sound file. Sound files can contain music, interviews, news reports — anything that you can hear.

Sound files, by the way, usually have the file extension AU or WAV. You can press Ctrl+Y to see technical information about the sound item, including its filename on the Gopher server.

When you double-click a sound item, Gopher asks for the directory and filename to put the item in on your hard disk. Use a filename with the same extension that the file has on the Gopher server. When you click OK, Gopher downloads the sound file and runs your sound viewer program. Presto! You hear the music, speech, or whatever.

If your PC has a soundboard and speakers, but you don't have a sound viewer program, (a sound viewer? we've reached metaphor meltdown), consult Chapter 18.

It's a World Wide Web page!

When you see the little globe icon, the Gopher menu item is a World Wide Web page — that is, it is a file designed to be viewed with WebSurfer or another World Wide Web browser program. Luckily, you've got one, namely WebSurfer, and it's described in detail in Chapter 17. (Chapter 16 describes the World Wide Web.)

World Wide Web pages are stored in a format called HTML. On PCs, the file extension is HTM.

If you want Gopher to run the WebSurfer program automatically when you retrieve a World Wide Web page, you have to tell it how. Follow these steps:

1. **Run Windows File Manager.**
2. **Choose File⇨Associate.**

   You see the Associate dialog box, shown in Figure 15-6. When File Manager knows, Gopher knows, too.

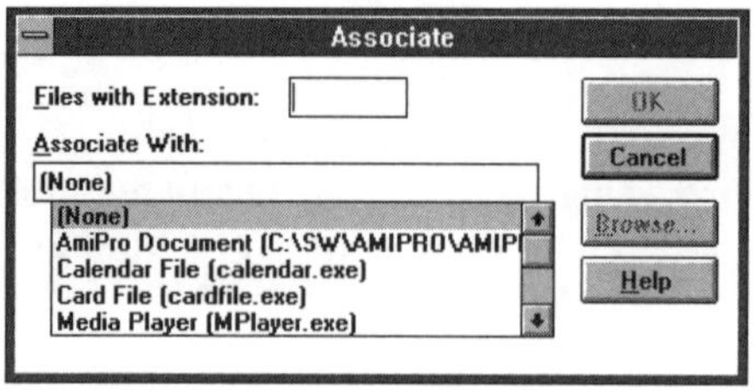

Figure 15-6: The Associate dialog box lets you tell File Manager what to run when it sees a World Wide Web page.

3. **Type** `HTM` **in the Files with Extension box and then press Tab.**

   In the Associate With box, File Manager shows the program that it runs to display HTML files — probably `(None)`.

4. **In the Associate With box, type the full path name of your WebSurfer program.**

   If you installed your Internet Chameleon software in a directory called `C:\NETMANAGE`, the program is called `C:\NETMANAGE\CHMOSAIC.EXE`.

   Alternatively, you can click the Browse button and look around on your hard disk for the WebSurfer program. Or switch to Windows Program Manager, click the WebSurfer icon once, press Alt+Enter to see its properties, copy the contents of the Command Line box, and click Cancel to leave the icon properties unchanged.

5. **Click OK.**

6. **Exit File Manager by choosing File⇨Exit.**

   Better yet, minimize File Manager by clicking the down-triangle button in its upper right-hand corner. (We like to leave File Manager running all the time; we never know when we're going to need it.)

Now File Manager knows what to do when you want to look at a file with the extension HTM, and File Manager tells Gopher. So you are ready to use Gopher to retrieve World Wide Web pages.

When you double-click a World Wide Web (HTML) menu item in Gopher, Gopher retrieves the item, runs WebSurfer automatically, and opens the World Wide Web page in it. Cool!

Searching with Gopher

When you see the little picture of a card file, you've got a search item. If you open the University of Minnesota Gopher menu, for example, you see a search item called something like Search Gopher Titles at the University of Minnesota. When you double-click the item, you see the Gopher Index Search window, shown in Figure 15-7.

Type one or more words that describe what you are looking for. For example, you could type **Brazil** to look for items in Gopher menus at the University of Minnesota that contain the word *Brazil*.

When you click OK, Gopher asks the Gopher server to perform your search. The items that the server finds appear as menu items indented below the original search item, as shown in Figure 15-8.

Figure 15-7: Searching for information with a Gopher search item.

Figure 15-8: Minnesota mama Gopher found a few items about Brazil.

Gopher search items don't work exactly the same way; the interpretation of any particular search key is entirely up to the Gopher server that performs the search. On most Gopher servers, if you type more than one word to search for, the search includes items that contain *all* the words that you typed. Some servers, however, give you all the items that include *any* of the words that you typed.

What if you want to search all of Gopherspace — not just the items in one particular Gopher server? People have written extremely clever programs that do just that. For information, see "Veronica, my darling," later in this chapter.

Leaping tall systems in a single bound

When you see a little gray picture of a terminal, the item is a *telnet* item. When you double-click one of these items, Gopher automatically runs Chameleon Telnet (discussed in Chapter 10) to connect you with a system that provides a service. More often than not, you have to log in to the remote system; if so, just before Gopher starts the connection, Gopher tells you the login name to use.

TIP

If your short-term memory isn't great, you may want to write down the login name that the telnetted-to system requires, because some time may pass before the system gets around to asking you for the login name.

When you finish, log out of the new system. If you can't figure out how to do that, choose Disconnect from the Telnet menu to cut the cord with the other computer; then choose Disconnect and Exit.

TIP

If you have trouble telnetting, find out what host computer Gopher's trying to telnet to, and try telnetting there yourself. After all, when Gopher telnets to a system, it's not doing anything magical; if Gopher can telnet somewhere, so can you. To display the host name, select the telnet item, press Ctrl+Y, and note the Host Name. Next time, you can telnet there yourself without Gopher's help.

If the telnet icon is dark blue instead of gray, the computer expects to talk to a special type of terminal: an IBM 3270. Chameleon Telnet can't pretend to be a 3270, so you need a special 3270-emulating telnet program called TN3270. See Chapter 19 for information on downloading and installing this program.

Other types of items

You may occasionally see other little icons to the left of menu items in Gopher. Refer to Figure 15-2 for a list of the icons. If you're not sure what an icon means, you can always try double-clicking the item to see what happens!

Searching Gopherspace

Hmmm . . . after you retrieve a bunch of Gopher menus, remembering what's where can be hard. Luckily, you can tell Chameleon Gopher to search the menu items that you retrieved, looking for a word or phrase. Follow these steps:

1. **Choose Item⇨Search or click the little picture of binoculars in the toolbar.**

   You see the GopherSpace Keyword Index dialog box, shown in Figure 15-9.

2. **Either type a word in the box at the top of the window or choose an item from the list.**

   If you type a word, as you type, Gopher skips down the list to the keyword that is closest to what you've typed so far. Also, the box at the bottom of the window shows all the Gopher items that contain the word you've typed.

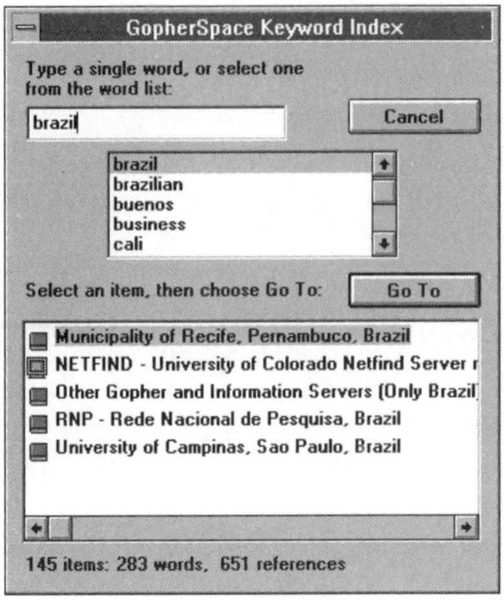

Figure 15-9: Searching the Gopher items you've already retrieved.

3. **Choose a Gopher item from the list at the bottom of the window, and click the Go To button.**

   You return to the Gopher window, and the menu item that you chose appears in the right side of the window.

Veronica, my darling

What if you are looking for information in Gopherspace, and you haven't retrieved it yet? Veronica comes to the rescue. Like Archie, Veronica has a big database of available services. Veronica tracks all the Gopher menus that can be accessed directly or (often, very) indirectly from the mother Gopher in Minnesota.

Using Veronica is easy; it's just another search item. You can find Veronica indented below the Other Gopher and Information Services item that appears in your Bookmark menu — it's probably called something like Search Titles in Gopherspace Using Veronica. Here's how to use Veronica:

1. **Double-click the Veronica menu item.**

   Gopher retrieves the Veronica menu, which looks something like Figure 15-10. If the menu contains FAQs (lists of frequently asked questions) or other text files of instructions, you may want to retrieve and read them.

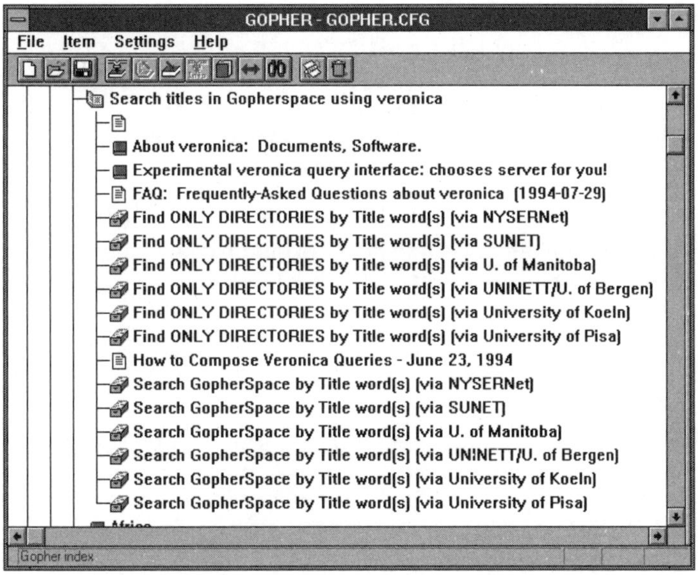

Figure 15-10: A Veronica menu with lots of items that perform searches of Gopherspace.

2. **Choose an item that searches Gopherspace by title (that is, by the name of the menu item).**

   There may be a number of such items — one for each Gopher server that offers the Veronica program. It doesn't matter which item you choose, because Veronica searches *all* of Gopherspace, not just the server it's on. If one server turns out to be busy or slow, you can try another one. Start with the server that is geographically nearest you.

   You see the same Gopher Index Search window that you saw when you performed other types of searches (refer to Figure 15-7).

3. **Type the word or words that you want to search for.**

4. **Click OK.**

   You see a Gopher Network Connection box while Gopher sends out the query and receives the response. Then you see the response: yet another menu, indented below the Veronica item that you chose.

The items that Veronica finds may include menus, text files, programs — you name it. You can tell what's what by the little icons that appear to the left of each item. For information on what to do with each type of item, refer to "What Do You Do When You Find Something?," earlier in this chapter.

If you get a message like `Too many connections, try again soon` or `Server refused connection, try again later`, the Veronica server that you chose is too busy to perform your search. Don't take it personally — either try again later or try another Veronica server. If you double-click the menu item for another Veronica server, the same search words that you typed the last time appear again in the search window. You can just click OK to repeat the search.

TIP

Veronica may well find the same item in a bunch of different places. It usually doesn't matter which item you use.

Rewriting the Map

When you start using Chameleon Gopher, its menu (or map) of Gopherspace contains the NetManage Gopher, a menu of Bookmarks, and a menu of Gopher Servers. The Bookmarks and Gopher Servers menus, however, have only one item apiece. You can add you own items to these menus to expedite finding the Gopher menus that you usually use.

Making book

As you move through Gopherspace, you often come to a menu that you want to revisit later. One way to do that is to carefully note the sequence of menus that led up to that one — but that's exactly the sort of thing that computers do better than people. Instead, you can create a Gopher *bookmark* to note your favorite places in Gopherspace.

To remember the current menu item, choose Item⇨Set Bookmark (or press Ctrl+B). Nothing seems to happen. But if you look in the Bookmarks section of your Gopherspace map, the menu item now appears there, too.

TIP

Why did they name it Veronica?

According to its authors, the name *Veronica* is just a coincidence — unrelated to Archie — because it's an acronym for the true name, which is *Very Easy Rodent-Oriented Net-wide Index to Computerized Archives.*

Another index searcher, however, is called *Jughead,* which is supposed to stand for *Jonzy's Universal Gopher Hierarchy Excavation And Display.* How gullible do they think we are? And what about Betty? And Moose?

Veronica tips

When you enter a word or words for Veronica to search for, try to be as specific as possible; otherwise, you may end up with hundreds or thousands of Gopher menu items, few of which you actually want. Typing several words is a good idea; that way, Veronica will find only items that contain *all* the words that you enter.

You can use the words *AND, OR,* and *NOT* in your search, too, as well as parentheses. If you are looking for recipes for Brazilian black beans, for example, you can use the following search instruction:

(black and beans) or feijoada

The preceding entry tells Veronica to find any item that contains the word *black* and *beans*, plus items that contain *feijoada* (the Brazilian name for a wonderful black-bean stew). The order in which the words appear in the menu item doesn't matter.

You can type an asterisk at the end of a word if you want to find all items that contain words starting with the word that you typed. If you enter **Brazil* beans**, for example, Veronica finds items that contain *Brazilian beans* and *Black beans Brazil style.*

You can also specify how many items Veronica tells you about. If you want to see only the first 50 items that Veronica finds, for example, you can add **-m50** to the end of your entry.

Finally, you can tell Veronica what type of items you are looking for by adding the following characters to the end of your search instructions:

- **-t0** (that's a zero) to find only text files
- **-t1** (that's a one) to find menus or directories
- **-t5** to find only PC programs
- **-tg** to find GIF images
- **-tI** (that's a capital *I*) to find images other than GIF files
- **-ts** to find sound clips
- **-th** to find HTML files (files designed for use on the World Wide Web, as described in Chapter 16).

We've come up with sets of bookmarks that are close to most of the items that we regularly use. The bookmarks allow us to get to our regular Gopher haunts quickly, starting from the Bookmark menu in the Gopherspace map.

Saving servers

If you find a nifty Gopher server that you'd like to add to your Gopher Servers menu, you can do it. You need to know the Internet address of the Gopher host computer, however. For example, `gopher.cpsr.org` is the Gopher server maintained by the organization Computer Professionals for Social Responsibility. Here's how to add a Gopher server to the Gopher Servers menu.

1. **Choose Item⇨Add Gopher Server.**

   You see the Add Gopher Server window, shown in Figure 15-11.

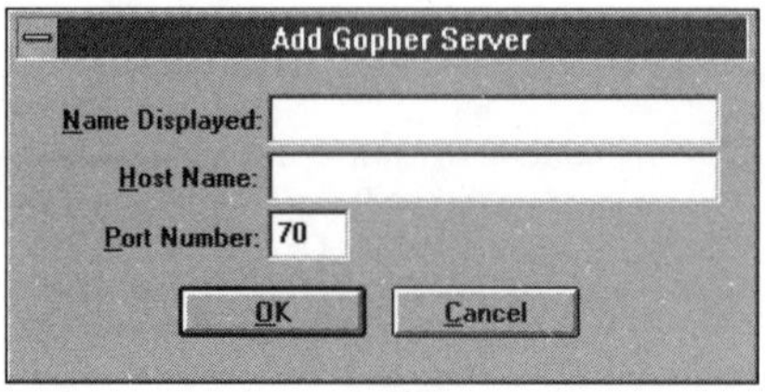

Figure 15-11: Adding your favorite Gopher servers to the Gopher Server menu.

2. **In the Name Displayed box, enter the name that you want to appear in the Gopher Server menu.**
3. **In the Host Name box, enter the Internet address of the Gopher server.**
4. **In the Port Number box, enter** `70`**.**

   Actually, the box probably already contains `70`, which turns out to be the standard port number for contacting Gophers.

5. **Click OK.**

   The server appears in your Gopher Servers menu, which is at the bottom of the Gopherspace menu.

TIP

For a list of Gopher servers, choose the item All the Gopher Servers in the World from the Other Gopher and Information Services item, which is in the Bookmarks menu. The server list is huge, and retrieving it can take several minutes, even after the information starts flowing.

TIP

To delete a Gopher server (or any other menu item), select it and then choose Item⇨Remove Item.

TIP

It's a breath mint! No, it's a floor wax! No, it's both!

The astute reader (you, of course) may be wondering why Archie and Gopher both exist. Both Archie and Gopher allow you to look for files and retrieve them. Don't the two programs really do the same thing?

Yes and no. Their original goals were quite different: Archie is an index to FTP files, and Gopher is a menuing system.

But the two systems turn out to be quite complementary. In Chapter 14, you saw lots of different ways to send a request to Archie (Chameleon Archie, mail, and so on). The Gopherologists figured that a Gopher search item is as good a way as any to send a request to Archie; they then arranged to intercept Archie's response so that the directory names that Archie returns turn into Gopher menus and the files turn into items. This arrangement enables you to use Gopher to retrieve the files that Archie found. A marriage made in heaven, no?

To find one of these Gopher-to-Archie gateways, use Veronica to search for the keyword `archie`. We don't list any here; the list of gateways changes so often that any list printed in this book would be obsolete by the time you read it.

Other Gopher Programs

Lots of other Windows versions of Gopher are available, including Gopherbook, which makes Gopher menus look like pages in a book; WinGopher, which makes each menu a separate subwindow; and HGOPHER (described in *MORE Internet for Dummies*). All these programs basically do the same thing — retrieve and display Gopher menus and files — but they do it in ways different enough that some people like one program a lot more than the others. For information on downloading and installing these programs, see Chapters 18 and 19.

The 5th Wave By Rich Tennant

"YOU MEAN TO TELL ME YOU KNEW THIS WAS SACRED INDIAN BURIAL GROUND AND YOU BUILT THE COMPUTER ROOM HERE ANYWAY?! YOU FOOL! YOU FOOL!"

Chapter 16

Swinging on the World Wide Web

In This Chapter

- What's the big deal?
- What is hypertext, and why do you care?
- What is WebSurfer?
- Another way around the Web

Telnet, FTP, Gopher — if you're beginning to think that there has to be an easier way, there is. One giant leap forward in making computers useful for ordinary mortals is the attempt to improve the interaction between computers and ordinary mortals. The efforts toward making computers do what humans would do seem to be much more fruitful than the typical approach of making humans act like computers.

The *World Wide Web* — or WWW or W3 or the Web, to its friends — is a major step forward in making the process of looking for information fast, powerful, and intuitive. WWW is based on a technology called *hypertext* — or now, more accurately, *hypermedia,* because it can handle graphics and sounds in addition to text. Hypertext was first described more than 25 years ago, but only now is it finding its way into widely used software.

Although hypertext concepts have been around for a while, creating the technology to bring them to life has been a challenge. So even though hypertext may be the coolest way to retrieve data, it's not necessarily the quickest. Setting up information for hypertext retrieval is still cumbersome, and that's one reason why more information isn't already available in hypertext form.

Hypertext: a reminiscence

The term and concept of *hypertext* were invented around 1969 by Ted Nelson, a famous computer visionary who has been thinking about the relationship between computers and literature for at least 25 years now, starting back when most people would have considered it stupid to think that such a relationship could exist. Twenty years ago, he claimed that people would have pocket computers with leatherette cases and racing stripes. We haven't seen any racing stripes yet, but otherwise, he was dead-on.

Back in 1970, Ted told us that we would all have little desk computers with inexpensive screens and super-whizzo graphical hypertext systems. "Naah," we said. "For hypertext, you'll want a mainframe with gobs of memory and a high-resolution screen." We were all right, of course, because what we have on our desks in 1994 are little computers that are faster than 1970s mainframes and that have more memory and better screens.

Various hypertext projects have come and gone over the years, including one at Brown University (of which Ted was part) and one at the Stanford Research Institute — which arguably was the most influential project in computing history because it developed screen windows and mice.

Ted's own hypertext system, Project Xanadu, has been in the works for more than 15 years, under a variety of financing and management setups, but with many of the same people slogging along and making it work. The project addresses many issues that other systems don't. In particular, Ted figured out how to pay authors for their work in a hypertext system, even when one document has pieces linked from others and the ensuing document consists almost entirely of pieces of other documents. For a decade, we have been hearing every year that Xanadu, and now a smaller Xanadu Light, will hit the streets the next year. This year, we hope that the Xanadu folks are right.

What's the Big Deal?

When you do research in an area that you know little about, you find yourself in a library, staring at the card catalog. You begin with one bit of information, such as a subject or a name. You look up one subject and begin reading the cards. New ideas flash into your mind — ways that you can continue your search with other subjects or other names. Even if you write down all the ideas, you inevitably have to pick one of them to follow; you then have to leave your current drawer and find the next, where you begin again. And again, your search may send you in an entirely different direction.

As you follow more and more leads, you may have to back up, look at choices that you made earlier, and see what would happen if you take a different tack. If you take careful notes, this process may be relatively easy, but chances are that you have to retrace many of your steps.

Hypertext organizes data to simplify this kind of information retrieval. It keeps one finger in one drawer and another finger in another drawer, so to speak, to help you to go down one path and then try a different one. Hypertext can have a hundred or more fingers in drawers all over the *planet.* (You might think of hypertext as being an extremely large — but friendly — alien centipede composed of information.)

In traditional libraries (both the kinds with books and the kinds in computers), information is organized hierarchically yet somewhat arbitrarily, in the order in which the information was entered into the system or in alphabetical order. These orders reflect nothing of the relationships among different pieces of information. In the world of hypertext, information is organized in relationship to other information. In fact, the relationships among different pieces of information often are much more valuable than the pieces themselves.

Hypertext also allows the same set of information to be arranged in multiple ways at the same time. In a conventional library, a book can be on only one shelf at a time. A book on mental health, for example, is shelved in the medicine or psychology section; it can't be in both places at the same time. Hypertext is not so limited; it's no problem to have links from both medical topics and psychological topics to the same document.

Suppose that you are interested in what influenced a particular historical person. You can begin by looking at the basic biographical information: where and when she was born, the names of her parents, her religion, and other basic stuff like that. Then you can expand on each fact by learning what else was happening at that time in her part of the world, what was happening in other parts of the world, and what influence her religion may have had on her. You draw a picture by pulling together all these pieces of information and understanding their connections — a picture that's hard to draw from just lists of names and dates.

A hypertext system creates the connections among pieces of information that enable you to find related information easily. As you draw the connections between pieces of information, you begin to envision the web created by the links between the pieces. What's so remarkable about WWW (the Web) is the fact that it connects pieces of information from around the world, on different machines, in different databases, all pretty much seamlessly — a feat that a card catalog would be hard-pressed to match.

Web pages can contain more than just text; they also can include pictures, sound, and even video clips. So you can not only read about your subject but see and hear about it, too.

What is WebSurfer?

Different WWW servers implement hypertext *browsing* programs differently. (These programs are called browsers rather than readers, partly because you usually spend more time puttering about the links than reading any individual document, and partly because all these programs potentially give you the ability to add links and comments of your own.) If you understand hypertext, you more easily understand how it works through any particular browser. Furthermore, if you find that the browser you're using is particularly difficult, you can try another. It's like underwear — you like what you like, and nobody can persuade you any differently.

Lucky you — you installed your own WWW browser, called WebSurfer, when you installed Internet Chameleon. You learn to use WebSurfer in Chapter 17. (Go ahead and skip there now if you are impatient; you won't hurt our feelings.) Chapter 17 shows you what WebSurfer is all about.

By the way, the most famous web-browser of all is called *Mosaic*. Mosaic is a fancy, mouse-driven, point-and-shoot browser invented at the National Center for Supercomputing Applications (NCSA). We're not quite sure what it has to do with supercomputing applications, but it has become extremely popular.

Note: WebSurfer and Mosaic do more or less the same thing, so when people talk about the cool places you can visit with Mosaic, you can go the same places with WebSurfer.

In WebSurfer, the hypertext links are highlighted. Use the mouse to click any highlighted word. WebSurfer retrieves a related page of information.

A Sample Web Crawl

Suppose that you are trying to decide which movie to rent tonight. You start at CERN's Virtual Library page, shown in Figure 16-1. (CERN is the group that invented the World Wide Web. See Chapter 17 for information on how to display this page on your own PC.)

Below the heading is an alphabetical list of topics. You scan down the list of topics until you come to the heading Movies, below which is the hypertext link `Movie database browser`. You click the link to display the screen shown in Figure 16-2.

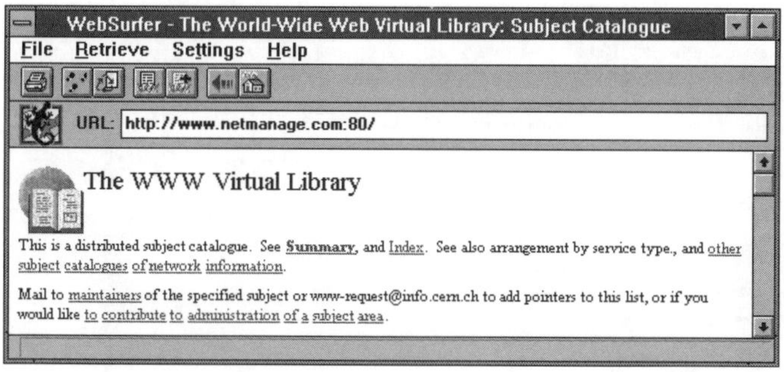

Figure 16-1: This page is like a table of contents for the Web.

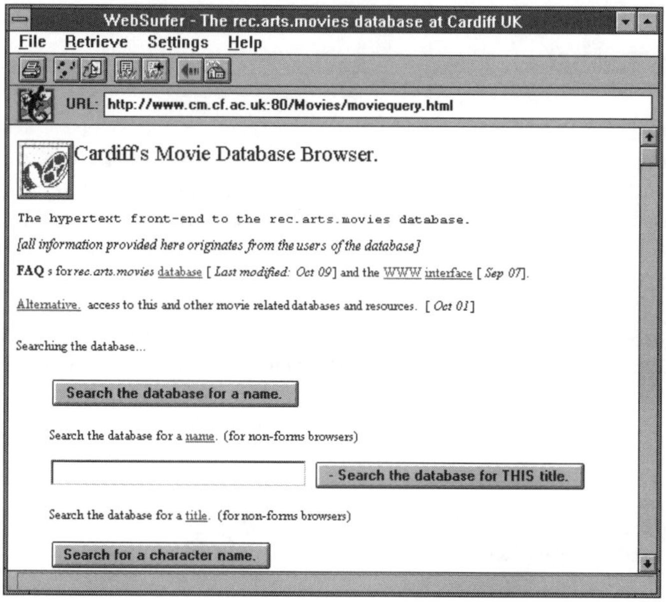

Figure 16-2: A great way to find about any movie, director, or actor.

Wow! Up pops Cardiff's Movie Database Browser. It seems to be British, based on the e-mail address provided for comments. Below this heading are several buttons and blanks that you can use to search for a specific movie, actor, or character (detailed instructions appear in Chapter 17). At the bottom of the page, you see "The rec.arts.movies top 40 films and bottom 40 films." (`Rec.arts.movies` is the Usenet newsgroup that talks about films.) This sounds like a good place for recommendations, so click top 40 films.

Voilà! There's the list of the best 40 films ever made, in the opinion of Internauts (see Figure 16-3). Each movie title is a hypertext link that leads to more information about that movie.

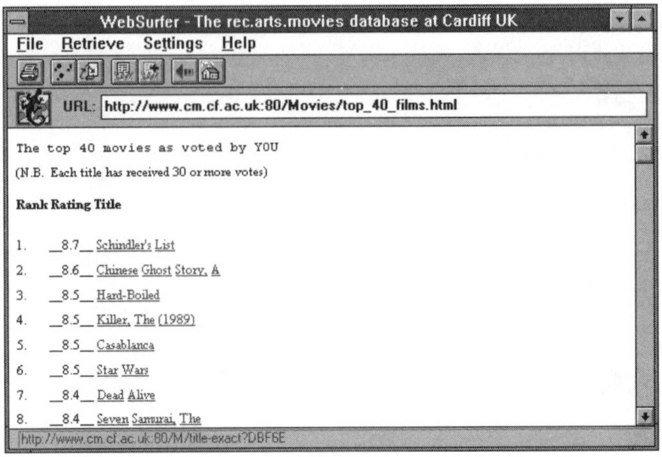

Figure 16-3: The best films ever made, according to Net nerds.

If you are interested in any of these movies, you can click its title to see the entire credits. Each name in the credits, of course, is also a hypertext link that you can click to find out what other films the person worked on. There are also links that tell you the plot, as well as links that allow you to say what you think of the movie.

Does that sound neat? It is! Although you may have to do some wandering around, you can find an amazing array of information by following the hypertext links from Web page to Web page. As you get more familiar with the Web, your searches get more efficient, because you know the most useful topic listings.

The Web Catches Gophers, Too

The material that WWW displays resides on many different servers around the world; WWW automatically contacts servers as necessary when you move to materials that those servers contain. In addition to providing a subject list as a starting point for Web walking, WWW provides access to many other network services, such as WAIS (see Chapter 20), telnet (Chapter 10), anonymous FTP (Chapter 12), Usenet newsgroups (Chapter 8), and Gopher (Chapter 15). The Web provides lists of all these kinds of servers (and indexes to these servers), so you can literally go from machine to machine and look at all that's available.

Battle of the titans: Gopher versus WAIS versus WWW

Okay, we've told you that you can use Gopher to search Archie and WAIS (described in Chapter 20), that you can use WWW to search Gopher, and that you can use WWW to search WAIS. If you can use any of them to search anything, which one should you use and when? Confusion reigns! You need guidance.

You're in luck: Guidance is our middle name. (Actually, John's middle name is Robert, but he's been thinking about changing it. Margy's never sure what her middle name is.) Following are some rules of thumb:

- Use Archie if you're trying to locate software or files available for FTP.
- Use Gopher if you're looking for something for which you suspect someone has built a Gopher menu. (After Gophering around for a while, you learn what to suspect.)
- Use WAIS to search documents by content.
- Use WWW if you're not sure what you're looking for, because the Web subsumes Archie, Gopher, and WAIS.
- Archie servers are all overloaded, so Archie is slow no matter how you use it. Use Chameleon Archie or e-mail as the mood strikes you.
- If you're not sure which Internet service to use, start with WWW. If you find that what you want is provided by Gopher or WAIS, switch.

Fame and Fortune

Another wonderful feature of WWW is the fact that the network is ever-expanding — and *you* can add to it. While we were viewing the information from the Gopher server, for example, WWW prompted us for our comments. WWW solicits comments at different levels so that you can really be involved in its growth. You can comment on the topic you're reading about, a new topic you want to discuss, WWW in general, the version of WWW that you're using, or whatever. You can enter your comments anonymously, if you want. WWW even allows you to request responses from subsequent readers.

Of course, if you really want to get serious about participating in WWW, you can create your own Web pages and run a Web server on your PC. But that's beyond the scope of this book — but we talk about that in detail in *Internet SECRETS*, coming soon from IDG Books.

Ms. Universe

Among the most useful innovations on the Web are what are known as *Universal Resource Locators,* always abbreviated as *URLs.* The point of a URL is to provide a short, consistent way to name any resource on the Net. Although URLs originally were intended for use only within WWW, they're so useful that you see them all over the place as a shorthand for FTP archives, Gopher menus, telnet servers, and (of course) WWW pages. Following is a typical URL:

```
http://sunsite.unc.edu/Dave/drfun.html
```

The `http` part says that this is a WWW page (if you care, it's *HyperText Transfer Protocol*). The name after the two slashes (`sunsite.unc.edu`) is the host name where the resource can be found, and the rest of the URL is the resource name on that host. Following is a typical URL for a Gopher menu:

```
gopher://fcc.gov/
```

The part after the two slashes is still the host name of the Gopher server. Nothing appears after the last slash in this case, which means that the URL refers to the top-level menu at the FCC Gopher server (the same FCC that regulates TV, radio, and telephone companies.) You can give this URL directly to WebSurfer or take it apart and give the host name (`fcc.gov`) to Chameleon Gopher.

The last kind of popular URL is one for a file in an anonymous FTP archive, like the following:

```
ftp://iecc.com/pub/jclt/sell.txt
```

Here, `iecc.com` is the host name, and `pub/jclt/sell.txt` is the filename on that host. Again, WebSurfer can use this URL directly, or you can use it yourself by starting Chameleon FTP, connecting to `iecc.com`, going to the directory `pub/jclt`, and retrieving the file `sell.txt`.

The People's Hypermedia

The Web is now well enough established that it is relatively easy for an individual (admittedly, an individual with some technical savvy and considerable patience) to create a WWW page. So, as you may well imagine, the results are some pretty funky pages. Figure 16-4, for example, is a page that a guy out in Santa Cruz created to keep his mother up-to-date on the activities of his kids.

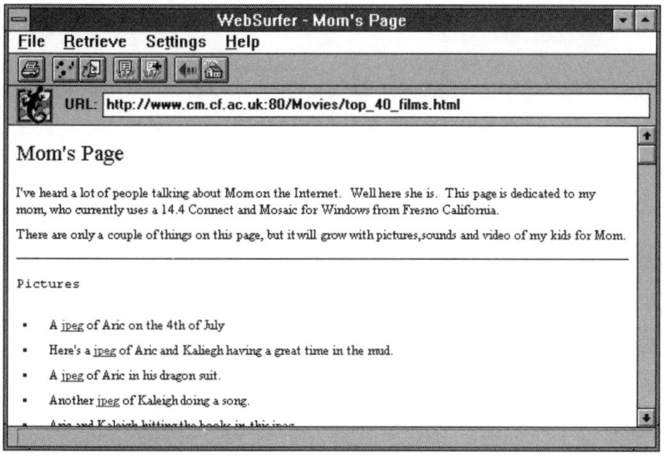

Figure 16-4: A page just for someone's mom.

Indexes Galore

TIP

Because any WWW page can link to any other Web page, we're starting to find a number of pages that exist solely to serve as indexes to collections of resources around the Net. One of the best is Scott Yanoff's Special Internet Connections page, which is updated twice a month.

Are you psyched up about the World Wide Web and WebSurfer now? Sure you are! The next chapter (drumroll, please) describes how to use WebSurfer.

Chapter 17

Using Chameleon WebSurfer

In This Chapter

- First, get some viewers
- Climbing on the Web
- Giving the Web a spin
- Tips for Web browsing
- Remembering your favorite Web pages
- Serious searching
- Grabbing files from the Web
- Changing the fonts that WebSurfer uses when displaying text
- Other Web-browsing programs

The World Wide Web (WWW) is the zoomiest, coolest Internet facility around. The Web contains lots of information, including pictures and other nontext stuff, in the form of *hypertext* (actually, *hypermedia*). As you read hypertext information, you can click words or buttons to zoom right to related information. We described the Web in some detail in Chapter 16.

To use the World Wide Web, you need WebSurfer, which comes with this book. You also need some *viewers* — programs that can display nontext information. If a page of information from the World Wide Web contains graphics in the form of a GIF file (a standard type of graphics file), you need a GIF file viewer to see it. Don't panic — it's easy to get and install viewers for all the common types of information that WWW pages contain.

TIP

For more information about Web applications like WebSurfer and the World Wide Web in general, read the Usenet newsgroups `comp.infosystems.www` and `alt.hypertext`. Also refer to Chapter 22 of *The Internet For Dummies* (IDG Books Worldwide).

First, Get Some Viewers

If you want to see GIF files, play WAV sound files, and otherwise experience the multimedia side of WebSurfer, you need some viewers. Chapter 18 describes how to get the viewers that you need. After you get a viewer, unzip it as needed, and tell File Manager about the files that the viewer works with (all these procedures are described in Chapter 18). WebSurfer can use the viewer, too.

We recommend that you get a viewer (we use the Lview program) to handle GIF and JPEG graphic files, which are common in Web pages. If your PC has a speaker, you may also want to get a sound player.

Now you are ready to do some Web swinging!

Climbing onto the Web

When you double-click the WebSurfer icon, you see the WebSurfer window, shown in Figure 17-1.

The WebSurfer window

Right below the menu bar are some interesting-looking buttons, which are described in Figure 17-1. Below the row of buttons are a graphic of a chameleon against a gorgeous pattern of colors (very tasteful) and a box that contains the URL (Universal Resource Locator) of the WWW page that you are viewing. (What's a URL? See the sidebar titled "Ms. Universe" in Chapter 16.)

Below that is a WWW page — initially, the NetManage TCP/IP for Windows page. You may want to make the WebSurfer window a little wider (by dragging its right border) so that you can see more of it. To see more of the page, you can also use the scroll bar to move the page up and down in its window.

TIP

If your Internet provider has a WWW home page (that is, a Web page that acts as a starting point for browsing the Web), you may see your provider's page rather than the NetManage page. Check it out — the page may contain information about services that you can get from your provider, hot Internet news, or other useful stuff. To see the NetManage TCP/IP for Windows page discussed here, click the Hotlist button (the burning page), which shows you a list of favorite remembered pages, and then choose the page from the list of pages.

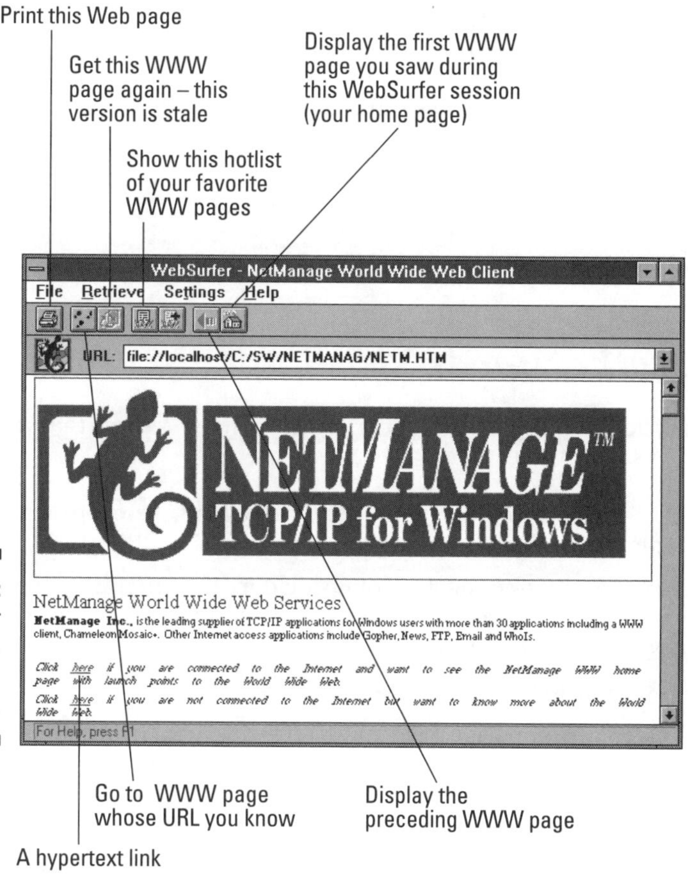

Figure 17-1: WebSurfer contains an introduction to itself.

Any word or phrase that appears underlined and in blue is a *link* — a button that you can click to see a different page. The page may be on your own PC (like the standard page shown in Figure 17-1), it may be on a World Wide Web server somewhere else in the world, or it may be a Gopher menu in disguise. When your mouse pointer points to a link, it turns into a little hand, and the URL of the link appears in the status bar at the bottom of the WebSurfer window.

TIP: You can run WebSurfer and look at its NetManage TCP/IP for Windows page without being connected to your Internet provider, because this page is stored on your own PC. However, if you're not connected, when you click a button that refers to a WWW page on a machine out on the Internet somewhere, WebSurfer tries — and fails — to connect to that machine. You see a cryptic message, complaining that WebSurfer can't resolve the Internet address of the page. Don't worry; just connect to your Internet provider and try again. If WebSurfer gets confused after failing to talk to the Internet, exit WebSurfer, connect to your Internet provider, and then run WebSurfer again.

Stop the music!

When you finish using WebSurfer, choose File⇨Exit to exit the program.

Some other pages

In this section, you do a bit of wandering through the Web, so that you can see how it looks. Follow these steps:

1. **Connect to your Internet provider by using the Custom program (see Chapter 3).**

   Actually, you can connect to your provider *after* you start running WebSurfer, if you like. You simply have to connect before you can retrieve any pages from the Internet.

2. **Run WebSurfer.**

   You see the NetManage page that is stored on your own computer. (In some cases, your provider may have arranged to see a different home page here.)

3. **Click on the link *here* in the sentence** `Click here if you are not connected to the Internet but want to know more about the World Wide Web.`

   You see a page titled Welcome to the NetManage World Wide Web (W3) Client.

4. **To see the main NetManage page stored on NetManage's own computer, click the link *here* in the sentence** `Click here to see the NetManage WWW page.`

   The little chameleon picture starts flashing psychedelic colors as WebSurfer retrieves the file that contains the Web page. There is a delay . . . still waiting . . . here we go . . . something must be happening . . . *aha!* You see the new Web page. The text appears first, and funny little symbols appear where pictures will go. Then the pictures appear one by one.

In this case, the new page is the NetManage TCP/IP Applications for Windows page (see Figure 17-2), which lives on NetManage's computer, not on your PC. The logo at the top may be the same as what's in the figure, but the rest will probably be different. Scroll down to see the latest news from NetManage.

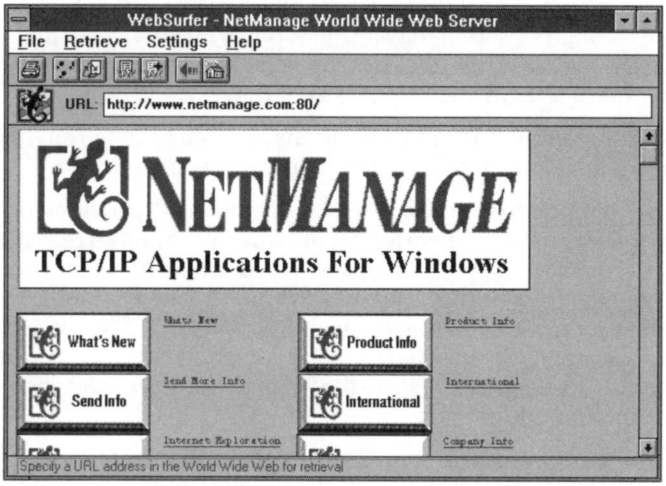

Figure 17-2: NetManage's home page, stored on their Web server.

It's a good idea to check out the NetManage page (the one stored on their computer, not the one on your PC, which is unlikely to change). On this page, NetManage may announce software upgrades or services for Chameleon users.

Tips for Browsing

Following are some tips to make your Web browsing faster and more fun:

- To see the last page you looked at, click the Previous Page button (a little blue arrow pointing left) in the toolbar. WebSurfer is so smart that it saves the pages you've already seen, so those pages appear right away. To return to the first page that you saw during this WebSurfer session, click the little house icon at the right end of the toolbar.
- To see a list of the pages that you've looked at since you started WebSurfer, choose Retrieve⇨History. You see the WebSurfer History dialog box, displaying a list of the pages that you've seen. To display a page again, double-click its title.

- Downloading the graphics files that some pages contain can take forever, especially over a phone line. If you don't care that much about graphics and would rather save time, you can tell WebSurfer not to bother with graphics files. Choose Settings⇨Preferences, select the Defer Image Display option, and click OK. Now you can't see the pictures, but you don't have to wait for them, either.
- If WebSurfer can't get through to the Web server that stores the page you want — the Web server may be busy, down for service, or just plain broken — you see one or two error messages. Just click the OK buttons to clear the messages and try again a few times.
- You can print the current Web page by choosing File⇨Print (or pressing Ctrl+P) or by clicking the printer icon on the toolbar.
- You don't have to stay connected to your Internet provider all the time that you are using WebSurfer — only when you want to retrieve a new page. To save money, you can retrieve a bunch of likely-looking pages, disconnect from the Net, and read the pages at your leisure. If you want WebSurfer to save Web pages even after you exit WebSurfer, so that you can look at those pages the next time you run WebSurfer, choose Settings⇨Preferences, choose the Save cached documents between sessions option, and click OK.
- You may run across a link on a Web page that refers to a Gopher menu rather than to another Web page. If you click on the link, WebSurfer runs Chameleon Gopher, which retrieves the Gopher menu.

Displaying Any Old WWW Page

If by chance you know the URL (the official technical name) of the WWW page that you want to see, it's easy to tell WebSurfer to get it for you. Follow these steps:

1. **Choose Retrieve⇨Go To URL.**

   WebSurfer asks for the URL.

2. **Type the URL.**

   Better yet, if you have the URL in a file on your computer somewhere, you can copy and paste the name by using the Windows Clipboard. If you have to type the name, however, be *very fastidious* about all those slashes and colons because, in a URL, every punctuation mark is sacred.

3. Click OK.

WebSurfer retrieves and displays the Web page.

Chapter 22 contains a bunch of fun Web pages that you may want to try.

Remembering Hot Places

After you find an interesting page, you need to remember how you got there, in case you want to go back there another time. No problem — WebSurfer allows you to add interesting pages to your *hotlist* so that you can return to those pages at any time. To add the current Web page to your hotlist, choose Retrieve⇨Add to Hotlist.

Later, to see your hotlist, click the icon on the toolbar of a piece of paper burning (get it?) — the fourth icon from the left. You see your hotlist in all its glory, as shown in Figure 17-3. (Sorry, this one isn't very hot.)

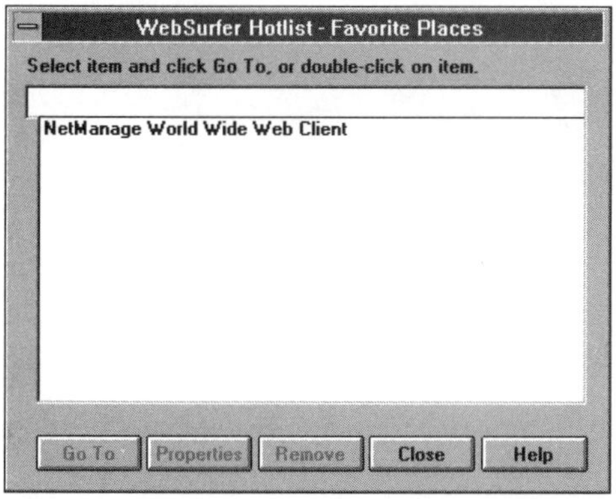

Figure 17-3: You'll have a hot time on the old Web tonight.

To see a Web page that is listed in your hotlist, just double-click its title.

If you don't like the title of a page that appears in your hotlist, you can change the title. This change doesn't affect the page itself — just the listing in the Hotlist. Select the page from the Hotlist, click the Properties button, and edit the Title setting. Then click OK to return to the Hotlist. The title may not change instantly, but it will be correct the next time that you display the Hotlist.

Serious Searching

"But where's all this information I keep hearing about?" we hear you cry. "I want to find out about agricultural practices in North Carolina!" Stay calm — it's out there. The problem is finding it.

A good place to start a series search is the Jump Point page, provided by NetManage. In the NetManage TCP/IP Applications for Windows page (refer to Figure 17-2), click the Jump Points button. Figure 17-4 shows the top of the Jump Points page.

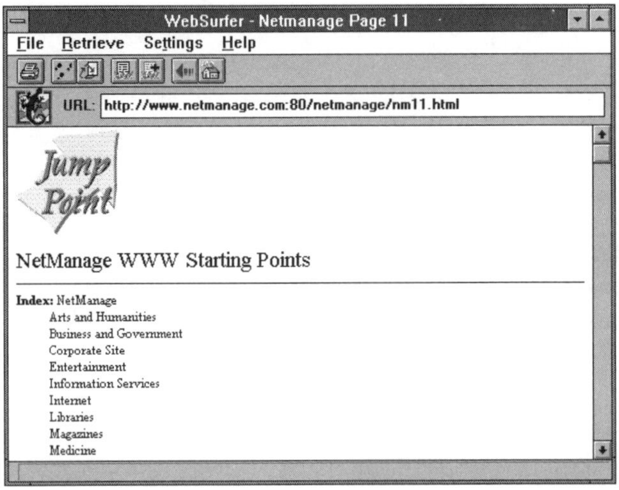

Figure 17-4: Your on-line library catalog, straight from NetManage.

If you have trouble finding the Jump Point page, choose Retrieve⇨Go To URL and enter the following URL in the box that Go To displays:

```
http://www.netmanage.com:80/netmanage/nm11.html
```

When you click OK, WebSurfer retrieves this page.

You can scroll down the list, click the subject areas that you want to see, and find an amazing array of information. Be sure to add the preceding page to your hotlist.

Another great page is CERN's Virtual Library page, which has the following URL:

```
http://info.cern.ch/hypertext/DataSources/bySubject/
          Overview.html
```

This page (shown in Figure 17-5) has a terrific collection of information and is well worth reading.

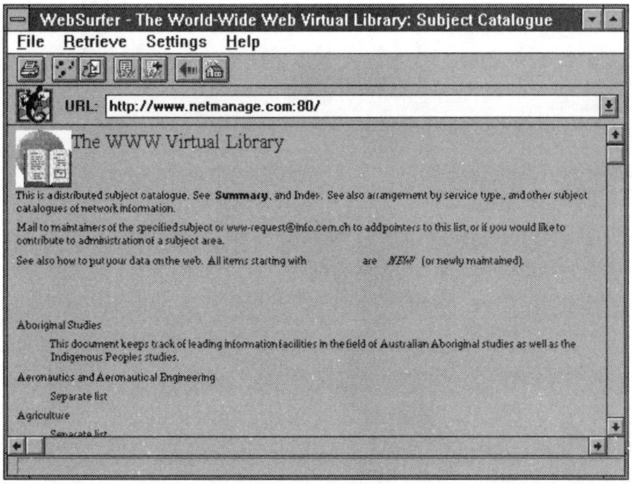

Figure 17-5: Another great library of Web pages, straight from Switzerland.

The Internet Resources List is great, too. That page has the following URL:

```
http://info.cern.ch/hypertext/DataSources/ByAccess.html
```

We put both of these pages on our hotlist right away.

Files on the Web

As if WebSurfer couldn't get you enough information already, you can use the program to get files from FTP sites. Here's how to do that:

1. **Go to an FTP URL.**

   If you want to look at the files on NetManage's own FTP server, start at the NetManage TCP/IP for Windows page on your own PC (it's in your Hotlist). Click the second *here* to see the Welcome to the NetManage World Wide Web (W3) Client page; then click *here* in the sentence `Click here to see the NetManage FTP site.`

   After a delay while WebSurfer contacts the FTP server, you see the list of the files and directories on the FTP server (see Figure 17-6). Each directory name is a link.

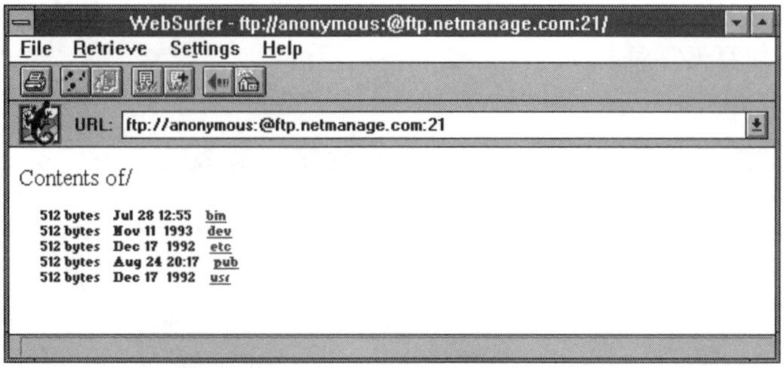

Figure 17-6: WebSurfer can show you a directory listing from an FTP server.

Another way to see FTP sites is to choose the Retrieve⇨Go To URL command and enter a URL that starts with *ftp*.

2. **Double-click directory names until you find a file that you want.**

   As you double-click each directory name, WebSurfer retrieves the listing of that directory. For all directories except the top-level one (the root), you also see a link called *Go one level up*, which returns you to the parent directory of the current directory.

3. **Double-click the file that you want to retrieve.**

   Again, no news is good news for a minute or two. If you retrieve a text file, WebSurfer displays it in Windows Notepad.

   If you retrieve a binary file (that is, anything but a text file), WebSurfer checks with the Windows File Manager and runs the appropriate program to display the file. If the file is a bitmap (BMP) file, for example, WebSurfer runs Windows Paintbrush and displays the bitmap file.

   If you want to save the file for good, be sure to use the File⇨Save As command in Notepad (or whatever viewer program you are using) to save the file with a different name than the temporary one that WebSurfer uses.

If you want to see a page in which you can browse through huge lists of FTP sites, go to the following URL:

```
http://hoohoo.ncsa.uiuc.edu:80/ftp-interface.html
```

FTP servers are frequently busy. If WebSurfer cannot get through, you see an error message. Try again later, preferably from 6 p.m. to 6 a.m. (local time for the server, not for you).

Searching for Info

You can use search programs, by way of WebSurfer, to search Gopherspace, FTP sites, and the Web itself. The following example uses the WebCrawler to search for Web pages on a given topic. Follow these steps:

1. **Display the NetManage Jump Points page.**

   For information on how to get there, refer to "Serious Searching," earlier in this chapter.

2. **Click** `Internet`**.**

   When you click this link, you move to the part of the Jump Points page that talks about Internet services.

3. **Click *here* in** `Click here for W3 searching`**.**

   You see the W3 Search Engines page, which contains a long list of ways to search the Internet.

4. **Scroll down the list to the heading Spider-based WWW Catalogs.**

   One of the great things about the Internet is the bizarre terminology that folks come up with. Because the WWW is a "web," a program that moves around it must be a *spider*! The WebCrawler folks wrote a program that crawls around the Web, collecting information about all the pages it finds, and then sticks that information in a huge database. You can search this database. The first entry in the Spider-based WWW Catalogs section allows you to use the WebCrawler (see Figure 17-7).

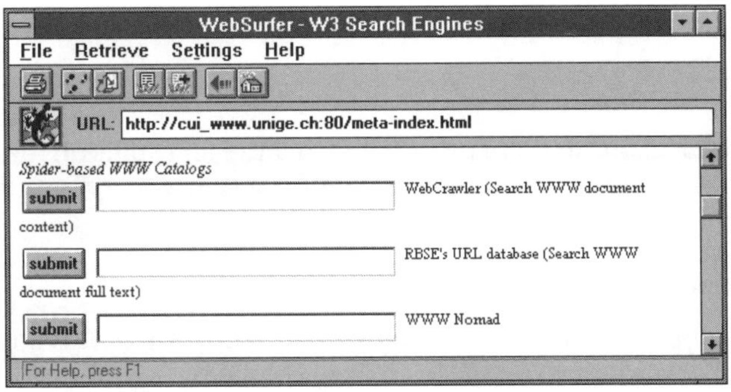

Figure 17-7: Fill in the blank and click the `submit` button to search the Web for a topic.

5. **In the WebCrawler (search WWW document content) box, enter a word or phrase that you want information about.**

   If you are thinking about moving to Brazil, for example, enter **Brazil.**

6. **Double-click the Submit button to the left of the WebCrawler item.**

   Almost instantly (how can the search be so fast?), you see a Web page displaying a list of related topics (see Figure 17-8).

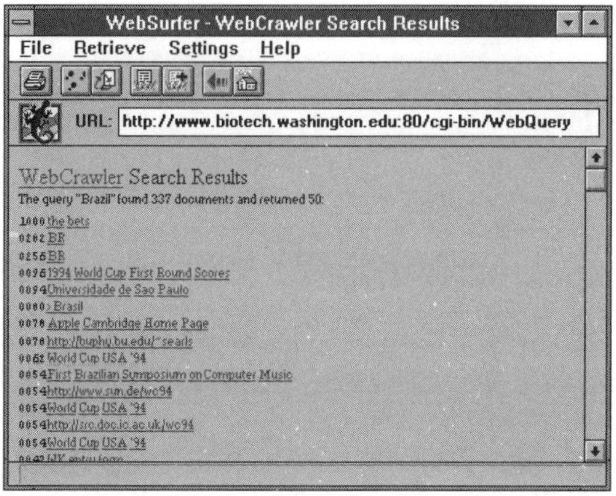

Figure 17-8: Lots of Web pages about Brazil.

TIP: For a fuller explanation of using the WebCrawler, click the `WebCrawler` link farther down in the W3 Search Engines page.

Changing the Fonts

If the text that WebSurfer displays is so big that the text spills off the right edge of the window, you can make the text smaller. You can also change the colors of regular text and links. Follow these steps:

1. **Choose Settings⇨Style Schemes.**

   You see the WebSurfer Style Schemes dialog box, shown in Figure 17-9. The Preview window, on the left side of the dialog box, shows how the various elements of a Web page appear on your screen. The right side of the dialog box is where you can make your formatting changes.

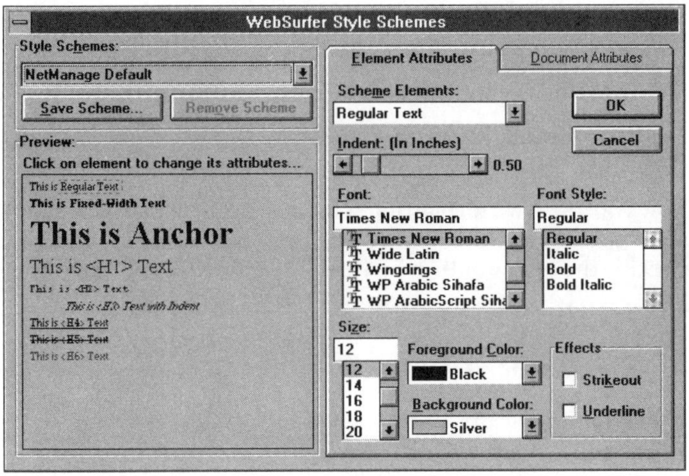

Figure 17-9: You can choose what fonts to use for all the elements of a Web page.

2. **Click the Document Attributes folder tab in the upper-right section of the dialog box.**

   Now you see settings that affect the way the whole Web page looks, not just one type of text. You can change the background color by clicking the Document Color option, but it's better not to; many Web pages are designed to have gray backgrounds and look a little funny with another color.

3. **To make all the fonts one point bigger, click the Increase button in the Overall Font Size section.**

   You can click this button more than once; WebSurfer makes all the fonts one point larger each time you click the button. You can see the difference in the Preview window.

4. **Click the Element Attributes folder tab.**

   Now you see settings that affect one type of text. In the Preview window, one of the lines of text (probably *This is Regular Text*) is outlined with a dotted line. Because this line is selected, the settings that you see are for regular text.

5. **For each type of text that you want to reformat, click the sample line in the Preview window and then change the formatting settings.**

   To make the titles smaller, for example, click *This is Title* in the Preview window, and then change the Size setting.

6. **When you finish making changes, save your new formatting scheme with a new name by clicking the Save Scheme button.**

   WebSurfer asks you for the name of the new formatting scheme.

7. **Type something like** `Margy's Scheme` **(if your name is Margy) and then click OK.**

   Now you have two formatting schemes: the original NetManage default scheme and your new one. You can switch between the schemes by clicking the arrow button to the right of the Style Schemes box (in the upper-left corner of the window) and then choosing the scheme that you want to use.

8. **When you finish, click OK.**

   WebSurfer displays a standard font dialog box from which you can choose the font and size. We usually leave the fonts alone because the NetManage people have chosen pretty well, but we make them a little bigger. (Are we going blind? Or just getting older?)

Other Web Browsers

Two other fine Web browsing programs are NCSA Mosaic (the most widely used Web browser and the ancestor of most other programs called Mosaic) and Cello. Both of these programs run under Windows, work with your WinSock SLIP connection to the Internet, and display WWW information on your screen, including graphics and other types of files. And they're *free* to boot. See Chapters 18 and 23 for more information about how to get them, or stick with Chameleon WebSurfer.

Part V

Neat Stuff from the Net

"I'M ALWAYS AMAZED AT THE TECHNOLOGICAL ADVANCES MADE AT PR FIRMS."

In this part . . .

This part is a compendium of ready references and useful facts (which implies, we suppose, that the other chapters are full of useless facts, but we hope not). It includes how to find and install swell free and shareware Internet software from the Net itself, as well as a bunch of fun and useful places to start your network explorations. Three handy Appendixes round out Part V.

Chapter 18

Grabbing Software over the Net

In This Chapter

- Uncompressing compressed files with WinZip
- Installing software in Windows Program Manager
- Associating programs with file extensions in File Manager
- Checking software for viruses

After you have installed Internet Chameleon, you are ready to grab software right off the Internet. Lots of programs are available as freeware or shareware by FTP.

First, though, you need to know a few things about downloading and running software from the Net, and this chapter tells you about them. You need a few well-chosen software tools, including a program to uncompress compressed files. Useful little programs like this are usually called *utilities* in computer jargon.

If you haven't read Chapter 12, read it now to find out how to use Chameleon FTP to copy files, including software, to your PC. When you are ready to download some software, see Chapter 19 for a list of interesting programs to try.

Where to Put Things

We recommend that you make a directory called something like `util` where you can put all the programs that you download. You can put them all in this directory, or you can create a subdirectory for each one — your choice. Just don't go sticking all this new software into the NetManage program directory or directories for other programs; when time comes to update your software, things will get too confusing.

To create a directory named `util`, run the Windows File Manager, choose File⇨Create Directory, and type **c:\util** in the Name box. When you click OK, you get a new directory.

TIP

We keep the floppy disks for our software in a big disk box. If our hard disk ever goes west and we have trouble restoring our tape backups, we can always use these floppy disks to reinstall our software. But what about the software that we get from the Net? Simple — we always copy the program files (usually, one big ZIP file) for the software we get from the Net to a floppy disk, label it, and add it to our program disk collection. This practice makes it easier to share downloaded software with friends, too.

Ready to Decompress: WinZip

You need an unzipping program to deal with compressed files, specifically those with the file extension ZIP (these files are called, amazingly, *ZIP files*). Programs with names like PKZIP, PKUNZIP, and UNZIP have been around for years, and you may already have one.

PKUNZIP and its brethren work fine, but they are DOS programs and not very convenient to use from Windows; it's annoying to use the MS-DOS icon every time you want to run one of these programs. Luckily, someone (a nice guy named Nico Mak) wrote a terrific little Windows program called WinZip that can both zip and unzip things for you right in Windows.

TIP

What about PKZIP and PKUNZIP?

If you've been zipping and unzipping files for a while, you probably have — and use — the PKZIP and PKUNZIP programs. These programs have been around much longer than WinZip has, and they run under DOS. The original version of WinZip, in fact, ran PKZIP and PKUNZIP behind the scenes to do the actual zipping and unzipping.

If you are an old-fashioned kind of person and want PKZIP and PKUNZIP, those programs are available by FTP. The FTP site `oak.oakland.edu` has them in the directory named `/pub/msdos/zip`, in a file named `pkz204g.exe`.

PKZIP and PKUNZIP are shareware. To register your copies, send $47 to PKWare, Inc., 7545 N. Port Washington Road, Glendale, WI 53217-3422. You can also register on-line with a credit card on the PKWare Support Bulletin Board System at 414-352-7176.

Grabbing WinZip

Installing WinZip involves three major steps: copy the files, unzip WinZip, and run the setup program.

TIP

If you already have WinZip (which is also available by mail or from various shareware outlets), skip this entire section. If you have and love PKZIP and PKUNZIP or UNZIP and don't mind running them from DOS, you can skip this section, too.

To connect to the FTP server at `ftp.cica.indiana.edu` and download `winzip55.exe` from the `win3/util` directory, follow these steps:

1. **Connect to the Internet.**

   That is, run the Custom program, as described in Chapter 3.

2. **When you are connected, run Chameleon FTP.**

3. **Choose Connect from the menu.**

   You see the Connect dialog box.

4. **In the Host box, enter** ftp.cica.indiana.edu.

5. **In the User box, enter** anonymous.

6. **In the Password box, enter your e-mail address.**

7. **Click OK to connect to the FTP server.**

   Chameleon FTP connects and gets a listing of the directories on the FTP server.

8. **In the Local part of the FTP window, change to a temporary directory, such as the `\temp` directory.**

   Don't specify the directory where you want to store the WinZip program in the long run; give the name of a temporary holding place for the program files.

9. **In the Remote part of the window, double-click `win`; then double-click `util`.**

   You move to the `win3/util` directory on the FTP server, which contains WinZip. FTP displays the names of files in the current directory.

10. **Scroll down until you see a file name that begins with WINZIP and has the extension EXE, and select it.**

    As of this writing, the latest version is called `winzip55.exe` (it may have another name if a newer version exists). This is a self-extracting file — that is, it can unzip itself.

11. **Make sure that Binary is selected in the Transfer box.**

12. **Click the left-pointing arrow to the left of the Copy label.**

    FTP copies the file from the FTP server to your PC.

13. **Choose Disconnect from the menu to disconnect from the FTP server.**

14. **Choose File⇨Exit to exit Chameleon FTP.**

    Or leave the program running if you'll be downloading more software soon.

If you have trouble getting the files from the `ftp.cica.indiana.edu` FTP server, you can use Archie to search for the file on other servers. Or FTP to `oak.oakland.edu` and look in the `/pub/msdos/windows3` directory. Or connect to the Internet For Dummies FTP server at `ftp.dummies.com`. When we wrote this book, WinZip 5.5 was the latest, greatest version. If a newer one comes out, we'll try to have it.

Uncompressing WinZip

Now you can unzip the EXE file that contains WinZip (say that three times fast!). Because you downloaded a self-extracting version of WinZip, it can unzip itself.

To uncompress WinZip, run File Manager; find the file `winzip55.exe`, which you just downloaded; and double-click the filename. The self-extracting part of the program starts and explodes into the WinZip program itself (named `winzip.exe`), a setup program, a Windows help file, and some text files.

At this point, you can delete `winzip55.exe`, perhaps after copying it to a floppy disk for your software disk archive.

Setting it up

WinZip 5.5 comes with its own little setup program, which gets it ready for you to use. Among other things, the setup program copies its files to a new directory (usually called `c:\windows\winzip`), creates an icon for WinZip in Program Manager, and tells File Manager to use WinZip to handle all your ZIP files. To install WinZip, follow these steps:

1. **In Windows File Manager, find the `setup.exe` program in the directory into which you put the WinZip program, and double-click it.**

   This action runs the WinZip setup program, which asks you what directory you want WinZip installed in. It usually suggests `c:\windows\winzip`; we prefer `c:\util\winzip`, ourselves.

2. **Correct the WinZip program if you don't like the directory that it suggests and then click OK.**

   You have to specify a different directory than the one where the files are now. When the setup program is done installing files, it displays a welcome message.

3. **Read the message, and then click OK.**

   Next, you see information about WinZip's license agreement.

4. **Read the information, and then click Yes.**

   You see a window that asks about unarchiving and uncompressing programs that work with WinZip (see Figure 18-1).

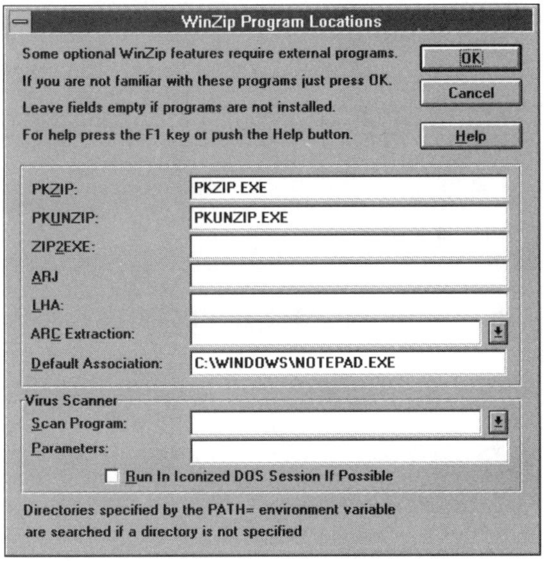

Figure 18-1: WinZip can automatically run other archiving and compression programs.

5. **Enter the directories and filenames of any compression programs that you know you have. If you don't know whether you have any, just leave everything as it is. Then click OK.**

   You see a message asking whether to create a program group and icons for WinZip.

6. **Click Yes.**

   WinZip creates a program group for WinZip. This program group contains icons for WinZip itself, as well as for its uninstall program and some help files.

You see a dialog box, asking how WinZip should work with File Manager (see Figure 18-2).

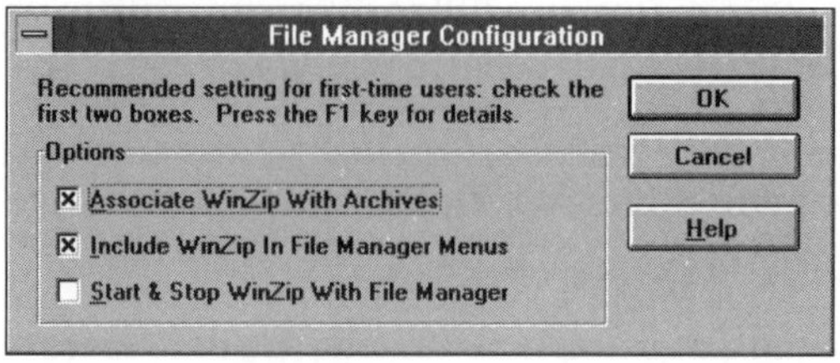

Figure 18-2: How should WinZip work with File Manager?

7. **Leave the first two boxes checked, and click OK.**

   You can click Help for more information on what these buttons do.

   WinZip associates itself with ZIP files in the mind of File Manager. That is, it tells File Manager that whenever you double-click a ZIP file, File Manager should run WinZip to handle the ZIP file. WinZip also adds a WinZip command to the File Manager menu bar. Cool!

   Finally, you see an upgrade notice, telling you ways in which WinZip 5.5 is niftier than previous versions.

8. **Click OK.**

   You see the WinZip window, shown in Figure 18-3.

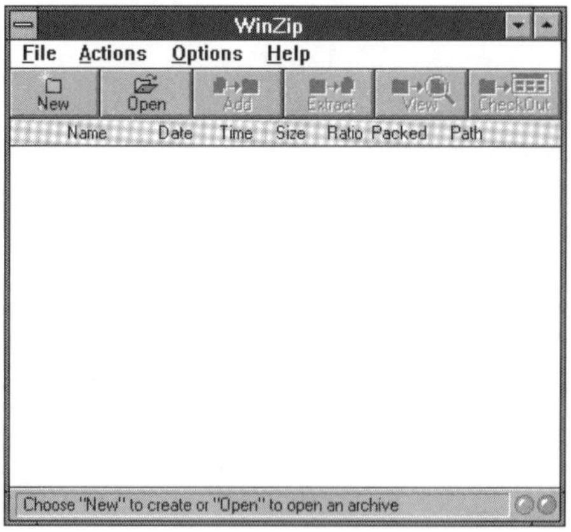

Figure 18-3: WinZip is ready to deal with your ZIP files.

Now File Manager knows that if you double-click a ZIP file, it should run WinZip to deal with it. Alternatively, you can run WinZip by double-clicking its icon. Very handy!

Remember that even though you got this program for free, it's shareware. If you like it, follow the instructions in the section "Doing Your Part" at the end of this chapter to register your copy.

What's in that ZIP file?

To open a ZIP file (which the WinZip folks call an *archive*), click the Open button on the toolbar, and then choose the directory and filename for the ZIP file. Poof! WinZip displays a list of the files in the archive, with their dates and sizes.

WinZip remembers the last four ZIP files that you opened and lists them at the bottom of the File menu, making it easy for you to reopen a ZIP file that you used recently.

Another way to open a ZIP file is to double-click its filename in File Manager. File Manager knows what to do with ZIP files: run WinZip!

Unzip it!

Sounds suggestive, we know, but it's not as much fun as it sounds. If you want to use a file from a ZIP file, after you open the ZIP file, you *extract* it — that is, you ask WinZip to uncompress the file and store it.

To extract a file, follow these steps:

1. **Choose it from the list of files.**

   You can choose a group of files that are listed together by clicking the first one and then Shift+clicking the last one. To select an additional file, Ctrl+click it.

2. **Click the Extract button on the toolbar.**

   The Extract dialog box asks which directory you want to put the file in and whether you want to extract all the files in the archive or just the one you selected (see Figure 18-4).

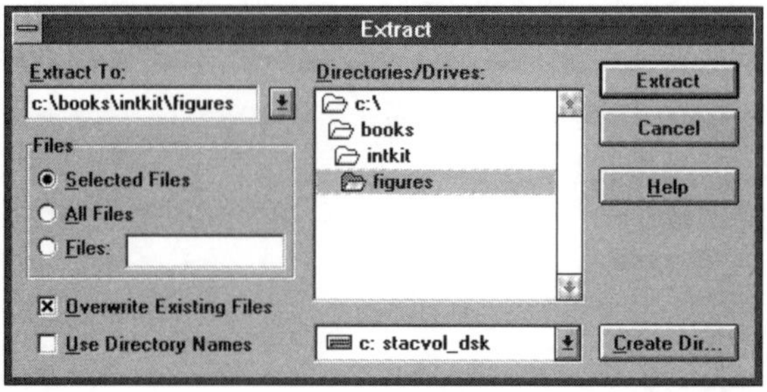

Figure 18-4: Where would you like WinZip to put your files?

3. **Select the directory in which you want to store the unzipped files.**
4. **Click OK.**

   WinZip unzips the file. The ZIP file is unchanged, but now you also have the uncompressed file (or files).

Zip it!

To add a file to a ZIP file, follow these steps:

1. **Open the ZIP file by clicking the Open button on the toolbar.**

   The list of filenames in the ZIP file appears in the WinZip window.

2. **Click the Add button on the toolbar.**

   You see the Add dialog box, shown in Figure 18-5.

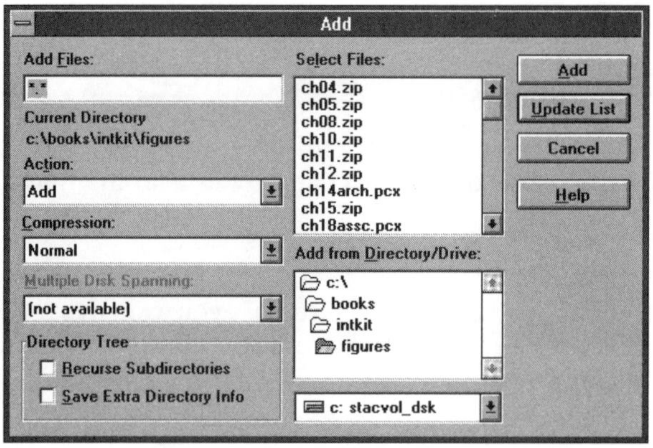

Figure 18-5: Adding a file to a ZIP file.

3. **Use the Add from Directory/Drive box to select the directory that contains the file (or files) that you want to add.**

   To choose the files, select them from the Select Files list.

4. **Choose a setting for the Action box.**

   Decide whether you want WinZip to compress the files into the ZIP file, leaving the original files untouched (Add), or whether you want WinZip to delete the original files after they have been added (Move).

5. **Click the Add or Move button to do the deed.**

Making your own ZIP file

To make a new ZIP file, follow these steps:

1. **Click the New button on the toolbar.**
2. **Choose the directory in which you want to store the new ZIP file, and enter a name for the file.**

   Make sure that the file extension is ZIP (or omit the file extension; WinZip adds ZIP itself).

3. **Click OK.**
4. **Add files to your new ZIP file, as explained in the preceding section.**

Zipped out?

When you finish zipping and unzipping, quit WinZip by choosing File⇨Exit.

TIP

If you later move WinZip to a different directory or just want to be sure that the associations are correct, choose Options⇨File Manager Configuration, check the Associate WinZip with Archives checkbox, and click OK.

TIP

News for hard-core downloaders

Nico Mak, the author of WinZip, points out a new feature of WinZip 5.5 that is especially useful for folks like yourself who grab software from the Internet. He says:

"After downloading and trying a lot of Windows programs, you'll find your hard disk gets filled quickly, even if you delete the program icons. This is because the SETUP or INSTALL programs for most programs silently copy files into various directories, including your Windows and System directories. They'll also modify your INI (initialization) files and sometimes the registration database. Simply deleting the icon doesn't get rid of these files.

"That's where WinZip's Install/Try/Uninstall feature comes in handy. It runs the install program in a ZIP file; gives you a chance to try the program; *optionally* deletes any new files, icons, and program groups; and restores any altered INI files, restoring your hard disk to its original state. If a ZIP file doesn't contain a SETUP or INSTALL program, the CheckOut feature provides a good way to try out software distributed in ZIP files. To use these features, just open a ZIP file and click the rightmost button (CheckOut) in the WinZip toolbar."

He's right — it's a great new feature!

Netting a Program

Now you are ready to grab software from the Net, unzip it as necessary, and make a little icon for it. This section gives you general instructions for getting a program off the Internet and installing it on your PC.

We are assuming that you know which program you want and that you know which FTP server has it. Chapter 19 contains a list of programs that we recommend, with information on which FTP servers you can find them on. The programs include mailers, newsreaders, Gopher programs, Web browsers, and viewers for use with Gopher and WebSurfer.

Getting hold of the program

To copy the file from the FTP server to your own computer, follow these steps:

1. **If you want to make a separate directory for the program, do so.**

   Otherwise, you can store the program in your `\util` directory.

2. **Connect to the Internet, as described in Chapter 3.**
3. **Run Chameleon FTP, and connect to the FTP server that has the program you want.**

4. **Choose the directory on the FTP server that contains the file you want and the directory on your computer in which to put it.**

   Use the Local part of the window to change to the directory on your computer where you want to store the files. Use the Remote part to change to the directory on the server that contains the files.

5. **Make sure that the Transfer is set to Binary.**

6. **In the Remote Files list, select the file(s) that you want to download.**

   To select more than one file, click the first one and then Ctrl+click the others.

7. **Click the left-pointing arrow to the left of the Copy label.**

   FTP downloads the file(s).

8. **Choose Disconnect from the menu; then choose File⇨Exit to leave Chameleon FTP.**

9. **Disconnect from the Internet to save connect charges, as described in Chapter 3.**

Unzipping the program files

Most programs are stored on FTP servers in ZIP files, both to save disk space on the FTP server and to save transfer time. If the program isn't in a ZIP file, skip this section. Here's how to unzip your ZIP file:

1. **In Windows File Manager, double-click the ZIP file.**

   This step runs WinZip and opens the ZIP file. WinZip shows you the files that the ZIP file contains.

2. **Click the Extract button on the toolbar.**

   You see the Extract dialog box.

3. **In the Extract To box, type the full path name of the directory in which you want the files to be stored.**

   Alternatively, you can use the directory box to its right to choose the directory.

4. **Choose All Files so that you extract all the files in the ZIP file.**

5. **Click Extract.**

   WinZip begins copying and uncompressing the files from the ZIP file to their new home. As long as WinZip is uncompressing files, the little light in the lower-right corner of the WinZip window remains red. When WinZip finishes, the light turns green. (Is this cute, or what?)

6. **To leave WinZip, choose File➪Exit.**
7. **Now that you have uncompressed the files that are in the ZIP file, delete the ZIP file if you need the space on your disk.**

TIP

If the ZIP file contains any file named READ.ME or README.TXT or anything else with a TXT or DOC extension, read it by using Windows Notepad or your word-processing program. The file may contain instructions for installing and configuring the program that are more accurate than what we are about to tell you.

Installing the program

Now the program is ready to run, but there is no icon for it. A few housekeeping tasks remain to be done. If the program uses files as input, associate the program with the appropriate file extension — that is, tell File Manager that when you double-click a file that has a particular file extension, you want File Manager to run this program to handle the file. These programs include editors, word processors, drawing programs, and other programs that store their data in files. For programs that don't work on input files, you don't need to do this, so skip to step 5.

Here's how to tell File Manager about the program and make an icon for it:

1. **In File Manager, choose File➪Associate.**

   You see the window shown in Figure 18-6.

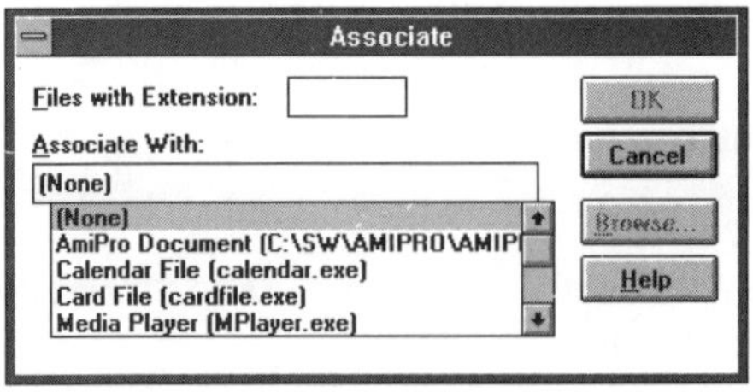

Figure 18-6: Associating programs with file extensions.

2. **In the Files with Extension box, type the file extension that the program uses; then press the Tab key.**

   File Manager shows you what program, if any, is currently associated with that type of file.

3. **In the Associate With box, type the full path name of the program.**
4. **Click OK.**

   Now you can make an icon for the program.
5. **Open both Program Manager and File Manager, and arrange the screen so that you can see the program group that you want to put the icon in (in Program Manager) and the program name (in File Manager).**
6. **Drag the program name from File Manager into Program Manager, and place it in the program group where you want it.**

   You see a new icon in your new program group.

Configuring the program

Now you can run the program by double-clicking its icon. Hooray!

You may have to tell the program, however, about your Internet address or your computer or who knows what before it can do its job. Refer to the text files, if any, that came with the program, or choose Help from the program's menu bar to get more information about how to configure and run your new program.

Now that you know how to install software that you get from the Internet, you're ready for the next topic: safe software.

Scanning for Viruses

We all know that you practice safe software — that is, you check every new program you get to make sure that it doesn't contain any hidden software viruses that might display obnoxious messages or trash your hard disk. If this is true of you, you can skip this section.

For the rest of you, it would be a good idea to use a virus-scanning program. You never know what naughty piece of code you may unwittingly FTP to your defenseless computer otherwise!

If you use MS-DOS 6.2 (or later)

DOS 6.2 comes with a virus checker built right into File Manager.

Follow these steps to use the virus checker:

1. **Run File Manager.**
2. **Choose Tools➪Antivirus.**

   You see the Microsoft Anti-Virus window.
3. **Choose a disk drive by choosing it from the Drives box.**
4. **Click the Detect and Clean button.**

   If you are scanning a large hard disk for viruses, this step can take several minutes.

TIP: It's a good idea to run Anti-Virus after you obtain and run any new piece of software. The FTP servers on the Internet make every effort to keep their software archives virus-free, but nobody is perfect. Don't get caught by some prankster's idea of a joke!

If you don't use MS-DOS 6.2

It costs about $10 to upgrade from DOS 6.0 or 6.1 to 6.2, so we suggest that you just do that. DOS 6.2 has lots of nice little features, and it installs easily and quickly.

If you don't want to do this, many virus-checkers are available on the Net. Use your FTP program to connect to `oak.oakland.edu`, and go to the `/pub/msdos/virus` directory. Follow the instructions in the rest of this chapter for downloading and installing software from the Net.

Doing Your Part

After you've used a new program for a while — perhaps for a few weeks — you should begin to feel guilty. Someone has gone to enormous effort to make this wonderful piece of software, and you haven't even said thank you. It's time to Do Your Part.

Free versus not-quite-free

Software that comes from the Internet falls into two broad categories:

- **Freeware:** given away for free. There may be restrictions on what you can do with it; most freeware owners don't allow you to resell their programs, for example. Many of the programs on the Internet are freeware.
- **Shareware:** given away for a limited trial period. If you plan to continue to use the program, you are honor-bound to pay for it. WinZip is a shareware program.

To find out which category your new program falls into, choose Help➪About or look for other menu choices that offer information about registering. WinZip, for example, has a command called Help➪Ordering Information.

If you are using a shareware program and you find it to be valuable, go ahead and pay up. Shareware never costs a great deal of money, and you become a registered user, entitled to receive information about updates and related programs. Besides, you feel great about what a wonderful, generous person you are. (***Note:*** Neither of the authors of this book distributes any shareware programs, so we have no vested interest.)

Registering WinZip

To pay by check, send $29 to Nico Mak, P.O. Box 919, Bristol, CT 06011-0919. To print an order form to submit to your company for payment, choose Help➪Ordering Information from the WinZip menu bar, and then choose File➪Print Topic from the WinZip Help menu bar. To pay by credit card, call the Public (software) Library at 800-2424-PsL or 713-524-6394. You can also mail credit-card orders to PsL at P.O. Box 35705, Houston, TX 77235-5705. To congratulate Mr. Mak on a job well done, you can e-mail him at `70056.241@compuserve.com`. Dedicated WinZip-pers may also want to order the attractive WinZip T-shirt or sweatshirt, which are suitable for all occasions.

Chapter 19

Other Cool Windows Internet Programs

In This Chapter

- WinSock-compatible programs that work with Internet Chameleon
- Viewers for use with Gopher and WebSurfer
- Other interesting stuff

The Internet has thousands of programs that are free for the taking. But what software is out there, and where is it? This chapter tells you about the software that we think you may find useful: other WinSock-compatible Internet applications, viewer programs that you can use with Gopher and WebSurfer, and other useful stuff.

Of course, lots of commercial Internet programs are coming out these days. But we don't need to tell you about them — you are probably already getting blitzed by advertising about them. And most of them are no better than the excellent package that comes with this book: Internet Chameleon.

Note: In many cases, we're not going to tell you the exact name of the file to download, because new versions of software come out all the time, with new version numbers, and the filenames usually change to match. Instead, we'll give you the first few letters of the filename, up to the version number. You won't have any trouble finding the files that we're talking about.

TIP: Many FTP software archives contain `readme` or `readme.txt` files, or you may see files with names like `00index.txt`, which usually contain information about the file in the current directory. Before you transfer any other files, download these files (using ASCII as the transfer type) and read them (using Windows Notepad or your word processor). The information in these files may be more up to date than what we've written here.

Sock Me Some WinSock Programs

We think that the programs that make up Internet Chameleon are terrific, but everyone has personal preferences. Here are other programs you can use instead. These are *WinSock* programs, which means that they're designed to work with *Windows Sockets*: a standard way to connect Windows programs to TCP/IP and the Internet. Fortunately, Chameleon has a swell built-in version of WinSock, so all these programs work with Chameleon.

For up-to-the-minute information on new WinSock programs, read the Usenet newsgroup `alt.winsock`. At the end of this chapter are suggestions for other ways to find out about new programs.

Mailers

These programs allow to you send and receive e-mail, as described in Chapter 5. You've already got Chameleon Mail, which does a nice job (see Chapter 4).

Win QVT/NET (described later in this chapter) also handles e-mail, as do many Usenet newsreaders.

Eudora

FTP to `ftp.qualcomm.com`, change to the `/quest/windows/eudora/1.4` directory, and download a ZIP file whose name begins with `eudora`. Or FTP to `gatekeeper.dec.com` and look in the `/.f/micro/msdos/win3/winsock` directory. Or FTP to `ftp.cica.indiana.edu` and look in the `/pub/pc/win3/winsock` directory. Or FTP to `sunsite.unc.edu` and look in the `/pub/micro/pc-stuff/ms-windows/winsock/apps` directory.

Eudora is a very popular commercial e-mail program written by Qualcomm Inc., and a scaled-down version is available as freeware. The freeware version doesn't handle automatic mail sorting, but it is otherwise very nice. The `Eudor2Info` EXE files in `/quest/windows/eudora` are self-extracting ZIP files that contain information about the commercial versions of the program. For more information about Eudora, send e-mail to `eudora-sales@qualcomm.com`. The commercial version isn't very expensive, and we know people who prefer it to Chameleon Mail.

Pegasus Mail

FTP to `risc.ua.edu`, change to the `/pub/network/pegasus` directory, and download a ZIP file whose name begins with `winpm`.

This popular freeware mail package doesn't have all the fancy features of either Chameleon Mail or Eudora, but the price is right: It's free. You can contact the author at `jford@seebeck.ua.edu`.

RFD Mail

FTP to `ftp.std.com`, change to the `/customers/software/rfdmail` directory, and download a ZIP file whose name begins with `rfdml` or `rfdmail`. Or FTP to `garbo.uwasa.fi` (yes, it's in Finland) and look in `/windows/comm`. Be sure to use version 1.22 or later.

This shareware mail program has been around for a while and just added SLIP/WinSock capabilities. For more information, send a note to the program's author, David Yon, at `rfdmail@world.std.com`.

Winelm

FTP to `ftp.cica.indiana.edu`, change to the `/pub/pc/win3/winsock` directory, and download `winelm.zip`. Or FTP to `gatekeeper.dec.com` and look in the `/.f/micro/msdos/win3/winsock` directory. Or FTP to `garbo.uwasa.fi` (yes, it's in Finland; use this site if you're in Europe) and look in `/windows/winsock`.

If you're an old UNIX wizard who is addicted to using the UNIX `elm` mailreader, this is just the program for you. Otherwise, forget it.

Newsreaders

These programs allow you to read Usenet newsgroups, as described in Chapter 7. You already have NEWTNews, an excellent newsreader (see Chapter 8).

Win QVT/NET (described later in this chapter) also handles Usenet news.

Trumpet

FTP to `ftp.utas.edu.au`, change to the `/pc/trumpet/wintrump` directory, and download a ZIP file whose name begins with `wtwsk`. Or FTP to `garbo.uwasa.fi` (yes, it's in Finland) and look in `/windows/winsock`. Or FTP to `ftp.cica.indiana.edu` and look in the `/pub/pc/win3/winsock` directory.

Trumpet is a widely-used shareware, WinSock-compatible newsreader written by Peter R. Tattam of the University of Tasmania. Don't confuse Trumpet the newsreader with Trumpet WinSock, a SLIP connection package (which you don't need, because you use Chameleon).

WinVN

FTP to ftp.cica.indiana.edu, change to the /pub/pc/win3/winsock directory, and download a ZIP file whose name starts with winvn. Or FTP to gatekeeper.dec.com and look in the /.f/micro/msdos/win3/winsock directory. Or FTP to sunsite.unc.edu and look in the /pub/micro/pc-stuff/ms-windows/winsock/apps directory. Or FTP to garbo.uwasa.fi (yes, it's in Finland) and look in the /windows/comm directory.

This public-domain newsreader handles threading (grouping related articles together), which can make newsreading a lot faster, and has a built-in uudecoder.

Telnet programs

These programs allow you to log in to remote computers, as described in Chapter 10. You've already got Chameleon Telnet, which works great, so we don't see much point in using any of the others. If you connect to IBM mainframe systems, however, you may want to try a 3270 version of Telnet, because that's the native terminal for IBM systems.

EWAN Telnet

FTP to ftp.lysator.liu.se (in Sweden), change to the /pub/msdos/windows directory, and download a ZIP file whose name starts with ewan. Or FTP to ftp.cica.indiana.edu and look in the /pub/pc/win3/winsock directory. Or FTP to gatekeeper.dec.com and look in the /.f/micro/msdos/win3/winsock directory. Or FTP to sunsite.unc.edu and look in the /pub/micro/pc-stuff/ms-windows/winsock/apps directory.

This is a fairly new freeware telnet program that can emulate a VT-100 terminal. You can even set the meanings of its function keys. Last time we checked, though, it was still pretty buggy.

QWS3270

FTP to ftp.cica.indiana.edu, change to the /pub/pc/win3/winsock directory, and download a ZIP file whose name begins with qws3270. Or FTP to gatekeeper.dec.com and look in the /.f/micro/msdos/win3/winsock directory. Or FTP to ftp.demon.co.uk (in the United Kingdom) and look in the /pub/ibmpc/winsock/apps/qws3270 directory. Or FTP to oak.oakland.edu and look in the /pub/msdos/winsock directory.

There are two versions of this program: one freeware and one shareware. Both versions can emulate the IBM 3270 terminal, something that your Chameleon Telnet program cannot do.

FTP programs

These programs allow you to connect to an FTP server and transfer files to or from your PC. You've already got Chameleon FTP, which works fine (see Chapter 12), both as an FTP client (that is, for downloading and uploading files from FTP servers) and as an FTP server.

Wftpd

FRP to `ftp.wst.com`, change to the `/pub/winsock/wftpd` directory, and download a ZIP file whose name begins with `wftpd`. Or FTP to `ftp.cica.indiana.edu` and look in the `/pub/pc/win3/winsock` directory. Or FTP to `gatekeeper.dec.com` and look in the `/.f/micro/msdos/win3/winsock` directory. Or FTP to `oak.oakland.edu` and look in the `/pub/msdos/winsock` directory.

This shareware FTP server allows your PC to become an FTP server and to provide files for other people to download.

WS_FTP

FTP to `ftp.usma.edu`, change to directory `/pub/msdos`, and download `ws_ftp.zip` (or any ZIP file whose name begins with `wsftp`). Or FTP to `garbo.uwasa.fi` (yes, it's in Finland) and look in `/windows/comm`. Or FTP to `ftp.cica.indiana.edu` and look in the `/pub/pc/win3/winsock` directory. Or FTP to `gatekeeper.dec.com` and look in the `/.f/micro/msdos/win3/winsock` directory.

WS_FTP is a very friendly FTP program written by John A. Junod at the United States Military Academy. In your connection profiles, you can include the local directory to put files into and the remote directory you want to get files from, which makes it quicker to get stuff from sites that you use frequently.

Archie

Archie client programs allow you to submit requests to search the Archie database (a database of all the files on almost all the FTP servers in the known universe) for files with a particular name. You've already got Chameleon Archie; Chapter 14 describes how to use it.

WSARCHIE

FTP to `ftp.demon.co.uk` (in the United Kingdom), change to the `/pub/ibmpc/winsock/apps/wsarchie` directory, and download a ZIP file whose name begins with `wsarch`. Or FTP to `ftp.cica.indiana.edu` and look in the `/pub/`

pc/win3/winsock directory. Or FTP to gatekeeper.dec.com and look in the /.f/micro/msdos/win3/winsock directory. Or FTP to oak.oakland.edu and look in the /pub/msdos/winsock directory.

This program is a nice, easy-to-use way to use Archie for finding files. It can be a lot faster than Chameleon Archie because it uses a different, more efficient method to send requests to Archie servers. We use it all the time.

Gopher

Gopher programs allow you to explore Gopherspace, moving from menu to menu until you find the information that you want. Chapter 15 explains it all for you, including how to use Chameleon Gopher, which you already have.

TIP

For up-to-date information on Gopher software and other Gopher-related stuff, read the Usenet newsgroup comp.infosystems.gopher.

GopherBook

NAVIGATE

FTP to sunsite.unc.edu; change to the /pub/micro/pc-stuff/ms-windows/winsock/apps directory; and download gophbook.zip, gophbk11.zip, or a file with a similar name. Or FTP to ftp.cica.indiana.edu and look in the /pub/pc/win3/winsock directory. Or FTP to gatekeeper.dec.com and look in the /.f/micro/msdos/win3/winsock directory.

In this freeware Gopher program, Gopher menus are displayed as pages in a book. The program was written by Kevin Gamiel.

HGopher

NAVIGATE

FTP to lister.cc.ic.ac.uk, change to the /pub/wingopher directory, and download a ZIP files whose name begins with hgoph. Or FTP to ftp.cica.indiana.edu and look in the /pub/pc/win3/winsock directory. Or FTP to gatekeeper.dec.com and look in the /.f/micro/msdos/win3/winsock directory. Or FTP to sunsite.unc.edu and look in the /pub/micro/pc-stuff/ms-windows/winsock/apps directory.

HGopher, which was written by Martyn Hampson in the United Kingdom, was among the first Gopher programs available for the PC. Because the program has been around the block a few times, it's very reliable and usable. It comes with a large help file. Version 2.3 is the last version in the public domain (that is, free); more-recent versions are commercial software. This program can have three connections open at the same time, which allows you to (for example) keep looking at menu pages while retrieving a large file.

WSGopher

FTP from sunsite.unc.edu, change to the /pub/micro/pc-stuff/ms-windows/winsock/apps directory, and download an EXE file whose name starts with wsg. Or FTP to tis.inel.gov and look in the /pub/wsgopher directory. Or FTP to boombox.micro.umn.edu and look in the /pub/gopher/Windows directory.

WSGopher is freeware and was written by Dave Brooks at EG&G, an engineering company. The program is widely used and has lots of nice features. Each Gopher menu appears as a subwindow on the Gopher screen. This arrangement allows you get to various menus quickly, but it can give you a very cluttered screen.

Web browsers

Web browsers allow you to explore the hypermedia universe of the World Wide Web, as described in Chapter 16. You've already got WebSurfer (see Chapter 17 for how to use it).

Cello

FTP to ftp.law.cornell.edu, change to the /pub/LII/Cello directory, and download cello.zip. Or FTP to gatekeeper.dec.com and look in the /.f/micro/msdos/win3/winsock directory. Or FTP to ftp.cica.indiana.edu and look in the /pub/pc/win3/winsock directory. Or FTP to garbo.uwasa.fi (yes, it's in Finland) and look in /windows/winsock.

This program is a simpler Web browser than NCSA Mosaic or WebSurfer, and it doesn't require Win32S. It was the second Windows browser (that we know of) for the Web, written by people at the Cornell Law School.

NCSA Mosaic

FTP to ftp.ncsa.uiuc.edu, change to the /Web/Mosaic/Windows directory, and download a ZIP file whose name begins with wmos. Or FTP to gatekeeper.dec.com and look in the /.f/micro/msdos/win3/winsock directory. Or FTP to garbo.uwasa.fi (yes, it's in Finland) and look in /windows/winsock. Or FTP to ftp.cica.indiana.edu and look in the /pub/pc/win3/winsock directory.

NCSA Mosaic is the original graphical Web browser, written by Chris Wilson and Jon Mittlehauser of the University of Illinois National Center for Supercomputing Applications. Chapter 14 of *MORE Internet For Dummies* (IDG Books Worldwide, written by us) contains a detailed description of how to download, install, and use NCSA Mosaic.

To run all but the earliest versions of NCSA Mosaic, you must also either run Windows NT or download and install Win32S, a program from Microsoft that allows NT-type software to run under regular Windows. You can download WIN32S, which is usually stored in the same directory as the Mosaic program, in a file named `win32s.zip`. (For details, see "Win32S," later in this chapter.)

WAIS

These programs allow you to use the WAIS system to search for files that contain specific words or phrases. Internet Chameleon doesn't come with a WAIS client program. Several of the programs listed in this section are described in detail in Chapter 20.

For up-to-date information on WAIS software and using WAIS, read the Usenet newsgroup `comp.infosystems.wais`.

EIWAIS (a/k/a. EINet WinWais)

FTP to `ftp.einet.net`, change to the `/einet/pc` directory, and download a file whose name begins with `EWAIS`. Or FTP to `wais.com` and look in the `/pub/freeware/dos` directory. Or FTP to `ftp.cica.indiana.edu` and look in the `/pub/pc/win3/winsock` directory. Or FTP to `gatekeeper.dec.com` and look in the `/.f/micro/msdos/win3/winsock` directory.

This is a shareware program, not freeware. It comes with graphics-viewer programs for GIF and JPEG files. We don't find it any better than the free versions listed in this section.

WAISMAN

FTP to `ftp.cnidr.org`, change to the `/pub/NIDR.tools/wais/pc/windows` directory, and download a ZIP file whose name begins with `waisman`.

WAISMAN was written at CNIDR (Clearinghouse for Networked Information Discovery), a North Carolina group that thinks about the sorts of things that WAIS does. We've heard that WAISMAN is no longer supported by its author, but it does work.

WinWAIS

FTP to `ridgisd.er.usgs.gov`, change to the `/software/wais` directory, and download a file whose name begins with `wwais`. Or FTP to `wais.com` and look in the `/pub/freeware/dos` directory.

WinWAIS, written at the U.S. Geological Survey, has a couple of spiffy features that are of extreme interest to geographers — for example, a built-in map of the world. It's the WAIS program that we use.

IRC

These programs allow you to waste unbelievable amounts of time chatting with other Internet users (mainly, bored undergraduates). Internet Chameleon doesn't come with an IRC client program; the manufacturer probably doesn't want to watch its programmer productivity go down the tubes!

IRC II for Windows

FTP to `ftp.cica.indiana.edu`, change to the `/pub/pc/win3/winsock` directory, and download the file `irciiwin.zip`. Or FTP to `gatekeeper.dec.com` and look in the `/.f/micro/msdos/win3/winsock` directory. Or FTP to `ftp.demon.co.uk` (in the United Kingdom) and look in the `/pub/ibmpc/winsock/apps/irciiwin` directory. Or FTP to `cs-ftp.bu.edu` and look in the `/irc/clients/pc/windows` directory.

This is a fairly new shareware IRC program.

WSIRC

FTP to `oak.oakland.edu`, change to the `/pub/msdos/winsock` directory, and download a ZIP file whose name begins with `wsirc`. Or FTP to `cs-ftp.bu.edu` and look in the `/irc/clients/pc/windows` directory. Or FTP to `garbo.uwasa.fi` (yes, it's in Finland) and look in `/windows/winsock`. Or FTP to `ftp.cica.indiana.edu` and look in the `/pub/pc/win3/winsock` directory. Or FTP to `gatekeeper.dec.com` and look in the `/.f/micro/msdos/win3/winsock` directory.

This shareware IRC client program, written by Caesar M. Samsi, is the best one that we've seen. A simpler freeware version (version 1.14-G) limits the number of simultaneous IRC connections that you can have.

MUD programs

We don't talk about MUDs much in this book, but here's a quick intro: MUDs (Multi-User Discussions or Multi-User Dungeons, depending on whom you ask) are programs that a bunch of people can use at the same time, usually logging in via telnet. Some MUDs are big free-for-all discussions; others are Dungeons and Dragons-style fantasy games; and others are educational, designed for kids.

To find out the names of host computers where MUDs are happening, read the `rec.games.mud.announce` Usenet newsgroup. (You also may want to read `rec.games.mud.admin` and `rec.games.mud.tiny` for general information about MUDs.) For FAQs (lists of frequently asked questions and their answers) about MUDs, FTP to `ftp.math.okstate.edu` and change to the `/pub/muds` directory.

Normally, you contact a MUD via telnet, but MUDs have become popular enough that several programs have been written specifically for telnetting to them and playing the game.

NAVIGATE

For MUD software, FTP to caisr2.caisr.cwru.edu, change to directory /pub/mud/clients, and look around for text files that may explain what's going on or for promising-looking ZIP files. Also try ftp.tcp.com, checking in the /pub/mud/Clients directory, or try ftp.math.okstate.edu, checking in the /pub/muds/clients/misc directory.

Miscellaneous Internet stuff

Win QVT/NET

NAVIGATE

FTP to biochemistry.bioc.cwru.edu, move to the /gopher/pub/qvtnet directory, and retrieve a file whose name starts with qvtws. Or FTP to ftp.cica.indiana.edu and look in the /pub/pc/win3/uploads directory. Or FTP to garbo.uwasa.fi (it's in Finland, for you Europeans out there), and look in the /windows/comm or /windows/winsock directory. Or FTP to gatekeeper.dec.com and look in the /.f/micro/msdos/win3/winsock directory.

Win QVT/NET is an all-purpose, multifunction program that does telnet, FTP, mail, news and has an FTP server and a cousin of FTP's called rcp — all in one package. The next version probably will include a cappuccino attachment. This package is big enough to need its own directory, so create one called \wnqvtnet.

WinTalk

NAVIGATE

FTP to ftp.elf.com, change to the /pub/wintalk directory, and download a ZIP file whose name begins with wtalk. Or FTP to ftp.cica.indiana.edu and look in the /pub/pc/win3/winsock directory. Or FTP to gatekeeper.dec.com and look in the /.f/micro/msdos/win3/winsock directory. Or FTP to oak.oakland.edu and look in the /pub/msdos/winsock directory.

This freeware program allows two-way, on-line communications with other Internauts who use the UNIX talk command (or other talk programs).

WS Host (Windows Socket Host)

NAVIGATE

FTP to ftp.cica.indiana.edu, change to the /pub/pc/win3/winsock directory, and download the file wshost.zip. Or FTP to gatekeeper.dec.com and look in the /.f/micro/msdos/win3/winsock directory.

This tiny little program has one, and only one, purpose: It translates a host name into a host number. If you want to know the host number for `dummies.com`, for example, WS Host can provide it — by contacting your DNS (domain name server) to ask, if you really must know.

Vying for Viewers

If you want to use Chameleon Gopher or WebSurfer to look at pretty pictures or hear lovely sounds, you need viewers that can handle the various image and sound formats that you'll run into. Be sure to follow the instructions in "Installing the program" in Chapter 18 to associate the programs with the file extensions that they can handle. See Chapter 15 for more about Gopher and Chapter 17 for details on WebSurfer.

NAVIGATE

The easiest place to get some viewers is by way of anonymous FTP from `ftp.law.cornell.edu`, in `/pub/LII/Cello`, or from `ftp.ncsa.uiuc.edu`, in `/Web/Mosaic/Windows/viewers`. This section describes some viewers that we have heard about or tried.

Seeing things

For viewing graphics files, you may need more than one viewer, because there are so many types of graphics files. The most common types are GIF and JPEG files. (You may encounter BMP and PCX files, too, but you don't have to worry about seeing them; Windows comes with Windows Paintbrush, which can display both BMP and PCX.)

Lview and Lview Pro

NAVIGATE

FTP to `oak.oakland.edu`, change to the `/pub/msdos/windows3` directory, and download a ZIP file whose name starts with `lview` (for Lview) or `lviewp` (for Lview Pro). Or FTP to `lister.cc.ic.ac.uk` (in the United Kingdom) and look in the `/pub/wingopher/viewers/image` directory. Or FTP to `ftp.law.cornell.edu` and look in the `/pub/LII/Cello` directory. Or FTP to `ftp.ncsa.uiuc.edu` and look in `/Web/Mosaic/Windows/viewers`.

Lview can display both GIF and JPEG files, and it's free. Lview Pro is a shareware version that can also run in 32-bit mode under Windows NT. (If you don't know what this means, don't worry about it; just forget about Lview Pro.) We use Lview.

WinGIF

FTP to `ftp.law.cornell.edu`, change to the `/pub/LII/Cello` directory, and download a ZIP file whose name starts with `wingif`. Or FTP to `oak.oakland.edu` and look in the `/pub/msdos/windows3` directory. Or FTP to `lister.cc.ic.ac.uk` (in the United Kingdom) and look in the `/pub/wingopher/viewers/image` directory.

WinGIF can display only GIF files, and it's shareware.

WinJPEG

FTP to `oak.oakland.edu`, change to the `/pub/msdos/windows3` directory, and download a ZIP file whose name starts with `winjp`. Or FTP to `ftp.cica.indiana.edu` and look in the `/pub/pc/win3/desktop` directory.

WinJPEG can handle JPEG files in addition to GIFs, and it's shareware.

Hearing voices

If your computer has a soundboard, you can play sound files (files with such file extensions as WAV, VOC, and AU). To play WAV files, you can use the Media Player or Sound Recorder programs (`mplayer.exe` and `soundrec.exe`, usually in your `c:\windows` directory) that come with Windows.

WHAM

FTP to `ftp.law.cornell.edu`, change to the `/pub/LII/Cello` directory, and download a ZIP file whose name starts with `wham`. Or FTP to `ftp.ncsa.uiuc.edu` and look in `/Web/Mosaic/Windows/viewers`.

WHAM is a good freeware sound player with lots of other features. Written by Andrew Bulhak in Australia, it can play WAV and other-format files.

WPLANY

FTP to `ftp.law.cornell.edu`, change to the `/pub/LII/Cello` directory, and download a ZIP file whose name starts with `wplny`. Or FTP to `lister.cc.ic.ac.uk` (in the United Kingdom) and look in the `/pub/wingopher/viewers/audio` directory. Or FTP to `ftp.ncsa.uiuc.edu` and look in `/Web/Mosaic/Windows/viewers`.

WPLANY is a good basic sound player. It's not fancy, but it can handle just about any sort of sound file found on the Net, including WAV and AU files.

Seeing ghosts

Movie files have the file extension AVI or MPG.

It takes a great deal of computing power to display a movie. If your computer isn't at least a 486, the movies show so slowly as to not be worth the bother.

MPEGWin

FTP to `ftp.cica.indiana.edu`, change to the `/pub/pc/win3/desktop` directory, and download a ZIP file whose name begins with `mpegw`.

MPegWin can handle movie files with the extension MPG.

VidVue

FTP to `wuarchive.wustl.edu`, change to the `/systems/ibmpc/win3/desktop` directory, and download a ZIP file whose name begins with `vidvue`. Or FTP to `ftp.cica.indiana.edu` and look in the `/pub/pc/win3/desktop` directory.

VidVue can display movie files with the file extension AVI.

Miscellany

The Internet is full of useful little utilities. Particularly handy are programs that can decompress the myriad of compression methods used on the many systems that connect to the Net. You've already got WinZIP, which can handle ZIP, ARC, ARJ, and LZH files (whatever they are). Following are some other programs that you may want to have up your sleeve.

Uudecoders

Uuencoded files have been translated into a bunch of ASCII characters so that they can be sent via Internet e-mail or posted in Usenet newsgroup articles. Your Chameleon Mail program can decode uuencoded files, but NEWTNews can't.

uu

FTP to `io.com`, look in the `/pub/usr/zboray/coding` directory, and download a ZIP file whose name begins with `uu`. Or FTP to `oak.oakland.edu` and look in the `/pub/msdos/decode` directory.

This is a small, quick, freeware uudecoding program that runs under DOS.

WinCode

FTP to `oak.oakland.edu`, change to the `/pub/msdos/windows3` directory, and download a ZIP file whose name begins with `wncode`. Or FTP to `ftp.cica.indiana.edu` and look in the `/pub/pc/win3/util` directory. Or FTP to `wuarchive.wustl.edu` and look in the `/systems/ibmpc/win3/util` directory.

WinCode is a nice Windows-based uuencoder and uudecoder.

UNIX uncompressors

Files that are compressed by UNIX users aren't in the same ZIP format that PCs use. Instead, they are in files with the file extension z or Z; other UNIX files have the extension gz (meaning that the files were compressed with the gzip program) or zoo.

gzip

FTP to `oak.oakland.edu`, change to the `/pub/msdos/compress` directory, and download a ZIP file whose name begins with `gzip`. Or FTP to `grind.isca.uiowa.edu` and look in the `/4/msdos/simtel/compress` directory. Or FTP to `pogue.admin.lsa.umich.edu` and look in the `/msdos/compression/gnuzip` directory.

This program is useful for dealing with files with the gz extension.

z and Z uncompressors

FTP to `oak.oakland.edu`, change to the `/pub/msdos/compress` directory, and download a ZIP file whose name begins with `comp`. Or FTP to `grind.isca.uiowa.edu` and look in the `/4/msdos/simtel/compress` directory. Or FTP to `pogue.admin.lsa.umich.edu` and look in the `/msdos/compression/unix` directory for either `cmp-ucmp.zip` or `compress.arc`. (Don't worry — WinZip can handle ARC files.)

Use this program to uncompress files with the Z or z extension.

zoo keepers

FTP to `pogue.admin.lsa.umich.edu`, change to the `/msdos/compression/zoo` directory, and download an EXE file whose name begins with `zoo`. Or FTP to `oak.oakland.edu` and look in the `/pub/msdos/zoo` directory.

Use this program for files with the ZOO extension.

Mac unstuffers

Macintoshes use different file compressors than PCs. Macs use files with extensions SIT (for StuffIt format), HQX (for BinHex format), and PIT (for PackIt format). Confusingly but usefully, these programs *run* on PCs but *read* files created on Macs.

HQX handlers

NAVIGATE

FTP to `oak.oakland.edu`, change to the `/pub/msdos/mac` directory, and download a ZIP file whose name starts with `binhex`. Or FTP to `ftp.cica.indiana.edu` and look in the `/pub/pc/win3/util` directory for a file named `unmacit.zip`.

This program can handle files into HQX (BinHex) format.

PIT unpackers

NAVIGATE

FTP to `pogue.admin.lsa.umich.edu`, change to the `/msdos/compression/macintosh` directory, and download a ZIP or ARC file whose name begins with `unpakit`. Or FTP to `oak.oakland.edu` and look in the `/pub/msdos/mac` directory.

Use this program for files with the PIT extension, created using PackIt.

SIT unstuffers

NAVIGATE

FTP to `pogue.admin.lsa.umich.edu` and look in the `/msdos/compression/macintosh` directory for an ARC file whose name begins with `unsit`. Or FTP to `oak.oakland.edu` and look in the `/pub/msdos/mac` directory. Or FTP to `ftp.cica.indiana.edu` and look in the `/pub/pc/win3/util` directory for a file named `unmacit.zip`.

This program can unstuff files in SIT archives.

Win32S

Win32S is Microsoft's extension to Microsoft Windows that lets you run 32-bit applications under existing versions of Windows. This program comes directly from Microsoft and can be legally downloaded and run by any licensed user of Windows 3.1 or Windows For Workgroups 3.11. It allows Windows to run software that is designed for use with Windows NT — that is, 32-bit software. You'll need it if you want to run NCSA Mosaic, among other programs.

FTP to `ftp.cica.indiana.edu`, change to the `/pub/pc/win3/util` directory, and download the file `win32s.zip`. Win32S is also available wherever you find NCSA Mosaic (described earlier in this chapter), because NCSA Mosaic requires Win32S to run.

To get information straight from the horse's mouth, so to speak, you may also want to FTP to `ftp.microsoft.com` and look around in the `/developr/win32dk` directory. You'd think that the latest, greatest versions would be here.

When you unzip the file, notice that some of the files should be extracted into a subdirectory named `disk1` and that other files should go into one named `disk2`. (Select the Use Directory Names option in the WinZip Extract dialog box, and WinZip will create these directories for you.) To install Win32S, exit all other Windows programs, but remain in Windows. From Program Manager, choose File⇨Run, and enter the program name `setup.exe`, which is in the `disk1` subdirectory that you just created.

Win32S also comes with a nearly unwinnable (by us, anyway) solitaire game. Because the game is a 32-bit program, if you can run it, Win32S is installed correctly. If you can win the game with any regularity, you deserve a Nobel prize. After extensive research, we found that we won twice in about 200 games.

Lost? Dumbfounded!

We suggest that if you have trouble finding the software listed in this chapter, you first use Archie to look for alternative sites for the files. If that doesn't work, FTP to `ftp.dummies.com` (yes, that's Internet For Dummies Central) and check for text files that contain updated lists of programs and sites, or other book updates. We may have the file you want, or we may have a text file that tells you where to look.

The Latest WinSock Programs

New WinSock programs (that is, Windows Internet applications) come out all the time. Luckily, two guys maintain extremely detailed lists of new WinSock software.

One list, maintained by Ed Sinkovits, is distributed monthly to the `net-happenings` mailing list (described in Chapter 6). WinSock programs are listed by type, including e-mail, newsreaders, Web browsers, and telnet programs. You'll also be able to find an expanded version of Ed's list in *Internet SECRETS*, coming soon from IDG Books.

You can grab the latest version of this excellent list any time via FTP. Connect to `ftp.cica.indiana.edu`, change to the `/pub/pc/win3/winsock` directory, and look for a ZIP file whose name begins with `winter`. The ZIP file includes the listing in two formats: one for Microsoft Word 6 (with the extension DOC) and one for Microsoft Windows Write (with the extension WRI).

The other list includes more types of programs, with file, source information, and comments. Send an e-mail message to `info@lcs.com` with the subject *FAQS*. Leave the body of the message blank. Or use WebSurfer to look at this Web page, at the following URL:

```
http://www.ramp.com/@tdlcs
```

The Most Popular FTP Servers

You can browse through a few FTP sites that provide lots of popular WinSock software, including those listed in Table 19-1. Or use WebSurfer to check out this Web page:

```
http://www.cica.indiana.edu
```

Some sites *mirror* the files at other sites — that is, they maintain exact copies of all the directories and files from another site. Through mirroring, more FTP servers are available to serve you the files that you need. You'll find that many of the sites listed in the table mirror the CICA files (from `ftp.cica.indiana.edu`) or SimTel, the "Coast-to-Coast Software Repository."

Table 19-1 FTP Servers with Useful WinSock Programs

FTP Server	*Directory*	*Location*
alpha.cso.uiuc.edu	/pub/mirror/win3/winsock	Illinois
archive.orst.edu	/pub/mirrors/ftp.cica.indiana.edu/win3	Oregon
dorm.rutgers.edu	/pub/msdos/winsock/apps	New Jersey
ftp.cc.monash.edu.au	/pub/win3/winsock	Australia
ftp.cdrom.com	/.2/SimTel/msdos/winsock	California
ftp.cica.indiana.edu	/pub/pc/win3/winsock	Indiana (busy)
ftp.cyf-kr.edu.pl	/pub/mirror/win3/winsock	Poland
ftp.demon.co.uk	/pub/ibmpc/winsock/apps	United Kingdom

(continued)

Table 19-1 *(continued)*

FTP Server	*Directory*	*Location*
ftp.funet.fi	/pub/msdos/SimTel	Finland
ftp.iij.ad.jp	/.4/win3/winsock	Japan
ftp.nectec.or.th	/pub/mirrors/SimTel or /pub/mirrors/cica	Thailand
ftp.uni-paderborn.de	/pcsoft/windows/winsock	Germany
ftp.uni-regensburg.de	/pub/pcsoft/windows/winsock	Germany
garbo.uwasa.fi	/windows/winsock and windows/comm	Finland
gatekeeper.dec.com	/.f/micro/msdos/win3/winsock	Massachusetts
info.nic.surfnet.nl	/mirror-archive	Netherlands
nctuccca.edu.tw	/PC/windows, /PC/simtel, or /PC/wuarchive	Taiwan
oak.oakland.edu	/pub/msdos/winsock	Michigan
polecat.law.indiana.edu	/pub/mirror/cica/pc/win3/winsock	Indiana
src.doc.ic.ac.uk	/pub/computing	United Kingdom
sunsite.unc.edu	/pub/micro/pc-stuff/ms-windows/winsock/apps	North Carolina
wuarchive.wustl.edu	/pub/pc/win3	Missouri (busy)

TIP

If you want to go for the gold, you can order a CD-ROM that contains the entire public-domain Windows-software archive from CICA (the folks at ftp.cica.indiana.edu, which has a mammoth number of programs of all types). For information, send e-mail to orders@cdrom.com, inquiring about the CICA Windows archive.

Chapter 20

We Have WAIS of Finding Your Information

In This Chapter

- "There are more things in heaven and earth, Horatio, than are dreamt of in your philosophy . . ."
- Finding documents by keyword
- Some great recipes

If you're keen on finding all there is to find about a given topic, it behooves you to learn to use WAIS, the software that knows its way around the databases of the world. *WAIS,* which stands for Wide Area Information Servers (pronounced "ways," incidentally), is a system designed for retrieving information from networks.

The developers of WAIS were information-retrieval and database gurus at Thinking Machines, Apple Computer, and Dow Jones (yes, the Dow Jones that publishes *The Wall Street Journal*). Although WAIS was developed to provide access to proprietary databases, such as the ones that Dow Jones sells, most of the information that is accessible by way of WAIS is available free, at this point. Thinking Machines even maintains a CM-5 Connection Machine supercomputer on the Internet for free WAIS access.

With WAIS, you enter a set of words that describe what you're looking for, and WAIS digs through whatever libraries you specify, looking for documents that match your request. Unlike Archie and Veronica, WAIS looks at the *contents* of documents rather than just the titles. This procedure requires the server to do much more work (that's one reason why Thinking Machines is involved — its supercomputer does this kind of searching well), but it makes it much easier to find what you want, because you don't have to depend on someone else to come up with properly descriptive titles for documents. WAIS can, in principle, also find pictures, sounds, and other kinds of files, although the WAIS databases are 99 percent text at the moment.

Why Z39.50 is good for you

In an anonymous building in Times Square in New York City, a little-known organization called the American National Standards Institute (ANSI) labors away to make our lives easier. For example, an ANSI standard for light bulbs ensures that no matter which brand of light bulb you buy, it fits into your socket at home.

The scheme that WAIS uses to communicate between its clients and servers is based, amazingly enough, on an official ANSI standard called Z39.50. (All the standards have strange names like that. This name simply means that it's the 50th standard approved by the 39th subgroup of the library-science division.)

Z39.50 defines rules for one computer to use when passing an information-retrieval query to another computer and the rules for passing back the result. Systems all over the world use Z39.50, because most libraries insist on it.

Splicing WAIS onto most existing information-retrieval systems that already speak Z39.50ese should be relatively simple, so you can expect to see many more WAIS sources as existing library databases get WAISized.

WAIS also uses *relevance feedback,* which means that after WAIS performs a search, it returns a list of documents that seem to match your request. You can look at some of those documents, and if WAIS didn't find quite what you want, you can identify a few of the documents that matched best (the most *relevant* ones) and tell WAIS to find stuff more like that.

Where Does WAIS Come From?

We were afraid you'd ask that. There's no WAIS program in Chameleon, so you have to improvise. Your improvisational riffs include the following:

- Telnetting to a public WAIS site
- Using WAIS from WebSurfer or Gopher
- Loading a real WinSock WAIS program

Of these possibilities, only the third is worth trying. The following sections explain why.

The world's ugliest program

A few Internet sites run a public WAIS client program, the best known of which is `quake.think.com`. You can telnet there and log in as `wais`, with no password. Unfortunately, that program is widely considered to be one of the most horribly unusable programs of any sort ever written. Rather than waste paper here trying to describe it, we'll just tell you not to bother with it. Besides, by the time you figure it out, you could more easily have loaded a real WAIS program on your own computer. (Gluttons for punishment will find the gory details in *The Internet for Dummies,* 2nd Edition and *The Internet for Dummies Quick Reference,* both published by IDG Books Worldwide.)

Gateways that usually aren't

One solution to WAIS's hard-to-use-ness would be to create some glue between WAIS and a program that people actually like, such as Gopher or WebSurfer. Some people have actually tried to do this. If you're a Chameleon Gopher user, you can select the Gopher Servers heading; then University of Minnesota, Other Gopher and Information Servers; then WAIS Based Information; and then List of All WAIS Sources. In theory, you should see great long menus full of Gopher search items, with one entry for each of the WAIS data sources that Gopher knows about. You click the source you want and then type your search words in the window that pops up; a list of matching documents appears. That's the theory, anyway — we've never actually gotten this procedure to work. Maybe you'll have more luck.

WebSurfer users are in roughly the same boat. In principle, you can find a Web-to-WAIS gateway at this URL:

```
http://info.cern.ch/hypertext/DataSources/WAIS/ByHost.html
```

(In WebSurfer, you select Retrieve➪Go to URL and then type this line.) In theory, you see a page full of WAIS databases that you can select and search; in practice, no such luck.

WAIS, at last

So how do you actually use WAIS? You load a real WAIS client program, that's how. Several Windows WAIS client programs are available. Because all these programs talk to the same WAIS servers with the same sets of documents, they all really do the same thing. We like WinWAIS, which was written at the U.S. Geological Survey (your taxes at play) and which has a couple of spiffy features of extreme interest to geographers, such as a built-in map of the world.

The following section tells you how to install WinWAIS.

Setting up WinWAIS

Setting up WinWAIS is a little bit tricky because it comes with about three dozen separate files. Follow these steps:

1. **Create a directory called `\apps\winwais` (or `\util\winwais`, or something like that).**

   WinWAIS is big enough that its files need their own directory.

2. **Connect to your SLIP provider, if you haven't already done so, and run the FTP program.**

3. **Connect to host `ridgisd.er.usgs.gov`.**

   Use `anonymous` as the user name and your e-mail address as the password.

4. **In the FTP program, on the remote host, change to the `software` directory; then change to the `wais` directory.**

5. **On the local system, change to the `\apps\winwais` directory (or to whatever directory you created in step 1).**

6. **Make sure that FTP is using binary mode and retrieve the file `wwais24.exe`.**

   That's the name for version 2.4. By the time you read this book, the program's authors may have a newer version named something like `wwais25.exe` or even `wwais30.exe`.

7. **Disconnect and exit FTP.**

   The EXE file is really a ZIP file that knows how to unzip itself.

8. **Start the Windows File Manager, if it's not already running, go to the** `\apps\winwais` **directory (or wherever you put the file); and then double-click** `wwais24.exe` **(or whatever the file is called).**

   This action runs the self-extractor and extracts the files. (Cautious people may want to run WinZip instead and use it to extract the files, in the unlikely event that someone spiked the file with a nasty virus.)

9. **If disk space is tight, you now can delete some of the extracted files, including** `setup.exe`, `wssetup.exe` **(two setup programs that you don't need if you're using WinSock), and** `wwais24.exe` **itself.**

10. **Create an icon for WinWAIS in the Program Manager.**

    The easiest way to do this is to drag the file `wais.exe` from the File Manager to one of the group windows in the Program Manager. If you do this correctly, the icon should be a little blue globe with a lightning bolt across it.

Hand-to-hand with WinWAIS

Getting WAIS to cough up some documents starts as a three-step process:

1. Identify some sources to use.
2. Search for some words, and get a list of documents.
3. Retrieve the documents that look interesting.

So how do you get your documents with WinWAIS? Double-click its icon (the globe with the lightning bolt) to display a screen that resembles Figure 20-1.

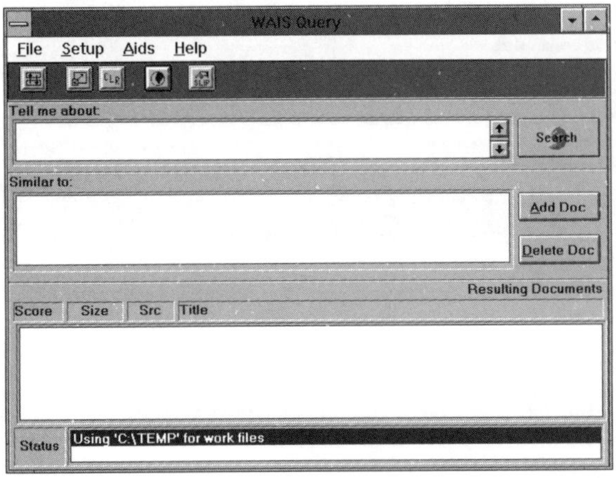

Figure 20-1: WinWAIS starts.

Let's go to the source

Before you can do any searching, you need to select some *sources*, or libraries of searchable documents. You can select sources in two ways. WinWAIS comes with two source lists, named WAIS and ALLSRC. The WAIS list contains only one source, but fortunately, it's the source directory that lists all the other sources. If you're not sure which source you want, you can use WAIS itself to look for likely sources. The other list, ALLSRC, contains a list of all of the well-known sources. Because new sources appear relatively infrequently, the sources in ALLSRC are pretty much the same ones that you could find by searching the directory of sources, so we'll find sources the easy way first.

To choose some sources, click the leftmost button in the row near the top of the WinWAIS window. You see the sources window, shown in Figure 20-2.

To switch to the ALLSRC list, click WAIS in the Source Group window. In the list that appears, click ALLSRC. The list of sources appears in the bottom window, as shown in Figure 20-3.

Now you can scroll through that list. When you see a source that you like, click it and drag it to the upper window to select it.

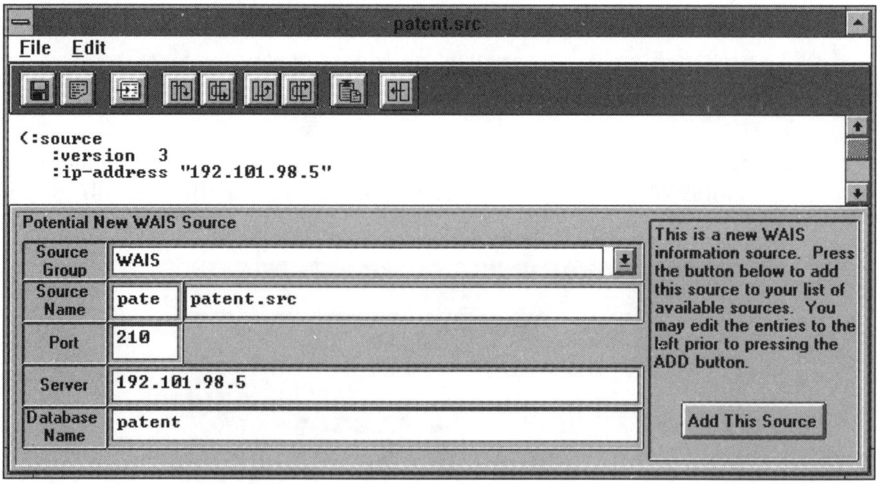

Figure 20-2: The WinWAIS sources window.

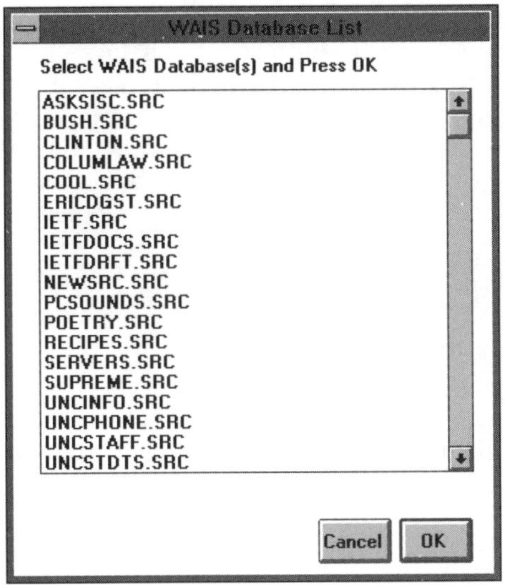

Figure 20-3: The list of sources.

TIP

You may think that the best way to find what you want is to use every possible source; there's even an All Sources button that you can use to select them all. Doing that, however, usually is a terrible idea. The problem is that WAIS searches each source separately, so if you have 50 sources and it takes 12 seconds to search each one, the total search will take more than 10 minutes — which is too long to wait unless you are a uniquely patient person. Also, the sources range over an enormous range of subjects. It seems pointless to include a source that contains, say, Australian biological abstracts if you're looking for presidential press conferences that mention the Information Supercollider. Try selecting one or two sources, and if you don't find what you need, select a few more.

If you want to look at presidential documents, for example, scroll down to White-House-Papers, drag it to the top window, and then click the Done button to go back to the main WinWAIS screen.

Are we ever going to do some real searching?

Sure we are; we thought you'd never ask. Click the large top window — the one to the left of the big Search button — and type some search words (say, **Iraq sanctions**). Then click Search, and WinWAIS does the search for you.

The progress of the search appears in the tiny window at the bottom of the screen. WinWAIS has to contact the server that contains the source, send the request to that server, wait while the server performs the search, and then receive the answers. If you're unlucky, WinWAIS may have trouble contacting the server, in which case you'll probably see a little window containing an inscrutable six-digit WinSock error code. Try the search again; some of the errors are what are known in network-ese as "transient" and may not occur on the second try.

A four-star performance

If the search goes as planned, the list of documents that best match the search words appears in the large Resulting Documents window. The found documents are scored like movies in a movie review, with one-star to four-star ratings. The scoring is specific to the search. Whichever document matches best is awarded four stars, even if it didn't match all that well.

To look at any of the found documents, double-click the document in the Resulting Documents window. WinWAIS retrieves and displays the document, as shown in Figure 20-4.

TIP

A bunch of buttons appear at the top of the document window. Some of these buttons are even useful, as the following list explains. (If you're a button-hater, all these buttons have menu equivalents; see the section "On the Button," next.)

- The leftmost button (floppy disk) saves the document to a file. You are asked for the filename before saving.
- The second button (torn curtain) prints the document.

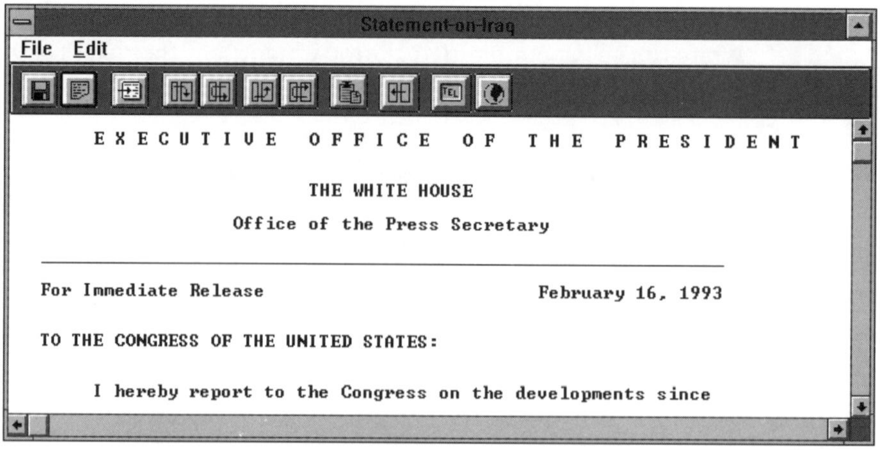

Figure 20-4: A presidential document.

- The third button (arrow stabbing a document) skips ahead in the document to the first place where your search words actually occur. Each time you click this button, you move to the next place where one of the words occurs.
- The next four buttons (various curved arrows and boxes) move to the preceding or following document, in various orders. The first button (right-turn arrow) gets the next document in the order in which the documents are stored on the server. The second button (U-turn) gets the next document in the order in which the documents are displayed in the list on the search screen — that is, from four stars down to one. The third and fourth buttons (left-turn and backward U-turn arrows, respectively) retrieve previous documents.
- The next-to-the last button (momma and baby Clipboards) copies selected document text to the Windows Clipboard.
- The last useful button (two boxes pinned together) mark selected text for relevance feedback, which we talk about in the following section.

TIP

To get rid of the document window, by the way, press F3 or double-click the button at the left end of the title bar.

On the button

TIP

If you use WinWAIS very much, you may find that the easiest way to control it is to use the keyboard instead of the mouse, because you have to type the search strings anyway. Table 20-1 is a keyboard cheat sheet:

Table 20-1 WinWAIS Keyboard Cheat Sheet

Key(s)	*Action*
F1	Show the Help screens
F3	Closes document window
F5	Finds search words in document window
F6	Adds selected text to relevance feedback
Shift+F6	Copies selected text to Clipboard
F7	Gets preceding document in source order
Alt+F7	Gets preceding document in listed order
F8	Gets following document in source order
Alt+F8	Gets following document in listed order
Arrow keys	Scrolls document up or down

That's irrelevant!

What's large and gray and works in the circus and has a long trunk? Oh, you heard that one when you were seven years old? Okay then, back to WAIS.

WAIS features relevance feedback, which is what you get when you take the trunk and wrap it all the way around to the... sorry, we forgot again. Relevance feedback allows you to take a document (or a piece of a document), give it back to WAIS, and tell WAIS to find more documents like it.

To select an entire document for relevance feedback, click the document you want in the search screen's Retrieved Documents window and then drag the document to the middle Similar To: window. To deselect the document, just drag it back ro Retrieved Documents. You can click the Add Doc and Delete Doc buttons, but dragging is easier (and much cooler).

To select part of the current document for relevance feedback, select the text and then click the Add section button (the one that looks like two bars pinned together).

After you set your list of relevant documents, click the Search button to redo your search, taking into account your relevance list. You may find that to find what you want, you need to add and remove search words and to add and remove relevant documents.

Back to the source

If you can't find the source that you need in the ALLSRC list, you need to search the Directory of Sources. Follow these steps:

1. **In the main screen, click the leftmost button.**

   The sources window appears.

2. **If the ALLSRC list of servers appears, click ALLSRC; then, when WAIS appears, click that.**

   You should see the Directory of Sources from WAIS.

3. **Drag the Directory of Sources from the bottom window to the top window, and then click Done.**

   This action tells WinWAIS that you want to search the directory of sources.

4. **Type some words that describe the kinds of documents that you want, and then click Search to search for likely sources.**

   The sources appear in the bottom window, scored from one star to four.

5. **Double-click a likely-looking source.**

   You see a special document window, as shown way back in Figure 20-2. The top part of the window is the text of the source file, which you can scroll through (very slowly) by using the scroll bar. After the computer glop at the top, the file usually contains a prose description of the source.

6. **If you like the source, click Add This Source to add it to your list of sources.**

7. **If you want to look at other sources in the list, use the buttons at the top of the window to move to the following or preceding source.**

8. **Close the window by pressing F3 or by clicking the button at the left end of the menu bar.**

Now the new source(s) are in your source list, and you can use them in future searches just like any other sources.

TIP

Keep in mind the difference between searching for sources and searching for documents. If you want to find information about patents for banana peelers, for example, you type a word like **patents** to look for sources. Then, when you find some sources, you type words like **banana** and **peelers** to search those sources.

Adding sources by hand

TECHNICAL STUFF

Sometimes you may find a reference to a swell new WAIS source in a mail message or a Usenet news article. If you're a careful typist, you can add a source yourself. Choose Setup⇨Sources to display a Source Editor window similar to the one shown in Figure 20-2; the difference is that you fill in the information yourself, as shown in Table 20-2.

Table 20-2	Manually Entering Sources
Field	***Entry***
Source Group	Leave the default entry (`WAIS`) alone.
Source Name	There are two subwindows in the field. In the smaller one, type a four-letter code that will be used to identify documents retrieved from this source in the Resulting Documents window. In the larger one, type a description of the source.
Port	Use the port number given in the description of the source (usually, 210).
Server	Enter the host name or host number of the server.
Database Name	Enter the database name exactly as given in the description of the source, being sure to use the same punctuation and spacing.

Then click Add to add the selected source to the list of available sources and click Done to close the window.

If you mess up in entering a source, you can fix it by coming back to the Source Editor window, clicking the source in question in the list at the top of the window (which fills in the fields with their current values), fixing the values that are wrong, and then clicking Change to store the changed version.

It isn't very useful, but it sure looks cool

WinWAIS was written at the U.S. Geological Survey, an outfit that is dedicated to maps. So you may not be amazed to hear that some features of WinWAIS are specifically designed for mapheads. If you click the globe button in the main screen (the second button from the right; it looks like a circle with a big black smudge), you see the Spatial Data Locator window, shown in Figure 20-5.

Using the arrows at the top of the window, you can rotate the globe and zoom in; you then can use the mouse to select regions on the globe. (Hint: When you change the rotation or zoom, click Redraw to redraw the globe to your new specifications.) When you close that window, WinWAIS adds to your current search some search terms that describe the area you selected in the Spatial Data Locator window. None of the WAIS sources that we've ever found can do anything useful with these spatial-data terms, but we presume that there are nonpublic WAIS servers chock full of USGS map information that can be selected geographically in this way.

Drawing the map can take a while. On our 486/33DX PC, it takes about five seconds; on a 386SX with no math coprocessor, it takes about 15 minutes. If you have a slow computer, you may want to skip this feature.

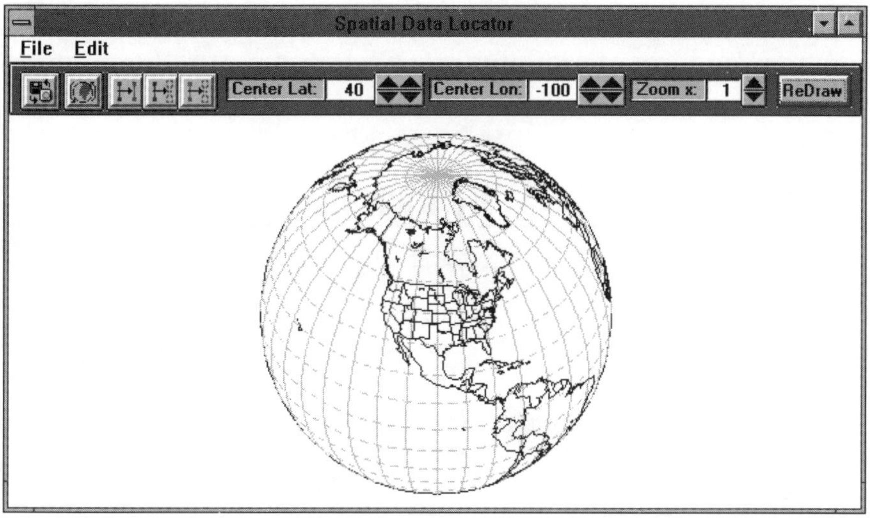

Figure 20-5: Around the world.

Other WAIS Programs

Other Windows WAIS clients are available on the Net; if you have a lot of time to waste, you may want to investigate them.

One client that we occasionally use is WAISMAN, available via FTP at `ftp.cnidr.org` in directory `/pub/NIDR.tools/wais/pc/windows` and file `waisman3.zip`. The main advantage of WAISMAN is that it can retrieve pictures and sounds as well as text. Not many WAIS sources are anything other than text, but if you stumble across one, WAISMAN is the program to use. For more details, see Chapter 13 of *MORE Internet for Dummies*.

Another program is EIWAIS, which is available via FTP on host `ftp.einet.net` in directory `/einet/pc` and file `EIWAIS155.EXE` (a self-extracting ZIP file.) EIWAIS is a perfectly decent WAIS client, but because it's somewhat larger than the others (and is shareware rather than freeware), we haven't used it much.

For further advice on WAIS, consult the Usenet newsgroup `comp.infosystems.wais` for a running discussion of WAIS in all its many forms.

The 5th Wave By Rich Tennant

"I JUST DON'T THINK THIS NEW SALES KID IS GONNA WORK OUT."

Chapter 21

Having a Problem?

In This Chapter

- Opportunities for embarrassment and humiliation
- Easy ways not to be embarrassed and humiliated

On the Internet, sometimes there are difficulties.

The Network's Dead, Jim!

Actually, it's probably not. Suppose that you try to use a service on some remote computer, and you can't get to it. You know that you didn't change anything on *your* computer, so the network or the remote computer must be kaput, right?

Not so fast. Many moving parts (conceptually speaking) lie between your computer and a computer on the other side of the country (or world). The Internet is a bunch of interconnected networks, so your data probably moves along a dozen different networks between here and there. In theory, then, any of those networks could cause a failure.

In practice, the networks in the middle are *high-speed, shared* networks with *multiple redundant paths, automatic rerouting, 24/7 monitoring,* and many other buzzword features that mean that the networks aren't likely to break and that even if they *do* break, bells start ringing in less than a second, network connections are rerouted, and people fix things.

Consider this: In more than 20 years, the Internet has experienced only one major backbone failure, and that was because of a software glitch, not because of cable failures. On the other hand, if you accidentally kick your computer's network connection out of the wall, who's going to notice but you? This chapter gives you a list of things to check.

Is your computer working?

Does your computer act normally when you tell it to do non-network things? Yes, we know this is an obvious question, but it never hurts to check. (True story: "Hello, help desk? My computer won't boot up." "Is it plugged into the wall correctly?" "I can't tell; the power failed and all the lights are out.")

Is your computer connected to your Internet provider?

The next step is to see whether you have any connection to the outside world. If you do, the best program to use is Chameleon Ping, which sends packets to another host that is supposed to echo them back. The Ping program depends on only the very lowest level of networking software, so if Ping can't reach another computer, that fact strongly suggests that there's been a network break or that the other computer is dead.

To test your network connection, run Ping and choose Start from the menu. Enter the Internet address of a nearby computer (such as your network provider), and then click OK. The resulting output looks something like Figure 21-1. (In a pinch, try Pinging a well-known computer, such as InterNIC's computer at `is.internic.net`.)

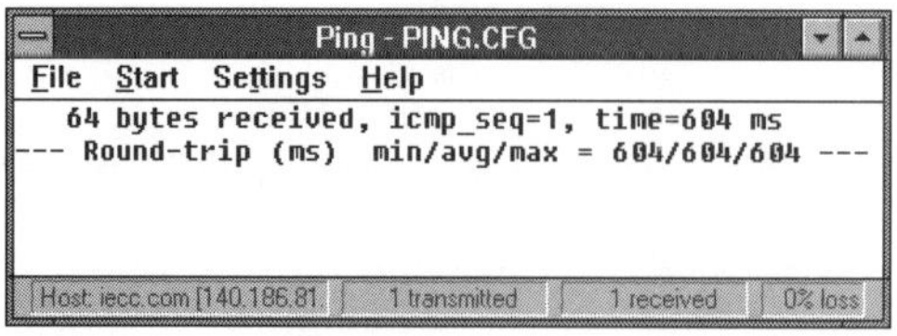

Figure 21-1: Pinging away.

Your Internet provider's address is shown in the Custom window (refer to Chapter 3 for information about running Custom). The address is the Domain Name listed at the bottom of the window.

Ping normally pings once and then waits. We find it more useful to choose Settings⇨Preferences, select the Continuous box, and click OK, so that the next time you start Ping, it runs until you click Stop or close the program.

The times that Ping reports are the approximate times it took for each message to reach the other computer and come back, measured in milliseconds (1/1,000 of a second, abbreviated as *ms*). For computers on the same Ethernet, the time should be in the vicinity of 10 ms. For computers on the other side of the world, it can be as much as 2,000 or 3,000 ms — two or three seconds. On a SLIP or PPP line, it should be 500 ms or so to your provider. Now and then, a ping can get lost in the network. If that happens only now and then, it's no problem. But if it happens frequently (more than 5 percent of the time), you have severe network congestion or — more likely — a flaky network connection with one of the computers.

If your computer tries to contact the other computer and can't, the most likely problem is that your computer isn't actually connected to your Internet provider. Using the Custom program, disconnect and connect again.

Are you connected to your name server?

If your computer claims that no such computer as the one that you're trying to contact exists, you may have lost contact with your *name server* — the computer that has the job of translating host names to four-part numeric addresses. Assuming that you know the numeric address of your Internet provider's machine, try contacting it by using the numeric address, typed as four numbers separated by periods.

To find out your Internet provider's numeric IP address, use the Custom program. Choose Services⇨Domain Servers. You'll see up to three listed. The four parts of the IP addresses are in different boxes — for example, 199, 0, 65, and 2. String the four parts together with periods to make an IP address — for example, `199.0.65.2`.

If your computer can ping your provider by using the numeric address but not the name, you have name-server trouble. (See "What's in a Name?," later in this chapter.) Contact your network provider (by voice, that is) and ask for help. If you can report that a numeric address works but the corresponding name doesn't, you narrow down the possibilities considerably.

Is the other end OK?

If you can get in touch with your Internet provider, that pretty much proves that your computer — and your provider's computer — are OK. The next thing to think about is whether the computer at the other end is on. In particular, what are the scheduled hours for that computer? Some services are available only part-time. The United States Library of Congress's LOCIS system, for example, is available only during library hours. Or maybe some maintenance is going on at the other end.

In what time zone is the other computer? If you're in Los Angeles, it may be 5 p.m. there, but if the other computer is in France, it's 2 a.m. there — a prime time for hardware and software maintenance.

Also, some companies use low-cost, dial-up access to connect their local network to the Internet, which means that they're on the Net only when someone at that company is using some outside network resource. Otherwise, that network is off the Net.

TIP

If you've determined that the other computer is indeed supposed to be available, maybe it's just broken. Try pinging some other computers. (The various network information centers or on-line services — such as `is.internic.net`, `compuserve.com`, and `delphi.com` — are good candidates.) If you can get to those computers, the network probably is OK. If you know someone where the computer you're trying to use is located, call him or her on the phone and ask whether there is a problem.

TIP

Things to know before your network breaks

It's much easier to diagnose network foul-ups if you gather a few important facts before it breaks. Following is a minimal set:

Your computer's host name: ______________

(The Custom window lists your host name and domain name. String those names together, separated by a period, and you have your computer's host name. For example, one author's host name is `meg`, and her domain name is `tiac.net`. Her host name is, therefore, `meg.tiac.net`.)

Its numeric IP address: ______________

(The Custom window lists your IP address, which looks something like `199.0.65.91`.)

Your name server's numeric IP address: ______________

(In Custom, choose Services⇨Domain Servers. You'll see up to three listed. The four parts of the IP addresses are in different boxes — for example, 199, 0, 65, and 2. String the four parts together with periods to make an IP address — for example, `199.0.65.2`.)

Another computer: ______________

(Such as `is.internic.net`.)

Its numeric address: ______________

(For InterNIC's computer, it's `192.153.156.15`. To find out the numeric address of a computer, ping it, and look on the status bar of the Ping window. If you can't see the whole thing, make the Ping window wider.)

What's in a Name?

Occasionally, you'll be running perfectly normally, and the program that you're using displays a strange message. What's going on?

The problem has to do with the way the Internet's Domain Naming System (DNS) works. When you tell a program to contact a computer by name, the program first has to find the corresponding numeric address for the name. To do that, it asks a local name server — a computer running a program that performs the translation. Because there are upward of three million named computers on the Net, no single name server knows all the names, as you may imagine. If you ask your local server for a name that it doesn't know, it goes out by way of the Net to find out about the name from other, better-connected servers.

Now and then, the process of translating a perfectly good name fails. Most likely, one of the Net messages got garbled, and your program got impatient and gave up waiting before the name server could get back to it with the name. The solution to this problem is quite simple: Just try again. The local server will have the translation details (the amounts of time are measured in fractions of a second), and your computer will get its numeric address the next time it asks.

If you get `address not found` errors two or three times in a row, the errors suggest that either the local network or the name server is broken. For suggestions about what to do in that case, refer to "The Network's Dead!" earlier in this chapter.

When Networks Go Bad

Actually, networks almost never go bad. But a few messages *do* mean that the network isn't doing what you want.

"Connection refused"

This message means just what it says: Your computer asked to talk to some other host, and the host said no. There are several possible reasons:

- **You tried to use a service that the host computer doesn't offer.** Not every Internet host offers every service. It's up to a host's manager to decide what services are available and what services aren't.

- **Some hosts don't offer any services at all.** For example, if you try to finger, FTP, telnet, or nearly anything else to `xuxa.iecc.com`, you get `Connection Refused`. It's nothing personal — `xuxa` lives in John's attic, and she won't connect to us, either, because she's a little old 286 PC that just routes data from one network to another. (She does respond to a ping, however, if you want to see that she exists.)
- **The host may accept requests only from certain addresses.** Frequently, for security reasons, a host accepts telnet and FTP only from other FTP hosts on the same network, which means that they're in the same organization.
- **In a few cases, services are available only during certain hours.** Many anonymous FTP servers are available only outside office hours so that the servers aren't slowed down while local users are trying to get work done.

"No route to host or Network unreachable"

Sometimes, this message actually means that no network connection exists between where you are and where the other host computer is. This situation may occur if one of the network routers near you or near the other host fails. More likely explanations are:

- **The numeric address of the host doesn't exist**. You may have typed an address incorrectly, a hard-coded address in a program may have changed, or some part of the database that translates host names to host numbers may be out of sync. (That database is, like much of the rest of the Internet, largely maintained by volunteers, who occasionally goof.)
- **A *firewall* system between you and the other host decided that you're not authorized to communicate with systems beyond it.** So as far as you're concerned, there really *is* no route from here to there. If the firewall is inside your organization, and you're trying to contact a host outside the organization, a special procedure to persuade the firewall that you're OK may be available. Failing that, unless you have pull with the people who run the firewall, you're probably out of luck.

. . . Utter silence . . .

Sometimes, you try to contact another host and get no response at all. This silence means that the host has a valid numeric address on an actual network somewhere, but the host itself doesn't exist — at least, not at the moment. (Think of a new subdivision street on which all the addresses are assigned but some lots are vacant.) Most often, this means that the host is down, so try again later.

Utter silence also may mean that the host exists and is working just fine but doesn't offer the service that you want, or that a firewall in front of the host declined to pass on your request. Ideally, a host computer should send an explicit `refused` message when it receives a request for a service that it doesn't offer; sometimes, though, it just ignores the request. Try Pinging the same address (refer to "Is your computer connected to your Internet provider?," earlier in this chapter). If that procedure works, you're being ignored.

If you think that the host is supposed to offer the service, you can send a polite message to its postmaster (using the e-mail address `postmaster@`*`hostname`*, where *hostname* is the name of the computer you are trying to use). Ask whether the host is broken or the service has been moved somewhere else.

What's My Address?

Before you begin sending out a great deal of e-mail and news articles, make sure that you know your electronic mailing address. Keep in mind that your address relative to the Internet as a whole may be different from your address within your company. For example, your in-company address may be

```
tom@calmari
```

but your address from the outside may be one of the following:

```
tom@calmari.mktg.nebraska.plexxcal.com
Thomas.A.Hendricks@plexxcal.com
```

or even

```
tom%calmari@mktg-gateway.plexxcal.com
```

TIP

One easy and nonembarrassing way to make sure that you have your address right is to send a message to an automated mail server (such as the Majordomo and LISTSERV mail servers discussed in Chapter 6). When the server sends you a response, look at the `To:` line in the response's message header to see what your address is. If you're at a loss for a mail server to use, send a message to The Internet For Dummies Central Headquarters at this address:

NAVIGATE

```
starter@dummies.com
```

While you're at it, add a few words about whether you like this book; messages go to both an automatic mail responder and to a mailbox where the authors can read your comments.

Don't Be a Pig

Because most Internet services are free (after you pay for the network connection), the popular ones can become slow and overloaded. Don't be a pig. Use what you need, but don't FTP megabytes of junk just because you think that you may need it someday.

A Not-So-CAPITAL Idea

Back in the Dark Ages of computing, nobody worried about uppercase and lowercase. Keypunches and terminals had only capital letters, so EVERYTHING WAS IN UPPERCASE, INCLUDING FILENAMES AND MAIL ADDRESSES. BUT IT SEEMED LIKE AN AWFUL LOT OF SHOUTING, SO AS SOON AS TERMINALS COULD HANDLE LOWERCASE, THEY switched to mixed case, which normal people use — at least some of them did.

The problem is that some computers (notably, those running UNIX) consider uppercase and lowercase letters to be different, whereas others (those running most other systems) consider the cases to be the same. On a UNIX system, for example, `README`, `ReadMe`, and `readme` are three different files, but on most other systems, they're merely three different ways to type the name of the file. When you are retrieving files by FTP, make sure that you type the name in the same mixture of uppercase and lowercase letters that appears in a directory listing. It can't hurt, and it may well help.

Another place where case occasionally causes trouble is in e-mail addresses. According to the official standard for e-mail addressing, case doesn't matter in the *domain* part of the address (the part after the @). But the *local* part (the part before the @) can be handled any way the recipient mail system wants. In theory, this means that a really perverse system could interpret `Fred@perverse.org` and `FRED@perverse.org` as being different mail addresses, although we have never seen a mail system that does so. In a few situations, you have to type the local part of the address in the same case that the recipient system uses; if the recipient's address is `fred`, it doesn't accept `Fred`. (These systems are gradually being stamped out, but a few still exist.)

TIP

Fortunately, a reliable rule of thumb is that systems that care about uppercase and lowercase addresses want the address to be in lowercase, so use `fred` to be sure.

How to Make Enemies by Way of E-Mail and News

By far, the quickest way to make a bad name for yourself is to send obnoxious e-mail or news. This subject is discussed to death in Chapters 5 and 6, but following is a short list of things not to do:

- **Don't send junk mail.** Just because it's easy to send e-mail to 10,000 people doesn't mean that it's a good idea. You can expect to find your mailbox clogged, minutes later, with 10,000 irate responses.
- **Don't send advertisements.** Traditionally, Internet e-mail is used for noncommercial purposes. It's perfectly okay to talk about work-related topics, but don't send out unsolicited ads to drum up business. If you do, expect to receive buckets of hate mail — and possibly expect your Internet provider to close your account.
- **Don't send junk news, either.** It's technically easy to send 10,000 copies of a message to every possible Usenet newsgroup to make sure that everyone in the world who reads news will see it. That practice is known as *spamming* (after the Monty Python "I don't like Spam" skit) and is universally loathed. Expect 100,000 irate messages, soon followed by the cancellation of your account.
- **Don't send any messages about dying boys, modem taxes, or chain letters.** Internet users have heard them all and don't want to hear them again. (See Chapter 5 for the sorry details.)
- **DON'T SEND MESSAGES IN UPPERCASE, LIKE THIS, BECAUSE PEOPLE WILL ASSUME THAT YOU'RE TOO DIM TO FIND — AND TURN OFF — THE CAPS LOCK KEY ON YOUR KEYBOARD.** Use uppercase and lowercase letters, just as you would on a typewriter. Some e-mail users evidently feel that neatness no longer counts, but they're wrong.
- **Don't forget: E-mail always comes across ruder or more obnoxious than you intend.** Over and over, people have discovered this important fact the hard way. E-mail is a funny medium, not really like the phone or paper mail. And it's unexpectedly easy to fly off the handle in response — so easy that the term for this is *flaming*. Don't flame. If you do, people assume that you're a flaming . . . um, well, you know what we mean.

Mailing List and Usenet News Etiquette

TIP

This subject is discussed in greater length in Chapters 6 and 7. Following is a brief review:

- Know the difference between the address that you use to get on or off a mailing list and the address that you use to send messages to the list itself.
- Read a mailing list or newsgroup for at least a week before you try to send anything to it, so that you understand what topics it covers and grasp the level of discussion. For example, a Usenet group called `comp.arch` is about computer architecture. But every month or so, some clueless newcomer who's never looked at the contents sends in a question about archiving programs. We're sure that you'll never make that kind of mistake now.
- Most lists have an introductory message, and most newsgroups periodically post one or more FAQ (frequently asked questions) messages that introduce the topic and answer the most commonly asked introductory questions. Before you send in your first question, make sure that it's not already answered for you.
- When you're responding to a message, if you include a copy of the original message, trim it down to the minimum needed.

Why FTP Mangled Your Files

Here's a mistake that everyone makes sooner or later: You use FTP to retrieve a program or a ZIP file, and the file is messed up. The program hangs, or the ZIP file doesn't unZIP. Is the disk broken? Is the network corrupt? Nope. You just forgot to tell FTP to transfer the file in *binary* mode, so FTP copied it in *ASCII* mode, under the mistaken impression that the file contained plain text. Just transfer the file again, this time in binary mode. (Click Binary in the FTP window before transferring the file.)

TIP

An easy way to check for this problem is to compare the size of the file on your computer to the size of the file on the computer from which you retrieved it. In binary mode, the copies should be exactly the same size. (You can click the arrow buttons to the left and right of the Info label in Chameleon FTP to see the file sizes.) If the size differs by a few percent (one copy is 87,837 bytes, and the other is 88,202, for example), you've been bitten by the ASCII copy gremlin. Don't be embarrassed — even experts forget this one from time to time.

The FTP That Wouldn't

Ninety percent of the time, when you copy a file with FTP, it works. When it doesn't work, 90 percent of the time it's because you copied a file in *ASCII* mode rather than *binary* mode (as described in the preceding section). In a few instances, though, FTP can't do what you want it to do for some other reason.

One reason is that on some computers — notably, Macintoshes — filenames can contain spaces. This is a problem for FTP programs on most other kinds of computers, which tend to screw up requests for names that contain spaces; in most cases, the programs assume that spaces separate one name in the command line from another. (A careful reading of the FTP spec shows that FTP programs are supposed to be capable of handling this, but most FTP programs were written long before Macs appeared on the Net in significant numbers.) The usual symptom is that you try to retrieve a file called `read me`, and FTP complains that there's no file called `read`. The only good way around this problem is to change the name of the file that you want to copy.

Dread Version Creep

Finally, there is *version creep*. All facilities on the Internet have evolved over the years. The older ones — such as telnet, FTP, and finger — have become quite stable, whereas the newer ones — such as Gopher, WAIS, and WWW — are still changing. Any successful facility is implemented dozens of times on dozens of different kinds of computers. That's why, for example, you can use telnet to log in to pretty much any kind of computer on the Net. Even though the computers' internal structures are quite different, they all provide compatible telnet servers.

In the more recent services, however, people add new features all the time. This means that you may occasionally get a strange message, such as `I'm sorry but . . . The Viewer: yet_to_be_written %i %p For view type;application/cso is disabled`. That message means that the remote Gopher has offered your system an item that your system doesn't know how to handle. The only solution to this problem is to get a more recent version of the Chameleon (or other) program that you are using.

As services become better understood and settle down, they change less often. For now, the more on the cutting edge something is, the more of a pain it is to keep up to date. (But really, are you surprised?)

Chapter 22

Ten Ways to Find Fun Things to Do

In This Chapter

- Fun
- Games
- Stuff like that

In this chapter, we lean back and relax (as if we weren't doing that already) and look at some of the fun and informal resources that the Net offers.

How to Get There

In case you haven't read Chapter 17, which describes WebSurfer, here's how you use the Uniform Resource Locators (URLs) — the strings that look like `http://dummies.com/` — in this chapter.

It's easy enough. Start WebSurfer, if it's not already running. Choose Retrieve⇨Go to URL. Then type the URL in the box that pops up, and click OK. You'll instantly be transported to . . . to . . . well, to somewhere.

For items that aren't World Wide Web pages, we tell you the name of the Usenet newsgroup to read or the computer to telnet to.

Travel

Internauts are a peripatetic crowd, always on the move. The Internet contains more information on travel than on anything else (except for information about the Net itself). Because the Net is truly global, tons of information about specific countries are available from the countries themselves.

The Global Network Navigator

`http://nearnet.gnn.com/gnn/meta/travel/index.html`

The Global Network Navigator has a whole section dedicated to travel, including a running series written by someone who's heading slowly around the world, filing reports by modem from his laptop. As of May 1994, he'd gotten to Nepal, someone had swiped his computer, and he was stuck. We hope that by the time you read this, he's gotten on his way again.

This server also has travel tips, country features, and ads from travel-related businesses.

The Avid Explorer

`http://www.explore.com`

This server is run by a travel agency offering cruises, expeditions, and other travel services.

U.S. State Department Travel Advisories

`http://www.stolaf.edu/network/travel-advisories.html`

Wondering how dangerous it is to go to Djibouti? The State Department publishes a travel advisory for every country in the world (except, for some reason, the United States), discussing travel facilities, entry requirements, political instability, medical facilities, and availability of U.S. embassies and consulates. (As developing African countries go, Djibouti's not particularly unsafe. You can call the embassy in Djibouti City at 35-39-95.)

TIP: This WWW page, at St. Olaf College, has links to all the current travel advisories, so you can Know Before You Go. Many experienced travelers find these advisories to be a bit alarmist (egad! you can't get Big Macs in Tombouctou!), so you may want to take them with a grain or two of salt.

The page also has links to the *CIA World Factbook*, which has political and economic information for countries all over the world, as well as links to home pages for a few countries.

Countries around the World

This section lists a bunch of informative home pages.

Down Under

You know, where they have have lots of beer and crocodiles and everybody's always upside-down.

Collected New Zealand Information

```
http://www.cs.cmu.edu:8001/Web/People/mjw/NZ/MainPage.html
```

This page has lots of information on beautiful New Zealand.

Guide to Australia

```
http://life.anu.edu.au/education/australia.html
```

Here's even more information on equally beautiful Australia: Geography, Environment, Culture (yes, there's more than beer), History, Travel, and Communications.

Europe

Here are some European hot spots in cyberspace.

The Germany Page

```
http://www.chemie.fu-berlin.de/adressen/brd.html
```

With typical German thoroughness, this page offers you links to much, much, more than any individual would want to know about Germany. Much of it's interesting and useful, of course.

Ireland: The Internet Collection

```
http://itdsrv1.ul.ie/Information/Ireland.html
```

It's time for news, advice, and opinions from the Emerald Isle.

Slovenia

```
http://www.ijs.si/slo.html
```

On the sunny side of the Alps, tucked among Italy, Austria, and Croatia, is Slovenia. It's a nice place; we were there in 1971 for a computer conference. Learn all about its past and present.

Information about the Netherlands

```
http://www.tno.nl/NL-www/nl-info.html
```

This page contains basic Dutch info, largely from the *CIA World Factbook*.

U.K. Information

```
http://www.cs.ucl.ac.uk/misc/uk/wfb.html
```

This page is also from the *CIA World Factbook*, but enriched by links to other, more specific information on counties and cities. You're only two clicks away from in-depth info on pubs in London.

Basic Information about Poland

```
http://info.fuw.edu.pl/poland-info.html
```

Here's the Polish page from the *CIA World Factbook*.

Switzerland Online Guide

```
http://heiwww.unige.ch/switzerland
```

It's the *CIA World Factbook* again (gee, it's almost as if only the CIA knows about anyplace!), enhanced with attractive photographs and other Swiss stuff.

Austria Online Guide

```
http://ravel.ifs.univie.ac.at/austria/austria_info.html
```

Guess what? It's the *CIA World Factbook* page about Austria! Wow!

Toot, toot!

Railroad lovers will find a wealth of choo-choo information on the Internet. Here's a sample:

The Railroad Page

```
http://www-cse.ucsd.edu/users/bowdidge/railroad/rail-
          home.html
```

This page contains information on mailing lists, FTP archives, commercial services, and on-line maps: everything for the well-informed rail fan.

The CalTrain Schedule

```
http://www.commerce.digital.com/palo-alto/CalTrain/form.html
```

This page provides an interactive schedule for the trains running between San Francisco and San Jose, California, and all intermediate stations.

The Funnies

Let's relax and read the funnies.

Dr. Fun

```
http://sunsite.unc.edu/Dave/drfun.html
Usenet newsgroup: alt.binaries.pictures.misc
```

The Internet has its own daily cartoon, *Dr. Fun*, in the tradition of *The Far Side*. *Dr. Fun* ranges from the strange to the extremely strange; one caption was "Silly String and Crazy Glue: a Deadly Combination." (The picture was not unlike what you'd expect.)

The doctor appears every weekday as an attractive full-color graphic. Don't miss him.

Dilbert and Doonesbury

`http://nearnet.gnn.com/gnn/news/comix/index.html`

The folks at GNN have a comics page featuring actual syndicated comics — at the moment, *Dilbert*, which is every nerd's favorite strip (because everything that he says about us nerds is true), and some classic *Doonesbury* strips about the Internet. You can find *Dr. Fun* from here, too.

Virtual Meetmarket

`http://wwa.com:1111/`

People in cyberspace are as sociable as those in real life, sometimes, so it was just a matter of time until the personals column appeared. Here it is. Each ad gets a page, as shown in Figure 22-1. There aren't a whole lot of ads yet, so at this point there's no charge to place and respond to ads. They say they may charge in the future.

WWW Calc

`http://guinan.gsfc.nasa.gov/Web/Calc.html`

Computer geeks have always delighted in making a big, expensive computer act like a greatly overpriced version of a common household or office appliance. (The On-line Internet Toaster was a big hit at a recent trade show.) WWW Calc takes the global resources of the World Wide Web and makes them simulate a $7.95 pocket calculator, only slower.

Try it out. Then forget about it.

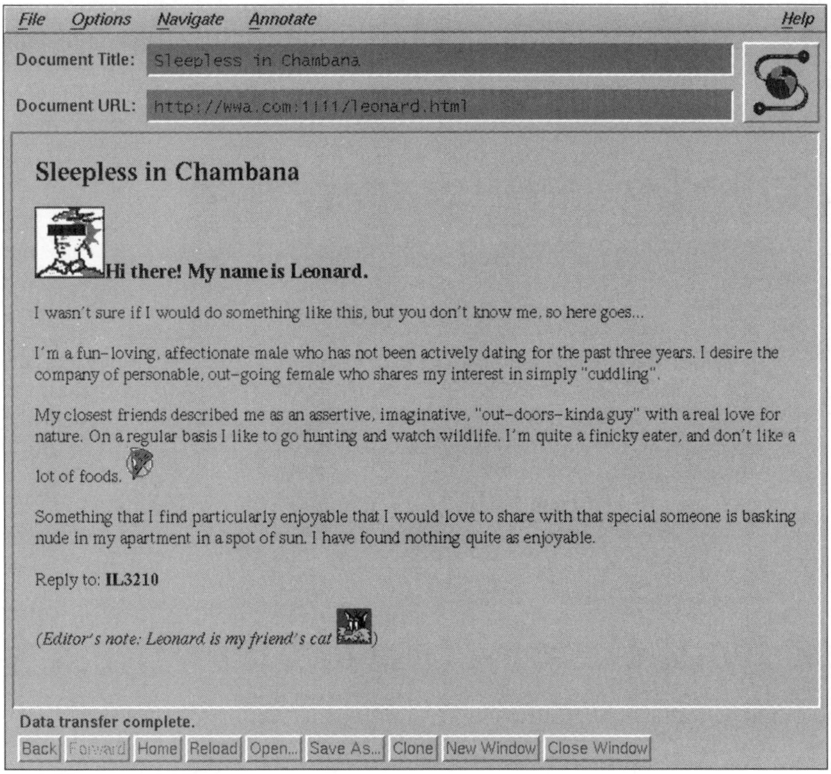

Figure 22-1: Where the elite meet.

The Metro Server

```
telnet to metro.jussieu.fr using port 10000
```

Are you troubled about getting lost on the subway? So long as you live in Vienna, Hong Kong, Montreal, Palermo, Toronto, Mexico City, Lille (France), Amsterdam, Lyons (France), Madrid, Marseilles, London, Paris, Boston, Toulouse (France), New York, Frankfurt, San Francisco, Munich, Washington (D.C.), or Athens, this is your lucky day. The Metro Server will figure out your route for you. Telnet in, and you immediately are in the Metro system. You tell the server the name of the city, the departing station, and the arriving station, and it'll give you the best route and the travel time.

When the server asks whether you want to use the X Window system, say no. You can abbreviate stations to the shortest portion of the name that isn't ambiguous.

Making Gopher Harder to Use

```
telnet to jh.ccs.neu.edu using port 1709
ftp://mailbase.ac.uk/pub/lists/unite/files/jays_house.txt
```

Part of the charm of Gopher is that it's easy to use: You just click menu items, and you get your stuff. Some people, however, seem to feel that information is worthwhile only if they have to work to get hold of it. If you're one of these people, MOO Gopher is just the ticket for you. This server is a Gopher client hidden inside a Multi-User Dungeon, so you have to look around and guess where to find things. There is some help, so it took us only two or three minutes to find some Gopher menus, but doubtless there were more that we didn't find.

And Now, Coming to a Network near You!

```
http://www.ncsa.uiuc.edu/radio/radio.html
http://www.cmf.nrl.navy.mil/radio/ITR.html
http://juggler.lanl.gov/itr.html
http://www.doc.ic.ac.uk/public/media/audio/ITR/
e-mail info@radio.com and sites@radio.com
```

The global village now has its own radio stations: Internet Talk Radio and Internet Town Hall, produced by the Internet Multicasting Service. Every week, ITR and ITH send out interviews, stories, and the occasional goofy sound clip. (One clip said, over portentous music, "The future . . . is tomorrow.") There's a weekly "Geek of the Week" interview with a network notable, as well as talks from the National Press Club and the occasional National Public Radio show. Most of it is well worth listening to. Some shows during a week in May 1994 included the following:

- **Common Ground:** The director of the special UN/OAS mission to Haiti discussed what went wrong.
- **HarperAudio**: Poet and novelist Robert Graves read from *The White Goddess*, a study of anthropology and mythology.

- **SoundBytes**: 12 Tone Geek, performed by house band Tungsten Maqaque (3.5 seconds long).
- **National Press Club**: Garrison Keillor discussed *Why I Decided Not to Run for President in 1996*.
- **HarperAudio**: S-F author Frank Herbert read from his classic *Dune* series.
- **Professor Neon's TV & Movie Mania**: Robert Justman, who directed and produced shows ranging from "The Outer Limits" to "Star Trek" and "Star Trek: The Next Generation," discussed the production of these shows.

If your computer can play sounds (most workstations, all Macs, and any PC with a sound card of some sort can), you can download the files and play them. Via the World Wide Web, you can use any of the four URLs above to get information and schedules. For actual FTP sites, send a message (contents unimportant) to `sites@radio.com`. We won't list sites here, because they change frequently. For a FAQ message that provides a more detailed overview of ITR and ITH, including info on how you can get the programs on cassette, send a message (contents unimportant) to `info@radio.com`.

Sound files are *REALLY, REALLY BIG*. An hour of sound fills up about 30MB of disk space. As the Multicasting Service's FAQ message says:

```
Oh, my! Do you mean to tell me that you expect me to download
          45MB of data? Are you nuts?
Yes.
```

You can make yourself extremely unpopular if you download 15MB files from a server on another continent in the middle of the day. So don't do that. Check the sites list to find a server close to you, and do your heavy-duty downloading at off-peak times: the middle of the night or on weekends.

Put up or shut up on the information superhighway

Back at the dawn of electronic history (around 1945), someone went around and asked people what they'd like to watch. The answers were along the lines of classic movies and plays, educational lectures, concerts — stuff like that. And what did we really watch? "I Love Lucy" and "Queen for a Day."

Recently, someone asked similar questions about what people would want access to on the coming Information Superhighway (known in some circles as the Information Supercollider). What do you know — classic movies and plays, educational lectures . . . you get the idea. Well, with the Internet Multicasting Service, we got what we asked for. Are we going to take advantage of it, or are we really waiting for "Internet Wheel of Fortune"?

Femmes Femmes Femmes Je Vous Aime!

`http://www.cnam.fr/bin.html/imageWWW`

This extraordinarily politically incorrect page features pictures, from France, of scantily clad ladies. It's all pretty innocent; we've seen more salacious stuff in *Vogue*. As one might imagine, it's quite popular. Controversial, too.

Horsing Around

`http://www.inslab.uky.edu/People/stevem/horses/KyDerbyInfo/kyderby.html`

It's the brightest jewel of the Triple Crown: the Kentucky Derby. This page includes the facts you need to know, such as that in 1994, number 6, Go For Gin, paid $20.20, $8.40, and $5.80. The server also provides news, events, and previous results.

Attention, Klutzes!

`http://www.hal.com/services/juggle/`

Ever want to learn how to juggle? The Juggling Information Service features news, advice, pictures, vendors of juggling equipment (flaming Indian clubs have to come from *somewhere*), software, and lots of gossip.

More Fun and Games

`http://wcl-rs.bham.ac.uk/~djh/index.html`

This page links Web pages, archived FAQ files, and everything else that the author could find on games and gaming. Want to know about playing Bolo on your Macintosh? Here's where to find out.

Food, Food, Wonderful Food

Finally, we get to something that we can all agree is interesting and important.

Where to Eat in the Hub of the Universe

```
http://www.osf.org:8001/boston-food/boston-food.html
Usenet newsgroup: ne.food
```

Hungry in Boston? This page lists hundreds of restaurants, with reviews constantly updated by readers' messages to Usenet. Most listings are linked to longer reviews, such as the following:

```
Emporio Armani Express [Italian] — Back Bay
More a scene than anything else, though the food is rather
good. For the men: dress like you're in advertising; for the
women: wear either no makeup or way too much. Feign an
attitude. They hired the most obsequious waiter I've _ever_
had, but you already guessed that. Have a drink in the bar
downstairs first. If you don't feel too alienated, have
dinner upstairs. (4/94)
```

On-line Coke Machines

There have been soda machines on the Net for almost as long as there's been a Net. Nothing annoys a hard-hacking nerd more than walking down the hall to get a life-sustaining, carbonated, sugared beverage, only to find out that the machine is empty — or, worse, was just filled and the soda is warm. To avert this unspeakable horror, machines were quickly networked for the benefit of local users. Of course, the Net being the Net, it's as easy to query a machine from 10,000 miles away as it is from 10 feet away.

The most common way to check on a Coke machine is with the Chameleon Finger program (described in Chapter 5). Among the most popular machines on the Net are `drink@drink.csh.rit.edu`, `coke@cs.cmu.edu`, `coke@xcf.berkeley.edu`, `pepsi@columbia.edu`, `cocacola@columbia.edu`, and `coke@ucc.gu.uwa.edu.au`. (When you use the Chameleon Finger program, enter the host name [the part of the address after the @] in the Host box, and the user name, the part of the address before the @, in the User box. Then click Finger.)

A typical response from the Carnegie-Mellon machine is:

```
[G.GP.CS.CMU.EDU]
Login name: coke                    In real life: Drink Coke
Directory: /usrgl/coke  Shell: /usr/cs/bin/csh
Plan:
Thu May 19 08:06:14 1994
M&M validity: 9          Coke validity: 9
  M & M             Buttons
  /—\        C: CC......................
  |   |    C: C...........  D: C...........
  |**** |    C: C...........  D: C...........
  |*****|    C: C...........  D: C...........
  |*****|            C: CCC.........
  \—/              S: C...........
   |      Key:
   |       0 = warm; 9 = 90% cold; C = cold; . = empty
   |       Leftmost soda/pop will be dispensed next
  _^_
```

The Trojan Room

```
http://www.cl.cam.ac.uk/coffee/coffee.html
```

In England, people evidently drink coffee rather than Coke, and there's no point going down the hall if the pot's empty. So in the finest hacker tradition, some academics at Cambridge University pointed a video camera at the coffeepot, using some extremely complicated software to digitize the picture once a second and send the image to their Web server (see Figure 22-2). Now people all over the world can tell whether, should they fly to Cambridge, there'll be coffee ready.

Figure 22-2: About half full.

TIP

Sometimes, the picture is pitch-black. Nothing's wrong; it's probably just the middle of the night, and someone's turned out the lights.

Appendix A

Listing of Software on the Starter Kit Disks

The floppy disks in the back of this book contain a complete version of Internet Chameleon, as well as a swell new automated sign-up program called Instant Internet. This appendix contains a list of the programs that you should have received.

Note: To install the programs, follow the instructions in Chapter 3.

Internet Chameleon is from NetManage, which can be contacted at `support@netmanage.com`.

Instant Internet

This program displays information about the Internet providers that have signed up to accept Instant Internet accounts. You use this program to sign up for a new Internet SLIP, CSLIP, or PPP account. The program also configures all the rest of the Internet Chameleon programs to work with this new account. The program is called `instinet.exe`. See Chapter 3 for information on how to run it.

After you have run Instant Internet and chosen an Internet provider, icons appear in Windows Program Manager for the rest of the programs listed in this appendix.

Chameleon Custom Program and NEWT

You use Custom to connect to and disconnect from your Internet provider by using the TCP/IP protocol over the phone. You leave Custom running all the time when you are connected to the Internet. The NEWT program runs behind the scenes; you see the NEWT icon while Custom is running. The program that runs when you click the Custom icon is called `custom.exe`. See Chapter 3 for information how to use Custom.

Chameleon Mail

Mail allows you to send and receive e-mail. It can store your messages in folders for future reference, and can handle MIME (multimedia) attachments to messages. The program is called `mail.exe`, and mail is stored in the `email` subdirectory of the NetManage program directory (usually `c:\netmanage`). See Chapter 4 for information on how to use Chameleon Mail.

Mail Utilities

This program allows you to fix broken Mail mailboxes, merge two mailboxes, or eliminate the wasted space that builds up in mailboxes. The program is called `dbutil.exe`. See the end of Chapter 4 for information on how to run it.

NEWTNews

NEWTNews is a Usenet newsreader. You can choose which newsgroups to participate in, select articles to read, respond to articles by e-mail, or post follow-up articles to the newsgroup. The program is called `newtnews.exe`. See Chapter 8 for information on how to use NEWTNews.

Chameleon Telnet

Telnet allows you to log in to other computers on the Internet. The program is called `telnet.exe`. See Chapter 10 for information on how to use it.

Chameleon FTP

This FTP program gives you access to the tens of thousands of files stored on FTP servers around the world. You can move around from directory to directory to see what's on each FTP server, and you can copy files to or from FTP servers. The program is called `ftp.exe`. See Chapter 12 for information on how to use it.

FTP Server

This program enables your lowly little PC to act as an FTP server, so that other people on the Internet can use their FTP programs to transfer files to and from your computer. The program is called `fts.exe`. See the sidebar at the end of Chapter 12 for information on how to use it.

Chameleon Archie

Archie enables you to search all the FTP servers in the world (or most of them, anyway), for the filename that you specify. The program is called `archie.exe`. See Chapter 14 for information on how to use it.

Chameleon Gopher

Gopher allows you to wander around in Gopherspace, moving from menu to menu, looking for useful information. You can use Gopher to find text files, graphics, and even programs. The program is called `gopher.exe`, and menus retrieved by Gopher are stored in the `gopher` subdirectory of the NetManage program directory. See Chapter 15 for information on how to use it.

WebSurfer

This program enables you to browse the World Wide Web, following hypertext links from Web page to Web page. You can also use it to read Usenet newsgroups, wander through Gopherspace, and review the files on FTP servers. The program is called `chmosaic.exe`, and graphics files retrieved by WebSurfer are stored in the `chmosaic` subdirectory of the NetManage program directory. Several Web pages come with the program and are stored in files with the extension HTM in the NetManage program directory. See Chapter 17 for information on how to use the program.

Chameleon Ping

This program enables you to send a "ping" message to any computer on the Internet and waits to receive a "pong" message in response. The program is called `ping.exe`. See Chapter 3 for information on how to use it to test your network connection.

Finger

Finger allows you to find out about a host computer on the Internet or about a particular person who uses that host computer. The program is called `finger.exe`. See Chapter 5 for information on how to use it.

Whois

This program uses the Whois system to find the e-mail addresses of people you specify. The program is called `whois.exe`. The Whois system mostly lists network adminstrators; see Chapter 5 for details.

The Readme icon in the Internet Chameleon program group displays a document named `inetcham.wri`, which is in Windows Write format. This document contains additional technical information about Internet Chameleon.

Appendix B

Manually Configuring Chameleon

In This Chapter

- How to install Internet Chameleon if you already have an Internet provider
- How to install Internet Chameleon if you want to use an Internet provider that is not displayed by the Instant Internet program
- What to do if your Internet provider changes, your e-mail address changes, or other important information changes

Using a Non-Instant Internet Provider

You can use the Internet Chameleon software that comes with this book even if you don't want to use one of the Internet providers that work with Instant Chameleon. This approach, however, has two drawbacks:

- **It's not so instant.** You need to configure your Internet Chameleon software yourself. Luckily, this appendix tells you how to do it.
- **It's going to cost some money.** If you use a provider of your own choosing, you have to pay NetManage to activate the Internet Chameleon software. Luckily, NetManage is still a great deal — the activation fee plus the cost of this book is still a lot less than you would pay otherwise for the complete, supported Internet software that you get.

The concept

Here's how it works:

1. You install the Internet Chameleon software.
2. You use Instant Internet to call up NetManage and get a free 30-day Internet account. For a fee, you can also get a full software license for the Internet Chameleon software. (When you connect to NetManage, the service quotes the current activation fee.)

3. You arrange for your own Internet account from the provider of your choice.
4. You configure the Internet Chameleon software to work with your new account instead of with NetManage.
5. You're ready to go!

In the following sections, we walk you through this process.

Installing the software

This part is easy; just follow the steps in "Installing Internet Chameleon" in Chapter 3. You end up with a program group in Windows Program Manager called Internet Chameleon. The group contains just two icons: Instant Internet and a Readme icon that displays lots of technical information.

Activating the software

To activate the software, you use Instant Internet to contact NetManage, the author of the Chameleon Internet software. (You can also refer to the "Instant Internet!" section of Chapter 3.) Follow these steps:

1. **Double-click the Instant Internet icon in the Internet Chameleon program group.**

   You see the Select Internet Provider window. Across the top of the window are tabs — one for each Internet provider that works with the Instant Internet program. One of them is for NetManage, which isn't really a regular Internet provider — they're the software company that wrote all these great Internet Chameleon programs.

2. **If the NetManage information isn't already visible, click the NetManage tab.**

   For more information about NetManage's deal (for registering your Internet Chameleon software and getting a demo Internet account), click the More Info button at the bottom of the window. After you read the text, click the Cancel button to return to the Select Internet Provider window.

3. **Click the Signup button.**

   You see the Instant Internet Account Sign-Up window. Two tabs appear at the top of the window; these tabs are named *Please fill out this registration form* and *Fill this additional form out as well.* The forms contain all the blanks that you need to fill in to tell NetManage all about yourself, where you live, and how you want to pay for activating the Internet Chameleon software.

Note: Be sure that no other communications program is running before you click Signup. Instant Internet is going to need your communications port and modem all to itself.

4. **Fill in the blanks.**

   You can always click the Help button if you have questions. Don't worry about the little pictures of phones, cables, and traffic lights — the program uses those pictures later to show you how it's doing while it communicates with NetManage.

5. **Click the Phone List button, and then choose the phone number that is the closest to you.**

   Because NetManage is a software company and not a full-fledged Internet provider, it doesn't have a national network of phone numbers.

6. **Click the tab that says Fill this additional form out as well.**

   You see another form, with more blanks.

7. **Fill in the blanks, if you have an existing Internet SLIP account and know the information it asks for.**

   If you don't have an account yet or don't know the information, don't worry. Later in this appendix, we'll tell you how to set the Internet Chameleon software up to work with your account. If you do have an account and your provider has given you a NetManage Provider ID, be sure to enter that so Instant Internet can configure you automatically.

8. **After you provide all the information in both forms, make sure that your modem is turned on (if it's an external modem). Also make sure that no other program is using the modem.**

   If you have a fax/modem, for example, close your fax software so that Instant Internet and your fax software don't argue about who's using the phone line. (It's a little like having teenagers in the house, actually.)

9. **Click the Send button.**

   Instant Internet figures out which of your communication ports connects to your modem, calls NetManage, transmits the information that you just typed, gets approval for your free 30-day account, and downloads your new Internet address and other configuration information. Most important, the program activates your Internet Chameleon software and configures the software to work with your new Internet account.

   You see a message that tells you when your account will be ready to use and that also provides your user name and other information. Write all of this information down in Table 3-1 in Chapter 3 or on the Cheat Sheet that comes in the front of the book.

10. **When Instant Internet finishes running, it creates a bunch of fantastic icons in your Internet Chameleon program group.**

    Your new, improved set of icons tells you that your software has been activated. You now have a fully supported software license for all these neat programs.

At this point, you can use your free NetManage account for 30 days. As soon as you get your permanent Internet account, you can switch over to that account, following the directions in the rest of this appendix.

Getting your own Internet account

Contact the Internet provider of your choice. Appendix C contains the names of some Internet providers outside the United States. You can also check the business section of your local paper for providers.

You may be able to get Internet access through your company or school. *Cool* — since that probably means that it's free.

Make sure that the Internet provider, or your company or school, gives you a SLIP, CSLIP, ISDN, or PPP account. Also make sure that the provider offers an SMTP mail gateway (for outgoing e-mail), a POP3 mail server (for incoming e-mail), and a news server (for Usenet newsgroups).

Ask your Internet provider for the information in Table B-1, which you will need when you configure the Internet Chameleon programs.

Table B-1 Information about Your Internet Connection

Information	*Description*	*Example*
Your own Internet	Your PC's own numeric Internet address. Although the address is for your computer, you get this number from your Internet provider.	`123.45.67.89`
Your own host name	The name of your own computer. When you get an account with an Internet provider, you usually get to choose this name. Make the name short, spellable, and perhaps cute.	`meg`
Your domain name	The name of your Internet provider's domain. The name looks like the last part of an Internet address and usually ends with `net` or `com` (in the United States, anyway).	`plebney.com`

Information	*Description*	*Example*
Your communications	The communications port on your own computer to which your modem is attached (usually, COM1 or COM2). Even if your modem lives inside your computer and doesn't look as though it is connected to a port, it is.	`COM1`
Your modem speed	The fastest speed at which both your modem and your Internet provider's modem can run. If your modem can run at 9,600 or 14,400 *bps* (bits per second) but your Internet provider can handle only 9,600, choose 9,600. Conversely, if your modem can do only 2,400 bps (which is going to seem really, really slow when you get connected), choose 2,400.	`14,400`
Your modem	The kind of modem that you have. Actually, WinSock packages are only dimly aware of the details on different kinds of modems. If you have a regular PC-type modem, it's probably similar enough to a Hayes model to fool Internet Chameleon.	`Hayes`
Phone number	The number that you call to connect to your Internet provider, exactly as you would dial it manually. If the number is long-distance, include 1 at the beginning. If you need to dial 9 and pause for a few seconds to get an outside line, include 9 and a comma at the beginning.	`1-617-637-1234`
Interface type	The exact type of interface used by the provider. The choices are SLIP, CSLIP, ISDN, and PPP. If you have a choice, use PPP. The next-best choice is CSLIP. The slowest option (but still OK) is SLIP. ISDN, when available, is twice as fast as any of the alternatives; its availability depends on your phone company, and it needs a special adapter to connect to the phone line.	`CSLIP`
User name	The name on your account with your Internet provider (also called a login name).	`myoung`

(continued)

Table B-1 *(continued)*

Information	*Description*	*Example*
User password	The password for your account.	`friedrice`
Startup command	The command that your Internet provider should run when you call in. Your provider can give you this command. If the provider starts SLIP right away when you log in, you may not need a startup command.	`SLIP`
Default gateway address	The numeric Internet address of the computer that passes your data to the rest of the network.	`123.45.67.89`
Domain name server address(es)	The numeric Internet address(es) of the computer(s) that can translate between regular Internet addresses and their numeric equivalents (for example, between `iecc.com` and `140.186.81.1`). Your Internet provider should give you one to three addresses.	`123.45.67.99`
Mail-gateway address	The Internet address of the computer that will handle your outgoing e-mail. A system called SMTP is used to send the mail along to the Internet for delivery.	`xuxa.iecc.com`
Mail-server address	The Internet address of the computer that will handle your incoming e-mail (most often the same as the mail gateway). Mail servers use a system called POP3.	`astrud.iecc.com`
Mailbox name	Usually the same as your user name. Your e-mail address will be the mailbox name followed by an at sign (@) and by the mail-server address (for example, `myoung@astrud.iecc.com`).	`myoung`
Mailbox password	Your Internet provider may allow you to give your mailbox a separate password.	`friedrice`
News server address	The Internet address of the computer that will provide your Usenet newsgroup information, using a system called NNTP.	`news.tiac.net`

Configuring Internet Chameleon for your account

Before you can use Internet Chameleon, you have to tell it all the fascinating facts that you just received from your Internet provider. To enter most of this information, you use a program called Custom.

Mercifully, NetManage, the Chameleon people, has already entered some of the information about many widely used Internet providers, so part of the work may have been done for you. The providers that Internet Chameleon knows something about are listed in Table B-2, along with the names of the configuration files. (By the time you read this book, NetManage may have added even more.) If your provider gave you a Provider ID and you entered it when using Instant Internet, most of the configuration information will already have been set up for you.

Table B-2 Internet Providers That Chameleon Knows About

Provider	*Configuration Filename*
ANSRemote	ANSREMOT.CFG
CERFNet	CERFNET.CFG
CICNet	CICNET.CFG
ClarkNet	CLARKNET.CFG
CRL	CRL.CFG
CyberGate	CYBRGATE.CFG
Digex	DIGEX.CFG
HookUp	HOOKUP.CFG
Iglou	IGLOU.CFG
InterAcc	INTERACC.CFG
InterRamp	INTERAMP.CFG
JVNCnet	JVNCNET.CFG
MRnet	MRNET.CFG
NetCom	NETCOM.CFG
NW Nexus	NWNEXUS.CFG
Olympus	OLYMPUS.CFG

(continued)

Table B-2 *(continued)*

Provider	*Configuration Filename*
OnRamp	ONRAMP.CFG
Panix	PANIX.CFG
Portal	PORTAL.CFG
PSINet	PSINET.CFG
UUNet's AlterNet	ALTERNET.CFG
WLN	WLN.CFG

To run Custom, double-click the Custom icon in the Internet Chameleon program group. This icon looks like a little crane. (Don't ask us why.)

If Internet Chameleon knows about your Internet provider

If you didn't give Instant Internet a Provider ID, follow these steps to enter some additional information in the configuration file for that provider:

1. **Choose File⇨Open and then select the configuration file for that provider.**

   Refer to Table B-2 for the name of the your provider's configuration file.

2. **Click OK to read the configuration file and add more information to it.**

   The information about the provider appears in the Custom window.

3. **Skip to "Either way" later in this appendix.**

If Internet Chameleon has never heard of your Internet provider

Don't despair. Follow these steps to create a configuration file for your provider:

1. **Choose File⇨New.**

   Custom creates a nice, blank configuration file for you.

2. **Choose Interface⇨Add.**

   You see the Add Interface window, shown in Figure B-1.

Figure B-1: Creating the configuration file for your Internet provider.

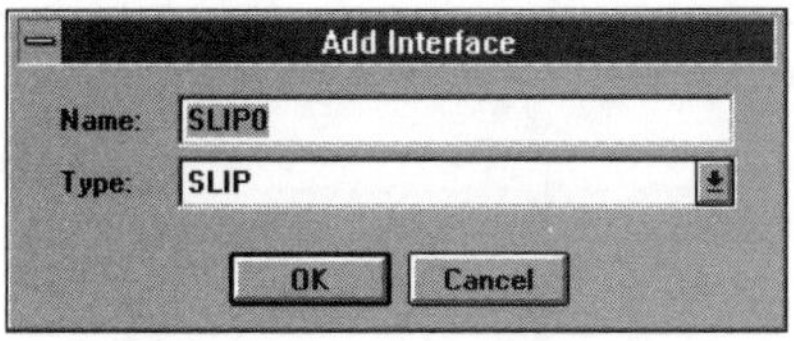

3. **In the Name box, enter the name of your Internet provider (or an abbreviation). Alternatively, accept the default name (`SLIP0`).**
4. **In the Type box, select the type of interface that your Internet provider uses (refer to Table B-1).**

   Your options are SLIP, CSLIP, ISDN, and PPP.
5. **Click the OK button.**

   Custom creates an interface of the type that you chose for this new configuration file.
6. **Choose File⇨Save As, and then give the configuration file a name. You can use as many as eight characters, with no spaces or punctuation.**

   We use TIAC (The Internet Access Company) in Bedford, Massachusetts, so we named our configuration file TIAC. Chameleon automatically adds the file extension CFG to the filename.
7. **Follow the steps in the "Either way" section.**

Either way

Now that you have a configuration file, either by opening one that Internet Chameleon already had or by creating a new one, you can enter your information into that file, using the information in Table B-1. Follow these steps:

1. **Run the Custom program if you're not already in it, and choose Setup⇨IP Address.**

   You see the bizarre-looking dialog box shown in Figure B-2.

   In the four little boxes, you enter the four parts of your personal Internet address. All Internet addresses come in four parts, separated by periods (for example, 199.0.65.91).

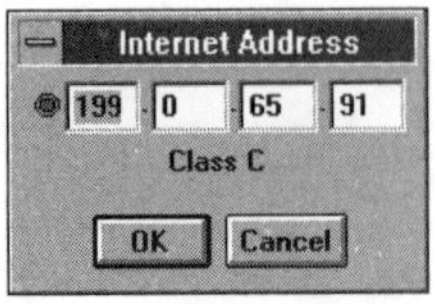

Figure B-2: A peculiar-looking way to enter your numeric Internet address.

2. **Enter each part in the appropriate box, and then click OK.**

   When the dialog box appears, you see the message `Class A`. After you enter the first of the four numbers in your Internet address, this message probably changes — ours says `Class C`. This message reflects how big and important an Internet address this is. For more information, see Chapter 2 in *The Internet For Dummies*.

3. **Choose Setup⇨Host Name, enter your own host name, and click OK.**

4. **Choose Setup⇨Domain Name, enter the domain name of your Internet provider, and click OK.**

5. **Choose Setup⇨Port.**

   You see the Port Settings dialog box, shown in Figure B-3. (Don't panic; we know that this dialog box displays a lot of horrific-looking gobbledygook.)

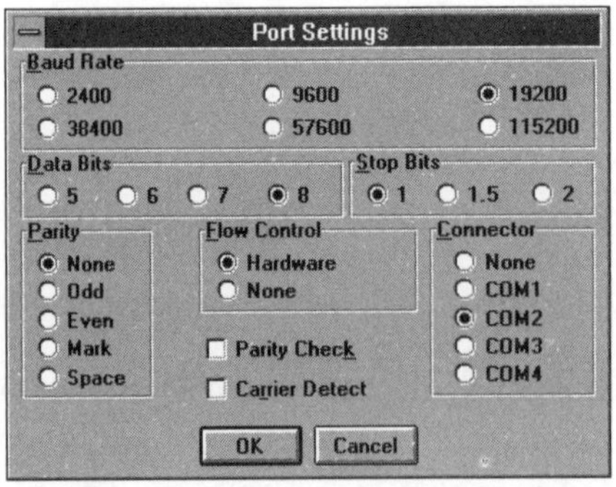

Figure B-3: The Port Settings dialog box.

6. **For the Connector setting, choose the communications port to which your modem is attached. For the Baud Rate setting, enter your modem's speed. Then click OK.**

   Leave everything else alone. Well, okay — if you *must* change something, you can select the Carrier Detect option so that Custom can tell when the phone hangs up. But that's all.

7. **Choose Setup⇨Modem.**

   You see the Modem Settings dialog box, shown in Figure B-4.

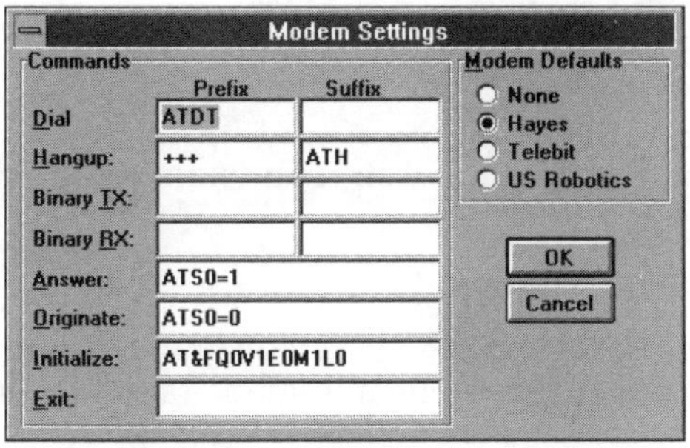

Figure B-4: What kind of modem do you have?

8. **Enter the type of modem you have (or the type that your modem acts like) in the Modem Defaults box, and then click OK.**

   Custom should automatically fill in the rest of the information.

9. **Choose Setup⇨Dial.**

   You see the Dial Settings dialog box, shown in Figure B-5.

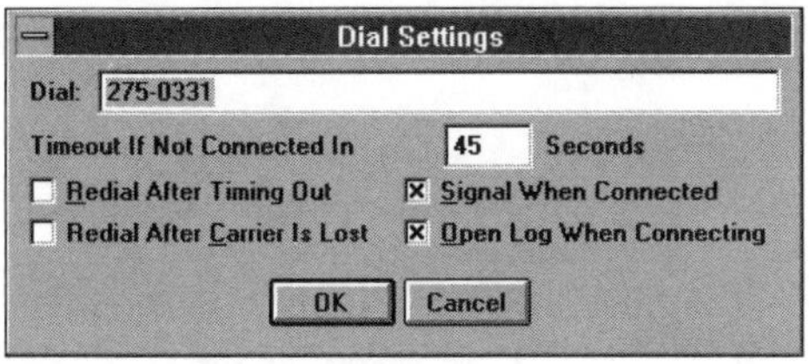

Figure B-5: Internet Chameleon has your number.

10. **Enter the phone number of your Internet provider exactly as you would dial it manually, and then click OK.**

    If you want Custom to open a Log window as it makes the connection so that you can see what's going on, click the Open Log When Connecting box. If you want Custom to keep trying if it can't get through, click the Redial After Timing Out box.

11. **Choose Setup⇨Login.**

    You see the Login Settings dialog box, shown in Figure B-6.

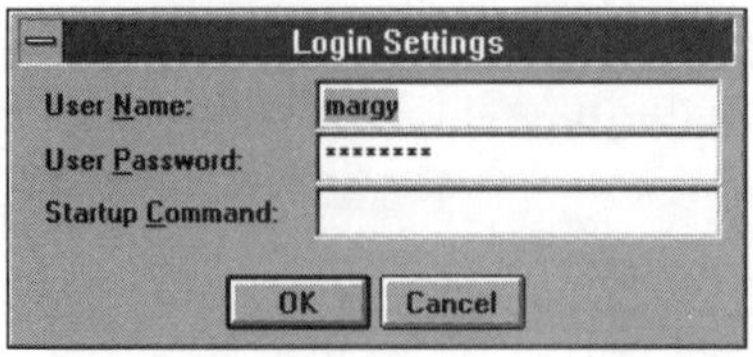

Figure B-6: Enter your login name here.

12. **Enter your user name, password, and start-up command in the blanks; then click OK.**
13. **Choose Services⇨Default Gateway.**

    This command may not be available — it is frequently gray and lifeless. If so, skip to step 15. If you use this command, you see another four-part box.
14. **Type the four-part numeric address of your provider's network gateway, and then click OK.**
15. **Choose Services⇨Domain Servers.**

    You see another bizarre dialog box, shown in Figure B-7.

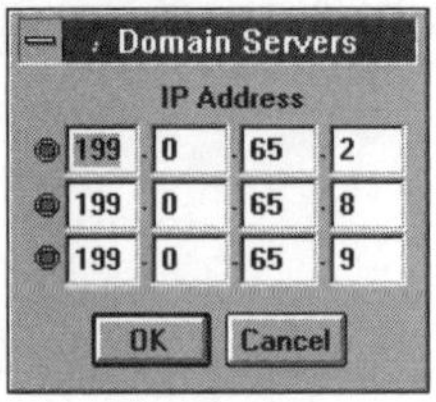

Figure B-7: Entering another incomprehensible numeric Internet address.

    The box has room for up to three numeric Internet addresses of your domain name servers: the one that you normally use, and two backups in case the regular one is dead.
16. **Enter the address(es), and then click OK.**

    You're almost finished, folks.
17. **Choose File⇨Save to save all the crucially important information that you just entered.**
18. **Exit the Custom program by choosing File⇨Exit.**

    Even if you plan to go ahead and try connecting to the Internet right away, you still have to exit the Custom program right now so that all the information you just entered goes into effect the next time you run Custom.

When you exit the Custom program, the NEWT program (which runs behind the scenes to handle communications with the Internet) is supposed to exit, too. The NEWT icon at the bottom of your screen should vanish; if the NEWT icon doesn't, exit Windows and restart Windows.

Now you should be ready to try connecting to your Internet provider. Follow the instructions in the section "Making a Connection" in Chapter 3. If you have problems, please call your Internet provider, *not* NetManage; the problem most likely is that one of the settings that you typed has to be adjusted, based on advice from your provider.

Configuring Your Mail

If your mail hasn't been set up by Instant Internet, the first time you run Chameleon Mail you have to create a mailbox for yourself. Chameleon Mail is ready to keep track of e-mail for several different people. When you run it for the first time, you act as the "Postmaster" and must create mailboxes for all the people who will use this copy of Chameleon Mail to read their mail.

In most cases, of course, *you* are the only person who will use this copy of Chameleon Mail. So you probably will have to create just one mailbox.

To set up mailbox, follow these steps:

1. **Double-click the Mail icon in the Chameleon program group in the Program Manager.**

   It's the one that looks like a little country-style mailbox.

   You see the little Mail Login dialog box, shown in Figure B-8. The program lets several people have their mailboxes on one PC, so you have to tell it who you are. At the bottom of the screen, a little Address Book icon appears too — we describe how to use it later in this chapter, in the section "Your Little Black Book."

2. **Leave the Username as *Postmaster* and leave the password blank. Click OK.**

   You see the Chameleon Mail window, shown in Figure B-9.

3. **Right now, Chameleon Mail thinks that you are someone named Postmaster. To fix that, choose Services⇨Mailboxes from the menu bar.**

   You see the Mailboxes window, shown in Figure B-10. It lists all the mailboxes that have been set up in your copy of Chameleon Mail — at this point, there is probably only one, named Postmaster.

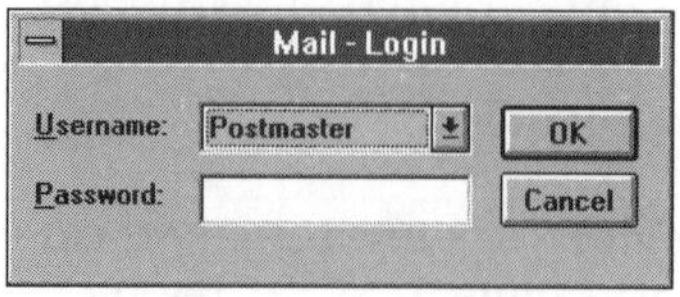

Figure B-8: Chameleon Mail wants to know exactly who you are.

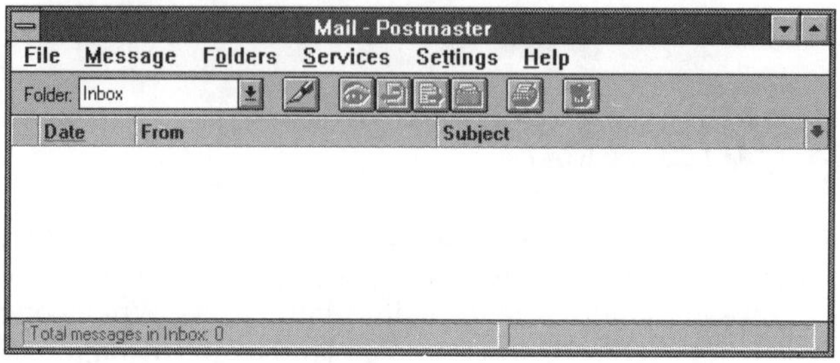

Figure B-9: Mission control for Chameleon Mail.

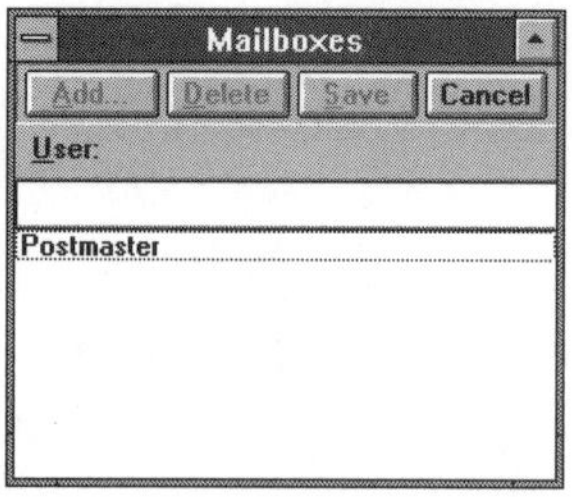

Figure B-10: Making a mailbox for yourself.

4. **In the User box, type the name you want to use for your mailbox.**

   For example, the mailbox name you have on your provider's system. (You can use any name you want here, but you have to remember it.)

5. **Click the Add button.**

   You see yet another dialog box, like the one in Figure B-11.

6. **In the Password box, enter the password you want to enter when you run Chameleon Mail.**

   If you are not worried about security, leave it blank. Your password, if you enter it, appears as asterisks so that no one can read it over your shoulder.

7. **In the In real life box, enter your full name.**

   This name appears on your outgoing mail, so spell it correctly.

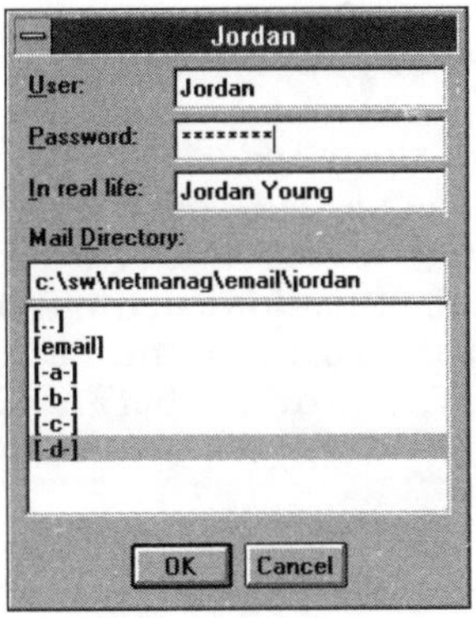

Figure B-11: Entering information about your mailbox.

8. **In the Mail Directory box, choose the directory in which you want your mail stored.**

   Chameleon Mail suggests that it create a subdirectory named EMAIL in the directory in which the Chameleon programs are stored (usually C:\NETMANAG). Then it plans to create a subdirectory of the new EMAIL directory with your user name. If the user is named Margy, for example, the mail directory is named C:\NETMANAG\EMAIL\MARGY.

   Sounds good to us, but if you would rather use a different directory in which to store your mail, just edit the pathname in the Mail Directory box.

9. **Click OK. Then click Yes to confirm that you want to make this new mailbox.**

   You return to the Mailboxes window, and the new mailbox appears on the list.

10. **Click the Save button to save the changes you have made to the mailboxes and leave the Mailbox window.**

    You're back in the main Mail window.

11. **Choose File⇨Exit to leave Chameleon Mail so that you can stop being Postmaster and log in as yourself.**

If several people plan to use the same computer to read their mail, create a separate mailbox for each one, following steps 4 through 9 for each person.

TIP

To change the password for your mailbox, choose Settings⇨Password. Chameleon Mail asks for your current password (to make sure that you are you) and your new password (which you enter twice, to avoid typos).

Changing Your Software Configuration

When you use the Instant Internet program to install your Internet Chameleon software, the program not only sets up an account with your Internet provider but also configures the various Internet Chameleon programs to work with your new account. Instant Internet inserts all the information listed in Table B-1 earlier in this appendix. Most of this information is used by the Custom program to make the Internet connection with your provider, but a few facts are needed by Chameleon Mail and NEWTNews.

The following sections show you how to change these settings if your situation changes — for example, if you change providers or connect your modem to a different port, or if your provider tells you that its news server's name has changed.

If your Internet address and name change

Instant Internet sets this stuff automatically. If you need to change it, here's where the information appears:

- Your own PC's numeric Internet address appears in the Custom window as your IP Address. (It may be blank, which is fine.) To change the address, choose Setup⇨IP Address from the menu in the Custom program, and then enter the four parts of your numeric address.
- Your PC's host name appears in the Custom window as the Host Name setting. (This may also be blank — not to worry.) Together with your Internet provider's domain name, the host name makes up your PC's Internet address (see the section "Who Are You?" at the end of Chapter 3). To change the host name, choose Setup⇨Host Name from the menu in the Custom program, and then enter the name.
- Your Internet provider's domain name appears in the Custom window as your Domain Name. To change the domain name, choose Setup⇨Domain Name from the menu in the Custom window, and then enter the name of your provider's domain.

If you change your modem

Instant Internet inserts the following information about your modem. The following list tells you how to change that information.

- Your modem is usually connected to a PC communications port named COM1, COM2, COM3, or COM4. (It doesn't matter whether the modem is internal or external.) The name of the communications port appears in the Custom window as part of the interface. To change this setting in Custom, choose Setup⇨Port; you see the Port Settings dialog box. In the Connector section, choose the communications port.
- Your modem speed also appears as part of the interface in the Custom window. The speed may be 9,600, 14,400, 19,200, or even 28,800. To change this setting in Custom, choose Setup⇨Port; you see the Port Settings dialog box. In the Baud Rate section, select the modem speed. (***Note:*** If you have a 14,400-baud modem, choose 19,200, because there is no setting for 14,400.)
- The kind of modem that you have matters, because different modems accept different commands. To see or change your modem type in Custom, choose Setup⇨Modem from the menu. The Modem Defaults setting shows the general type of modem. If you change it, the modem commands in the rest of the dialog box change. If you have an unusual modem that uses different commands from the modems listed, you may have to consult your modem manual and enter modem commands yourself in the various boxes in the Commands section of the dialog box. (We sincerely hope that you won't have to!)

If you change the way you connect to your Internet provider

Instant Internet sets the following options to tell Custom how to connect to your provider:

- The telephone number of your Internet provider appears as the Dial setting in the Custom window. To change the phone number in Custom, choose Setup⇨Dial from the menu. In the Dial box, enter the phone number to dial. Most modems ignore spaces and dashes, so you can include those characters to make the number more readable. Most modems interpret commas as being one-second pauses, which you may need if your modem should pause while dialing to get an outside line.
- The type of connection that you have with your Internet provider can be SLIP, CSLIP, ISDN, or PPP, depending on what your provider specifies. At the bottom of the Custom window is a list of the interfaces that you use for this Internet provider; most people use only one interface. Look in the Type column. To change this setting in Custom, you must create a new interface by choosing Interface⇨Add from the menu. You see the Add Interface window (refer to Figure B-1). In the Name box, enter the name of your Internet provider (or an abbreviation) or accept the default name (`SLIP0`). In the Type box, choose the type of interface that your Internet provider uses.

- Your user name is usually your first name, last name, initials, or some other variation on your name. To change the user name in Custom, choose Setup⇨Login from the menu; you see the Login Settings dialog box. Enter your new user name in the User Name box.
- Your user password is the password for your Internet account. You never have to type the password; Custom does this for you. Your password appears (sort of) in the Login Settings dialog box. (To see this dialog box in Custom, choose Setup⇨Login from the menu.) Actually, you just see a bunch of asterisks, for security reasons. To change the password, type a new password in the box. Type very carefully, because you can't see what you are doing.
- Your startup command tells your Internet provider to start communicating with you via SLIP, CSLIP, ISDN, or PPP as soon as you log in. Some providers don't require a command; they just start right up. To change the command in Custom, choose Setup⇨Login from the menu, and enter the new command in the Startup Command box.

If your provider's network gateway or domain name server changes

Your Internet provider has a network gateway, which is the computer that connects your PC to the rest of the Internet. It also has one or more *domain name servers* (DNS). These servers are host computers that translate between Internet addresses (for example, `dummies.com`) and numeric addresses (for example, `140.186.81.6`). To see or change these settings, choose Services⇨Default Gateway or Services⇨Domain Servers from the Custom menu.

If your mail server or mail gateway changes

Instant Internet tells the Chameleon Mail program how your Internet provider handles incoming and outgoing mail, as follows:

- Your mail gateway (SMTP server) is the computer whose job is to send your outgoing mail out to the Internet for distribution. To see or change the address of the gateway, run Chameleon Mail and choose Settings⇨Network⇨Mail Gateway.
- Your mail server (POP3 server) is the computer whose job is to receive mail for you and other users. To see or change the address of the server, run Chameleon Mail, and choose Settings⇨Network⇨Mail Server.

- Your mailbox name is usually the same as your user name. To see or change the name, run Chameleon Mail, and choose Settings⇨Networld⇨Mail Server. The mailbox name appears in the box named User (confusingly enough).
- Some Internet providers allow you to give your mailbox a separate password so that other people can't read your mail. To see or change this password, run Chameleon Mail and choose Settings⇨Networld⇨Mail Server.

If your news server changes

Your news server is the computer whose job is to provide you the latest Usenet newsgroup articles. To see this server, run NEWTNews, choose Disconnect, and choose Disconnect again. Then choose Connect. You see the news-server address. To use a different news server, enter its Internet address and then click OK to reconnect to the same news server.

Other Things That May Go Wrong

This section tells you about a few miscellaneous things that you may need to do.

How to change the password for your account

You never have to type your password, but changing it now and then is a good idea. For directions on changing your password, call your Internet provider or send e-mail to your provider's support address.

How to unlock your mailbox

If you lose your network connection while Chameleon Mail is retrieving your mail from the mailbox, you may get an error message the next time you try to get your mail. The reason is that your mail server locks your mailbox while you are retrieving mail, so that incoming mail won't foul things up. If the mail server "forgets" to unlock the mailbox, you can't send or receive any mail. Call your Internet provider right away and ask the provider to unlock your mailbox; until the mailbox is unlocked, any new mail that arrives may be discarded.

Appendix C

International Internet Providers

Because some of the Instant Internet providers have numbers only in the United States (although you might want to call them to check this, or click on the More Info button to read their text files — you never know when they might expand), here is a list of providers in countries other than the U.S. The list isn't complete, but it should give you some starting points.

TIP: This list is far from complete, and address and phone numbers may have changed. We'll try to update this list as we get corrections and new names. If you are having trouble finding a provider, you may be able to get newer info from us by looking on our Web page, whose URL is `http://dummies.com/`. (See Chapter 17 to find out how to use URLs.)

Australia

InterConnect Australia

Locations: Adelaide, Brisbane, Canberra, Melbourne, Perth, and Sydney

Phone: (03)528-2239 from Melbourne or (008)818-262 from elsewhere in Australia

E-mail: `sales@interconnect.com.au`

DIALix Services

Locations: Adelaide, Brisbane, Canberra, Melbourne, Perth, and Sydney

Phone: (02)948-6995 or (09)244-2433 or (041)111-4388 or (1800)642-433

E-mail: `justin@dialix.com` or `justin@dialix.oz.au`

OzEmail Pty. Ltd.

Locations: Adelaide, Canberra, Darwin, Brisbane, Melbourne, Newcastle, Perth, and Sydney

Phone: (02)437-45500 or (1800)805-874 (in Australia)

Fax: (02)437-5500

E-mail: sales@ozemail.com.au

Belgium

EUnet Belgium

Locations: Brussels, Ghent, Leuven, Antwerp, Kortrijk, Liege, and Hasselt

Phone: (016)23.60.99

Fax: (016)23.20.79

Email: sales@Belgium.EU.net

Canada

UUNET Canada

Locations: Vancouver, Toronto, Calgary, Ottawa, Edmonton, Montreal, London, Quebec City, Kitchener, and Halifax

Phone: (416)368-6621 or (800)463-8123

Fax: (416)368-1350

E-mail: info@uunet.ca

France

EUnet France

Location: Paris

Phone: (01)53.81.60.60

Fax: (01)45.74.52.79

E-mail: contact@France.EU.net

Oleane

Locations: Paris, Strasbourg, and Grenoble

Phone: (01)43.28.32.32

Fax: (01)43.28.46.21

E-mail: info-internet@oleane.net

World-NET

Location: Paris

Phone: (01)40.37.32.67 or (01)60.20.85.14

E-mail: info@World-net.sct.fr

Germany

EUnet Germany

E-mail: info@germany.EU.net

Italy

EUnet Italy IUnet

Location: Milan, Turin, Rome, Genoa, Trieste, and Padua

Phone: (02)27.00.25.28

Fax: (02)27.00.13.22

E-mail: sales@Italy.EU.net

Japan

twics

Location: Direct-dial in 03 (Tokyo), but Tympas packet network access from 40 other Japanese cities

Phone: (03)3351-5977

Fax: (03)3353-6096

Dial-up: (03)3351-8244 (log in as guest)

E-mail: info@twics.com

Mexico

We don't know of any public Mexican Internet providers. If you hear of one, please drop us a line at starter@dummies.com!

Netherlands

EUnet The Netherlands

Location: Amsterdam

E-mail: beheer@Netherlands.EU.net

NetLand

Location: Amsterdam

Phone: (020)694-8287

Fax: (020)694-3664

Dial-up: (020)694-0350 (log in as `new` or `info`)

E-mail: `info@netland.nl`

Stichting Knoware

Locations: Utrecht, Amsterdam, Rotterdam, Den Haag, Zoetermeer, Leiden, and Delft

Phone: (030)89-67-75

E-mail: `knoware@knoware.nl`

Stichting NEST

Location: Amsterdam, Amstelveen, and Schiphol

Phone: (020)626-5566

E-mail: `info@nest.nl`

Simplex

Location: Amsterdam

Phone: (020)693-2433

Fax: (020)668-5486

Dial-up: (020)665-3388 (log in as `new` or `info`)

E-mail: `simplex@simplex.nl`

NLNet

Locations: Amsterdam, Haarlem, Almere, Zaandam, Weesp, Ouderkerk a/d Amstel, and Zeewolde

Phone: (020)663-9366

Fax: (020)665-5311

E-mail: `info@NL.net`

Norway

EUnet Norway

Location: Oslo, Bergen, Trondheim, Stavanger, and Bronnoysund

Phone: (022)958327

Fax: (022)604427

E-mail: sales@Norway.EU.net

South Africa

Internetworking Cape (INCA)

E-mail: info@inca.za

Spain

EUnet Spain

Location: Madrid, Barcelona, Malaga, Sevilla, Valladolid, and Bilbao

Phone: (01)413.48.56

Fax: (01)413.49.01

E-mail: info@eunet.es

Switzerland

EUnet Switzerland

Location: Zurich, Basel, Bern, Geneva, Lugano, and Lausanne

Phone: (01)291-4580

Fax: (01)291-4642

E-mail: info@eunet.ch

SWITCH - Swiss Academic and Research Network

Location: Zurich

Phone: (01)268-1515

Fax: (01)268-1568

E-mail: `info@switch.ch`

United Kingdom (U.K.)

CityScape

Locations: London, Birmingham, Bristol, Cambridge, Edinburgh, and Manchester

Phone: (01223)566-950

Fax: (01223)566-951

E-mail: `sales@cityscape.co.uk`

Compulink Information eXchange (CIX)

Location: London

Phone: (0181)390-8446

Fax: (0181)390-6561

E-mail: `cixadmin@cix.compulink.co.uk`

DEMON

Locations: London, Warrington, Liverpool, Manchester, Sunderland, Leeds, Bradford, Hull Clough, Sheffield, Birmingham, Isle of Wight, Cambridge, Saffron Walden, Reading, and Edinburgh

Phone: (0181)349-0063

Fax: (0181)349-0309

E-mail: `internet@demon.net`

The Direct Connection (TDC)

Location: London, Bristol, Birmingham, Cambridge, Edinburgh, and Manchester

Phone: (081)317-0100

Fax: (081)317-3886

Dial-up: (081)317-2222 (log in as `demo`)

E-mail: `sales@dircon.co.uk`

EUnet GB

Location: Aberdeen, Birmingham, Bracknell, Canterbury, Cambridge, Glasgow, London, and Manchester

Phone: (01227)266-466

Fax: (01227)266-477

E-Mail: `sales@Britain.EU.net`

PIPEX: Public IP Exchange

Locations: London, Cambridge, and Edinburgh

Phone: (0223)250-120

Fax: (0223) 250-121

E-mail: `sales@pipex.net`

Index

• A •

abbreviations, e-mail, 96
Account Registration Complete dialog box, 33
Account Sign-Up window, Instant Internet, 30-31
accounts, getting Internet, 360-362
Add dialog box, WinZip, 286
Address Book icon, 369
Address Book window, Chameleon Mail, 59
address book
  creating, 59-60
  mailing lists, 60-61
  using, 60
addresses
  changes, 372
  e-mail, 44-48
  entering, 366
agriculture databases, 174
alt (alternative) newsgroup listing, 152, 154-155
alt.binaries.pictures.erotica, 118
alt.sex, 142
AlterNet, 19
America Online (AOL), 18, 86
anonymous FTP, 184-185, 187, 202
ANSI terminal emulation, 160
Applelink, 86
Arachnet Electronic Journal of Virtual Culture, WV, 206
Archie, 12-13, 215-230
  case sensitive searches, 218
  customizing, 224
  e-mail, 227-228
  exact search method, 225
  file search limitations, 220
  file search types, 218-219
  regex search method, 225
  regular expression searches, 218
  retrieving files, 220-221
  search methods, 225
  search strings, 224-225
  servers listing, 222
  starting, 216-217
  sub search method, 225
  subcase search method, 225
  teleneting to Archie server, 223-224
  troubleshooting, 217-218
  variables, 226
  whatis service, 221, 226-227
Archie Preferences dialog box, 220
Archie window, 216
archive files, 198, 200-202
archives, mirrored, 203
articles
  anatomy, 119-121
  distributions, 120-121
  header, 119
  message ID, 119
  message numbers, 120
  rot13, 119
  sending, 113-114
  text files, 18
  threads, 120
ASCII file, 190
Associate dialog box, Windows, 242
associations
  file, 65
  Gopher, 239
AT&T Mail, 86
Attachment Description dialog box, 63-64
Attachments⇨Delete command, Chameleon Mail, 65
Attachments⇨Modify command, Chameleon Mail, 65

Attachments⇨New command, Chameleon Mail, 63
Attachments⇨Save command, Chameleon Mail, 65
Attachments⇨View command, Chameleon Mail, 65
attachments, saving as separate file, 65
Australia, home pages, 341
Australian National University FTP server, 206
aviation database, 177
Avid explorer, 340

• B •

bang path address, 90
BBS (bulletin board system), 15, 113
binary files, 61, 118, 190
binary mode, 336
BinHex encoded files, 62
bionet newsgroup, 152
bit newsgroup, 152
BITNET, 87
  LISTSERV program, 99-103
BIX, 87
biz newsgroup, 152
book databases, 177-178
book
  icons, 4-5
  included software, 2
  introduction, 1-6
  organization, 3-4
  overview, 1
  user level, 3
  using, 2-3
bookmarks, Gopher, 234, 248-249
bulletin boards, 12
  Internet provider, 17
  Usenet, 12

• C •

cache, Gopher, 237
CARL book database, 177
CCITT, 90
Cello program, 276, 301
chain letters, 94-95
Chameleon Custom
  disconnecting, 38-39
  troubleshooting, 36-37
Chameleon Finger, 76-80
  organizational directories, 79
  starting, 76-79
Chameleon Mail
  address book, 59-61
  attaching files to e-mail, 61-67
  Cancel button, 53
  confirming e-mail address, 47
  creating signatures, 53-54
  customizing, 71-72
  Delete button, 57
  deleting folders, 69
  deleting messages, 57
  determining e-mail address, 40
  entering message text, 52
  exiting, 50
  folders, 67-70
  Forward button, 57
  forwarding messages, 57
  Mail Login window, 49
  Mail window, 49-50
  mail-sorting rules, 70-71
  mailing lists, 60-61
  outbox, 54
  Print button, 53, 57
  printing messages, 57
  printing outgoing messages, 55
  reading e-mail messages, 56
  receiving attached files, 65
  receiving e-mail, 56-57
  renaming folders, 69
  Reply button, 56-57
  replying to messages, 56-57
  saving attachments as separate file, 65
  saving messages, 67
  Send button, 52-55
  sending mail, 51-55

setting up, 48-50
starting, 49
Trash folder, 70
uudecoding uuencoded messages, 132
uuencoded files, 65-67
viewing outbox messages, 55
Chameleon Ping program, 328
Chess server, 181
CityScape service provider, 383
clari newsgroup hierarchy, 153, 156
ClariNet newsgroup, 156
Clemson Forestry and Agriculture Network database, 175
codes
mailing lists, 108-109
Rot13, 131
Telnet, 171
coffee pot, 350-351
commands
appearance in book, 3
Archie e-mail, 228
Archie
help, 224
maxhits, 225
prog, 225
set search, 225
Settings⇨Log, 217
Settings⇨Preferences, 220
Show, 224
whatis, 221, 226-227
case sensitive, 3
Chameleon Custom, File⇨Exit, 39
Chameleon Finger
Edit⇨Copy, 79
File⇨Print, 78
Settings⇨Verbose, 78
Chameleon Mail
Attachments⇨Delete, 65
Attachments⇨Modify, 65
Attachments⇨New, 63
Attachments⇨Save, 65
Attachments⇨View, 65
Edit⇨Save 'From' Address, 76
Feelings, 52
File⇨Exit, 50
File⇨Insert File, 62
File⇨Print, 57
Folders⇨Create, 68
Folders⇨Delete, 69
Folders⇨Folder List, 68
Folders⇨Open, 68
Folders⇨Rename, 69
Message⇨Append to File, 67
Message⇨Copy to File, 67
Message⇨Create, 51
Message⇨Delete, 57
Message⇨Forward, 57
Message⇨Move to Folder, 69
Message⇨Reply, 57
Message⇨Retrieve Mail, 56
Message⇨Send, 52
Message⇨Uudecode, 132
Message⇨uuencode, 66
Message⇨View, 56
Services⇨Address, 60
Services⇨Address Book, 51-52, 59
Services⇨Empty Trash, 70
Services⇨Outbox, 55
Services⇨Rules, 70
Settings⇨Preferences, 71
Settings⇨Signature, 40, 53
Settings⇨Timers, 54
File Manager, File⇨Associate, 65
File⇨Exit, 368, 371
File⇨Open, 364
File⇨Save, 368
File⇨Save As, 365
FTP, Settings⇨Connection Profile, 193
Gopher
Help⇨Diagnose Connections, 236
Help⇨Symbol Legend, 234
Item⇨Add Gopher Server, 250
Item⇨Item Properties, 236
Item⇨Remove Item, 237, 250
Item⇨Retrieve, 235
Item⇨Retrieve Item, 237
Item⇨Search, 245
Item⇨Set Bookmark, 248

Interface⇨Add, 364, 374
Internet Chameleon
  Setup⇨Dial, 35
  Setup⇨Log, 35
NEWTNews
  File⇨Save To File, 130
  Groups⇨Catch Up, 137
  Groups⇨Check New Groups, 139
  Groups⇨List All, 138
  Groups⇨Unsubscribe, 137
  Messages⇨Clear Flag, 130
  Messages⇨Follup/E-Mail, 133, 135-136
  Messages⇨Mark Unread, 130
  Messages⇨Set Flag, 130
  Messages⇨View, 129
  Settings⇨Preferences, 137
Retrieve⇨Go to URLs, 339
Services⇨Default Gateway, 368
Services⇨Domain Servers, 368
Services⇨Malboxes, 369
Settings⇨Network⇨Mail Gateway, 374
Settings⇨Network⇨Mail Server, 374-375
Setup⇨Dial, 373
Setup⇨domain Name, 366
Setup⇨Host Name, 366
Setup⇨IP address, 365
Setup⇨Login, 367
Setup⇨Port, 366
Telnet
  Disconnect, 164
  Disconnect and Exit, 164
  Edit⇨Copy, 165
  File⇨Capture, 164
  File⇨Print, 164
  File⇨Printer Auto Mode, 164
  Settings⇨Connection Profile, 165
  Settings⇨Preferences, 167
WebSurfer
  Retrieve⇨Add to Hotlist, 269
  Retrieve⇨Go To URL, 268
  Retrieve⇨History, 267
  Settings⇨Style Schemes, 274
Windows
  File⇨Associate, 242
  File⇨Create Directory, 280
  File⇨Run, 27
  Options⇨File Manager Configuration, 287
  Tools⇨Antivirus, 292
WinZip
  File⇨Print Topic, 293
  Help⇨Ordering Information, 293
commercial services, 178-180
communications software, 16
comp, newsgroup names, 116
comp.compilers, 142
compress program, 201
compressed files, 198, 200-202
Compulink Information eXchange (CIX) service provider, 383
CompuServe, 18, 87, 179
computer group newsgroups listing, 142-146
computers
  remote (host), 159, 189
  terminal, 159
  using as FTP Server, 196
configuration file, service provider, 365
configurations, saving software, 372-375
configuring
  Chameleon, 357-376
  mail, 369-371
Connect dialog box, FTP, 185-186
Connect To dialog box, Telnet, 162
Connection Profile dialog box, Telnet, 165-166
Connection Profile window, FTP, 193
connection profile, Telnet, 165-167
Consumer Access Services database, 177
CR Labs, 179
CSLIP (Compressed Serial Line Internet Protocol), 19
Custom window, 328
  Disconnect button, 38
  Internet Chameleon, 35
  Setup⇨Dial command, 35

• D •

Dartmouth College Library, 173
data files, 198-199
databases
  agriculture/nutrition, 174-175
  aviation, 177
  book, 177-178
  geography, 175
  ham-radio, 175-176
  history, 176
  outerspace, 176-177
DELPHI Internet, 18-19, 88, 179
DEMON service provider, 383
Dial settings dialog box, 367
DIALix Services service provider, 377
digests, exploding, 105
directory of sources, 322
directory paths, file download, 189-190
directory, download, 279-280
Disconnect and Exit command, Telnet, 164
Disconnect command, Telnet, 164
distributions, 120-121
  possible list, 120-121
domain, 80
domain name server (DNS), 374
download directory, 279-280
downloading etiquette, 334
DUATS aviation database, 177

• E •

e-mail, 12
  abbreviations, 96
  address, 44-48, 333
  addressing, 51-52
  addressing with address book, 59-60
  Archie, 227-228
  attaching files to, 61-67
  chain letters, 94-95
  commands, Archie, 228
  deleting messages, 57
  entering text, 52
  etiquette, 92-95, 336
  flaming, 93
  forwarding messages, 57
  including uuencoded files, 65-67
  mail services, 12
  mailing lists, 12
  on-line systems, 86-92
  printing messages, 57
  privacy issues, 95
  programs, 73
  reading messages, 56
  receiving, 56-57
  receiving attached files, 65
  replying to messages, 56-57
  responding to newsgroup articles, 133-136
  saving attachments as separate file, 65
  saving messages, 67
  sending, 51-55
  signatures, 53-54
  smiley faces in, 93
  sorting, 70-71
  timing mail gateway connections, 54-55
  timing mail retrieval connections, 54
  viewing in outbox, 55
e-mail address
  access.usask.ca, 174
  alt.hypertext, 263
  archive.umich.edu, 205
  astro.temple.edu, 180
  authors of this book, 5, 40, 47, 75
  biochemistry.bioc.cwru.edu, 304
  byrd.mu.wvnet.edu, 206
  caen.fr.eu.undernet.org, 180
  callsign.cs.buffalo.edu, 176
  columbia.ilc.com, 177
  comp.infosystems.www, 263
  comp.text.tex, 199
  comp.text.troff, 199
  components of, 46
  compuserve.com, 179
  confirming, 40
  Coombs.anu.edu.au, 206
  crl.com, 179
  cs.ubc.ca, 211
  culine.colorado.edu, 181

delphi.com, 179
determining own, 76
determining your, 47
domain, 80
duats.gtefsd.com, 177
esrin.esa.it, 176-177
etext.archive.umich.edu, 210
eureka.clemson.edu, 175
exuokmax.ecn.uoknor.edu, 180
finding, 75-96
fpt.ncsa.uiuc.edu, 301
ftp.cc.umanitoba.ca, 211
ftp.cica.indiana.edu, 281, 297-298, 303-304, 307, 310-311
ftp.cnidr.org, 302
ftp.cu.nih.gov, 207
ftp.cwru.edu, 208
ftp.demon.co.uk, 299
ftp.einet.net, 302
ftp.elf.com, 304
ftp.internic.net, 205
ftp.law.cornell.edu, 301, 305-306
ftp.lysator.liu.se, 298
ftp.ncsz.uiuc.edc, 305
ftp.neosoft.com, 211
ftp.netcom.com, 209
ftp.qualcomm.com, 73, 296
ftp.senate.gov, 209
ftp.std.com, 297
ftp.usma.edu, 299
ftp.utas.edu.au, 297
ftp.uwp.edu, 210
ftp.voa.gov, 210
ftp.wst.com, 299
gatekeeper.dec.com, 211
geophys.washington.edu, 175
glis.cr.usgs.gov, 175
gopher.cpsr.org, 249
hellspark.wharton.upenn.edu, 181
hermes.merit.edu, 178
herxl.tat.physik.uni-tuebingen.de, 181
hollis.harvard.edu, 173
host numbers, 46
iecc!starter., Internet for Dummies address, 90
iecc.com, 207
info.anu.edu.au, 174
info.ccit.arizona.edu, 174
InterNIC, 205
io.com, 307
irc.nsysu.edu.tw, 180
irc.tuzvo.sk, 180
laguna.epcc.edu, 174
library.dartmouth.edu, 173
library.vuw.ac.nz, 174
library.wustl.edu, 178
lister.cc.ic.ac.uk, 300
locis.loc.gov, 172-173
mail exchange, 78
martini.eecs.umich.edu, 175
meg.tiac.net, 40
mhpower@mit.edu, 82
mthvax.cs.miami.edu, 211
MX addresses, 78
nctuccca.edu.tw, 174
netcom.com, 179
news.announce.newusers, 126
next7.cas.muohio.edu, 181
nic@vnet.ibm.com, 85
nis.nsf.net, 205
nri.reston.va.us. port 185, 85
ns.risc.net, 175
NSFNET, 205
nssdc.gsfc.nasa.gov, 176
oak.oakland.edu, 205, 209, 280, 282
oak.oakland.edu, 303, 305-309
obelix.wu-wien.ac.at, 180
orbis.yale.edu, 173
pac.carl.org, 177
pc.usl.edu, 176
pctravel.com, 179
pldsg3.gsfc.nasa.gov, 177
pogue.admin.lsa.umich.edu, 308-309
postmaster, 80
president@whitehouse.gov, 46
princeton.edu, 206

psupen.psu.edu, 174
quote.com, 180
rafael.metiu.uscb.edu, 181
ridgisd.er.usgs.gov, 302
risc.ua.edu, 296
rtfm.mit.edu, 204
sci.dixie.edu, 180
seabass.st.usm.edu, 181
sipb.mit.edu, 81
spacelink.msfc.nasa.gov, 176
sri.com, 205
starter@dummies.com, 5, 40, 47, 75
sulaw.law.su.oz.au, 209
sumex-aim.stanford.edu, 205
sunsite.unc.edu, 300-301
telnet ics.uoknor.edu, 181
ten reasons not to call someone for address, 77
ukanaix.cc.ukans.edu, 176
utas.edu.au, 73
UUCP, 90
whois.internic.net, 80
wordsworth.com, 178
world.std.com, 179
wuarchive.wustl.edu, 204, 307
X.400, 91-92
Earthquake info database, 175
Easylink, 88
Edit⇨Copy command
Chameleon Finger, 79
Telnet, 165
Edit⇨Save 'From' Address command, Chameleon Mail, 76
EIWAIS program, 302, 325
electronic address, know it, 333
Ellnet Belgium service provider, 378
Ellnet France service provider, 379
Ellnet Germany service provider, 379
Ellnet Italy IUnet service provider, 380
Ellnet Norway service provider, 382
Ellnet Spain service provider, 382
Ellnet Switzerland service provider, 382
Ellnet The Netherlands service provider, 380
elm, UNIX mail program, 160
emacs, UNIX text editor, 160
emulation, terminal, 160
entertainment/games services, 180-181
etiquette, e-mail, 91-95
Eudora program, 73, 296
EUnet GB service provider, 384
Europe, home pages, 341-342
European Space Agency database, 176-177
EWAN Telnet program, 298
exact search method, 225
executable files, 198, 200
Extract dialog box, WinZip, 285-286

• F •

Feelings command, Chameleon Mail, 52
FIDONET, 88
FIFE database, 177
file associations, 239
File Manager, 242
File to Attach dialog box, 63
file transfer, 184
File⇨Associate command
File Manager, 65
Windows, 242
File⇨Capture file command, Telnet, 164
File⇨Create Directory command, Windows, 280
File⇨Exit command, 368, 371
Chameleon Custom, 39
Chameleon Mail, 50
File⇨Insert File command, Chameleon Mail, 62
File⇨Open command, 364
File⇨Print command
Chameleon Finger, 78
Chameleon Mail, 57
Telnet, 164
File⇨Print Topic command, WinZip, 293
File⇨Printer Auto Mode command, Telnet, 164
File⇨Run command, Windows, 27
File⇨Save As command, 365

File⇨SAve command, 368
File⇨Save To File command, NEWTNews, 130
files
archive, 198, 200-202
ASCII, 190
associations, 65
attaching to e-mail, 61-67
binary, 61, 118, 190
BinHex encoded, 62
compressed, 198, 200-202
copying from FTP server, 191-192
copying to FTP server, 192
data, 198-199
downloading, 288-289
downloading with WebSurfer, 271-272
executable, 198, 200
extracting, 285-286, 289-290
GIF, 240
group of, 118-119
INETCHAM.WRI, 41
kill, 117
mangled by FTP, 336-337
PostScript document, 200
README, 203
receiving attached, 65
retrieving with Archie, 220-221
saving newsgroup articles as, 130
search types, 218-219
self-extracting, 282
shar (shell archive), 132
text, 197, 199-200
types of, 197-199
uuencoding, 62, 65-67
whois-servers.list, 81
winzip55.exe, 282
ZIP, 285
zipping, 286-287
Finger window, 77
copying information between programs, 79
Finger button, 77
Host box, 77
User box, 78
flags, newsgroup, 128, 130
flaming, 93
Folder List window, Chameleon Mail, 68
Folders⇨Create command, Chameleon Mail, 68
Folders⇨Delete command, Chameleon Mail, 69
Folders⇨Folder List command, Chameleon Mail, 68
Folders⇨Open command, Chameleon Mail, 68
Folders⇨Rename command, Chameleon Mail, 69
folders
Chameleon Mail, 67-70
creating, 68
deleting, 69
filing messages, 69
naming conventions, 68
renaming, 69
Trash, 70
viewing contents, 68-69
food, 349
freeware, registering, 292
Frequent Flyers mailing list, 109
FTP (file-transfer protocol), 13, 184, 196, 202
anonymous, 184-185, 187, 202
anonymous log in, 203
connection profile, 193-195
copying files from FTP server, 191-192
copying files to FTP server, 192
customizing, 193-195
deleting files, 192
disconnecting, 193
file download directory paths, 189-190
file transfer rules, 202
file transfer speed, 192
file types, 190
finding remote computer files, 189
image mode, 190
locating remote computer files, 189
mangled files, 336-337
mirrored archives, 203

renaming files, 192
servers list, 203-211
starting, 185-187
troubleshooting file transfers, 195-196
FTP server, 183, 196, 311-312
behavioral brain sciences, 206
compilers, 207
congressional mail, 209
Coombs Papers, 206
downloading files from, 288-289
EJVC, 306
ftp.cica.indiana.edu, 281
law libraries, 209
news, 210
NIH, 207
NSFNET, 205
recipes, 211
RTFM, 204
Supreme Court rulings, 208
travel tips, 211
tv/movie guide, 210
UUNET, 204
WUARCHIVE, 204
FTP window, 188
ftp.qualcomm.com, 73
fun, finding things to do, 339
funnies, 343-345

• G •

games/entertainment services, 180-181
garbage, 160
gateway systems, 178
gatewayed mailing lists, 108
GEnie, 88
Geographic Server database, 175
geography databases, 175
Ghostscript program, 200
Ghostview program, 200
GIF files, 240
format, 198
viewer, 240, 263
GL file format, 198
GLIS (Global Land Use Info System) database, 175
Global Network Navigator, 340
gnu newsgroup, 153
Gopher, 12-13
accessing through World Wide Web, 258-259
adding servers, 250
associations, 239
blue/red book icon, 240
bookmarks, 234, 248-249
browsing, 237-238
cache, 237
card file icon, 243
closing menus/menu items, 237
customizing, 248-251
deleting items, 237
exiting, 238
globe icon, 242
history, 232
HTML file format, 242
keyword searches, 245-246
NetManage, 234
PC program icon, 241
picture icon, 240
red book icon, 240
saving servers, 249-251
searches, 243-248
selecting information, 235-236
servers, 234
speaker icon, 241-242
Telnet access, 244-245
terminal icon, 244-245
text icon, 240
troubleshooting, 236
Veronica searches, 246-249
vs WAIS vs WWW, 259
World Wide Web access, 242-243
Gopher window, 233-234
Gopherbook program, 251, 300
GopherSpace Keyword Index dialog box, 245-246
graphics viewers, 263-264

Groups⇨Catch Up command, NEWTNews, 137
Groups⇨Check New Groups command, NEWTNews, 139
Groups⇨List All command, NEWTNews, 138
Groups⇨Unsubscribe command, NEWTNews, 137
gzip program, 201, 308

• H •

ham-radio databases, 175-176
hardware requirements, 26
Harvard Library, 173
headers, article, 119
help command, Archie, 224
Help⇨Diagnose Connection command, Gopher, 236
Help⇨Ordering Information command, WinZip, 293
Help⇨Symbol Legend command, Gopher, 234
hepnet newsgroup, 153
HGOPHER program, 251, 300
History dialog box, WebSurfer, 267-268
home pages, countries, 341-342
host computers, 46
  getting information with Finger, 76-80
  host numbers, 46
  host (remote) computer, 159
hotlist, WebSurfer, 269
HQX handlers program, 308
HTML file format, 242
hypermedia, 13
  WWW, 253
hypertext, 13
  WWW, 253-255
hytelnet service, 174

• I •

I.E.C.C., MA, 207
IBM 3270 terminal emulation, 160
icons
  Address Book, 369
  Gopher
    blue/red book, 240
    card file, 243
    globe, 242
    PC program, 241
    picture, 240
    red book, 240
    speaker, 241-242
    terminal, 244-245
    text, 240
  Instant Internet, 30
  Internet Chameleon, 28, 32
    Archie, 216
    Custom, 35
    Finger, 76
    FTP, 185
    Gopher, 233
    Mail, 49
    NEWT, 35
    NEWTNews, 123
    Ping, 37
    Readme, 41
    Telnet, 162
    WebSurfer, 264
    Whois, 81
  Program Manager, 28
  trashcan, 57
  used in book, 4-5
  white folded-paper icon, 56
  yellow envelope icon, 56
IEEE newsgroup, 153
indexes, WWW (World Wide Web), 261
INETCHAM.WRI file, 41
installation, 25-29
Instant Internet, 2, 30-34, 122, 358-360
  Account Sign-Up window, 30-31
  browsing providers, 30

Help button, 31
Internet SLIP providers, 22
ISDN telephone connection, 33
Phone List button, 31
providers, 30
Restart Later button, 33
Restart Now button, 33
Send button, 31
Signup button, 30
troubleshooting problems, 34
InterConnect Australia service provider, 377
Interface⇨Add command, 364, 374
International Internet providers, 377-384
Internet
bulletin boards, 12
connecting, 15-24
e-mail, 12
file transfer programs, 184
getting an account, 360-362
gopher, 12-13
hypermedia, 13
hypertext, 13
information retrieval, 12-13
IRC (Internet Relay Chat), 13-14
making a connection, 34-36
newsgroups, 12
on-line conversation, 13-14
opening SLIP account, 29
overview, 9-14
socially unstratified, 11
uses for, 11-14
using other computers (Telnet), 13
Internet address
see also addresses
changes, 372
determining your PC's, 39-40
Internet Chameleon, 2
activation requirements, 2
Archie icon, 216
Archie program, 215-230
configuring for account, 363-364
Custom icon, 35
Finger icon, 76
FTP icon, 185
FTP program, 183-196
FTP Server program, 196
Gopher icon, 233
Gopher program, 231-252
hardware requirements, 26
installing, 25-29
instant service provider 357-371
Internet providers known about, 363
LAN version, 22
manually configuring, 357-376
NEWT, 29
NEWTNews, 123-140
NEWTNews icon, 123
provider information, 360-362
Readme icon, 41
service provider knowledge, 364-369
software, 358-360
Telnet icon, 162
Telnet program, 159-170
WebSurfer icon, 264
WebSurfer program, 256, 264-276
Whois icon, 81
Whois program, 80-85
Internet Network Information Center, CA FTP server, 205
Internet provider, 16-22
browsing, 30
bulletin boards, 17
changing connections, 373-375
choosing, 22
connection types, 373
e-mail storage, 47-48
instant, 357
mail gateway, 47
mail server, 47
money-saving tips, 58
on-line services, 18
phone number, 35
shell systems, 18-19
sign-up agreements, 32
SLIP systems, 19-21
Internet Relay Chat, 180
Internet services, telnet, 159-170

Internet Talk Radio (ITR), 346-347
Internet Town Hall (ITH), 346-347
Internet Use mailing list, 109
Internetworking Cape (INCA) service provider, 382
InterRamp, 19
introduction, 1-6
IRC (Internet Relay Chat), 13-14
IRC II for Windows program, 303
ISDN telephone connection, 33
Item⇨Add Gopher Server command, Gopher, 250
Item⇨Item Properties command, Gopher, 236
Item⇨Remove Item command, Gopher, 237, 250
Item⇨Retrieve command, Gopher, 235
Item⇨Retrieve Item command, Gopher, 237
Item⇨Search command, Gopher, 245
Item⇨Set Bookmark command, Gopher, 248

• J •

JPEG file format, 198
JPEG file viewer, 264

• K •

k12 newsgroup, 153
keyboard combinations
  Ctrl+A (Attach), 63
  Ctrl+B (Bookmark), 248
  Ctrl+C (Copy), 79, 130
  Ctrl+D (Delete), 57
  Ctrl+F (Flag), 130
  Ctrl+F (Forward), 57
  Ctrl+I (Insert), 62
  Ctrl+L (List), 68
  Ctrl+M (Move), 69
  Ctrl+R (Respond), 133, 136
  Ctrl+R (Retrieve), 237
  Ctrl+S (Save), 130
  Ctrl+Shift+F (Clear Flag), 130
  Ctrl+T (Retrieve Mail), 56
  Ctrl+U (Catch Up), 137
  Ctrl+W (View), 56, 129
  Ctrl+Y (Properties), 236
keyboard functions, 321
kill files, 117
Knowbot program, 85

• L •

LAN (local area network), 15
libraries, 172-174
  hytelnet service, 174
Library of Congress, 172-173
links
  WebSurfer, 265
  automating, 113
LISTSERV program, 99-103
  address naming conventions, 101
  bounced messages, 101
  contacting list owner, 100
  getting on/off a list, 99-101
  tricks, 101-103
  vs Majordomo, 105
lower case letters, 334
Lview Pro program, 305
Lview program, 305

• M •

mail
  see also Chameleon Mail
  configuring, 369-371
  services, 12
mail exchange (MX addresses), 78
mail gateway, 47
  changes, 374-375
Mail Login dialog box, 369
mail programs, UNIX, 160
mail robot (mailbot), 75
Mail Rules dialog box, Chameleon Mail, 70
mail server, 47
  changes, 374-375

Mail Signature window, Chameleon Mail, 53
mailbox
  setting up, 369-371
  unlocking, 375
mailing lists, 12, 97-112
  bounced messages, 106
  codes, 108-109
  creating, 60-61
  digested, 105
  digests, 105
  Frequent Flyers, 109
  gatewayed, 108
  getting on/off, 98
  Internet Use, 109
  LISTSERV, 99-103
  maintainer, 98
  Majordomo 103-105
  manual/automatic, 98
  moderated, 106
  Net-happenings, 109
  Net-stuff, 110
  replying to messages, 107
  Risks Digest, 110
  Roots, 110
  Scout Report, 110
  sending messages to, 105-107
  Sorehand, 110
  Telecom Digest, 111
  Tourism Discussion, 111
  types of, 108-109
  undigestification, 105
  vs Usenet News, 108
  Weather Talk, 111
  White House Press Releases, 111
maintainer, mailing lists, 98
Majordomo program, 103-105
  contacting list owner, 104
  getting on/off a list, 103
  vs LISTSERV, 105
manual mailing lists, getting on/off, 98-99
Massachusetts Institute of Technology, MA FTP server, 204
maxhits command, Archie, 225
MCI Mail, 80
meg.tiac.net, 40
MERIT Network gateway system, 178
message ID, article, 119
message numbers, articles, 120
Message⇨Append to File command, Chameleon Mail, 67
Message⇨Copy to File command, Chameleon Mail, 67
Message⇨Create command, Chameleon Mail, 51
Message⇨Delete command, Chameleon Mail, 57
Message⇨Forward command, Chameleon Mail, 57
Message⇨Move to Folder command, Chameleon Mail, 69
Message⇨Reply command, Chameleon Mail, 57
Message⇨Retrieve Mail command, Chameleon Mail, 56
Message⇨Send command, Chameleon Mail, 52
Message⇨Uudecode command, Chameleon Mail, 132
Message⇨uuencode command, Chameleon Mail, 66
Message⇨View command, Chameleon Mail, 56
Messages⇨Clear Flag command, NEWTNews, 130
Messages⇨Followup/E-Mail command, NEWTNews, 133, 135-136
Messages⇨Mark Unread command, NEWTNews, 130
Messages⇨Set Flag command, NEWTNews, 130
Messages⇨View command, NEWTNews, 129
messages
  attaching files to, 63-65
  Connection refused, 331-332
  Failure to connect to POP server, 56

Fetching list of newsgroups, 124
filing in folders, 69
Gopher server returned no information, 236
Network unreachable, 332
No message received, 38
No route to host, 332
Save changes to Untitled?, 238
saving e-mail, 67
sending to mailing lists, 105-107
Server connection timed out, 236
Server refused connection, try again later, 248
SLIP connection initiated, 37
Too many connections, try again soon, 248
Unable to connect to host, 78
Unable to resolve host, 78, 81
unable to start viewer. Check file associations., 240
uuencoded, 131-132
mhpower@mit.edu, 82
MIME (Multi-purpose Internet Mail Extensions), 62
messages, 118
mirrored archives, 203
misc (miscellaneous) newsgroups listing, 116, 146-147
modems, 16
changing, 372-373
disabling call-waiting, 16
operating speed, 16-17
type dialog box, 367
moderated mailing lists, 106
Mosaic program, 256, 276, 301
MPEG file format, 198
MPEGWin program, 307
MS-DOS 6.2, virus scanning, 292
MUD programs, 303-304

• N •

name servers, 331
connections, 329
names
changes, 372
newsgroups, 115-116
Names dialog box, Chameleon Mail, 51-52
NASA database, 176
National Science Foundation c/o MERIT, MI FTP server, 205
NCSA (National Center for Supercomputing Applications), 256
NCSA Mosaic, *see* Mosaic program
Net news 113
Net, *see* Internet
Net-happenings mailing list, 109
Net-stuff mailing list, 110
NETCOM, 18-19, 179
NETCOM On-Line Communications Services, 209
Netland service provider, 381
NetManage Gopher, 234
NetManage Inc, Internet Chameleon, 2
NetManage TCP/IP for Windows, 264-267
network gateway changes, 374
Network Go, 181
networks, 9
go bad, 331-333
no response, 327
New Message window, Chameleon Mail, 51
News etiquette, 336
news server, 122
news.announce.newusers, 126, 141
news.answers, 141
newsgroups, 12, 113-122
adding new, 139
alt (alternative) groups, 152, 154-155
alt.hypertext, 263
alt.sex, 142
arranged in hierarchies, 115-116

bing, 152
bionet, 152
bit, 152
clari (ClariNet), 153, 156
comp (computer) groups, 142-146
comp.compilers, 142
comp.infosystems.www, 263
comp.text.tex, 199
comp.text.troff, 199
copying articles between Windows programs, 130
flagging articles, 130
gnu, 153
hepnet, 153
IEEE, 153
k12, 153
listings, 141-156
misc (miscellaneous) groups, 146-147
names, 115-116
news.announce.newusers, 141
news.answers, 141
printing articles, 130-131
reading articles, 128-131
rec (recreation) groups, 147-149
rec.humor.funny, 142
regional, 116-117
relcom, 153
replying to articles, 130
responding to articles, 133-136
saving article to file, 130
saving articles, 130-131
sci (science) groups, 150
shar files, 132
skipping unread articles, 137
soc (social) groups, 151
subscribing to, 114, 124-126
talk groups, 152
unsubscribing, 114
uuencoded articles, 131-132
vmsnet, 153

newsreaders
Trumpet, 139
WinQVT/Net, 140
WinVN, 140

NEWT (NetManage Enhanced Windows TCP/IP) program, 29, 369

NEWTNews, 12, 115, 122
adding new groups, 139
copying articles between Windows programs, 130
customizing, 137-138
exiting, 127
flagging articles, 130
flags, 128
main window, 126-127
options, 137-138
password, 124
Print button, 130
printing articles, 130-131
reading newsgroup articles, 128-131
replying to articles, 130
responding to articles, 133-136
Rot13 encoded articles, 131
running, 127-128
running for first time, 123-126
Save button, 130
saving newsgroup articles, 130-131
shar files, 132
skipping unread articles, 137
subscribing to newsgroups, 124-126
toolbar, 129
uuencoded articles, 131-132

nic@vnet.ibm.com, IBM mail server, 85
NLNet service provider, 381
non-instant Internet provider, 357-371
activating software, 358-360
concept, 357
getting an account, 360-362
installing software, 358
nri.reston.va.us. port 185, Knowbot server, 85
numeric Internet address, entering, 366
nutrition databases, 174

• O •

Oak Software Repository, Oakland University, Rochester, MI, 205, 209
Oleane service provider, 379
on-line coke machines, 349-350
on-line services, 18
  America Online (AOL), 86
  Applelink, 86
  AT&T Mail, 86
  BITNET, 87
  BIX, 87
  CompuServe, 87
  Delphi, 88
  Easylink, 88
  FIDONET, 88
  GEnie, 88
  MCI Mail, 89
  Prodigy, 89
  Sprintmail (Telemail), 89
  UUCP, 89-90
  UUNET Communications, 90
  X.400 address, 90-92
operating systems, UNIX, 19
Options⇨File Manager Configuration command, Windows, 287
organizational directories, 79
outbox, Chameleon Mail, 54
OzEmail Pty. Ltd. service provider, 378

• P •

passwords
  changing, 375
  determining, 41
  NEWTNews, 124
PC Travel, 179
Pegasus Mail, 296-297
PENpages database, 174
personals column, 344
phone line, 16
phone numbers, Internet provider, 35
pine, UNIX mail program, 160
Ping window, 37-38
Ping, testing communications link, 37-38
Pipeline, 18
PIPEX: Public IP Exchange, 384
PIT unpackers program, 309
PKUNZIP program, 201, 280
PKZIP program, 198, 201, 280
POP3 (Post Office Protocol Ver 3), 48
POP3 server, 374
Port Settings dialog box, 366
ports, Telnet, 161-162
postmaster, 80
PostScript document files, 200
PPP (Point-to-Point Protocol), 19
Preferences dialog box, 137
  Chameleon Mail, 71-72
president@whitehouse.gov, 46
Princeton University, NJ, FTP server, 206
printing
  contents of Finger window, 77
  current WebSurfer page, 268
  e-mail messages, 57
  newsgroup articles, 130-131
  outgoing e-mail messages, 55
Prodigy, 18, 89
prog command, Archie, 225
Program Manager, 27-28
  Mail Utilities, 72
programs
  see also software
  Archie, 12-13, 215-230
  Cello, 276, 301
  Chameleon WebSurfer, 2
  compress, 201
  configuring, 291
  Custom, 35-37
  downloading, 279-284
  e-mail, 73
  EIWAIS, 302
  Eudora, 296
  EWAN Telnet, 298
  Finger, 76-80
  freeware, 292

FTP servers, 196, 311-312, 355
Ghostscript, 200
Ghostview, 200
Gopher, 231-252
GopherBook, 251, 300
gzip, 201, 308
HGOPHER, 251, 300
HQX handlers, 308
installing, 290-291
Internet, 295-312
IRC II for Windows, 303
Knowbot, 85
LISTSERV, 99-103
Lview, 305
Lview Pro, 305
Majordomo, 103-105
Mosaic, 256, 276, 301
MPEGWin, 307
MUD, 303-304
Pegasus Mail, 296-297
Ping, 37-38
PIT unpackers, 309
PKUNZIP, 201, 280
PKZIP, 198, 201, 280
QWS3270, 169, 298
registering shareware, 292
RFD Mail, 297
shareware, 292
SIT unstuffers, 309
Stufitt, 201-202
Telnet, 159-170, 354
TeX, 199
troff, 199
Trumpet, 140, 297
UU, 307
version creep, 337
VidVue, 307
WAIS, 313-326
WAISMAN, 302
Wasrchie, 229
WebSurfer, 242-243, 256, 264-276, 355-356
Wftpd, 299
WHAM, 306
Win QVT/NET, 169, 304
Win32S, 309-310
WinCode, 308
Winelm, 297
WinGIF, 306
WinGopher, 251
WinJPEG, 306
WinQVT/Net, 140
WinSock, 23, 296-305
WinTalk, 304
WinVN, 140, 298
WinWAIS, 302, 313-326
WinZip, 198, 201, 280-288
WPLANY, 306
WS Host, 304-305
WS_FTP, 299
WSARCHIE, 299-300
WSGopher, 301
WSIRC, 303
Z uncompress, 308
z uncompress, 308
ZIP, 201
zoo keepers, 308
providers
selecting with Instant Internet, 30-33
sign-up agreements, 32

• Q •

quake.think.com, 315
quartz.rutgers.edu, 210
QUOTE.COM, 180
QWS3270 program, 169, 298

• R •

railroads, 343
README files, 203
rec (recreation) newsgroup listing, 147-149
rec, newsgroup names, 116
rec.humor.funny, 142
regex search method, 225
regional groups, 116-117

regular expression file search, 218
relcom newsgroup, 153
relevance feedback, 314, 322
remote (host) computer, 159
remote computer, locating files, 189
restaurant referrals, 349
Retrieve⇨Add to Hotlist command, WebSurfer, 269
Retrieve⇨Go To URL command, WebSurfer, 268, 339
Retrieve⇨History command, WebSurfer, 267
RFD Mail program, 297
Risks Digest mailing list, 110
Roots mailing list, 110
rot13 articles, 119
Rot13 code, 131
rules, mail-sorting, 70-71
Run dialog box, 27
Rutgers University FTP server, 210

• S •

sci (science) newsgroup listing, 150
  newsgroup names, 116
Scout Report mailing list, 110
Scrabble, 181
Search dialog box, Archie, 219
search methods, 225
search string, 231
searches
  Gopher, 243-248
  types of, 218-219
  WebSurfer, 270-274
searching, errors, 320
servers list, Whois, 81-84
servers
  FTP, 183, 311-312
  FTP listing, 203-211
  Gopher, 234
  saving with Gopher, 249-251
service providers
  see also Internet provider
  changing connections, 373-375
  international, 377-384
  network gateway changes, 374
Services⇨Address Book command, Chameleon Mail, 50-60
Services⇨Default Gateway command, 368
Services⇨Domain Servers command, 368
Services⇨Empty Trash command, Chameleon Mail, 70
Services⇨Mailboxes command, 369
Services⇨Outbox command, Chameleon Mail, 55
Services⇨Rules command, Chameleon Mail, 70
set search command, Archie, 225
Settings⇨Connection Profile command
  FTP, 193
  Telnet, 165
Settings⇨Log command, Archie, 217
Settings⇨Network⇨Mail Gateway command, 374
Settings⇨Network⇨Mail Server command, 374-375
Settings⇨Preferences command
  Archie, 220
  Chameleon Mail, 71
  NEWTNews, 137
  Telnet, 167
Settings⇨Signature command, Chameleon Mail, 40, 53
Settings⇨Style Schemes command, WebSurfer, 274
Settings⇨Timers command, Chameleon Mail, 54
Settings⇨Verbose command, Chameleon Finger, 78
Setup dialog box, 27
Setup⇨Dial command, 35, 373
Setup⇨Domain Name command, 366
Setup⇨Host Name command, 366
Setup⇨IP address command, 365
Setup⇨Log command, Internet Chameleon, 35
Setup⇨Login command, 367

Setup⇨Port command, 366
shar (shell archive) file, 132
shar files, 118-119
shareware, registering, 292
shell archive files, 118-119
shell systems, 18-19
  vs SLIP, 21
show command, Archie, 224
signatures, creating, 53-54
Simplex service provider, 381
sipb.mit.edu, 81
SIT unstuffers program, 309
slash (/), with X.400 attributes, 91-92
SLIP (Serial Line Internet Protocol), 19
  vs shell systems, 21
SLIP account
  information sheet, 33
  opening, 29
  payment methods, 29
SLIP providers, 122
SLIP systems, 19-21
smiley faces, 93
SMTP (Simple Mail Transfer Protocol), 48
  server, 374
soc (social) newsgroup listing, 151
  newsgroup names, 116
software
  see also programs
  activating non-instant Internet provider, 358-360
  Archie, 12-13
  Chameleon Custom/NEWT, 354
  Chameleon FTP, 355
  Chameleon Gopher, 355
  Chameleon Mail, 354
  Chameleon Ping, 356
  communications, 16
  downloading, 279-294
  e-mail programs, 73
  included with book, 2
  installing for non-instant Internet provider, 358
  Mail utilities, 354
  NETNews, 354
  Whois, 356
software configurations
  addresses, changing, 372
  domain name server, 374
  mail gateway changes, 374-375
  mail server changes, 374-375
  mailbox, unlocking, 375
  modems, changing, 372
  name gateway changes, 374
  names, changing, 372-373
  news server changes, 375
  passwords, changing, 375
  saving, 372-375
Sorehand mailing list, 110
sound documents, viewing, 320
sources
  adding, 322-323
  adding by hand, 323-325
Spacelink database, 176
Sports info, 181
Sprintmail (Telemail), 89
SRI International, CA, 205
Stanford University FTP server, 205
Starter Kit software, 353-356
starter@dummies.com, Internet for Dummies address, 5, 40, 47, 75
Stichting Knoware service provider, 381
Stichting NEST service provider, 381
Stufitt program, 201-202
Style Schemes dialog box, WebSurfer, 274-275
sub search method, 225
subcase search method, 225
Subscribe - All Groups window, 124-125
Subscribe - New Groups window, NEWTNews, 139
subscribing newsgroups, 114
SWITCH service provider, 383
Sydney University Law School, Sydney, AUS FTP server, 209

• T •

talk newsgroup listing, 152
talk, newsgroup names, 116
Telecom Digest mailing list, 111
Telemail (Sprintmail), 89
teletype machines, 161
Telnet, 13, 159-170
  accessing with Gopher, 244-245
  ANSI terminal emulation, 160
  Archie servers, 222-224
  codes, 171
  commercial services, 178-180
  connection profile, 165-167
  copying information to/from another Windows program, 165
  customizing, 167-169
  databases, 174-178
  emulation, 160
  exiting, 164
  games/entertainment services, 180-181
  garbage, 160
  gateway systems, 178
  hytelnet service, 174
  IBM 3270 terminal emulation, 160
  libraries, 172-174
  options, 167-169
  port 13, 162
  port 23, 161
  saving incoming text to a file, 164
  starting, 162-163
  terminal computer, 159
  terminal emulation, 160
  V-T100 terminal emulation, 160
ten ways to find fun, 339-351
  Avid Explorer, 340
  coffee machine, 350-351
  countries, 341-342
  food, 349
  fun and games, 348
  funnies, 343-345
  girls, girls, girls, 348
  Global Network Navigator, 340
  Gopher, 346
  horsing around, 348
  Internet Talk Radio (ITR), 346-347
  Internet Town Hall (ITH), 346-347
  juggling, 348
  Metro server, 345-346
  navigating, 339-341
  on-line coke machines, 349-350
  personals column, 344
  railroads, 343
  restaurant referrals, 349
  travel, 339
  Trojan room, 350-351
  US State department Travel advisories, 340
terminal computer, 159
terminal emulation, 160
Terminal Preferences dialog box, Telnet, 167-168
TeX program, 199
text editors, UNIX, 160
text files, 197, 199-200
The Direct Connection (TDC) service provider, 384
Thought for the Day, 180
threads, articles, 120
Timers window, Chameleon Mail, 54-55
toolbars, NEWTNews, 129
Tools⇨Antivirus command, Windows, 292
Tourism Discussion mailing list, 111
Trash folder, 70
troff program, 199
troubleshooting, 327-337
  bad networks, 331-333
  check host/server hours, 320-330
  check your computer, 328
  choose when to download, 334
  computer connected to Internet provider, 328
  connection refused, 331-332
  e-mail don'ts, 335
  know your electronic address, 333
  letter case, 334

name server, connections, 329
names, 331
network unreachable, 332
networks down?, 327
news don'ts, 335
no response, 332-333
no route to host, 332
things to know before the networks break, 330
version creep, 337
when networks go bad, 331-333
Trumpet newsreader, 139
Trumpet program, 73, 297
Tubingen Game Server, The, 181
twics service provider, 380

• U •

undigestification, 105
United States Senate FTP server, 209
University of Kansas database, 176
University of Manitoba, Winnipeg, CAN FTP server, 211
University of Michigan FTP server, 205
University of Wisconsin at Kenosha, WI FTP server, 210
UNIX operating system, 19
mail programs, 160
regular expressions, 219
shar files, 118-119
text editors, 160
unsubscribing newsgroups, 114
uppercase letters, 334
URL (Universal Resource Locators), 260
US State department Travel advisories, 340
Usenet, 12, 113
see also newsgroups
hierarchies, official names, 116
News, vs mailing lists, 108
newsgroups, 113-122
origination, 115
Rot13 code, 131
user name, as postmaster, 369
users, login list, 77-78
utas.edu.au, 73
UU program, 307
UUCP address, 89-90
uudecode program, 118
uuencoded messages, 131-132
uuencoding binary files, 118
uuencoding files, 62, 65-67
size limitations, 66
UUNET Canada service provider, 378
UUNET Communications, 90

• V •

V-T100 terminal emulation, 160
variables, Archie, 226
Veronica searches, Gopher, 246-249
vi, UNIX text editor, 160
Victoria University of Wellington Library, 174
VidVue program, 307
viewers
GIF file, 240, 263
graphics, 263-264
JPEG, 264
viruses, scanning for, 291-292
vmsnet newsgroup, 153
Voice of America FTP server, 210

• W •

WAIS (Wide Area Information Servers), 313-326
gateways that aren't, 316
how to get it, 314
load good program, 316
other programs, 325
ugly program, 315
vs Gopher vs WWW, 259
WAISMAN program, 302, 325
Washington University, Missouri FTP server, 204

Weather Talk mailing list, 111
WebSurfer program, 2, 242-243, 256, 264-276
  browsing, 266-268
  changing fonts, 274-276
  customizing, 274-276
  displaying WWW page, 268-269
  downloading files, 271-272
  exiting, 266
  hotlist, 269
  information searches, 270-274
  links, 265
  pages, 266-267
  printing current page, 268
  viewers, 263
WebSurfer window, 264-265
Wftpd program, 299
WHAM program, 306
whatis command, Archie, 221, 226-227
White House Press Releases mailing list, 111
Whois program, 80-85
  servers list, 81-84
Whois window, 81
  Host box, 81
  User box, 81
  Whois button, 81
whois-servers.list file, 81
whois.internic.net, 80
Win QVT/NET program, 169, 304
Win32S program, 309-310
WinCode program, 308
Windows
  Clipboard
    copying information between programs, 165
    copying newsgroup articles to, 130
  copying newsgroup articles between programs, 130
  File Manager, 242
  installing programs, 290-291
  Program Manager, 27-28
    Mail Utilities, 72
windows
  Archie, 216
  Chameleon mail
    Address Book, 59
    Folder List, 68
    Mail, 49-50
    Mail Login, 49
    Mail Signature, 53
    New Message, 51
    Timers, 54-55
  Custom, 328
  Finger, 77
  FTP, 188
    Connection Profile, 193
  Gopher, 233-234
  Instant Internet, Account Sign-Up, 30-31
  Internet Chameleon, Custom, 35
  NEWTNews, 126-127
    Subscribe - New Groups, 139
  Ping, 37-38
  Subscribe - All Groups, 124-125
  WebSurfer, 264-265
  Whois, 81
  WinWAIS source, 318
  WinZip, 284
Winelm program, 297
WinGIF program, 306
WinGopher program, 251
WinJPEG program, 306
WinQVT/Net newsreader, 140
WinSock programs, 23, 296-305
  Archie, 299-300
  FTP, 299
  Gopher, 300
  IRC, 303
  Mac unstuffers, 309
  mailers, 296-297
  movies, 307
  MUD, 303-304
  newsreaders, 297-298
  obtaining update lists, 310-311
  Telnet, 298

UNIX uncompressors, 308
uudecoders, 307-308
viewers, 305-307
voice, 306
WAIS, 302
web browsers, 301-302
Win32S, 309-310
WinTalk program, 304
WinVN newsreader, 140
WinVN program, 298
WinWAIS program, 302
adding sources, 322-325
buttons, 320-321
directory of sources, 322-223
finding sources, 318
hand to hand, 317-325
other programs, 325
relevance feedback, 322
searching, 319
selecting sources, 319-320
setting up, 316-317
successful searching, 320-321
using, 317-325
WinWAIS sources window, 318
WinZip program, 198, 201, 280-288
creating a zip file, 287
customizing, 282-285
exiting, 287
extracting files, 285-286
installing, 281-282
opening ZIP file, 285
registering, 293
self-extracting file, 282
uncompressing, 282
zipping files, 286-287
WinZip window, 284
winzip55.exe file, 281-282
Wordsworth Books database, 178
World Wide Web, see WWW
World Window Gateway at Washington University, 178
World, The, 18-19, 179
World-NET service provider, 379
WPLANY program, 306
WS Host program, 304-305
WS_FTP program, 299
Wsarchie program, 229, 299-300
WSGopher program, 301
WSIRC program, 303
WWW (World Wide Web), 2, 13, 253-261
accessing with Gopher, 242-243
browsing, 256-258
creating pages, 260-261
Gopher access, 258-259
hypermedia, 253
hypertext, 253-255
indexes, 261
information retrieval, 255
naming resources, 260
soliciting comments, 259-260
Universal Resource Locators (URL), 260
uses for, 254-255
vs Gopher vs WAIS, 259
WWW Calc, 344
wysiwyg (what you see is what you get), 199

• X •

X.400 address, 90-92
attributes list, 91

• Y •

Yale Library, 173

• Z •

Z uncompress program, 308
z uncompress program, 308
Z39.50 standard, ANSI, 314
ZIP file, opening, 285
ZIP program, 201
zoo keepers program, 308

DUMMIES PRESS

11/11/94

The fun & easy way to learn about computers and more!

SUPER STAR

Windows 3.1 For Dummies,™ 2nd Edition
by Andy Rathbone

ISBN: 1-56884-182-5
$16.95 USA/$22.95 Canada

SUPER STAR

MORE Windows For Dummies™
by Andy Rathbone

ISBN: 1-56884-048-9
$19.95 USA/$26.95 Canada

SUPER STAR

DOS For Dummies,® 2nd Edition
by Dan Gookin

ISBN: 1-878058-75-4
$16.95 USA/$21.95 Canada

IX
FINALIST
Ninth Annual Computer Press Awards 1993

The Internet For Dummies™ 2nd Edition
by John R. Levine & Carol Baroudi

ISBN: 1-56884-222-8
$19.99 USA/$26.99 Canada

NATIONAL BESTSELLER!

Personal Finance For Dummies™
by Eric Tyson

ISBN: 1-56884-150-7
$16.95 USA/$21.95 Canada

VIII
FINALIST
Eighth Annual Computer Press Awards 1992

PCs For Dummies,™ 2nd Edition
by Dan Gookin & Andy Rathbone

ISBN: 1-56884-078-0
$16.95 USA/$21.95 Canada

SUPER STAR

Macs For Dummies,® 2nd Edition
by David Pogue

ISBN: 1-56884-051-9
$19.95 USA/$26.95 Canada

Here's a complete listing of IDG's *...For Dummies* Titles

Title	Author	ISBN	Price
DATABASE			
Access 2 For Dummies™	by Scott Palmer	1-56884-090-X	$19.95 USA/$26.95 Canada
Access Programming For Dummies™	by Rob Krumm	1-56884-091-8	$19.95 USA/$26.95 Canada
Approach 3 For Windows For Dummies™	by Doug Lowe	1-56884-233-3	$19.99 USA/$26.99 Canada
dBASE For DOS For Dummies™	by Scott Palmer & Michael Stabler	1-56884-188-4	$19.95 USA/$26.95 Canada
dBASE For Windows For Dummies™	by Scott Palmer	1-56884-179-5	$19.95 USA/$26.95 Canada
dBASE 5 For Windows Programming For Dummies™	by Ted Coombs & Jason Coombs	1-56884-215-5	$19.99 USA/$26.99 Canada
FoxPro 2.6 For Windows For Dummies™	by John Kaufeld	1-56884-187-6	$19.95 USA/$26.95 Canada
Paradox 5 For Windows For Dummies™	by John Kaufeld	1-56884-185-X	$19.95 USA/$26.95 Canada
DESKTOP PUBLISHING / ILLUSTRATION / GRAPHICS			
CorelDRAW! 5 For Dummies™	by Deke McClelland	1-56884-157-4	$19.95 USA/$26.95 Canada
CorelDRAW! For Dummies™	by Deke McClelland	1-56884-042-X	$19.95 USA/$26.95 Canada
Harvard Graphics 2 For Windows For Dummies™	by Roger C. Parker	1-56884-092-6	$19.95 USA/$26.95 Canada
PageMaker 5 For Macs For Dummies™	by Galen Gruman	1-56884-178-7	$19.95 USA/$26.95 Canada
PageMaker 5 For Windows For Dummies™	by Deke McClelland & Galen Gruman	1-56884-160-4	$19.95 USA/$26.95 Canada
QuarkXPress 3.3 For Dummies™	by Galen Gruman & Barbara Assadi	1-56884-217-1	$19.99 USA/$26.99 Canada
FINANCE / PERSONAL FINANCE / TEST TAKING REFERENCE			
QuickBooks 3 For Dummies™	by Stephen L. Nelson	1-56884-227-9	$19.99 USA/$26.99 Canada
Quicken 8 For DOS For Dummies™, 2nd Edition	by Stephen L. Nelson	1-56884-210-4	$19.95 USA/$26.95 Canada
Quicken 5 For Macs For Dummies™	by Stephen L. Nelson	1-56884-211-2	$19.95 USA/$26.95 Canada
Quicken 4 For Windows For Dummies™, 2nd Edition	by Stephen L. Nelson	1-56884-209-0	$19.95 USA/$26.95 Canada
The SAT I For Dummies™	by Suzee Vlk	1-56884-213-9	$14.99 USA/$20.99 Canada
GROUPWARE / INTEGRATED			
Lotus Notes 3/3.1 For Dummies™	by Paul Freeland & Stephen Londergan	1-56884-212-0	$19.95 USA/$26.95 Canada
Microsoft Office 4 For Windows For Dummies™	by Roger C. Parker	1-56884-183-3	$19.95 USA/$26.95 Canada
Microsoft Works 3 For Windows For Dummies™	by David C. Kay	1-56884-214-7	$19.99 USA/$26.99 Canada

FOR MORE INFORMATION OR TO ORDER, PLEASE CALL ▸ 800 762 2974

For volume discounts & special orders please call Tony Real, Special Sales, at 415. 312. 0650

Title	Author	ISBN	Price
INTERNET / COMMUNICATIONS / NETWORKING			11/11/94
CompuServe For Dummies™	by Wallace Wang	1-56884-181-7	$19.95 USA/$26.95 Canada
Modems For Dummies™, 2nd Edition	by Tina Rathbone	1-56884-223-6	$19.99 USA/$26.99 Canada
Modems For Dummies™	by Tina Rathbone	1-56884-001-2	$19.95 USA/$26.95 Canada
MORE Internet For Dummies™	by John R. Levine & Margaret Levine Young	1-56884-164-7	$19.95 USA/$26.95 Canada
NetWare For Dummies™	by Ed Tittel & Deni Connor	1-56884-003-9	$19.95 USA/$26.95 Canada
Networking For Dummies™	by Doug Lowe	1-56884-079-9	$19.95 USA/$26.95 Canada
ProComm Plus 2 For Windows For Dummies™	by Wallace Wang	1-56884-219-8	$19.99 USA/$26.99 Canada
The Internet For Dummies™, 2nd Edition	by John R. Levine & Carol Baroudi	1-56884-222-8	$19.99 USA/$26.99 Canada
The Internet For Macs For Dummies™	by Charles Seiter	1-56884-184-1	$19.95 USA/$26.95 Canada
MACINTOSH			
Macs For Dummies®	by David Pogue	1-56884-173-6	$19.95 USA/$26.95 Canada
Macintosh System 7.5 For Dummies™	by Bob LeVitus	1-56884-197-3	$19.95 USA/$26.95 Canada
MORE Macs For Dummies™	by David Pogue	1-56884-087-X	$19.95 USA/$26.95 Canada
PageMaker 5 For Macs For Dummies™	by Galen Gruman	1-56884-178-7	$19.95 USA/$26.95 Canada
QuarkXPress 3.3 For Dummies™	by Galen Gruman & Barbara Assadi	1-56884-217-1	$19.99 USA/$26.99 Canada
Upgrading and Fixing Macs For Dummies™	by Kearney Rietmann & Frank Higgins	1-56884-189-2	$19.95 USA/$26.95 Canada
MULTIMEDIA			
Multimedia & CD-ROMs For Dummies™, Interactive Multimedia Value Pack	by Andy Rathbone	1-56884-225-2	$29.95 USA/$39.95 Canada
Multimedia & CD-ROMs For Dummies™	by Andy Rathbone	1-56884-089-6	$19.95 USA/$26.95 Canada
OPERATING SYSTEMS / DOS			
MORE DOS For Dummies™	by Dan Gookin	1-56884-046-2	$19.95 USA/$26.95 Canada
S.O.S. For DOS™	by Katherine Murray	1-56884-043-8	$12.95 USA/$16.95 Canada
OS/2 For Dummies™	by Andy Rathbone	1-878058-76-2	$19.95 USA/$26.95 Canada
UNIX			
UNIX For Dummies™	by John R. Levine & Margaret Levine Young	1-878058-58-4	$19.95 USA/$26.95 Canada
WINDOWS			
S.O.S. For Windows™	by Katherine Murray	1-56884-045-4	$12.95 USA/$16.95 Canada
MORE Windows 3.1 For Dummies™, 3rd Edition	by Andy Rathbone	1-56884-240-6	$19.99 USA/$26.99 Canada
PCs / HARDWARE			
Illustrated Computer Dictionary For Dummies™	by Dan Gookin, Wally Wang, & Chris Van Buren	1-56884-004-7	$12.95 USA/$16.95 Canada
Upgrading and Fixing PCs For Dummies™	by Andy Rathbone	1-56884-002-0	$19.95 USA/$26.95 Canada
PRESENTATION / AUTOCAD			
AutoCAD For Dummies™	by Bud Smith	1-56884-191-4	$19.95 USA/$26.95 Canada
PowerPoint 4 For Windows For Dummies™	by Doug Lowe	1-56884-161-2	$16.95 USA/$22.95 Canada
PROGRAMMING			
Borland C++ For Dummies™	by Michael Hyman	1-56884-162-0	$19.95 USA/$26.95 Canada
"Borland's New Language Product" For Dummies™	by Neil Rubenking	1-56884-200-7	$19.95 USA/$26.95 Canada
C For Dummies™	by Dan Gookin	1-878058-78-9	$19.95 USA/$26.95 Canada
C++ For Dummies™	by Stephen R. Davis	1-56884-163-9	$19.95 USA/$26.95 Canada
Mac Programming For Dummies™	by Dan Parks Sydow	1-56884-173-6	$19.95 USA/$26.95 Canada
QBasic Programming For Dummies™	by Douglas Hergert	1-56884-093-4	$19.95 USA/$26.95 Canada
Visual Basic "X" For Dummies™, 2nd Edition	by Wallace Wang	1-56884-230-9	$19.99 USA/$26.99 Canada
Visual Basic 3 For Dummies™	by Wallace Wang	1-56884-076-4	$19.95 USA/$26.95 Canada
SPREADSHEET			
1-2-3 For Dummies™	by Greg Harvey	1-878058-60-6	$16.95 USA/$21.95 Canada
1-2-3 For Windows 5 For Dummies™, 2nd Edition	by John Walkenbach	1-56884-216-3	$16.95 USA/$21.95 Canada
1-2-3 For Windows For Dummies™	by John Walkenbach	1-56884-052-7	$16.95 USA/$21.95 Canada
Excel 5 For Macs For Dummies™	by Greg Harvey	1-56884-186-8	$19.95 USA/$26.95 Canada
Excel For Dummies™, 2nd Edition	by Greg Harvey	1-56884-050-0	$16.95 USA/$21.95 Canada
MORE Excel 5 For Windows For Dummies™	by Greg Harvey	1-56884-207-4	$19.95 USA/$26.95 Canada
Quattro Pro 6 For Windows For Dummies™	by John Walkenbach	1-56884-174-4	$19.95 USA/$26.95 Canada
Quattro Pro For DOS For Dummies™	by John Walkenbach	1-56884-023-3	$16.95 USA/$21.95 Canada
UTILITIES / VCRs & CAMCORDERS			
Norton Utilities 8 For Dummies™	by Beth Slick	1-56884-166-3	$19.95 USA/$26.95 Canada
VCRs & Camcorders For Dummies™	by Andy Rathbone & Gordon McComb	1-56884-229-5	$14.99 USA/$20.99 Canada
WORD PROCESSING			
Ami Pro For Dummies™	by Jim Meade	1-56884-049-7	$19.95 USA/$26.95 Canada
MORE Word For Windows 6 For Dummies™	by Doug Lowe	1-56884-165-5	$19.95 USA/$26.95 Canada
MORE WordPerfect 6 For Windows For Dummies™	by Margaret Levine Young & David C. Kay	1-56884-206-6	$19.95 USA/$26.95 Canada
MORE WordPerfect 6 For DOS For Dummies™	by Wallace Wang, edited by Dan Gookin	1-56884-047-0	$19.95 USA/$26.95 Canada
S.O.S. For WordPerfect™	by Katherine Murray	1-56884-053-5	$12.95 USA/$16.95 Canada
Word 6 For Macs For Dummies™	by Dan Gookin	1-56884-190-6	$19.95 USA/$26.95 Canada
Word For Windows 6 For Dummies™	by Dan Gookin	1-56884-075-6	$16.95 USA/$21.95 Canada
Word For Windows For Dummies™	by Dan Gookin	1-878058-86-X	$16.95 USA/$21.95 Canada
WordPerfect 6 For Dummies™	by Dan Gookin	1-878058-77-0	$16.95 USA/$21.95 Canada
WordPerfect For Dummies™	by Dan Gookin	1-878058-52-5	$16.95 USA/$21.95 Canada
WordPerfect For Windows For Dummies™	by Margaret Levine Young & David C. Kay	1-56884-032-2	$16.95 USA/$21.95 Canada

FOR MORE INFORMATION OR TO ORDER, PLEASE CALL ▸ 800. 762. 2974

For volume discounts & special orders please call Tony Real, Special Sales, at 415. 312. 0650

DUMMIES QUICK REFERENCES

11/11/94

Fun, Fast, & Cheap!

NEW!

CorelDRAW! 5 For Dummies™ Quick Reference
by Raymond E. Werner

ISBN: 1-56884-952-4
$9.99 USA/$12.99 Canada

NEW!

Windows "X" For Dummies™ Quick Reference, 3rd Edition
by Greg Harvey

ISBN: 1-56884-964-8
$9.99 USA/$12.99 Canada

SUPER STAR

Word For Windows 6 For Dummies™ Quick Reference
by George Lynch

ISBN: 1-56884-095-0
$8.95 USA/$12.95 Canada

SUPER STAR

WordPerfect For DOS For Dummies™ Quick Reference
by Greg Harvey

ISBN: 1-56884-009-8
$8.95 USA/$11.95 Canada

Title	Author	ISBN	Price
DATABASE			
Access 2 For Dummies™ Quick Reference	by Stuart A. Stuple	1-56884-167-1	$8.95 USA/$11.95 Canada
dBASE 5 For DOS For Dummies™ Quick Reference	by Barry Sosinsky	1-56884-954-0	$9.99 USA/$12.99 Canada
dBASE 5 For Windows For Dummies™ Quick Reference	by Stuart J. Stuple	1-56884-953-2	$9.99 USA/$12.99 Canada
Paradox 5 For Windows For Dummies™ Quick Reference	by Scott Palmer	1-56884-960-5	$9.99 USA/$12.99 Canada
DESKTOP PUBLISHING / ILLUSTRATION/GRAPHICS			
Harvard Graphics 3 For Windows For Dummies™ Quick Reference	by Raymond E. Werner	1-56884-962-1	$9.99 USA/$12.99 Canada
FINANCE / PERSONAL FINANCE			
Quicken 4 For Windows For Dummies™ Quick Reference	by Stephen L. Nelson	1-56884-950-8	$9.95 USA/$12.95 Canada
GROUPWARE / INTEGRATED			
Microsoft Office 4 For Windows For Dummies™ Quick Reference	by Doug Lowe	1-56884-958-3	$9.99 USA/$12.99 Canada
Microsoft Works For Windows 3 For Dummies™ Quick Reference	by Michael Partington	1-56884-959-1	$9.99 USA/$12.99 Canada
INTERNET / COMMUNICATIONS / NETWORKING			
The Internet For Dummies™ Quick Reference	by John R. Levine	1-56884-168-X	$8.95 USA/$11.95 Canada
MACINTOSH			
Macintosh System 7.5 For Dummies™ Quick Reference	by Stuart J. Stuple	1-56884-956-7	$9.99 USA/$12.99 Canada
OPERATING SYSTEMS / DOS			
DOS For Dummies® Quick Reference	by Greg Harvey	1-56884-007-1	$8.95 USA/$11.95 Canada
UNIX			
UNIX For Dummies™ Quick Reference	by Margaret Levine Young & John R. Levine	1-56884-094-2	$8.95 USA/$11.95 Canada
WINDOWS			
Windows 3.1 For Dummies™ Quick Reference, 2nd Edition	by Greg Harvey	1-56884-951-6	$8.95 USA/$11.95 Canada
PRESENTATION / AUTOCAD			
AutoCAD For Dummies™ Quick Reference	by Bud Smith	1-56884-198-1	$9.95 USA/$12.95 Canada
SPREADSHEET			
1-2-3 For Dummies™ Quick Reference	by John Walkenbach	1-56884-027-6	$8.95 USA/$11.95 Canada
1-2-3 For Windows 5 For Dummies™ Quick Reference	by John Walkenbach	1-56884-957-5	$9.95 USA/$12.95 Canada
Excel For Windows For Dummies™ Quick Reference, 2nd Edition	by John Walkenbach	1-56884-096-9	$8.95 USA/$11.95 Canada
Quattro Pro 6 For Windows For Dummies™ Quick Reference	by Stuart A. Stuple	1-56884-172-8	$9.95 USA/$12.95 Canada
WORD PROCESSING			
Word For Windows 6 For Dummies™ Quick Reference	by George Lynch	1-56884-095-0	$8.95 USA/$11.95 Canada
WordPerfect For Windows For Dummies™ Quick Reference	by Greg Harvey	1-56884-039-X	$8.95 USA/$11.95 Canada

FOR MORE INFORMATION OR TO ORDER, PLEASE CALL ▸ 800. 762. 2974

For volume discounts & special orders please call Tony Real, Special Sales, at 415. 312. 0650

11/11/94

Windows 3.1 SECRETS™
by Brian Livingston
ISBN: 1-878058-43-6
$39.95 USA/$52.95 Canada
Includes Software.

MORE Windows 3.1 SECRETS™
by Brian Livingston
ISBN: 1-56884-019-5
$39.95 USA/$52.95 Canada
Includes Software.

Windows GIZMOS™
by Brian Livingston & Margie Livingston
ISBN: 1-878058-66-5
$39.95 USA/$52.95 Canada
Includes Software.

Windows 3.1 Connectivity SECRETS™
by Runnoe Connally, David Rorabaugh, & Sheldon Hall
ISBN: 1-56884-030-6
$49.95 USA/$64.95 Canada
Includes Software.

Windows 3.1 Configuration SECRETS™
by Valda Hilley & James Blakely
ISBN: 1-56884-026-8
$49.95 USA/$64.95 Canada
Includes Software.

Internet SECRETS™
by John R. Levine & Carol Baroudi
ISBN: 1-56884-452-2
$39.99 USA/$54.99 Canada
Includes Software.
Available: January 1995

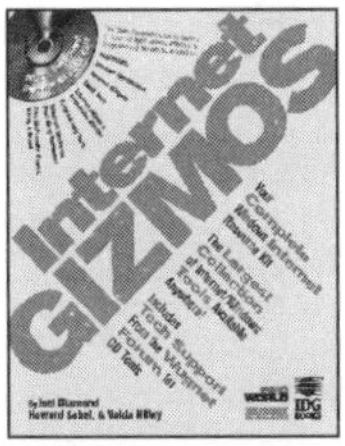

Internet GIZMOS™ For Windows
by Joel Diamond, Howard Sobel, & Valda Hilley
ISBN: 1-56884-451-4
$39.99 USA/$54.99 Canada
Includes Software.
Available: December 1994

IX
WINNER
Ninth Annual Computer Press Awards 1993

Network Security SECRETS™
by David Stang & Sylvia Moon
ISBN: 1-56884-021-7
Int'l. ISBN: 1-56884-151-5
$49.95 USA/$64.95 Canada
Includes Software.

PC SECRETS™
by Caroline M. Halliday
ISBN: 1-878058-49-5
$39.95 USA/$52.95 Canada
Includes Software.

WordPerfect 6 SECRETS™
by Roger C. Parker & David A. Holzgang
ISBN: 1-56884-040-3
$39.95 USA/$52.95 Canada
Includes Software.

DOS 6 SECRETS™
by Robert D. Ainsbury
ISBN: 1-878058-70-3
$39.95 USA/$52.95 Canada
Includes Software.

Paradox 4 Power Programming SECRETS,™ 2nd Edition
by Gregory B. Salcedo & Martin W. Rudy
ISBN: 1-878058-54-1
$44.95 USA/$59.95 Canada
Includes Software.

Paradox For Windows "X" Power Programming SECRETS™
by Gregory B. Salcedo & Martin W. Rudy
ISBN: 1-56884-085-3
$44.95 USA/$59.95 Canada
Includes Software.

IX
FINALIST
Ninth Annual Computer Press Awards 1993

Hard Disk SECRETS™
by John M. Goodman, Ph.D.
ISBN: 1-878058-64-9
$39.95 USA/$52.95 Canada
Includes Software.

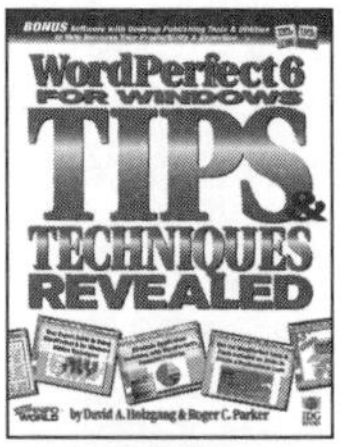

WordPerfect 6 For Windows Tips & Techniques Revealed
by David A. Holzgang & Roger C. Parker
ISBN: 1-56884-202-3
$39.95 USA/$52.95 Canada
Includes Software.

Excel 5 For Windows Power Programming Techniques
by John Walkenbach
ISBN: 1-56884-303-8
$39.95 USA/$52.95 Canada
Includes Software.
Available: November 1994

INFO WORLD

...SECRETS™

FOR MORE INFORMATION OR TO ORDER, PLEASE CALL ▸ 800. 762. 2974

For volume discounts & special orders please call Tony Real, Special Sales, at 415. 312. 0650

PC WORLD

11/11/94

"A lot easier to use than the book Excel gives you!"

Lisa Schmeckpeper, New Berlin, WI, on PC World Excel 5 For Windows Handbook

Official Hayes Modem Communications Companion

by Caroline M. Halliday

ISBN: 1-56884-072-1

$29.95 USA/$39.95 Canada

Includes software.

PC World Excel 5 For Windows Handbook, 2nd Edition

by John Walkenbach & Dave Maguiness

ISBN: 1-56884-056-X

$34.95 USA/$44.95 Canada

Includes software.

BESTSELLER!

PC World DOS 6 Handbook, 2nd Edition

by John Socha, Clint Hicks, & Devra Hall

ISBN: 1-878058-79-7

$34.95 USA/$44.95 Canada

Includes software.

PC World Word For Windows 6 Handbook

by Brent Heslop & David Angell

ISBN: 1-56884-054-3

$34.95 USA/$44.95 Canada

Includes software.

BESTSELLER!

PC World Microsoft Access 2 Bible, 2nd Edition

by Cary N. Prague & Michael R. Irwin

ISBN: 1-56884-086-1

$39.95 USA/$52.95 Canada

Includes software.

"Easy and enjoyable to read, well structured and so detailed you cannot fail to learn! It's the best computer book I have ever used."

John Wildsmith, Gateshead, England, on PC World Microsoft Access 2 Bible, 2nd Edition

PC World WordPerfect 6 Handbook

by Greg Harvey

ISBN: 1-878058-80-0

$34.95 USA/$44.95 Canada

Includes software.

QuarkXPress For Windows Designer Handbook

by Barbara Assadi & Galen Gruman

ISBN: 1-878058-45-2

$29.95 USA/$39.95 Canada

NATIONAL BESTSELLER!

Official XTree Companion, 3rd Edition

by Beth Slick

ISBN: 1-878058-57-6

$19.95 USA/$26.95 Canada

NATIONAL BESTSELLER!

PC World DOS 6 Command Reference and Problem Solver

by John Socha & Devra Hall

ISBN: 1-56884-055-1

$24.95 USA/$32.95 Canada

SUPER STAR

Client/Server Strategies: A Survival Guide for Corporate Reengineers

by David Vaskevitch

ISBN: 1-56884-064-0

$29.95 USA/$39.95 Canada

"*PC World Word For Windows 6 Handbook* is very easy to follow with lots of 'hands on' examples. The 'Task at a Glance' is very helpful!"

Jacqueline Martens, Tacoma, WA

"Thanks for publishing this book! It's the best money I've spent this year!"

Robert D. Templeton, Ft. Worth, TX, on MORE Windows 3.1 SECRETS

FOR MORE INFORMATION OR TO ORDER, PLEASE CALL ▸ 800 . 762 . 2974

For volume discounts & special orders please call Tony Real, Special Sales, at 415. 312. 0650

ORDER FORM

11/11/94

IDG BOOKS

Order Center: **(800) 762-2974** *(8 a.m.–6 p.m., EST, weekdays)*

Quantity	ISBN	Title	Price	Total

Shipping & Handling Charges

	Description	First book	Each additional book	Total
Domestic	Normal	$4.50	$1.50	$
	Two Day Air	$8.50	$2.50	$
	Overnight	$18.00	$3.00	$
International	Surface	$8.00	$8.00	$
	Airmail	$16.00	$16.00	$
	DHL Air	$17.00	$17.00	$

*For large quantities call for shipping & handling charges.
**Prices are subject to change without notice.

Ship to:

Name ______________________________

Company ______________________________

Address ______________________________

City/State/Zip ______________________________

Daytime Phone ______________________________

Payment: ☐ Check to IDG Books (US Funds Only)

☐ VISA ☐ MasterCard ☐ American Express

Card # ______________________ Expires __________

Signature ______________________________

Subtotal __________

CA residents add applicable sales tax __________

IN, MA, and MD residents add 5% sales tax __________

IL residents add 6.25% sales tax __________

RI residents add 7% sales tax __________

TX residents add 8.25% sales tax __________

Shipping __________

Total __________

Please send this order form to:

IDG Books Worldwide
7260 Shadeland Station, Suite 100
Indianapolis, IN 46256

Allow up to 3 weeks for delivery.
Thank you!

IDG BOOKS WORLDWIDE LICENSE AGREEMENT

4. **Limited Warranty.** IDG Warrants that the Software and disk(s) are free from defects in materials and workmanship for a period of sixty (60) days from the date of purchase of this Book. If IDG receives notification within the warranty period of defects in material or workmanship, IDG will replace the defective disk(s). IDG's entire liability and your exclusive remedy shall be limited to replacement of the Software, which is returned to IDG with a copy of your receipt. This Limited Warranty is void if failure of the Software has resulted from accident, abuse, or misapplication. Any replacement Software will be warranted for the remainder of the original warranty period or thirty (30) days, whichever is longer.

5. **No Other Warranties.** To the maximum extent permitted by applicable law, IDG and the author disclaim all other warranties, express or implied, including but not limited to implied warranties of merchantability and fitness for a particular purpose, with respect to the Software, the programs, the source code contained therein, and/or the techniques described in this Book. This limited warranty gives you specific legal rights. You may have others which vary from state/jurisdiction to state/jurisdiction.

6. **No Liability For Consequential Damages.** To the extent permitted by applicable law, in no event shall IDG or the author be liable for any damages whatsoever (including without limitation, damages for loss of business profits, business interruption, loss of business information, or any other pecuniary loss) arising out of the use of or inability to use the Book or the Software, even if IDG has been advised of the possibility of such damages. Because some states/jurisdictions do not allow the exclusion or limitation of liability for consequential or incidental damages, the above limitation may not apply to you.

Disk Installation Instructions

1. Insert the Internet Chameleon Disk 1 in the disk drive.
2. In the Windows Program Manager, choose File⇨Run from the menu.
3. Type `a:` in the Command Line box, and click OK. Chameleon asks where to install the software. Click Continue to accept its suggestion of C:.
4. When you're asked for a disk, stick the disk it wants into the same disk drive you've been using and click Continue.
5. Click OK when the installation program says that it's done.
6. In the Program Manager, double-click the Internet Chameleon icon to see the Chameleon program group.
7. Double-click on Instant Internet to get signed up for an Internet account.

These instructions are also printed on the Cheat Sheet for your convenience. For full software installation details, see Chapter 3.